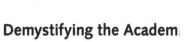

Demystifying the Academi

Demystifying the Academic Research Enterprise

Becoming a Successful Scholar in a Complex and Competitive Environment

Kelvin K. Droegemeier

The MIT Press
Cambridge, Massachusetts
London, England

The MIT Press would like to thank the anonymous peer reviewers who provided comments on drafts of this book. The generous work of academic experts is essential for establishing the authority and quality of our publications. We acknowledge with gratitude the contributions of these otherwise uncredited readers.

This book was set in Times Roman by Westchester Publishing Services, Danbury, CT. Printed and bound in the United States of America.

Library of Congress Cataloging-in-Publication Data

Names: Droegemeier, Kelvin, 1958– author.
Title: Demystifying the academic research enterprise : becoming a successful scholar in a
    complex and competitive environment / Kelvin K. Droegemeier.
Description: Cambridge, Massachusetts : The MIT Press, [2023] | Includes bibliographical
    references and index.
Identifiers: LCCN 2022062131 (print) | LCCN 2022062132 (ebook) | ISBN 9780262547079
    (paperback) | ISBN 9780262377218 (epub) | ISBN 9780262377201 (pdf)
Subjects: LCSH: Universities and colleges—Research—United States. | Research—Moral and
    ethical aspects—United States. | Research—Methodology. | Learning and scholarship—
    United States.
Classification: LCC LB2326.3 .D76 2023 (print) | LCC LB2326.3 (ebook) | DDC 378.0072—
    dc23/eng/20230512
LC record available at https://lccn.loc.gov/2022062131
LC ebook record available at https://lccn.loc.gov/2022062132

10 9 8 7 6 5 4 3 2 1

To my incredible wife and best friend, Lisa, who has been and remains an untiring supporter of my ambitions and dreams, a dedicated servant of God, and a role model for all. Her loving guidance and enduring faith in my abilities shaped both me and this work.

Contents

List of Acronyms   xi
Foreword   xv
Preface   xvii
Acknowledgments   xxi

Introduction   1

1   Deep in Our Bones: Why and Where We Perform Research
and Creative Activity   5
Chapter Overview and Learning Objectives   5
1.1   The Root of Curiosity and Emergence of Structured Inquiry   6
1.2   The Lexicon of Research: Understanding and Misunderstanding   7
1.3   The Many Homes of Research and Creative Activity   10
1.4   From Individual Researcher to a Globally Engaged Team   12
1.5   Outcomes, Impacts, and Assessing Purpose and Value   13
1.6   Research Leadership at Academic Institutions   15
Assess Your Comprehension   23
Exercises to Deepen Your Understanding   24

2   The Money Trail: Funding for Research and Creative Activity   27
Chapter Overview and Learning Objectives   27
2.1   Sources of Funding and Historical Trends   27
2.2   Determining Research Priorities and Budgets   33
2.3   Identifying and Understanding Mechanisms for Obtaining Funding   42
2.4   The Future of Research Funding   45
Assess Your Comprehension   48
Exercises to Deepen Your Understanding   49

3   Perception and Reality: Public Attitudes, Understanding,
and Use of Research   51
Chapter Overview and Learning Objectives   51
3.1   Research and the Social Compact with the General Public   51
3.2   Factors Shaping Public Understanding of Research   55

3.3   Balancing Progress in Research with Belief Systems and Ethics   56
3.4   The Use and Misuse of Research Results in Policy   58
3.5   All Academic Disciplines Created Equal?   62
3.6   Research and Creative Activity as the Foundation of Innovation   64
Assess Your Comprehension   67
Exercises to Deepen Your Understanding   68

4   **Essential Concepts: Performing Research and Creative Activity   71**
Chapter Overview and Learning Objectives   71
4.1   General Framework   72
4.2   The Scientific Method   75
4.3   The Historical Method   78
4.4   Indigenous Methods   79
4.5   Integrating Research and Education   81
4.6   Broader Application of Research Methods: Citizen Science and
       Daily Life   83
4.7   Reproducibility, Reliability, and Replicability of Research Results   84
4.8   Surprise, Surprise! Serendipity in Research and Creative Activity   88
Assess Your Comprehension   92
Exercises to Deepen Your Understanding   93

5   **Becoming a Detective: Finding What You Need and Using
     It Effectively   95**
Chapter Overview and Learning Objectives   95
5.1   Becoming Familiar with Previous Work   95
5.2   Assessing Your Need, Identifying Sources, and Collecting/Protecting
       Resources   98
5.3   Source Validation, Quality Assurance, and Control   99
5.4   Analysis and Synthesis   102
Assess Your Comprehension   104
Exercises to Deepen Your Understanding   104

6   **Diving into the Pool: Research Proposals, Evaluation Processes,
     and Project Management   107**
Chapter Overview and Learning Objectives   107
6.1   Structure and Value of the Research Proposal   107
6.2   Research Project Budget and Sharing the Costs of Research   111
6.3   Proposal Submission and Evaluation Processes   116
6.4   Managing a Research Project   119
Assess Your Comprehension   120
Exercises to Deepen Your Understanding   121

7   **The Give-and-Take of Criticism: Subjecting Research to Scrutiny
     via Peer/Merit Review   125**
Chapter Overview and Learning Objectives   125
7.1   Importance, History, and Forms of Scrutinizing Research
       and Creative Activity   125

7.2   Definition and Purpose of Peer/Merit Review   127
7.3   Principles and Processes of Peer/Merit Review   129
7.4   Strengths and Weaknesses of Peer/Merit Review   135
7.5   Variations on Classical Peer/Merit Review   138
7.6   Using Criticism Effectively   140
Assess Your Comprehension   142
Exercises to Deepen Your Understanding   143

8   We See the World Differently: Bias and Differing Views   145
Chapter Overview and Learning Objectives   145
8.1   Defining and Understanding Bias   146
8.2   Types of Bias and Their Impacts: The Research Process   147
8.3   Types of Bias and Their Impacts: Peer/Merit Review   151
8.4   Approaches for Mitigating Bias   153
8.5   Differing Points of View: Agencies, Publishers, the Research Community,
       the Public, and Law/Policy Makers   154
Assess Your Comprehension   156
Exercises to Deepen Your Understanding   157

9   Honesty Is the Best Policy: Ethical Conduct and
     Research Integrity   159
Chapter Overview and Learning Objectives   159
9.1   Importance of Responsible Conduct of Research   160
9.2   Ethics and Morality and Applying Ethical Behavior to Research   162
9.3   Research Misconduct and Associated Consequences   163
9.4   Creating and Maintaining an Ethical Program of Scholarship   166
Assess Your Comprehension   168
Exercises to Deepen Your Understanding   169

10   Better Safe than Sorry: Research Compliance   171
Chapter Overview and Learning Objectives   171
10.1   History and Purpose of Research Compliance   172
10.2   The Universe of Research Compliance   173
10.3   Research Security: A Balancing Act between Promotion
       and Protection   179
10.4   Creation and Enforcement of Research Rules and Regulations   182
10.5   Your Role in Understanding and Meeting Compliance Rules
       and Regulations   185
10.6   Recent Reforms: Ensuring Effective Compliance without
       Undue Burden   186
Assess Your Comprehension   190
Exercises to Deepen Your Understanding   192

11   Show Time: Making Your Work Known to Multiple Audiences   195
Chapter Overview and Learning Objectives   195
11.1   Importance of Communicating Scholarly Outcomes   195
11.2   Traditional and Open Access Frameworks   196

11.3   Publicly Accessible Publications and Data   200
11.4   Communicating with Expert Audiences   202
11.5   Communicating with General Audiences   204
11.6   Special Circumstances and Other Helpful Hints   207
Assess Your Comprehension   208
Exercises to Deepen Your Understanding   209

12   **Yours, Mine, and Ours: Ownership of Research Outcomes   213**
Chapter Overview and Learning Objectives   213
12.1   Context, Definition, and Importance of Intellectual Property   213
12.2   Types of Intellectual Property Protection   217
12.3   Policies, Procedures, and Challenges in the Academic Enterprise   220
12.4   Disposition of Intellectual Property   223
12.5   The Value to Society of Academic Intellectual Property   227
Assess Your Comprehension   229
Exercises to Deepen Your Understanding   234

13   **I Need You and You Need Me: Collaboration, Multidisciplinary Inquiry,
and Academic-Corporate Partnerships   237**
Chapter Overview and Learning Objectives   237
13.1   Lexicon, Challenges, and Opportunities of Collaboration   238
13.2   Disciplinary Research and Education in a Multidisciplinary World   241
13.3   Characteristics of Successful Teams   244
13.4   Developing Teams and Engaging Boundary-Spanning Problems   247
13.5   Multisector Collaborations and Academic-Corporate Partnerships   251
13.6   Establishing an Academic-Corporate Partnership   255
13.7   Beyond Research in Academic-Corporate Partnerships   259
Assess Your Comprehension   262
Exercises to Deepen Your Understanding   263

14   **A Glass Half Empty or Half Full: Challenges and Opportunities for the
US Academic Research Enterprise   267**
Chapter Overview and Learning Objectives   267
14.1   Comparisons between the US and Other Nations   267
14.2   US Education Statistics   272
14.3   Challenges Facing the US Academic Research Enterprise   276
14.4   Looking Ahead   278
Assess Your Comprehension   278
Exercises to Deepen Your Understanding   279

Afterword   283
Notes   285
References   289
Author Biography   311
Index   313

Acronyms

2 C.F.R. § 200	Title 2 of the US Code of Federal Regulations, Part 200
AA	American Airlines
AAALAC	Association for Assessment and Accreditation of Laboratory Animal Care
AAHRPP	Association for the Accreditation of Human Research Protection Programs
AAMC	Association of American Medical Colleges
A&M	Agricultural and mechanical
AAU	Association of American Universities
ACE	American Council on Education
ADVANCE	Increasing the Participation and Advancement of Women in Academic Science and Engineering Careers
AIRI	Association of Independent Research Institutes
APC	Article processing charge
APLU	Association of Public and Land-grant Universities
AUTM	Association of University Technology Managers
BAA	Broad agency announcement
BRAIN	Brain Research through Advancing Innovative Neurotechnologies
CAPS	Center for Analysis and Prediction of Storms
CARR	Coordinating Administrative Research Requirements
CBR	Congressional Budget Resolution
CITI	Collaborative Institutional Training Initiative
COGR	Council on Governmental Relations
COI	Conflict of interest
COMPETES	Creating Opportunities to Meaningfully Promote Excellence in Technology, Education, and Science
CoR	Council on Research

CORD-19	COVID-19 Open Research Dataset
COVID-19	Coronavirus disease
CR	Continuing Budget Resolution
CRS	Congressional Research Service
CUI	Controlled Unclassified Information
CY	Calendar year
DBER	Discipline-based education research
DHHS	Department of Health and Human Services
DNA	Deoxyribonucleic acid
DOD	Department of Defense
DOE	Department of Energy
D/PU	Doctoral/Professional Universities, Carnegie Classification of Institutions of Higher Education
EHSO	Environmental Health and Safety Office
EPSCoR	Established Program to Stimulate Competitive Research
ERI	Emerging research institution
EU	European Union
FAIR	Findability, accessibility, interoperability, and reuse of digital assets
F&A	Facilities and administrative costs
FDP	Federal Demonstration Partnership
FFRDC	Federally Funded Research and Development Center
FTE	Full-time equivalent
FY	Fiscal year
GDP	Gross domestic product
GPS	Global positioning system
GRANTED	Growing Research Access for Nationally Transformative Equity and Diversity
GUIRR	Government-University-Industry Research Roundtable
HBCU	Historically Black College and University
HIPAA	Health Insurance Portability and Accountability Act
HSI	Hispanic Serving Institution
IACUC	Institutional Animal Care and Use Committee
IBC	Institutional Biosafety Committee
I-Corps	Innovation Corps
IG	Inspector general
IP	Intellectual property
IR&D	Internal research and development
IRB	Institutional Review Board

JCORE	Joint Committee on the Research Environment
M1	Master's Colleges and Universities—Larger programs, Carnegie Classification of Institutions of Higher Education
M2	Master's Colleges and Universities—Medium programs, Carnegie Classification of Institutions of Higher Education
M3	Master's Colleges and Universities—Smaller programs, Carnegie Classification of Institutions of Higher Education
MSI	Minority Serving Institution
NASA	National Aeronautics and Space Administration
NASEM	National Academies of Science, Engineering, and Medicine
NCA	National Council on the Arts
NCURA	National Council of University Research Administrators
NEA	National Endowment for the Arts
NEH	National Endowment for the Humanities
NIH	National Institutes of Health
NIST	National Institute of Standards and Technology
NOAA	National Oceanic and Atmospheric Administration
NORDP	National Organization of Research Development Professionals
NPRM	Notice of Proposed Rulemaking
NSB	National Science Board
NSC	National Security Council
NSF	National Science Foundation
NSPM	National Security Presidential Memorandum
NSTC	National Science and Technology Council
OECD	Organisation for Economic Co-operation and Development
OIRA	Office of Information and Regulatory Affairs
OMB	Office of Management and Budget
ORI	Office of Research Integrity
OSP	Office of sponsored programs
OSTP	Office of Science and Technology Policy
PCAST	President's Council of Advisors on Science and Technology
PD	Project director
PHI	Personal health information
PI	Principal investigator
PPP	Purchasing power parity
PUI	Primarily Undergraduate Institution
PYI	Presidential Young Investigator
QA	Quality assurance

QC	Quality control
R1	Doctoral Universities–Very high research activity, Carnegie Classification of Institutions of Higher Education
R2	Doctoral Universities–High research activity, Carnegie Classification of Institutions of Higher Education
R2O	Research to operations
R&D	Research and development
RAS	Research administrative services
RCN	Research Coordination Networks program
RCR	Responsible conduct of research
RD	Research development
RDT&E	Research, development, test, and evaluation
RECR	Responsible and ethical conduct of research
RFI	Request for Information
ROW	Rest of world
SBIR	Small Business Innovation Research program
SEI	Science and Engineering Indicators
SETI	Search for Extraterrestial Intelligence
SRAI	Society of Research Administrators International
SRO	Senior research officer
STEAM	Science, technology, engineering, arts, and mathematics
STEM	Science, technology, engineering and mathematics
STTR	Small Business Technology Transfer program
STW	Skilled technical workforce
TCU	Tribal College and University
TED	Technology, Entertainment and Design
UIDP	University-Industry Demonstration Partnership
US	United States
USPTO	United States Patent and Trademark Office
VC	Venture capital

Foreword

We are indeed at a pivotal moment as a nation as we chart a bold future toward accelerating our progress in science and technology to ensure a vibrant society and economy. Research enterprises that inspire, nurture, and develop world-class ideas and talent across the broad socioeconomic, demographic, and geographic diversity of our nation are exceedingly important in the vanguard of innovation and competitiveness.

This is an excellent, exhaustive, unique, and timely treatise covering all aspects of research and creative endeavors. Dr. Droegemeier has done a superb job of capturing and representing data, information, and knowledge about what it takes to build successful and sustainable enterprises. This coverage spans the range from an individual researcher building highest-quality research ideas to large research enterprises at the institutional level focused on inspiration and impact.

Dr. Droegemeier's vast knowledge and experience are clearly reflected throughout this book. The thoughtful inclusion of summary notes for assessing comprehension and the valuable exercises at the end of every chapter are bound to reinforce understanding and inspire new ideas.

Having served as a member of national boards and councils such as the National Science Board and as chair of the Council on Research at the Association of Public and Land-grant Universities, I have realized the importance of a focused exposure and training of the important elements needed to build innovative research programs and impactful research enterprises. In addition, due to my roles as a faculty researcher, academic mentor, department chair, and vice president for research, I see tremendous value in this book, especially for the following individuals:

- Graduate students who aspire to build a career in research.
- Young researchers and faculty members who are keen to build a strong research program, translating their ideas into successful projects.

- Senior researchers and administrators at a unit level who want to mentor students, faculty, and researchers to succeed in their research endeavors.

- Members of research teams who aspire to develop shared knowledge working across disciplines.

- Research staff at various levels at an institution who are motivated to serve their researchers by helping them access opportunities, configure ideas into successful projects and proposals, and build effective budgeting and execution of the projects.

- Institutional research leaders like vice presidents/vice chancellors for research who are interested in succeeding in their roles with a commitment to building a strong research office that serves the students, faculty, and researchers.

- Individuals from outside academia who want to understand the drivers and motivators for research advancement in academic enterprises to create impact.

In summary, Dr. Droegemeier's several decades of rich experience as a prolific researcher, a strong research administrator, and an innovative national science leader have resulted in this one-of-a-kind book that is bound to serve generations of researchers, practitioners, research staff, and academic administrators. His passion and commitment for serving the research community is evidenced by his efforts to make this book freely accessible to everyone across our nation.

Dr. Sethuraman (Panch) Panchanathan
February 4, 2022

Preface

I have been blessed to spend my entire professional career in academia and have loved every minute of it! The opportunities to impart knowledge to future generations and to challenge individuals to think creatively, learn how to tackle important problems, and operate with the highest standards of integrity are beyond exhilarating. Especially rewarding is collaborating with others to create new knowledge by unlocking the secrets of this amazing world in which we live. Indeed, working at a comprehensive R1 research university, I have come to appreciate deeply that those secrets avail themselves not only in the laboratory, clinic, or fabrication facility, but also in the studio, on the stage, and from our past and present society.

I also have come to understand that exceptional scholarly work, performed by exceptionally talented individuals, can be found not only in our nation's most highly ranked comprehensive institutions but also in Minority Serving Institutions (MSIs), emerging research institutions (ERIs), and institutions that historically have focused principally on instruction but are becoming more active in research (e.g., Primarily Undergraduate Institutions [PUIs] and community colleges). Yet, in all situations, becoming a successful scholar—irrespective of discipline and institution—requires a great deal of understanding about a wide array of topics in addition to the expertise required to master a given field of study, such as the value, necessity, and types of research and creative activity; public attitudes toward scholarly work and associated outcomes; priority setting within funding sources; formulating ideas and identifying funding; research methods; collecting data or materials; writing competitive grant proposals; publishing and communicating outcomes; understanding and following ethical rules of conduct; navigating the labyrinth of intellectual property and compliance regulations; multidisciplinary inquiry; using research outcomes in policy; collaboration and working in teams; diversity, equity, and inclusion; and the future of research. Typically, understanding of these and other topics comes about quite slowly, mostly through years of direct experience conducting research, presuming one is sufficiently fortunate to be affiliated with a well-resourced institution. Where is the educational resource that addresses these and other issues? Sadly, I found none.

What I did find, however, was myself repeatedly explaining the finer points of the aforementioned topics to my undergraduate and graduate students, postdocs, and early career faculty colleagues, frustrated that no mechanism existed to give them an advantage I did not have. Namely, a way to compress decades of experiential learning—gained by those who have long walked the path of conducting research and participated in policy, education, and other dimensions of the scholarly enterprise—into a dramatically shorter time, thereby allowing nascent researchers to be more productive and engaged earlier in their career.

I also found, in many cases, that next-generation researchers at MSIs, ERIs, and PUIs not only have relatively limited exposure to the aforementioned topics, but also that their institutions frequently lack the administrative support frameworks to assist their scholarly endeavors. As greater attention is being paid nationally to redress long-standing deficiencies in supporting research at these types of institutions, it is important to understand that building their research capacity and capability requires more than funding for research. It also requires access by researchers to administrative resources, such as those for processing research grant proposals, reporting project outcomes to agencies, dealing with the broad array of compliance rules and regulations (including research security), and supporting intellectual property and commercialization. And it requires solid working knowledge, by next-generation researchers, of the related topics noted previously so these individuals can be highly competitive and successful as early as possible in their careers.

Consequently, I decided to develop an online course covering topics I considered most crucial to the success of academic scholars at all stages of their work, and subsequently write this book containing similar material. These resources, and especially this book, are not a how-to guide for researchers, but rather an educational resource for understanding important concepts in the context of one's own research and personal circumstances—concepts that can make a difference between success and failure.

With this book I hope to achieve two goals.

First, to enhance and greatly accelerate understanding, by those pursuing careers of scholarship in all academic disciplines and at all types and sizes of institutions, regarding the topics noted above, which are both increasingly important as well as complex in today's research and creative activity enterprise. And to do so in a manner that is accessible to undergraduate students, graduate students, postdoctoral scholars, early career faculty, and other researchers in academia, private industry, the nonprofit sector, and state and federal research organizations. I also believe the information will be useful to midcareer and senior faculty, research administrators, funding organization program officers, congressional staff, corporate and nonprofit organization researchers, law and policymakers charged with stewarding America's research enterprise, the media, and the general public.

The second overall goal is to democratize understanding of the aforementioned topics across the broad span of America's scholarly enterprise, particularly with regard to organizations, institutions, and individuals traditionally underserved, underrepresented, and underresourced. I, like so many others, have found extraordinary talent and achievement where traditional measures of success and potential, as well as personal circumstances, least suggest they exist. These institutions and individuals must be given every opportunity and resource to contribute.

As America continues to be challenged in its competitive research position on the international stage, and as America works to ensure opportunity for all who wish to pursue scholarly research and creative activity, this book serves as a practical tool for ensuring individual as well as institutional success. This will result in greater equity and strength, and thus greater competitiveness overall, for America's research enterprise.

Acknowledgments

This book, and the associated online course from which it was created, reflect the hard work over a period of some four years by an exceptional team of enthusiastic, passionate, and skilled experts at the University of Oklahoma (OU) and NextThought, LLC (NT).

I wish to express my sincere appreciation to Meleah Meadows, former NT Director of Operations, who was a champion for this work from day one and helped me navigate numerous complex issues. She always found a way to "get to yes," and always saw the potential to help future researchers and the broader research enterprise. Janelle Bevin, former NT Head of Video Productions, was exceptionally helpful in producing the online videos, and I am grateful for the professionalism, creativity, and patience of these two individuals in making my dream a reality. Meleah and Janelle are among the most creative people I have ever met and have been an absolute joy to work with!

Dr. Alicia Knoedler, former OU Executive Associate Vice President for Research and now Head of the Office of Integrative Activities at the National Science Foundation, was an essential partner in every aspect of the project, bringing amazing ideas that were uniquely hers as well as thoughtful critiques that greatly improved the final product. When she saw the need for improvements, she helped identify ways to implement them, and she spotted issues I never would have seen in a million years. Her background in cognitive psychology, coupled with mine in physical science, represented the perfect combination for spanning the spectrum of most every topic or challenge that arose. From Dr. Knoedler I learned more than I can recount and learned to think in ways I had never considered. Others should be so fortunate to work with someone of her capability.

Dr. Chris Nguyen, hired first as an OU graduate student and then later as a postdoctoral fellow, lent tremendous expertise and creativity in collecting and organizing supplemental materials, helping develop exercises, and providing input on numerous other aspects of the project. Max Bevan, Head of Sales at NT, has been a wonderful partner as well, helping bring the online asset over the finish line despite considerable headwinds all along the way.

Dr. Lori Snyder, OU Professor of Psychology, provided important editorial comments on several topics, and Dr. Susan Walden, former Director of the OU Office of Undergraduate Research, was especially helpful in the early stages as I was conceiving the project. Melany Dickens, OU Associate Vice President for Research and Partnerships, lent her extraordinary talents as a logistician in several aspects of the project, especially marketing and contracting. Heather Joseph, Executive Director of SPARC (Scholarly Publishing and Academic Resource Coalition), provided extremely valuable insight and edits regarding all things open access. Jim Bratton, former Director of the OU Office of Technology Development, provided helpful guidance about the complex topic of intellectual property. Tobin Smith, Vice President for Science Policy and Global Affairs at the Association of American Universities, provided very helpful suggestions concerning the federal research and development budget process. And Dr. Laura McMeeking, Director of the STEM Center and Associate Professor at Colorado State University, provided very helpful edits regarding the book and peer reviewer comments about it, as did Matt Hourihan, former Director of the R&D Budget and Policy Program at the American Association for the Advancement of Science.

I extend my deepest thanks and admiration to the remarkable individual who conceived of NT and built the extraordinary family it is today. With a passion for online learning and keen insight and technical knowledge regarding how to utilize technology to personalize and enrich learning, Ken Parker is a force of nature. He also is one of the most brilliant, well read and thoughtful individuals I have ever met. Thank you, Ken, for being a great friend and mentor, and for supporting my crazy ideas!

I also am most grateful to Dr. Edwin Adlerman, one of my former graduate students and an undergraduate alumnus of MIT, for graciously providing publication subvention funding via a gift to the MIT Press, and to David Hoffner of Upsidedown Design for expertly redrafting the figures from their original sources.

The manuscript was expertly evaluated by three anonymous peer reviewers, and their thoughtful comments and suggestions greatly improved the final product. Reviewing a book manuscript requires considerable time and care, so to my three unknown colleagues, you have my heartfelt thanks. My editor at MIT Press, Susan Buckley, was the consummate professional, patiently guiding me through the submission and review steps and answering my numerous questions. John Donohue and Alison Britton at Westchester Publishing Services expertly handled the copyediting and production processes.

Finally, I am deeply appreciative of my dear friend and colleague, Nicholas S. Hathaway, former OU Executive Vice President, for his strong support, and especially for the funding he directed toward creating the online course as part of OU's contract with NT.

Introduction

The academic research enterprise. That easily uttered phrase—foundational to our health, prosperity, economic and national security, and quality of life—defines an exceedingly complex and historically vital component of society that is interpreted quite differently by its many stakeholder groups.

To faculty and other professional researchers, it connotes an intellectually stimulating, multi-institutional, multigenerational, multicultural, and rewarding enterprise that underpins their professional lives; supports the creation and dissemination of new knowledge; and educates the next generation of scholars, entrepreneurs, inventors, and technologists. To postdoctoral researchers, it represents the environment within which to develop additional professional skills, independence, knowledge, and relationships that help frame a future of contributions in the academy, industry, or government. To graduate students, it means an educational system that supports study of an interesting topic and preparation of a thesis or dissertation, along with publishing, performing, or exhibiting the outcomes as a step toward pursuing multiple career options. To undergraduate students, it means a broad education underpinned by several courses in their chosen field or fields of study, possible involvement in a mentored research project, and even presenting work at a conference or publishing a paper or two before graduating. And yet to many students—far too many students—it means an opportunity that cannot be seized owing to a variety of socioeconomic, cultural, and/or financial circumstances. Consequently, this limits or even eliminates the ability of such individuals to participate in America's scholarly enterprise and thus become important players in our nation's future.

The view of the academic research enterprise is notably different for those who facilitate research rather than perform it. To senior research officers, such as vice presidents and vice chancellors for research, it means helping faculty and students succeed in creating and disseminating new knowledge, building areas of excellence, and increasing external grant and contract funding to their institution. It also means engaging with federal agencies to understand future directions of research nationally, including budgets that support research, and influencing those directions via interactions with members of Congress, the executive branch, and other organizations, such as professional societies. To research administrators, the academic research enterprise means an array of rules and regulations, audits, last-minute proposal submissions, and complex negotiations and award management activities including patents and licenses. To private companies, it represents the seed corn of innovation, a major source of intellectual property, and most importantly, the origin of a well-equipped workforce. To funding agencies and private foundations, it represents the repository of talent where investments, usually in response to grant proposals, lead to discoveries, solutions to complex problems, and the next generation of researchers, entrepreneurs, inventors, and technologists. And to the general public, it means a respected, albeit somewhat mysterious element of society that yields outcomes generally viewed as beneficial.

Although these and other groups view the academic research enterprise through vastly different lenses, they share, with the arguable exception of the general public, one important characteristic: *learning about and applying, in practical ways, the many complex elements of this enterprise incrementally, as their career progresses.* Sometimes this learning is provided by a mentor, a workshop, formal certification training, or colleagues. But in most cases, when it comes to researchers, the learning takes place over long periods of time via direct experience, which can lead to unnecessary delays, frustration, false starts, and missteps that sometimes have serious consequences.

As a partial remedy, this book provides a comprehensive examination of key practical topics to enable aspiring as well as early-career researchers (undergraduate students, graduate students, postdoctoral researchers, early career faculty, and research staff) across all disciplines—from art history to zoology—and all types and sizes of institutions, to begin mastering important professional capabilities far earlier in their career than normally would be the case. The content, complementary to knowledge received as part of formal education and training in research, is assembled in a manner that highlights interrelationships among topics, augmented and contextualized with nearly four decades of experience by the author in research and national policy. The chapters need not be read in sequence, and can even be used piecemeal, as standalone references. Although the book emphasizes the academic research enterprise, the topics addressed are equally valuable for researchers in the government, corporate, and nonprofit sectors.

Importantly, this book is not a how-to guide or instruction manual for next-generation or current researchers. Rather, it is an educational resource for developing and understanding researcher roles, responsibilities, and opportunities in the context of the reader's own scholarly program and personal circumstances. As such, this book has been written for individuals at large, comprehensive doctoral research universities and doctoral/professional universities (Carnegie R1, R2, and D/PU classification; http://carnegieclassifications.acenet.edu), master's colleges and universities (Carnegie M1 to M3 classification), MSIs, ERIs, and institutions that historically have focused principally on instruction but are becoming more active in research (e.g., PUIs and community colleges). Particular emphasis is given to individuals at the latter institutions, which have relatively limited exposure to the topics contained herein because their institutions often lack the resources and administrative support frameworks to assist their scholarly endeavors.

This book also places scholars in a broad national and international context—not as passive recipients of a system already in place, but as key participants in a system in which their active engagement is essential for helping set priorities, determine policies, drive systemic change, and advance knowledge for the success of the enterprise as a whole.

Chapter 1 sets the stage by addressing foundational issues such as the role of curiosity in research and creative activity; the spectrum of research from fundamental to highly applied and translational; how, where, and by whom research is performed; ways in which outcomes and impacts of research are assessed and valued; and the manner in which academic research administration and services are structured. All research requires funding, and thus chapter 2 is devoted to sources of funding for research, the setting of priorities by research funding organizations, the federal research and development budget process, and strategies for obtaining funding.

Because the bulk of fundamental or curiosity-driven research and creative activity in the US is funded by taxpayers via federal agencies, the general public has a vested interest in research and its outcomes. This topic is addressed in chapter 3, along with factors that shape public understanding, the manner in which belief systems influence public views, and how research results are used in public policy.

Chapters 4–6 focus on the processes associated with proposing and performing research, starting with an array of research methods and extending to finding, creating, and analyzing data as well as research grant proposal development, evaluation, and project management. Subjecting research to scrutiny via the peer review process is addressed in chapter 7, including how to use criticism effectively to advance both individual as well as broader goals. Chapter 8 builds on this topic by discussing bias and multiple points of view in the research enterprise, and chapter 9 addresses the important topic of ethical conduct in research, the roles and responsibilities of researchers, and consequences that can arise if research misconduct occurs.

Chapter 10 describes the complex universe of research policies and compliance, the roles and responsibilities of researchers, and activities now underway to reduce unnecessary administrative burden, while chapter 11 focuses on approaches for communicating research outcomes to multiple audiences. Chapter 12 delves into the complexities of intellectual property ownership and protection, and ways in which intellectual property can be utilized to advance personal goals as well as the economy, national security, and quality of life.

Many of today's most intellectually stimulating and compelling challenges reside not within a particular discipline, but rather at the boundaries of multiple disciplines. Chapter 13 describes challenges and opportunities of collaboration and working in multidisciplinary teams, as well as the value and structure of academic-corporate partnerships. The book concludes in chapter 14 with a look ahead, including an array of research and education funding and output statistics that place the US in an international context.

A set of questions is provided at the end of each chapter to help assess the reader's comprehension of the material presented, along with several exercises to deepen the reader's understanding via hands-on experience. As noted in the exercises themselves, the amount of time and resources required, and level of guidance needed, vary by topic and activity. A Facilitator Guide also is available online at https://mitpress.mit.edu/9780262547079 to assist in supervising the comprehension assessment questions and exercises.

1

Deep in Our Bones: Why and Where We Perform Research and Creative Activity

Chapter Overview and Learning Objectives

From providing a platform for understanding our history to conveying our ideas and emotions through artistic expression to exploring the most foundational questions of the universe, research and creative activity allow us to expand the frontiers of knowledge. They inspire us to pursue the impossible, unite us around shared goals, and guide us through life by providing solutions, comfort, and joy.

This chapter provides a foundation to the book by introducing the concepts of research and creative activity—where they take place, how they contribute to society, and how research administrative services (RAS) are organized at colleges and universities. After reading this chapter, you should

- Understand the meaning of the terms "research" and "creative activity" and the role played by curiosity in them;
- Be able to differentiate among the various subclassifications of research;
- Understand the sectors in which research takes place;
- Appreciate the roles of individuals and teams in performing research;
- Understand the importance of taxpayer funding in supporting fundamental research and the value to society of research outcomes;
- Realize that a delicate balance exists between focusing on the practical, quantifiable value to society of research and the need to engage in research and creative activity for the sole purpose of contributing to a body of knowledge and expression;
- Recognize the importance of incorporating multiple perspectives and expertise through a multidisciplinary, globally engaged approach to research in order to solve the world's most complex problems; and

- Understand how RAS are structured at colleges and universities, and options for obtaining needed resources if your institution does not provide them.

1.1   The Root of Curiosity and Emergence of Structured Inquiry

One of the world's most creative individuals, Walt Disney, said "We keep moving forward, opening new doors, and doing new things, because we're curious—and curiosity keeps leading us down new paths" (Walt Disney Archives n.d.). Physicist Albert Einstein said, "The important thing is to not stop questioning. Curiosity has its own reason for existence" (Miller 1955, 64). And author Zora Neale Hurston said, "Research is formalized curiosity. It is poking and prying with a purpose" (Hurston 1942, 182).

Curiosity! If I were to come up with a single word that embodies what research and creative activity are all about, that would be it.

Think of it! What is the earliest thing we do as children? We "get into things" when we begin to crawl and walk! This clearly demonstrates that curiosity is not something we develop over time, but rather is a fundamental part of our humanity. We are born curious! But what makes us curious? Animals are curious too. However, humans have the ability to utilize their curiosity to investigate and understand, express creatively, innovate, explain, and build upon that understanding. Thus, significant value, both quantitative and qualitative, exists in our curiosity—a point we will revisit in chapter 3.

Albert Einstein also is presumed to have said, "If we knew what we were doing, it would not be called research, would it?" This quote nicely captures the link between research and curiosity. However, the notion can be misleading because, in fact, we do know what we are doing when conducting research, as we will see in chapter 4. In fact, pursuing curiosity and getting paid to do it—which is what researchers do—may seem frivolous. However, the benefits of research are all around us. Examples include smartphones, laptop computers, flat-screen televisions, commercial and military airplanes, radars that detect the formation of tornadoes, and clothes that do not wrinkle.

These and other technologies, born out of research, do not reflect the totality of what research is about. Portraying the world in art is a form of research, as noted in the next section, providing insight into people and culture. You might wonder why we make paintings of things we can both see and photograph. It is because paintings capture more than the image—they capture the expressive intent of the artist in sometimes subtle but important ways. We also express abstract ideas and emotions in art and dance, as well as capture history, preserve culture, and show important aspects of society such as conflict, tension, and change. Studying our past helps us understand the present and also the future. We are curious why people thought and behaved in certain ways, and sometimes we can only appreciate those things when viewed through the lens of history.

Despite the beauty and importance of curiosity, when it comes to research, curiosity cannot be pursued in an arbitrary manner. Consequently, beginning over two thousand years ago, philosophers such as Aristotle created structured approaches for studying the natural world, understanding the past, and creating music and plays. Rules and steps exist in research not only because we want to make sure we are correct in our understanding, but also because we want to build upon the work of others or interpret their work in our own way.

We test hypotheses, not only in the chemistry laboratory, but also in the dance studio. We test theories about the natural world to determine whether certain events occur randomly or for some other reason. Even some of the things we encounter continuously, and take for granted, such as gravity, are not fully understood.

It is important to recognize, however, that today's structured approaches to research—the rules and steps we follow—do not deny the tremendous value of lore, Indigenous knowledge, and tradition in research. Indeed, as discussed in chapter 4, these and other approaches to understanding the world increasingly are being embraced as a means for enhancing the overall research process.

The beauty of inquiry is that learning never stops, even though some questions may get answered. Yet in reality, research rarely provides immutable answers, but rather conveys the state of our understanding at any given time. Sometimes, we make major breakthroughs, but most of the time, our knowledge advances incrementally, one new revelation at a time. As Laurence Sterne noted, "The desire of knowledge, like the thirst for riches, increases ever with the acquisition of it" (Sterne 1759).

1.2   The Lexicon of Research: Understanding and Misunderstanding

The word "research" has a rather cumbersome but important formal definition in modern application. It generally refers to systematic "investigation or experimentation aimed at the discovery and interpretation of facts, revision of accepted theories or laws in the light of new facts, or practical application of such new or revised theories or laws" ("Research" n.d.). Wow!

Let us unpack this.

The key points here are "systematic," which means a structured approach that follows established or accepted steps and processes; "discovery," which means either creating new understanding or refining existing understanding; and also "practical application," which includes the translation of new and/or previous research outcomes into new services, devices, procedures, processes, or activities that might benefit society.

A close cousin of research is the term "creative activity," which often is used in colleges and research universities. It makes clear that research is not solely the domain of the physical sciences, life sciences, engineering, social and behavioral sciences, and medicine, but also includes areas such as the humanities, and the arts and fine arts (e.g., English and other languages, literature, history, classics and letters, art, music, theater). One thus frequently hears "research and creative activity" used together in the context of academic scholarship.

However, this separation is a bit unfortunate because individuals working in fields such as science and engineering (often referred to as STEM disciplines, encompassing science, technology, engineering, and mathematics) apply a great deal of creativity in their work. Likewise, fields such as history and the arts test hypotheses about the past—for example, regarding human movement and expression in musicals (STEM is sometimes expanded to STEAM to include the arts, though not simply by adding it but rather by integrating it with the other elements of STEM). A better term to encompass all of research and creative activity is "scholarship," which covers all the bases but can be confused with special awards of funding to pay for education. The incorporation of lore and other sources and approaches enriches the broad concept of scholarship.

Throughout this book, I use the terms "research" and "research and creative activity" synonymously unless otherwise noted.

Having described the formal definition of research and creative activity, it is important to recognize that three subclassifications exist in research, often termed basic or fundamental research, applied research, and development (table 1.1). As shown in the table, basic research simply refers to research performed without a clear practical use in mind. That is why we also call it fundamental, discovery- or curiosity-based research—to make clear it is not "basic" in the sense of being simple. Studying the structure of atoms, the fundamental properties of materials and compounds, and the nature of black holes are good examples of fundamental research. The federal government funds the bulk of fundamental research in the US, and we examine in chapter 2 the broader spectrum of research funding.

The second subclassification, known as applied research, often is referred to as use-inspired research. It emphasizes using the outcomes of fundamental and other research for solving problems or developing new processes, products, or techniques that have practical value for a specific application or purpose. Often this purpose is linked directly to societal value or economic or

Table 1.1
US government executive branch definitions of research.

Basic research is systematic study directed toward a fuller knowledge or understanding of the fundamental aspects of phenomena and of observable facts without specific applications toward processes or products in mind. Basic research, however, may include activities with broad applications in mind.

Applied research is systematic study to gain knowledge or understanding necessary to determine the means by which a recognized and specific need may be met.

Experimental development is creative and systematic work, drawing on knowledge gained from research and practical experience, which is directed at producing new products or processes or improving existing products or processes. Like research, experimental development will result in gaining additional knowledge.

Research and development (R&D) equipment includes acquisition or design and production of movable equipment, such as spectrometers, research satellites, detectors, and other instruments. At a minimum, this category includes programs devoted to the purchase or construction of research and development equipment.

Research and development facilities include the acquisition, design, and construction of, or major repairs or alterations to, all physical facilities for use in R&D activities. Facilities include land, buildings, and fixed capital equipment, regardless of whether the facilities are to be used by the government or by a private organization, and regardless of where title to the property may rest. This category includes such fixed facilities as reactors, wind tunnels, and particle accelerators.

Source: Office of Management and Budget (2018a, 205).

business benefit. Examples of applied research include the development of a heart pacemaker using available circuitry, batteries, and medical implantation procedures.

The third and final subclassification is development, which sometimes is broken into applied development and product development. Here, multiple alternatives to a particular application are evaluated and the best chosen to go forward based upon which have the fewest risks or possibilities of failure. At this point, market forces come into play as some alternatives may be more expensive or less marketable than others. Note that the US government recently replaced "development" with "experimental development" (table 1.1).

If you think the above classification is complex, the US Department of Defense (DOD) has taken it a step further, both in terms of expanding the framework of fundamental research to applied research to development, but also structuring it via a numbering system that runs from categories 6.1 to 6.7.

As shown in table 1.2, category 6.1 is basic research, while 6.7 represents upgrades to operational capabilities. A new category, 6.8, now covers pilot programs in software and digital technology. Traditionally, a logical, linear progression has been envisioned to exist in which basic research begets applied research begets development and then leads to products. In chapter 3, however, we show that the real world is far more complicated.

Table 1.2
US Department of Defense research, development, test, and evaluation budget activity codes and descriptions.

Code	Description
6.1	Basic research
6.2	Applied research
6.3	Advanced technology development
6.4	Advanced component development and prototypes
6.5	System development and demonstration
6.6	RDT&E management support
6.7	Operational system development
6.8	Software and digital technology pilot programs

Source: Congressional Research Service (2021a).

In addition to these classifications of research is the notion of translational research. Usually applied in the context of human health, a precise overall definition has yet to be agreed upon. However, in general, translational research—which can be applied in domains broader than health—involves research that rapidly translates discoveries and research outcomes into practice for the benefit of society. Examples include fundamental discoveries in tumor structure that lead to new cancer therapies and research using radar data in computer models of the atmosphere to improve the prediction of severe storms (an example of R2O, or research to operations transition; http://vlab.noaa.gov/web/osti-r2o).

Another term commonly used in the context of research is "innovation." It generally is accepted that innovation describes the process by which research outcomes, technologies, and ideas are converted into goods, services, processes, or other things having value for society. For example, Apple did not fund or conduct the fundamental research that led to what lies inside an iPhone (like the battery, touch screen, electronic circuitry, wireless technology). Rather, Apple brilliantly innovated using all of these things and more to produce a product that has transformed society in ways unimaginable just a decade ago. The next time you use your smart device to make a call, surf the Internet, or send a text message, think of all of the research and innovation that made possible those capabilities.

1.3 The Many Homes of Research and Creative Activity

Having established motives for research and creative activity as well as the associated classifications, consider where research actually takes place. The "how" of research—that is, research methods and the rules and procedures discussed in the previous section—is addressed in chapter 4.

The bulk of fundamental research in the US is performed at research universities. This includes comprehensive institutions that offer doctoral, master's and baccalaureate degrees (Carnegie R1 and R2 classification; http://carnegieclassifications.acenet.edu) and have the performance of research and creative activity as part of their mission, along with teaching, community engagement, and public and professional service. Such institutions also tend to have excellent research support resources (section 1.6). Research also is performed at institutions that offer only doctoral/professional, master's or baccalaureate degrees (Carnegie D/PU and M1 to M3 classification), or that focus principally on instruction (PUIs and community colleges). The latter institutions tend to have fewer administrative support resources, though increasingly are becoming more active in research via their own strategic directions as well as special funding opportunities offered by federal agencies and other sources.

Historically, demonstrated success in research and creative activity was one of the most important requirements for receiving academic tenure[1] at comprehensive institutions. Yet a tension has long existed between teaching and research in evaluating faculty performance and awarding tenure, with success in research tending to dominate, even though mentoring students in research clearly involves teaching. At other types of institutions, and even now many comprehensives, teaching is the clear metric by which tenure is awarded, even though faculty often perform research as well. The importance of instruction more generally now is recognized as a key value proposition for tenure across all types of higher education institutions, and an increasing amount of research is being conducted by undergraduate students, sometimes in classroom settings.

In addition to conducting the bulk of fundamental research in the US, academic institutions also conduct applied research, especially in disciplines such as business, engineering, law, journalism, and education, though such scholarly areas also do their share of basic research.

As detailed in chapter 2, the federal government traditionally has been the largest funder of fundamental research owing to the lack of a clear purpose for its outcomes and thus the financial risk it poses were it funded principally by the private sector. Many federal agencies—so-called mission agencies—conduct research in their own laboratories and centers, and this sort of work is called intramural research. Examples include, for the US Department of Energy (DOE) (http://energy.gov), National Laboratories such as Los Alamos, Sandia, Lawrence Livermore, Oak Ridge, and the National Renewable Energy Laboratory; for the National Oceanic and Atmospheric Administration (NOAA) (http://noaa.gov), its National Severe Storms Laboratory; and for the US DOD (http://defense.gov), the Army Research Laboratory and Naval Research

Laboratory. These and other agencies also fund research at academic institutions and private companies by providing them with competitive grants and contracts (chapter 6), and such work is termed "extramural" research because it is performed outside of government-owned and -operated organizations.

For-profit private companies conduct huge amounts of research as well (chapter 2), mostly in the areas of applied R&D that leads to products and services that can be commercialized. Use of company funds for this purpose is often termed IR&D, which stands for internal R&D. The sectors where such research most often takes place include chemicals, computers and electronics, aerospace, defense, automotive, and software.

An example of a major for-profit research organization, which unfortunately no longer exists, is the venerable Bell Laboratories, where the transistor was first demonstrated. Today, Google, another massive for-profit organization, conducts large amounts of research on topics ranging from self-driving cars to high-altitude balloons for advanced communication.

Independent research institutes are another important part of the research landscape. Typically, they are funded via philanthropy and focus on very specific topics such as poverty, global health, the environment, and social justice. The more familiar examples in science include the Howard Hughes Medical Institute (http://hhmi.org), Cold Spring Harbor Laboratory (http://cshl.edu), and the Danforth Plant Science Center (http://danforthcenter.org). Additionally, numerous private foundations also provide significant funding for research conducted in academia (chapter 2).

In the area of the arts, fine arts, and humanities, a vast array of nonprofit and philanthropic-based organizations fund research and creative activity. These organizations exist at the community level, as well as the state and national levels. Most depend upon some form of public support, with occasional funding from federal agencies via grants. Several are organized as coalitions, consortia, or performing companies. As described further in chapter 3, this area of the research and creative activity enterprise has far fewer opportunities for federal support yet is vitally important to society.

1.4 From Individual Researcher to a Globally Engaged Team

Because research and creative activity—irrespective of discipline or idea—ultimately spring forth from human curiosity or societal need, the pathway to discovery, interpretation, or answers rests with people. Yet, the manner in which people tackle research problems depends upon a number of factors.

For example, if you wish to study a particular problem or pursue an idea, the first question you must ask yourself—assuming the problem or idea is viable—is whether you have sufficient expertise to do so by yourself. For the moment, we are setting aside issues such as funding, necessary equipment, space, and so on. In other words, is the scope of the problem within your own skill set?

Historically, scholars tended to work on their own, pursuing their ideas and sharing their findings with others via publications, presentations, and performances. Many problems still can be tackled in this manner, which is the so-called single investigator approach that often leads to the highly coveted sole author journal article, recital, or book. Yet, single investigators almost always build upon work performed previously, perhaps as far back as several decades. Even Albert Einstein, who published many single-author papers, benefited from the work of others in establishing his theories.

In many cases, however, problems are so broad in scope or so complex that they require capabilities and knowledge well beyond what a single individual possesses, even if they have been in the field for several decades. For example, the oft-asked question "What causes tornadoes to form?" is so complex that, to be answered, it requires experts in the fields of fluid dynamics, thermodynamics, mathematics, engineering, physics, and computer science. And even then, once the cause or causes become known, the ultimate goal is to prevent people from dying, which involves research in human behavior, communication science, and sociology. In other words, to keep people from dying in tornadoes, many disciplines must come together to study the problem in an integrative, holistic manner. We discuss collaborations, team-oriented scholarly activity, and "convergent research" in chapter 13.

Additionally, the solution to a problem in one part of the world, or in one industry, may not be applicable in other contexts for many reasons—such as culture, religion, economic conditions, or corporate philosophy. In such cases, it is necessary to engage researchers across broad domains and regions in order to bring the necessary perspectives and expertise to bear on the problem.

Climate change is a good example. Although the fundamental physics of climate change apply to the planet as a whole, the manner in which these changes are manifest, and the impacts they have, are highly variable and local. Thus, understanding and mitigating the impacts of climate change require not only a multidisciplinary approach, but a globally engaged one as well.

1.5 Outcomes, Impacts, and Assessing Purpose and Value

The performance of research and creative activity requires funding—ranging from the salary of those performing the work to funding for space, equipment, instruments, technicians, graduate and undergraduate students, materials, publications, performances, exhibits, professional meetings, and travel.

Consequently, those providing the funding—which includes taxpayers (usually via federal agencies or foundations), companies, and philanthropists—want to ensure the work is of the highest quality, is relevant, adheres to the highest ethical standards, and has meaningful value and impact.

Unfortunately, it is not always easy, as noted further in chapter 3, to connect the dots from fundamental research to marketable product or public service. Also difficult is accepting the fact that, in many cases, years to decades pass before a fundamental research outcome makes a transformational impact on society, as did the iPhone, the global positioning system (GPS), the laptop computer, and the Internet. Nor is it always easy to argue for the great value wrought to society by the arts, fine arts, and humanities. Paintings, performances, and the study of ancient cultures may not cure cancer, but they are as important to our humanity as the activities that seek to find such cures. Indeed, modern medicine increasingly includes the arts in a holistic approach to therapy, with very impressive results.

The historical social compact between the taxpayer and the research enterprise, which has allowed our society to thrive, is being questioned today. Why? Generally, as a result of budget challenges, which lead to less tolerance for funding research (by Congress in particular) that does not demonstrably produce outcomes of immediate practical value. It has been said that, had researchers at the start of the Industrial Revolution listened to what society thought was most important, the steam engine, telegraph, and airplane would have been long delayed.

Assessing the value of research to society is a very difficult task and needs to consider not one aspect of research but the entire process—from idea to outcome. Not surprisingly, it is a mistake to presume all value can be monetized, or that practical outcomes are the sine qua non of research. It equally is unwise to assume all research will produce beneficial or positive results. Failure is an essential element of fundamental research and even product commercialization, and boldness of ideas and risk of failure are inseparable. And failure is never without the learning it brings. Charles Kettering aptly captured this sentiment in a quote often incorrectly attributed to C. S. Lewis, "Failures, repeated failures, are finger posts on the road to achievement. One fails forward toward success" (O'Flaherty 2018, 37).

Perhaps it is most appropriate to speak not in terms of the value of research, but rather the purpose. For even seemingly esoteric studies in pure mathematics, investigations into the evolution of obscure languages, or the study of an essentially unknown artist, have a purpose in contributing to the body of knowledge and expression we know as research and creative activity. Judging which such efforts should be funded, though an imperfect task performed via peer or merit review (chapters 6 and 7), has served the US well and made us the envy of the world. Indeed, we should measure the associated outcomes and impacts of research that can be quantified, but also be comfortable knowing those things that are more qualitative in character are of tremendous value to society as well.

1.6   Research Leadership at Academic Institutions

Throughout this book, I mention numerous resources provided by academic institutions to support the scholarly endeavors of students, faculty, and other researchers. However, not every institution is able to provide these resources, and even if they do, the variation across institutions can be significant. As a student conducting research for the first time, or as a postdoctoral researcher or early career faculty member, it is important that you understand how academic institutions organize their research administration leadership and resources so you can benefit from them to the maximum extent possible. And even more important is that you understand where to turn if your institution does not or cannot provide the resources you need.

At the highest levels of institutional leadership, most colleges and universities have a similar administrative structure. Namely, a chancellor or president who serves as the chief executive officer of the campus (some colleges and universities are part of a system, led by a chancellor or president). They also have a provost (also often carrying the title senior vice president), who serves as the chief academic officer of the campus, along with academic deans, who oversee individual colleges typically organized by discipline or groupings of disciplines (e.g., engineering, arts and science, fine arts, business, social and behavioral sciences, graduate studies). Rounding out the leadership are department chairs, heads, or directors, who oversee individual academic units (e.g., department of modern languages).

Numerous other positions exist as well, such as chief legal counsel, chief diversity officer, vice president or vice chancellor for student affairs, and directors of centers and institutes. Members of the senior leadership team (president or chancellor and vice presidents or vice chancellors) function as executive officers, most of whom report directly to the president or chancellor and compose the cabinet.

The institutions themselves are governed by boards of regents, trustees, or overseers, the members of which usually are selected by the governor (in the case of public institutions), though sometimes are elected by alumni, the citizenry, or the boards themselves. Such governing bodies have full legal authority over the institution and function as its fiduciary, subject to federal and state laws. They hire the president or chancellor, authorize the awarding of degrees, create and enforce policy, approve strategic plans, budgets, and the academic curriculum, approve hiring of all faculty and staff (though at some institutions, the president/chancellor or provost have this responsibility), and in general are responsible for overall institutional success.

Because the aforementioned positions and structures are common to most colleges and universities, their roles and responsibilities generally are understood by faculty and staff. Although an undergraduate student, graduate student, and postdoctoral scholar may generally be aware of this institutional structure, they tend to be more familiar with individuals or offices directly impacting their scholarly work—namely, their college dean, department chair or director, and faculty mentor. Students and postdocs also interact with and thus tend to be most familiar with the financial aid office, learning and writing center, center for student life, and student social and intramural athletic organizations.

Ironically, one leadership position that is among those least understood is the senior research officer (SRO). Despite being responsible for one of the three major dimensions of academic institutional success (teaching, research, and service/community engagement), the role of the SRO can be somewhat of a mystery. Why? Because in contrast to the aforementioned senior leadership positions, the SRO function, scope of responsibility, and level of resources provided can vary dramatically from institution to institution. Some SROs are responsible solely for research while others have numerous additional responsibilities, including research compliance (chapter 10), graduate education, and economic development (chapter 12).

Depending upon the size and type of academic institution, the SRO may hold the title of vice president or vice chancellor for research (as well as dean if overseeing a graduate college or program), reporting directly to the president or provost. In some cases, especially for smaller institutions, the SRO is an associate vice president or vice provost and even a midlevel staff position.

Not surprisingly, executive officers, faculty, and staff view the SRO through vastly different lenses. Presidents/chancellors and provosts generally view the SRO as someone who can dramatically and sustainably increase external research funding to the institution in the form of grants and contracts (chapter 6) and intellectual property licenses (chapter 12) and can also oversee graduate student and postdoctoral policies—all of which can lead to improved institutional outcomes and rankings. Deans, department chairs/directors, and faculty generally view the SRO as someone who provides services to support the preparation and submission of grant proposals, and the management of grants once awarded. They also see the SRO as providing matching funding for externally sponsored grants and contracts, funding for the purchase and repair of equipment, space for scholarly activity, start-up funds for new faculty hires, and support for travel and publishing, exhibiting, or performing scholarly outcomes.

Graduate and undergraduate students, and postdoctoral scholars, rarely interact with the SRO during their professional development. However, if they wish to pursue careers as academic scholars or even work in government or industry (which frequently have a position equivalent to an SRO), they quickly come to understand that the SRO is a key resource for their success. Consequently, it is important for you, as a next-generation researcher, to become familiar with the SRO so you can make maximum use of the associated resources both during your formal studies and afterward in your professional endeavors.

The actual roles and responsibilities of the SRO position can best be organized within the six general categories shown below. A summary of the activities associated with each follows. Note again that not all categories are present within all institutions, and consequently, throughout this book, suggestions are provided so you can obtain the resources you need when they do not exist at your own institution.

- Institutional strategic planning
- Research development
- Research administrative services
- Internal funding
- Economic development and community engagement
- Research compliance and integrity

Institutional strategic planning   Most colleges and universities have comprehensive strategic plans encompassing academic success and student achievement, research and creative activity, community engagement, affordability and accessibility, diversity enhancement, local and regional impact, economic development, and other topics. The SRO leads the component of the plan involving research and creative activity (and contributes to others as well, especially economic development), often resulting in three to five pillars of institutional strategic emphasis in research based upon factors such as historical strengths, a desire to create new areas of excellence, and alignment with national, regional, state, and local activities and directions. The research component of the plan frequently contains a list of goals, objectives, and strategies or tactics for attaining them, along with required resources, usually in the form of new funding and/or facilities, as well as metrics for assessing progress.

The most effective strategic plans are developed by obtaining input from all stakeholders, including next-generation researchers. Consequently, it is important for you, as such an individual, to be aware of your institution's planning activities and to become involved with them. Do not wait to be asked! Be proactive, because the future of America's research enterprise belongs to you—and you can most effectively steward it by engaging strategically in helping determine its future directions as early as possible in your career.

Research development   A relatively new capability that has emerged in many colleges and universities during the past decade, and that has grown dramatically in recent years, is research development (RD), which involves assisting faculty and postdoctoral scholars, and sometimes graduate students, in planning their scholarly activities. This includes but is not limited to identifying overall career goals and the scholarly activities along the way needed to achieve them; developing and framing ideas as the foundation of scholarly work (i.e., ideation); identifying appropriate sources of external funding; developing competitive grant proposals containing persuasive narratives that contextualize the work to be done and how the expected outcomes will contribute to the existing body of knowledge; identifying collaborators and building teams; guiding the development of research partnerships; creating mechanisms to broaden the participation of traditionally underrepresented groups and enhancing diversity, equity, inclusion, and belonging as part of the research process; identifying research impacts broader than those associated with the research itself; and understanding how a given project contributes to a scholar's overall career plan.

Some institutions have RD offices or centers with professional staff to assist in the activities mentioned above. As a student, postdoctoral scholar, or early career (and even mid- or late-career) faculty member, you should determine if and where your institution provides such resources. And if it does not, consult the SRO to understand the mechanisms available to you to help plan your specific research activities and place them in the context of your career goals. One valuable resource is the National Organization of Research Development Professionals (NORDP) (http://nordp.org), comprising more than one thousand RD professionals across hundreds of academic institutions, nonprofit organizations, and private companies.

Research administrative services   One of the most long-standing and important components of the SRO scope of responsibility is the provision of services supporting the processing of researcher grant proposals submitted to external funding sources (chapter 6), and the subsequent management of associated grants and contracts after they are awarded. Indeed, if one views RD as everything leading up to and including the preparation of the intellectual content of a grant proposal, RAS represent everything that follows. That is, development of the proposal budget and all other information required by the funding source, followed by actual submission of the proposal to the funding source according to applicable policies and laws. Once a grant proposal or contract is funded, RAS helps ensure compliance with the "terms and conditions" of the awarding organization, including budget management, preparation and submission of progress reports, data capture, and monitoring of subcontracts to collaborators.

Typically, the RAS function is executed within an institution's office of sponsored programs (OSP), which usually has a reporting line to the SRO. When such an office does not exist, the principal investigator of the grant or contract is responsible for the aforementioned activities—a significant burden to be sure, and one that places the scholar at considerable risk owing to the numerous details contained in terms and conditions and the legal ramifications of violating them. Fortunately, staff within the OSP are highly skilled and many are formally credentialed. Also, in most institutions, only a few individuals in the OSP, including the SRO, have the legal authority to submit proposals on behalf of the institution and thus obligate it formally to the terms and conditions contained within.

If your institution does not have an OSP and you require the sorts of services it provides, contact your SRO or equivalent to determine how your needs can best be met. Some academic institutions, especially those that are resource-challenged, are partnering with larger institutions to provide SRO capabilities. Such multi-institutional shared services models provide economies of scale, thus improving the ability of all institutions to actively participate in America's research enterprise. They also promote a framework for developing multi-institutional research collaborations (chapter 13). Additionally, as in the case of RD, RAS has a number of supporting professional organizations, especially the National Council of University Research Administrators (NCURA; http://ncura .edu) and the Society of Research Administrators International (SRA International; http://srainternational.org/home). And finally, as noted in section 10.6, efforts are underway within the federal government to improve research administrative resources across the national academic enterprise.

Internal funding   One of the most important roles of the SRO is to strategically allocate funding from internal resources[2] to support the scholarly endeavors of its students, postdoctoral scholars, and faculty. Although the capture of funding from external sources, such as federal agencies (e.g., the National Science Foundation [NSF; http://nsf.gov], the National Endowment for the Arts [NEA; http://nea.gov], the National Endowment for the Humanities [NEH; http://neh.gov], and the National Institutes of Health [NIH;

http://nih.gov]) and private nonprofit foundations (e.g., the John Templeton Foundation [http://templeton.org], the Bill and Melinda Gates Foundation [http://gatesfoundation.org], the James S. McDonnell Foundation [http://jsmf .org], the Alfred P. Sloan Foundation [http://sloan.org], the W. M. Keck Foundation [http://wmkeck.org], the Mellon Foundation [http://mellon.org], and the Ford Foundation [http://fordfoundation.org]) is the desired goal for most scholars, *internal funding* is critically important for several reasons.

First, scholars often need seed funding to obtain preliminary results in pursuit of a new research idea or project, especially one that is outside the mainstream of their expertise, so as to best position them to compete for external funding. The internal funding may support travel to interview subjects, collect data, attend a meeting, meet with potential collaborators, or view archives. It also may involve supporting a student for a short period of time to perform preliminary research.

Second, funds frequently are needed for publishing, exhibiting, presenting, or performing scholarly outcomes. Although costs for such items can be included in most external grants, some disciplines—especially the arts, fine arts, and humanities—have far less access to such external funding and therefore must rely upon institutional support. This is especially true for the publication of books, which are a principal mode of communicating scholarly outcomes for the humanities, but for which institutional subvention fees to publishers sometimes are needed given the often relatively limited distribution of such work.

Third, researchers often require funding to travel to professional conferences and meetings, give invited presentations or exhibitions, and serve on committees or as journal editors. Fourth, some external funding sources require institutional cost sharing as part of the proposal budget (section 6.2). That is, for every dollar obtained from the external funding source, the institution must provide a certain level of resources, either cash or in-kind. Fifth, researchers look to the SRO for assistance in purchasing and maintaining equipment such as microscopes, fabrication machinery, stage lighting and sound equipment, and video and audio recording equipment for interviews or other types of human subject or animal research. SROs also typically contribute funding to start-up packages for new faculty, retention packages for existing faculty, and space rental as needed if scholarly work is not performed in buildings owned by the institution. Bridge funding for students supported on external grants and contracts to ensure continuity of work across awards is another important contribution made by SROs.

Researchers early in their career, including students, typically have access to a broad array of funding, both internal and external to their institution. This includes funding for presenting results at conferences, support for materials, and professional development training. Contact your SRO or equivalent, or your academic advisor, to determine the sources available to you, and ask for assistance in obtaining them.

Economic development and community engagement Increasingly, most SROs are charged with technology transfer and economic development (indeed, most SROs now carry the title of vice president or vice chancellor for research and economic development). In these roles, the SRO oversees the institution's portfolio of intellectual property (chapter 12), and makes decisions about licensing, intellectual property protection, and possibly institutional investment in companies spun out of the institution. The SRO also collaborates with local, state, and regional officials and organizations to maximize the impact of institutional research outcomes on economic development. In some cases, this might involve seeking federal funding with a consortium of corporate and/or academic partners to establish a regional research hub, say in artificial intelligence or advanced manufacturing (chapter 13). Or, it might involve partnering with philanthropic organizations to create a local center for the performing arts or a cultural museum.

In all cases, the SRO represents to external stakeholders the academic institution's scholarly portfolio and works to ensure that it is benefiting society to the maximum extent possible. Indeed, most institutions report annually on their economic and other impacts to the community and state in which they are located. The Carnegie Foundation for the Advancement of Teaching (http://www.carnegiefoundation.org) and the American Council on Education (ACE; http://acenet.edu), now sponsor elective classifications for community engagement to highlight "those institutions that have made extraordinary commitments to their public purpose."

As a next-generation scholar, you should both understand and be able to explain how your work contributes more broadly to society, beyond the contributions made to your specific discipline (chapter 11). Contact your SRO or equivalent to understand the economic development and community engagement programs in which your institution participates and learn how you can become involved with them. Maybe you can partner with a local school to assist students or help teach classes in your area of expertise. Or maybe you can begin an afterschool program for disadvantaged youth. Whatever you do, look beyond yourself and find ways of becoming a contributor to the world around you rather than only a consumer.

Research integrity and compliance Two of the most important yet time-consuming dimensions of the SRO position are research integrity and research compliance.[3] So important are these topics to scholarly endeavors that entire chapters in this book are devoted to them (chapters 9 and 10, respectively). Insofar as the SRO position is concerned, research integrity involves ensuring research is performed following the highest standards of professional ethics and accountability, with the institutional provost usually charged with adjudicating cases of alleged misconduct. Research compliance involves oversight of personnel, activities, facilities, and committees to ensure that applicable institutional policies, as well as state and federal policies and laws, are followed.

As noted in chapter 10, the overall purpose of research compliance is to drive human behavior in desired directions such that scholarly activities are conducted with the highest standards of ethics, integrity, safety, and security. The universe of research compliance is huge and includes but is not limited to the following: protocols for research involving human and animal subjects; training in the responsible conduct of research; disclosure and management of potential personal and institutional conflicts of interest; laboratory and radiation safety; bioethics; management of controlled and toxic substances used in research; clinical trials; protection of data containing information that is sensitive, classified, or otherwise restricted; export controls and research security; intellectual property disclosure, protection and licensing; reporting to funding agencies; and negotiation of grant and contract terms and conditions.

The size, scope and importance of these and other research compliance topics places extraordinary demands of time and expertise on the SRO and associated staff, as well as on funding organizations such as federal agencies and especially on academic scholars. Indeed, three national surveys (Rockwell 2009; Federal Demonstration Project 2014; Schneider 2020), conducted roughly seven years apart, consistently found that college and university faculty spend 42 to 44 percent of their time on administrative activities associated with federal grant funding, unrelated to the research being conducted. That is a very large number and one that needs to be reduced. Every researcher agrees with the need for research compliance. However, it is important that research compliance policies and laws be thoughtfully formulated and informed by those who perform research, be implemented appropriately, and be regularly evaluated to ensure they are meeting their intended purpose.

While serving as director of the White House Office of Science and Technology Policy (OSTP; http://whitehouse.gov/ostp), I initiated a major effort within the National Science and Technology Council (NSTC; http://whitehouse .gov/ostp/nstc) to address the administrative workload associated with research compliance. Known as Coordinating Administrative Research Requirements (CARR), it operated as a subcommittee of the NSTC Joint Committee on the Research Environment (JCORE; National Science and Technology Council

2019) and built upon work of the National Science Board (2014) (NSB; http://nsf.gov/nsb). Although some progress was made, the task is enormous and continues. It is imperative that the extraordinarily large amount of time academic scholars spend on research compliance be addressed by eliminating compliance rules and regulations that have outlived their purpose or are providing no practical benefit. Others should be streamlined and unified in order to minimize the time burden for researchers, personnel costs for academic institutions and funding organizations, and duplication across funding sources (especially federal agencies).

As a next-generation scholar, you should actively participate in efforts to reduce the research administrative workload while ensuring research remains accountable and is conducted with the highest standards of ethics, integrity, safety, and security. To learn more, contact your SRO or national organizations such as the Council on Governmental Relations (COGR; http://cogr.edu), which is a consortium of academic institutions, teaching and research hospitals, and independent research organizations that works to ensure the effectiveness of policies for research and creative activity. Determine if your institution is a COGR member, and if so, speak with those who attend COGR meetings so they can direct you to the many valuable resources COGR provides.

Finally, a study I led in 2016, while chairing the Council on Research (CoR) of the Association of Public and Land-grant Universities (APLU; http://aplu.org), involved a national survey to evaluate the roles of SROs at American research universities. The published results (Droegemeier et al. 2017) showed a number of interesting observations, perhaps the most disturbing of which is the lack of diversity in SROs across the country. At that time, 80 percent were male and 91 percent were White. Only 1 percent were Black or African American, and 5 percent were Asian. The results were not terribly sensitive to institutional Carnegie classification or Land-grant status. Although progress has been made during the past several years, a great deal more work needs to be done to improve SRO diversity and to better encourage and prepare individuals from all backgrounds to become SROs.

Assess Your Comprehension

1. Define the word "research" and list ways in which it differs from or is symbiotic with "creative activity."

2. Describe the role played by curiosity in fundamental research and creative activity.

3. What is "fundamental" or "basic" research and how does it differ from "applied" or "use-inspired" research?

4. What is meant by the term "innovation" and how does it relate to research and creative activity?

5. What is translational research and how does it differ from other types of research?

6. By what type of organization is the bulk of fundamental research performed in the US?

7. The largest amount of funding for fundamental research in the US is provided by what source?

8. List the principal types of organizations responsible for performing research and development in the US.

9. Describe why scholarly activities in some disciplines, such as arts and humanities, often are not valued as highly as activities in science, engineering, and technology.

10. Why is it often difficult to show clear linkages between fundamental research outcomes and products and services that benefit society?

11. Why is the SRO position at academic institutions often not as well understood compared to positions such as president, provost, and dean?

12. List the principal responsibilities of, and services offered by, the SRO at academic institutions.

Exercises to Deepen Your Understanding

Exercise 1: All research and creative activity endeavors are valuable to society and contribute to our understanding of the world, regardless of the discipline in which they occur, or whether they are based solely on curiosity or seek to solve a specific problem. For this exercise, develop research questions that most interest you for both a basic (curiosity-inspired) and an applied research project. Discuss the significance, potential value to the discipline(s) involved, and relevance to society more broadly of obtaining answers to these questions. In so doing, provide a context for the work that needs to be performed with emphasis on how it would build upon previous research.

Exercise 2: In the US, twenty-six federal agencies fund research, as do numerous private foundations. Select one federal research funding agency and one private foundation and use information from their websites and other available sources to compare and contrast their approaches to supporting research and creative activity. Feel free to choose a particular topic that is supported by both organizations (e.g., brain cancer, clean energy technology, environmental sustainability, world hunger, disease), and consider issues such as eligibility on the part of the researcher and their organization, the amount of funding available, the number of projects to be funded, project duration, and any special requirements or restrictions that might exist. What surprised you most about the information you gathered, and what, if anything, might you recommend as improvements to the funding organizations?

Exercise 3: Use the Internet to identify and explore a product, service, creation, or work in the world today that traces its origin to academic research. Describe how the item you selected evolved over time and the manner in which university research outcomes resulted in its creation and utilization. Also, discuss the impact of this item on society, using, as appropriate, both qualitative and quantitative measures.

Exercise 4: Use the Internet to locate a journal article in your field of study authored by a single individual, and compare and contrast the scope, methodology, and overall relevance and significance of this article with another authored by five or more individuals. What conclusions can you draw from this comparison, and what did you notice about the number of authors per article as you searched for the two required in this exercise?

Exercise 5: The US research enterprise consists of an array of government, academic, corporate, and nonprofit institutions that both fund research as well as perform it. Among this array are a number of independent research institutes. Identify several of them and compare and contrast their missions and structures with those of federal agencies. A good starting point for identifying the former is the Association of Independent Research Institutes (AIRI; http://www.airi.org/home). A list of federal agencies that fund research and development across all disciplines may be found at the Grants .gov website under the tab "Grant-Making Agencies." What differences did you find most surprising or interesting, and to what extent do you feel independent research institutes and federal agencies could improve their respective capabilities by borrowing certain features from each other?

Exercise 6: Visit the websites of the senior research officer (SRO) (e.g., vice president for research, vice chancellor for research) at six to ten academic institutions having the characteristics shown below and develop a table for the research support services they offer based upon those described in section 1.6. How do the services vary by institution? Which institutions have the greatest array of services, and what types of services are most common? Least common? To what extent does your scholarly work intersect with the services? Suppose you are located at an institution (select one from your list) that has relatively few research support services. Examine the website of that institution to determine what steps would you take to locate needed support services.

Characteristics of institutions to be examined are shown below (consult the Carnegie Classification website at http://carnegieclassifications.iu.edu /classification_descriptions/basic.php to understand the terms used below and to select the institutions you wish to examine).

- Public Carnegie R1 (Very high research activity) institution
- Private Carnegie R1 (Very high research activity) institution
- Public Carnegie R2 (High research activity) institution
- Private Carnegie R2 (High research activity) institution
- Public Carnegie M1 (Master's Colleges and Universities—Larger programs) institution
- Public Carnegie M2 (Master's Colleges and Universities—Medium programs) institution
- Public Carnegie M3 (Master's Colleges and Universities—Smaller programs) institution
- Tribal Colleges and Universities (TCUs)
- Hispanic Serving Institutions (HSIs)
- Historically Black Colleges and Universities (HBCUs)

2

The Money Trail: Funding for Research and Creative Activity

Chapter Overview and Learning Objectives

Irrespective of discipline, topic studied, or methods utilized, all research and creative activities require funding and often other types of resources. This chapter describes various sources and types of available funding, including historical trends and the complexities of how budgets of research sponsors are developed, prioritized, and funded. It further discusses how R&D funding in the US compares with that of other nations, the federal R&D budget process, strategies for identifying funding and applying for it, and how funding might change in the future. After reading this chapter, you should

- Understand the differences among various entities that fund research and creative activity, as well as the mechanisms by which such funding is sought and awarded;
- Understand differences in how research budgets are determined across various sectors, in STEM and non-STEM areas, as well as the key areas or topics that are prioritized by organizations in each;
- Be able to explain the process by which the R&D component of the federal budget is created; and
- Recognize future challenges in allocating appropriate federal funding to various topics across all disciplines and appreciate the importance of our nation's competitive position in the global research enterprise.

2.1 Sources of Funding and Historical Trends

Research and creative activity take many forms, utilize a wide array of approaches, and occur in disciplines ranging from art to zoology. But the one thing all research and creativity endeavors have in common is the need for resources. More specifically, funding for academic R&D is needed to support faculty salaries, graduate and undergraduate students, postdoctoral fellows, technicians, administrative personnel, supplies, equipment, services, facilities, travel, and dissemination of outcomes (chapter 6).

The array of funding available for research and creative activity is quite large and spans sources that include federal, state, and local government organizations, for-profit corporations, private nonprofit foundations, individual philanthropists, the general public (e.g., crowd funding), and even the personal resources of those performing the research. As you might imagine, the assets, roles, and expectations of each of these sources also vary widely.

For example, twenty-six US federal agencies provide funding in the form of competitive and other types of grants, including the preponderance of support for basic or fundamental research (figure 2.1).[1] They also fund applied research and development toward specific agency missions and priorities. On the other hand, private companies fund mostly applied research and development that directly contributes to creating new or improving existing products and services.

State and local government funding for research often is directed at specific programs and themes relevant to growing the local economy or enhancing quality of life through investments in the arts and fine arts. Nonprofit foundations typically fund work in specific areas of interest to the person or persons who established and often direct the foundation. Examples include poverty, social justice, the environment, equity and inclusion, health, education, and the arts, fine arts, and humanities. Specific foundation topics can change every few years and sometimes are linked to current events.

It is instructive to examine historical trends in research funding in the US—which almost entirely is directed toward STEM fields—and how they compare with those of other countries. Figure 2.2 illustrates how the US federal government funded the bulk of R&D in the 1950s and 1960s, and how just the reverse is true today—with private industry funding now representing nearly three-quarters of all R&D. Examining where this R&D actually takes place (figure 2.3), one finds, not surprisingly, that industry dominates, with universities playing an important role, though largely in the area of fundamental research (figure 2.4). However, academic institutions are expanding their portfolios in applied R&D, as I facilitated when I was vice president for research at my institution, not only as a way to expand the opportunity space for researchers, but also to contribute in more direct ways to the creation of products and services that benefit society. Additionally, such work naturally provides opportunities for partnering with the private sector (chapter 13).

To a large extent, these data illustrate the manner in which federal investments in fundamental research have led—over many decades—to private

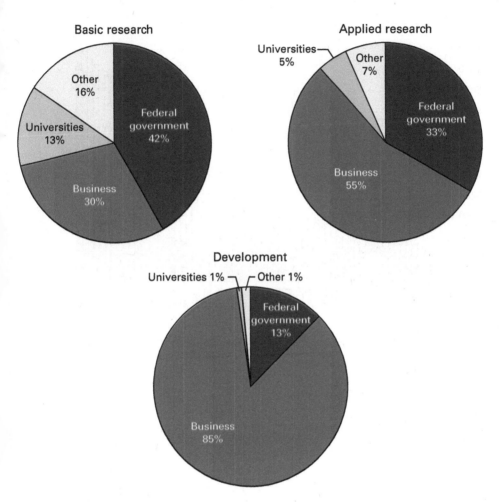

Figure 2.1
Composition of US basic (fundamental) research, applied research, and development by funding sector, 2017. *Source*: Congressional Research Service (2020b).

sector innovation and increased funding by the private sector of applied research and development (figures 2.1 and 2.4). Indeed, the fact that the US now boasts trillion-dollar private companies reinforces this fact. Yet, as noted below and in chapter 14, federal investment in fundamental research has lagged behind that of other countries, causing concern for US global competitiveness.

Focusing on US universities in particular, most of the external funding they receive for R&D comes from the federal government (figure 2.5). In the past few years, federal R&D expenditures by universities have been increasing (National Center for Science and Engineering Statistics 2022). As discussed below, the

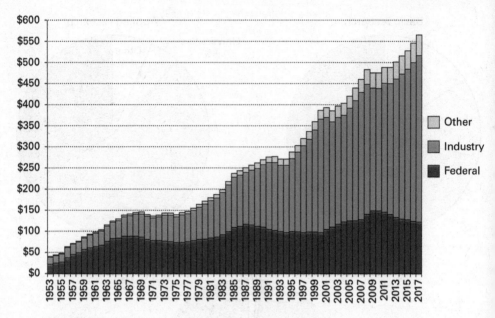

Figure 2.2
US R&D by funding source (expenditures in billions of fiscal year [FY] 2019 dollars). *Source*:
American Association for the Advancement of Science (2018).

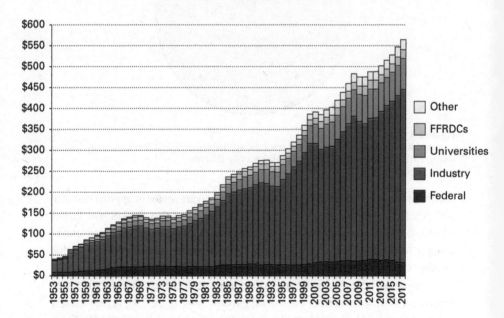

Figure 2.3
US R&D by performer (expenditures in billions of FY 2019 dollars). *Source*: American Association for the Advancement of Science (2018).

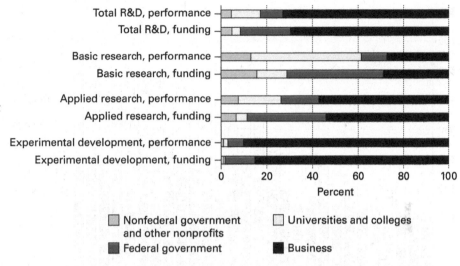

Figure 2.4
US R&D by type, performer, and funding. *Source*: National Science Board (2020f).

bulk of such funding is directed toward STEM fields. Funding to universities for non-STEM scholarly activities—in addition to the much smaller level of dollars received from federal agencies—often takes the form of highly competitive and prestigious fellowships, such as Fulbright Fellowships (http://us.fulbrightonline .org), American Council of Learned Societies fellowships (http://www.acls.org /competitions/acls-fellowships), National Endowment for the Humanities fellow- ships (http://www.neh.gov/grants/research/fellowships), MacArthur Foundation fellowships (http://www.macfound.org/programs/fellows), and Rockefeller Foun- dation fellowships (http://www.rockefellerfoundation.org).

An interesting, and in some contexts troubling trend evident over the past two decades is the increasing amount of institutional funds directed by uni- versities toward research (figure 2.5)—now representing nearly 25 percent of the total research dollars they expend. Some of this is planned investment, such as for new research facilities and equipment, whereas some is directed toward a host of otherwise unfunded federal, state and institutional compli- ance mandates and unrecoverable facilities and administrative costs (sections 6.2 and 10.6).

Globally, total US investment in R&D as a percent of its total gross domes- tic product (GDP) was relatively flat between 2008 and 2015 (figure 2.6) but has increased steadily since and now is well above 3 percent. Although China continues to increase dramatically, it remains well below 3 percent. R&D is a collaborative global enterprise, and as someone once said, research anywhere

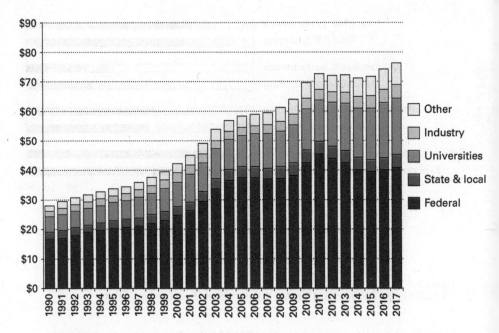

Figure 2.5
US university R&D funding by source (expenditures in billions of FY 2018 dollars). *Source*:
American Association for the Advancement of Science (2018).

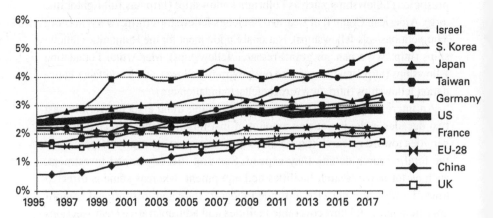

Figure 2.6
US gross R&D as a percentage of gross domestic product. *Source*: American Association for the
Advancement of Science (2020).

is good for research everywhere. Consequently, the US must continue to grow its investments in step with the economy and with that of its collaborators and competitors, and also continue its efforts to balance openness of its research enterprise with securing its research assets against malign foreign government interference (section 10.3).

A massive array of other information regarding current estimates and historical trends in budgets and expenditures by funder, performer, nation, economy, discipline, technology sector, and other attributes may be found online. As a next-generation scholar, it is in your best interest to become familiar with domestic R&D budgets and trends and how they compare internationally. Although several additional budget and other measures are described in chapter 14, sources I consult most frequently are shown below.

- Americans for the Arts (http://americansforthearts.org)
- American Association for the Advancement of Science (AAAS) (http://aaas.org)
- American Institute of Physics (http://aip.org)
- Consortium of Social Science Organizations (http://cossa.org)
- National Humanities Alliance (http://nhalliance.org)
- National Science Board (http://nsf.gov/nsb)

2.2   Determining Research Priorities and Budgets

Having examined a variety of trend data in the preceding section, you may wonder how research budgets are determined—not only in federal agencies, but also in other organizations that fund research and creative activity. How are priorities determined and who decides the amount of money needed to fund them? To say the least, it is a complicated process, involving many organizations, that plays out over long periods of time. Before diving into the details, let us examine the federal budget from the broadest perspective.

Figure 2.7 shows total outlays (estimated expenditures) by major category for the federal FY 2019 budget in billions of dollars. Overall, the pie can be divided into two broad categories: *mandatory spending*, which represents costs that must be paid (Social Security, Medicare, Medicaid, net interest on the national debt, and other items), as well as *discretionary spending*, which further is divided into defense and nondefense categories. R&D is included in the discretionary spending category, and the process by which Congress appropriates funding each year across twelve bills is described below.

The programs within the mandatory spending category often are referred to as entitlement programs because individuals receiving the associated funds

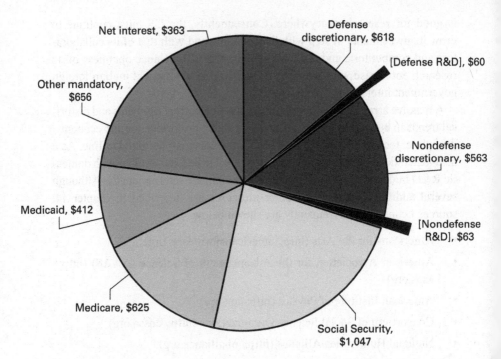

Figure 2.7
Total outlays (expenditures) by major category for the federal FY 2019 budget in billions of dollars. *Source*: Hourihan (2018).

are entitled to them by virtue of federal law. Costs within mandatory programs generally increase year over year as the population ages and as other social programs are added, which means the discretionary programs either must shrink to accommodate those increases, or additional funds must be appropriated by Congress, thus increasing the national debt. Because R&D is included in the discretionary spending category, it is caught between two politically challenging issues: managing growth of mandatory spending and increasing the national debt.

Historically, the ratio between R&D spending and total discretionary spending (figure 2.8) has been relatively constant since the late 1970s, with nondefense R&D—which is most relevant for academic institutions—remaining at approximately 11 percent in recent years. The constancy of this ratio over time indicates that R&D spending follows closely the overall discretionary budget. Consequently, as mandatory programs grow, and presuming only modest increases in the national debt, R&D spending decreases.

Within that broad context, the starting point for federal R&D funding is the President's Budget, which typically is issued in early February for the fiscal

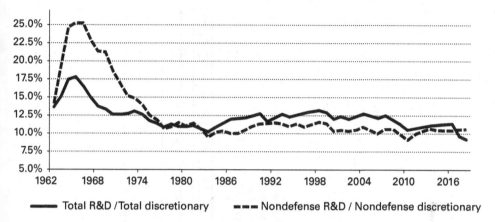

Figure 2.8
Ratio of total US federal R&D spending to total discretionary spending (solid curve) and ratio of US federal nondefense R&D spending to total nondefense discretionary spending (dashed curve). *Source*: Hourihan and Parkes (2019).

year beginning the following October. However, to fully understand the process, it is important to back up and examine how the president's budget itself is formulated.

Figure 2.9 shows key steps within the overall federal R&D budget process using a generic calendar indicating both calendar years (CY; January 1 through December 31) and federal fiscal years (FY; October 1 through September 30), with the symbol X representing any given year, such as 2022.

Federal R&D agencies begin to develop their budget priorities for FY $X + 2$ in the spring of CY X based upon written guidance from the White House Office of Management and Budget (OMB; http://whitehouse.gov/omb/), their own multiyear strategic plans, input from agency advisory committees (the members of which are drawn from academia, industry, and nonprofit organizations), and other sources. In addition to serving on agency advisory committees, academic and other scholars play other important roles in suggesting priorities for federal funding agencies, such as NEA and NSF, by holding workshops, engaging the public in meetings, and mobilizing community and congressional support for what they believe are critical areas of scholarly endeavor that need to be pursued. Agencies pay close attention because the individuals making the recommendations—mostly academic scholars—are on the "front lines" of research and have their fingers on the pulse of their disciplines. This is particularly true of workshops held and studies conducted by the National Academies of Science, Engineering, and Medicine (NASEM). Such activities are important in catalyzing broad interest and support and sometimes end up becoming national priorities for the President's Budget.

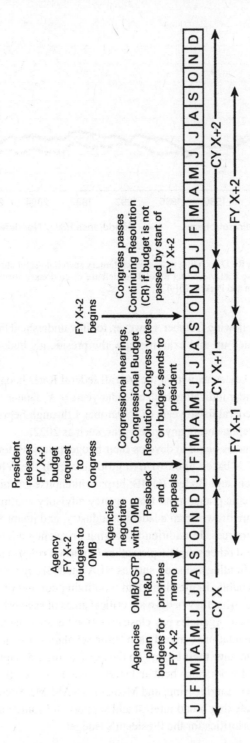

Figure 2.9
The process of developing the US federal R&D budget. CY and FY represent calendar and fiscal years, respectively, and X is a generic placeholder for any given year, such as 2022.

It is important to recognize that the federal budget covers only a single fiscal year. However, in some cases, agencies fund large, complex and expensive projects (e.g., satellites, space- and ground-based telescopes, ships, particle accelerators) that extend over a decade or longer. Often, these projects involve several agencies, which greatly increases the complexity of planning and coordination. Examples include multidecadal "grand challenges," such as the Cancer Moonshot and BRAIN (Brain Research through Advancing Innovative Neurotechnologies) Initiative. In such cases, out-year estimates of funding are included in agency budget planning.

Congress often holds hearings throughout the year on a wide array of important topics relevant to R&D. This includes but is not limited to STEM education and workforce development, critical research areas (e.g., nanotechnology, artificial intelligence, hydrogen fusion, new materials and drugs and their related development by industry), improving diversity, and the cost of higher education. The research community, and especially academic scholars, have an opportunity to participate in these and other activities to help shape the future of America's research and education enterprise. As a next-generation scholar, you should stay abreast of developments and seek ways to become involved. You need not be a senior scholar to do so because all perspectives are vitally important.

During summer of CY X, usually July or August, OMB and OSTP—both of which are "components" of The Executive Office of the President—jointly issue an R&D priorities memo to federal agencies. This memo identifies executive branch R&D priorities and processes to which agencies are directed[2] in formulating their budgets for FY X + 2. In the past, priorities have included national security, energy and the environment, space exploration, industries of the future, clean energy, climate change, nanotechnology, cybersecurity, and STEM education. Also included in the memo are priorities that cut across the key topical areas, such as workforce development, diversity enhancement, and multisector partnerships.

Agencies then submit their proposed FY X + 2 budgets to OMB in September of CY X and spend the next few months negotiating with OMB via a process known as passback and appeals. It is important to recognize the importance and power of OMB, not only in the budgeting process but also in regulatory policy (chapter 10). Indeed, each federal agency has multiple OMB budget examiners who evaluate, in great detail, all aspects of the agency budget submission and coordinate appeals and passback. Among the many items considered, this evaluation includes the extent to which agencies met their goals from the previous fiscal year.

Using all of this information, OMB then works with other organizations in the executive branch to prepare the President's Budget Request to Congress, which is released in early February of CY X+1. This budget specifies, in great detail, executive branch policies and priorities and serves only as a roadmap for Congress to consider. Congress has the final word in budgeting because it has the legal authority to authorize and appropriate funding to federal agencies. This leads to the oft-heard phrase, "Congress has the power of the purse."

Following release of the President's Budget in February, two important actions take place. First, congressional budget committees and subcommittees hold hearings about the President's Budget. Each congressional committee, supported by a sizable professional staff, is chaired by a member from the majority party, with a ranking member serving as the senior representative from the minority party. Membership is nearly evenly split between the two parties (along with independents, who usually caucus with one of the majority parties), though with the majority party having the most members. Budget subcommittee chairs often are referred to as "cardinals" because of the power they hold regarding budget priorities. Indeed, congressional budgets often reflect the personal preferences of cardinals, as well as congressional leadership (speaker of the US House of Representatives, majority leader of the US Senate, and to a lesser extent, the minority leaders of the House and Senate).

In R&D budget hearings, relevant federal agency heads and other senior officials testify about their respective components of the President's Budget. Frequently, Congress disagrees with the President's priorities and budget levels, leading to sometimes confrontational hearings. Yet for the most part, these hearings are productive and provide the research community with an early indication of how Congress may act.

The second important action following release of the President's Budget is a series of hearings, also held by Congress, regarding budget bills it has drafted to inform its own overall budget plan, known as the Congressional Budget Resolution (CBR). This resolution, which is a relatively simple document (compared to the President's Budget), lays out top-line spending numbers (known as 302b allocations) for each of the twelve appropriation bills. The US House of Representatives and US Senate Budget Committees each create their own version of the CBR. Once passed by these committees, the resolutions move to the floors of their respective chambers for a vote. Any differences are dealt with in a joint House-Senate conference, with the final single resolution voted on by both chambers. Note that the CBR is not a formal bill, as would be signed by the president to establish a law, but rather a framework for the budget upon which Congress ultimately will vote.

In preparing the CBR, Congress seeks input from a wide array of stakeholders, including subject matter experts drawn from universities (e.g., executive officers, faculty, senior researchers), private companies, and nonprofit organizations across the nation. Lobbyists, who are hired by private companies, interest groups, universities, and other organizations, play a key role by advocating for their clients' priorities to individual members and also to committee staff. Some lobbyists are former members of Congress or senior staff members who know their way around Washington. Other input on the CBR is obtained from professional societies, such as NASEM, and perhaps most importantly from member constituents.

You, as a researcher—especially if you are relatively early in your career—should work with your institution's governmental relations official to determine how you can best advocate for the research and education enterprise broadly and perhaps your own area of scholarly work in particular. Members of Congress generally love meeting with their constituents, and often such meetings are held by member staffers rather than the members themselves. If you have the opportunity to meet with a member, learn about their background, interests, committees on which they serve, priorities (usually listed on their websites), and recent legislative activities (e.g., bills passed or sponsored). This will help you place your remarks in the context of their own activity. It is never a good idea to bring to a member an issue completely unfamiliar to them, or one that is incongruent or even at odds with something in their portfolio. Do not get into the technical weeds with a member, but rather make only one or two key points and be succinct, letting them ask questions. Numerous documents have been developed to assist researchers in interacting with Congress (e.g., White and Carney 2011), and chapter 11 provides additional information about presenting your research to general audiences.

Several of the twelve congressional spending bills comprising the federal budget contain funding for R&D, though the funding is spread across multiple agencies, as well as multiple congressional jurisdictions and subcommittees. It also is spread across numerous disciplines (figure 2.10). This complicates the budgeting process and often leads to confusion and delays.[3] However, once the major committees of jurisdiction over a particular component of the budget—in the form of a bill—reach agreement in both the US House and US Senate—they vote.

Quite frequently, the House and Senate versions of bills are notably different and have different titles. As a result, the differences must be reconciled in a conference involving members from both chambers. This is true not only for the broad authorization and appropriation bills, but also for other bills written along the way.

For example, smaller bills frequently are written that relate to R&D laws already in place. They modify existing wording, add new text, and bring in new requirements, policies, and work to be done. Sometimes these changes are

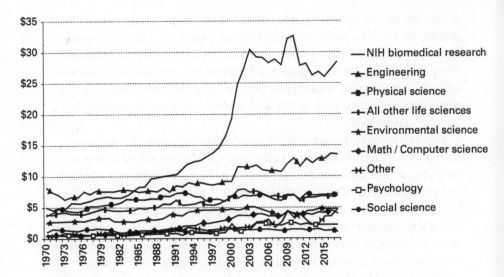

Figure 2.10
Trends in US federal research funding by discipline (obligations in billions of constant FY 2019 dollars). *Source*: American Association for the Advancement of Science (2018).

made as amendments during committee deliberations, or even on the floor, but quite often they exist as stand-alone bills. The latter format allows members to take credit as sponsors and cosponsors, which can be especially important if the bill has demonstrable impacts on their district or state.

If, after hearings, deliberations, and conference committee discussions both houses of Congress pass a given bill on the floor of their respective chambers, the final version goes to the president's desk to be signed into law. In some situations, the funding actually appropriated bears little resemblance to that requested in the President's Budget, irrespective of which parties hold the White House and the two branches of Congress. If Congress is unable to come to agreement on the twelve bills individually, an omnibus package is created in which the totality of the twelve bills is combined into a single bolus of funding across the federal government.

If Congress does not finish its work prior to the start of the new fiscal year on October 1, the US government either shuts down temporarily or Congress passes a short-term Continuing Budget Resolution (CR; figure 2.9). In a CR, federal agencies continue receiving funding, though at levels or rates equal to those in the previous year's budget, with some exceptions. According to the Pew Research Center (figure 2.11), the last time Congress approved all twelve spending bills by October 1 was in fiscal year 1997 (i.e., by October 1, 1996).

Although the CR can serve as an effective stopgap measure, it generally is disliked by funding agencies and researchers alike because no new programs

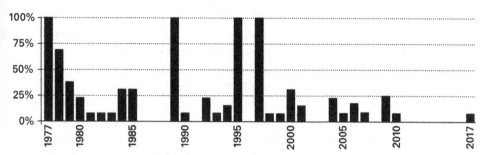

Figure 2.11
Percentage of stand-alone appropriations bills enacted by the US Congress on or before October 1
of each federal fiscal year. *Source*: Desilver (2018).

can be initiated unless otherwise specified in the resolution's language, and
because it provides less certainty regarding how research funding agencies can
plan for allocating funds throughout the coming fiscal year.

One final resource in the toolbox of Congress is "directed spending" or the
"earmark." Rule XXI, clause 9 in the US House of Representatives defines the
congressional earmark as "a provision or report language included primarily
at the request of a Member, Delegate, Resident Commissioner, or Senator providing, authorizing or recommending a specific amount of discretionary budget
authority, credit authority, or other spending authority for a contract, loan, loan
guarantee, grant, loan authority, or other expenditure with or to an entity, or
targeted to a specific State, locality or congressional district, other than through
a statutory or administrative formula driven or competitive award process"
(Congressional Research Service 2021b).

More simply stated, earmarks represent one mechanism for members of Congress to direct funding to their state for specific projects. Although some argue
this is entirely appropriate and in fact is a key member responsibility, others
argue it is wasteful because, historically, earmarks have not proceeded through
the regular competitive award process (chapter 7). This is why earmarks sometimes are referred to as "pork-barrel spending." Although several well-known
scandals occurring in the early 2000s led to the institution of a moratorium on
earmarks by the 112th Congress (2011–2012), both Republicans and Democrats
voted in 2021 to restore earmarks, though with a modified process.

At the state level, support for research is far less complex and usually directed
toward priorities involving job growth and other forms of economic development or quality of life enhancement. Many states have organizations that fund
competitive research grants, both in the sciences and in the arts and humanities.
Some direct small portions of tax revenues toward strategic research investments such as hiring faculty at research universities, funding equipment, and
providing cost sharing for grant proposals.

Corporate R&D is focused almost exclusively on work that leads to new products and services for commercialization. These funds often are referred to as IR&D. Although corporate investment in R&D has increased dramatically over the past thirty years (figure 2.2), the proportion of this increase going to research universities has been nearly flat (figure 2.5). Several reasons for this exist (chapter 13), and efforts now are underway to simplify and streamline mechanisms for private companies to engage with universities in R&D.

With regard to private foundations, the overall role of a foundation typically is set by the founder, and funding priorities follow in kind. For example, the Mellon Foundation works to strengthen, promote, and defend contributions of the humanities and the arts to human flourishing, while the Ford Foundation focuses on civil rights, education, arts and culture, human rights, poverty reduction, and urban development. The Bill and Melinda Gates Foundation addresses global challenges that improve lives via investing in health, education, and sustainability, and the W. M. Keck Foundation focuses on funding potentially transformative science and engineering research, medical research, and education.

As you can see, the funding ecosystem in the US is wonderfully diverse yet also very complex. In the next section, we discuss strategies for wading through this array of options to identify sources of funding ideally suited to a given idea or project.

2.3 Identifying and Understanding Mechanisms for Obtaining Funding

Suppose you have an interesting idea that requires research, and you wish to pursue it but need funding. The idea might involve trying to understand how people reacted, or failed to react, to an approaching hurricane. It might involve an entirely new approach to a classic Shakespeare play or the study of a Native American language that faces extinction. Or, it might involve studying a supernova thousands of light years away or creating a new sensor that can detect cancer simply by contacting the skin. What's next? Where do you turn to find funding, and what are your chances of receiving it?

Before starting your search, it is important to understand the nature of the work to be done and the approach to be taken. Why? Because certain funding sources are better suited for your project than others. Is your project curiosity-driven (the supernova example), or does it involve innovating a new product (the cancer sensor)? Once you have a clear sense of your goals and the approaches to be used, you then can explore funding options by visiting the websites of various federal agencies, nonprofit foundations, and even for-profit companies.

Fundamental or curiosity-driven research typically is funded by the federal government (figure 2.1), so the space of possibilities for the supernova study quickly can be narrowed to relevant agencies, such as NSF or the National Aeronautics and Space Administration (NASA; http://nasa.gov), and to certain nonprofit foundations, such as the Keck Foundation. Very few if any private companies would fund this type of study. Sometimes, federal agencies issue announcements of opportunity with associated deadlines, and these announcements target specific areas of research, such as coupled human-natural systems. Such announcements are advertised almost continuously, and you can sign up to receive notifications based upon your indicated areas of interest (see below).

Federal broad agency announcements (BAAs) represent another mechanism of funding, but in most such cases, the opportunity tends to be very specific and represents a need to be met by a specific agency. We revisit this point in the next section.

Private foundations often issue calls for research proposals, as do federal organizations such as NEA, NEH, and state and municipal funding organizations. Submission of an "unsolicited" proposal is sometimes possible as well, which means you pitch your idea to the funder, though not as part of a particular announcement of opportunity.

Because for-profit private companies are not funding agencies, they almost never issue solicitations. And the manner in which one engages with them is quite different from that of federal and state agencies and usually involves an early discussion about how the work to be done would benefit their business (section 13.6). Businesses typically only invest in activities that are low-risk and understandably have a high probability of making money. Additionally, a variety of issues involving intellectual property arise when receiving funding from a private company, and we discuss them in chapter 12.

In today's highly connected society, numerous mechanisms exist for you to learn, via the Internet, about funding opportunities that might be appropriate for supporting your scholarly work. For example, many federal agencies offer free online subscription services that will notify you of funding opportunities based upon specific criteria you specify, such as keywords in your research area, budget floors and ceilings, and domestic and international collaborations. Agencies also maintain extensive databases of work funded previously so you can evaluate the extent to which your project might be additive or duplicative. The US government also provides such services across all agencies and disciplines (see http://grants.gov and http://research.gov).

Professional disciplinary societies, broader-based societies and consortia of societies, as well as individual academic institutions, sometimes operate listservs and provide subscription services and other tools for notifying researchers about funding as well as related education and outreach opportunities. The advent of artificial intelligence and machine learning is likely to transform all such mechanisms by aggregating data from a wide array of sources (see the example from coronavirus disease 2019 [COVID-19] in section 11.3), including the published literature, and synthesizing it to create gap analyses and even generate hypotheses automatically. As a next-generation researcher, you should explore these free services and take maximum advantage of them not only to identify support for your own work, but also to maintain a working knowledge of the directions research is taking based upon work various funding organizations are supporting or seeking to support.

In most cases, funders of research and creative activity provide money on a competitive basis. That is, you have to submit your idea in the form of a grant proposal (chapter 6), and that proposal is evaluated in some manner against other submissions, with the "best" submission or set of submissions chosen for funding. In some cases, funding is provided on a noncompetitive basis, such as in a block grant, and so-called set asides exist to support certain activities, such as enhancing small businesses. Examples in this category include the Small Business Innovation Research (SBIR) and Small Business Technology Transfer (STTR) programs, which are operated by multiple federal research agencies. The federal Established Program to Stimulate Competitive Research (EPSCoR) was created in 1978 to help build research capacity within entire states (referred to by EPSCoR as jurisdictions) that tend to be less competitive overall for federal funding than their peers.

The mechanisms by which funding is provided for research are almost as varied as the sources of funding themselves. Research assistance grants, which can range from one to ten years in duration, are commonly used by federal agencies to support research and creative activity in academia and at private companies. Sometimes the entire amount of funding is provided up front (standard grant), while in other cases, it is given on a yearly basis (continuing award). In all cases, rigorous reviews are conducted regularly to ensure progress is being made as planned and that funds are being spent appropriately. As described in chapter 6, grants typically involve the sharing of costs between the organization providing the funding and the one receiving it. The reason is that both the provider of the funding, and the organization receiving it, obtain value from the research. This is known as the mutuality of interest principle.

Another common funding mechanism is the contract. It differs from a grant in that contracts involve the generation of value principally to the funding organization, and consequently, the funding organization usually funds the full cost of the project. Also, contracts have specific deliverables, whereas grants have expected outcomes that cannot be guaranteed up front. A number of other funding vehicles exist, such as cooperative agreements, collaborative awards, gifts, fellowships, and crowdfunding, and more information about these can be found on the Internet.

One important issue is worth noting in the context of a gift, such as a cash donation to an academic institution to support research. Such a gift usually is tax deductible, but in order to obtain the tax advantage, the funding agreement cannot specify a deliverable from the project or give specific guidance about what is to be done. That is, there cannot be a quid pro quo.

Finally, all grants, contracts, and other funding instruments, come with specific terms and conditions that must be met under federal and state laws, and also policies of the receiving and funding organizations.

As an example, suppose a faculty member or student is part of a university and receives a grant to fund their idea. Although the award of funding is made to the university, the faculty or student investigator—not the institution—is personally and legally responsible for ensuring all laws and procedures are followed. Fortunately, most universities and other organizations have individuals on staff to assist with such compliance, which is described further in chapters 6 and 10. For those that do not, recommendations are made throughout the remainder of the book regarding how to obtain assistance with project management and compliance.

2.4   The Future of Research Funding

Since the dawn of America's multisector research enterprise immediately following World War II (section 3.1), federal funding for research and creative activity has been an important and hotly debated topic across all stakeholders. The historical trends described earlier in this chapter indicate that, overall, federal funding for research has increased very slightly over time (with peaks roughly every twenty years followed by decreases—figure 2.2), though as a percentage of gross domestic product, it has decreased rather dramatically (figure 2.12).

One of the greatest challenges faced by researchers is uncertainty of research budgets within the organizations upon which they depend most, especially federal agencies. This lack of stability and predictability in budgets is exacerbated by the historically large federal deficit (i.e., the yearly shortfall between spending and available funding) and debt (the total accumulated funds yet to be paid to creditors), the large and growing component of the federal budget devoted to fixed-cost or entitlement programs such as Medicaid, Medicare, and Social Security, and other important priorities within the federal budget such as national defense and homeland security.

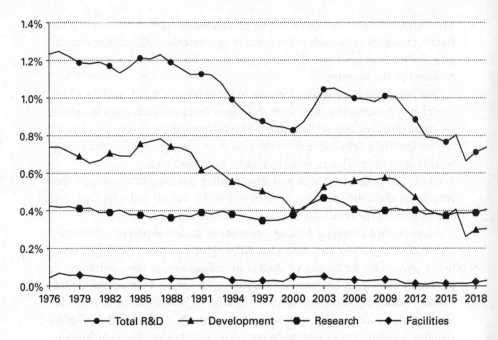

Figure 2.12
US Federal R&D funding as a percent of gross domestic product. *Source*: American Association for the Advancement of Science (2018).

Numerous reports have been written during the past several years about the importance of research to the nation. Among the most prominent and impactful have been the two *Rising above the Gathering Storm* reports (National Academies of Science, Engineering and Medicine 2007, 2010), a report on research universities and the future of America (National Research Council 2012b), and two reports, produced by the American Academy of Arts and Sciences (2014, 2020), which speak to the importance of restoring the foundation of the basic or inquiry-driven research enterprise as part of the American Dream.

Not surprisingly, politics plays a significant role in determining the future of federal agency research budgets. For that reason, among others, calls have been made to study science policy so that more effective approaches can be applied. In fact, NSF used to offer a grant funding program called the Science of Science and Innovation Policy that was designed to help the nation take a more structured and thoughtful approach toward setting research budgets and developing related policies. Recently, it was expanded and now is known as the Science of Science: Discovery, Communication and Impact.

So, what does the future hold? Although no one has a crystal ball (chapter 14), funding for research and creative activity generally has bipartisan support.

This support has been reinforced recently in light of the extraordinary role played by science and technology R&D in addressing the many challenges associated with the COVID-19 pandemic (e.g., vaccine and therapeutic development, technology for remote education and work, application of artificial intelligence and machine learning, evaluation of environmental factors affecting the coronavirus).

For the first time in decades, extraordinary investments are planned in key federal R&D agencies, such as NIH, NSF, the National Institute of Standards and Technology (NIST), and the US Department of Energy Office of Science, as shown collectively in the nondefense discretionary component of figure 2.13. The ability for America to sustain these levels of funding—if history is prologue—will be difficult to envision, as shown in 2024 and beyond in figure 2.13, given the nation's unprecedented debt and continuing large yearly deficits, along with increasing emphasis on enhancing entitlement programs. We explore these issues in greater detail in chapter 14.

For these and other reasons, increasing attention is being given to partnerships (chapter 13) among academic institutions, private companies, state and

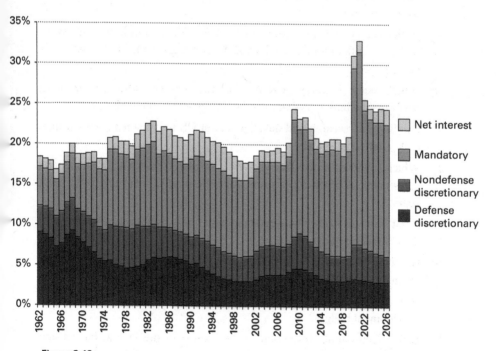

Figure 2.13
US federal spending as a percent of gross domestic product. Values from 2022 and beyond are projections. *Source*: Hourihan (2021).

federal agencies, and nonprofit organizations to ensure America's research enterprise remains robust and internationally competitive. The arts, fine arts, and humanities represent a tiny fraction of research budgets and often are the first areas of funding to be seen by some as wasteful or unnecessary. As will be repeated many times throughout this book, such disciplines lie at the core of the human experience and their activities not only should be preserved but also enhanced (chapter 14).

Assess Your Comprehension

1. How many US federal agencies fund research and creative activity?
2. What is a mission agency and how does it compare to non-mission agencies?
3. How many nonprofit foundations in the US fund research and creative activity?
4. Which sector (industry, government, academia, nonprofit organizations) funds the bulk of fundamental research, applied research, and development in the US?
5. Which sector (industry, government, academia, nonprofit organizations) funds the bulk of total research and development in the US? What is that percentage?
6. Which sector (industry, government, academia, nonprofit organizations) performs the bulk of research and development in the US?
7. Funding for research and development at US universities comes principally from what source?
8. Which countries showed the greatest growth in research and development investment, as a percent of gross domestic product, over the past twenty years?
9. What is the difference between mandatory and discretionary spending in the US federal budget?
10. Describe the process by which the US federal research and development budget is created.
11. How are universities involved in developing the US federal research and development budget?
12. Define Continuing Resolution in the context of the federal budget and describe its strengths and shortcomings with regard to the nation's research enterprise.

13. Describe how corporate research and development differs from that conducted in the public sector (e.g., by universities).

14. Describe how federal funding for research varies among broad disciplinary categories.

15. How do private foundations differ from other organizations in providing funding for research and development?

16. What is a broad agency announcement (BAA)?

17. What is a research grant and how does it differ from a research proposal?

18. How does a research grant differ from a research contract?

19. How do solicited proposals differ from unsolicited proposals?

20. How does a standard research grant differ from a continuing award, and what advantages and limitations exist for each in the eyes of the funding organization and the recipient of funding?

21. Who at a university is legally responsible for assuring all terms and conditions are met in a grant awarded for research?

22. Describe overall historical trends for research and development funding in the US and possible implications for the future of the nation's economy.

Exercises to Deepen Your Understanding

Exercise 1: The US House of Representatives Committee on Science, Space and Technology (HSST) authorizes funding for agencies such as the National Science Foundation (NSF), the National Aeronautics and Space Administration (NASA), and the National Oceanic and Atmospheric Administration (NOAA). Select one of these agencies and, for a selected fiscal year, follow the process by which its budget for research and related activities was determined, debated, and then approved. Start with the president's budget and then proceed to House budget bills, HSST hearings, and HSST and House committee and subcommittee meetings, ending with actions by the full House.

Exercise 2: Using the Internet, locate the last ten to fifteen years of yearly research and development (R&D) priority memos issued jointly by the White House Office of Management and Budget (OMB) and Office of Science and Technology Policy (OSTP). Examine carefully how the stated priorities have changed over time and the extent to which certain priorities have persisted or been modified to reflect the views of the president and society at large. See if you can connect priorities in the R&D memo with specific programs in one or two federal agencies.

Exercise 3: The Federal Register is an important mechanism by which the federal government seeks input on a wide array of topics, from STEM education to research and advanced technology. Specifically, Requests for Information (RFIs) are issued regularly by agencies and anyone may respond. On the Internet, search the Federal Register for RFI topics that are of interest to you and examine the questions asked by federal agencies. Although agencies typically do not publicly address the input they receive, they frequently summarize and publish that input. To the extent possible, evaluate that input in the context of your own ideas and develop suggestions you would have provided.

Exercise 4: In the US, twenty-six federal agencies fund research, as do numerous private foundations. Select one federal research funding agency, or one private foundation, and identify from their associated websites a call for proposals on a topic that most interests you. Develop an *outline* for the proposal that addresses the following:

- What questions are you seeking to address, and what work has been performed previously that contextualizes these questions and provides a clear rationale and motivation for addressing them?
- If your work involves one or more hypotheses (section 4.2) to be tested, state them.
- How will you actually conduct the research being proposed?
- What resources will you need?
- What is a reasonable timeline for your project?
- What challenges do you anticipate and how will you overcome them?
- How does your proposed work add to the existing body of knowledge?
- How will this work contribute to society?

Exercise 5: Because R&D funding is included in the discretionary portion of the US federal budget, it often is caught between the two competing challenges of growing mandatory spending (e.g., for Medicare, Medicaid, Social Security, and other programs) and a huge and growing national debt. Evaluate arguments on both sides of this complex issue from White House and congressional documents, press reports, and the work of nonprofit organizations (i.e., think tanks). What trends exist in philosophy and actions among these and other stakeholders, and to what extent do you believe the future of federal research and development funding might eventually be limited by national debt and mandatory spending?

3

Perception and Reality: Public Attitudes, Understanding, and Use of Research

Chapter Overview and Learning Objectives

Although research and creative activity benefit society in a variety of ways, attitudes toward these endeavors, and use of their outcomes, vary among stakeholder groups—in some cases dramatically. This chapter describes how research is viewed by the general public as well as factors that can undermine public trust in research findings and the overall value of research. It also describes models of innovation and emphasizes the need to view research through a broad lens, to ultimately instill a culture of collaboration across multiple fields to advance knowledge and understanding. After reading this chapter, you should

- Understand the social compact between taxpayers and researchers in the context of fundamental research;
- Describe public attitudes toward research and its application, and the factors shaping those attitudes;
- Explain how progress in research must be balanced with belief systems and ethics and how such factors influence public policy;
- Describe how research results can be used, and misused, in policy;
- Explain how our current system of disciplines arose and the challenges such a system poses for research;
- Describe the linear and cyclic models of innovation; and
- Explain the roles of research and creative activity in society, particularly in serving as the foundation for innovations that improve economic and national security as well as quality of life.

3.1   Research and the Social Compact with the General Public

As described in chapter 1, research and creative activity span a wide spectrum of types, funders, and performers (table 1.1). At one end is curiosity-driven, fundamental or "basic" research, which involves studying the world in which we live simply because we want to understand more about it. It also involves creating works of art and culture that enrich the human experience. At the other end are applied research and development, which involves innovating basic research results to create products and services that provide practical benefits to society.

Fundamental research takes place mostly at universities, whereas applied research and development occur mostly in government laboratories and private companies (figure 2.4).[1] Applied research and development are funded (figure 2.1) mainly by the federal government, say for military applications (figure 3.1), and by private industry. Conversely, fundamental research is funded principally by the federal government (figure 2.1)—using taxpayer dollars—because the outcomes of such work are far too uncertain, and the associated risks of success usually are far beyond those a company is willing to accept. That is, companies must make money to survive, and uncertainty

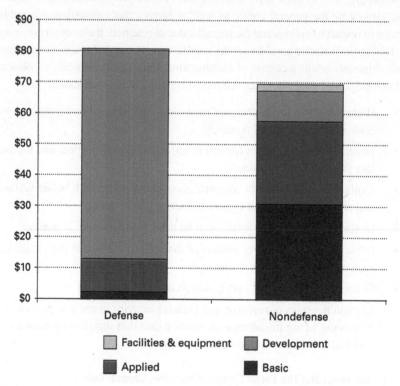

Figure 3.1
US FY 2017 base budget R&D by character. *Source*: Hourihan and Parkes (2016).

and risk are factors companies try to minimize. Yet fundamental research is critical to companies because its outcomes represent the "seed corn" or starting point from which private sector innovation flows.

Because taxpayer dollars support a great deal of fundamental research—to the tune of tens of billions of dollars per year—citizens who provide this funding, namely, the general public via taxation, must be assured the money is used as effectively as possible. In this spirit, an implicit "social compact" of trust, between the general public and those performing fundamental research, emerged after World War II. The compact holds researchers and federal funding agencies accountable as responsible and trustworthy stewards of these dollars.

The emergence of this social compact, and arguably the start of the modern research enterprise, were marked by a highly visionary treatise titled *Science: The Endless Frontier*. It was written by Dr. Vannevar Bush (Bush 1945), President Franklin D. Roosevelt's de facto science advisor and head of the Office of Scientific Research and Development. Recognizing the critical value of research in aiding the Allied war effort, President Roosevelt reasoned these same capabilities—which were organized principally within the highly secretive Manhattan Project—could provide tremendous benefits to civil society if transitioned into the open framework of academia. Consequently, the president charged Dr. Bush in 1944 with developing a plan for such a transition, and Bush underpinned it with three key foundational elements: the essential value of basic or discovery research in advancing national interests and the role of the federal government in supporting it; the importance of developing scientific talent for the future; and the need to remove as many restrictions as possible to promote the open exchange of scientific ideas, information and results.

An important outcome of Bush's report was establishment in 1950 of NSF, an independent federal agency which today funds the bulk of our nation's non-clinical fundamental research.[2] NIH was formally established in 1948, though its origin dates back to 1887. As the name implies, NIH funds fundamental research and its translation into clinical practice in all areas of human health.

Within the arts and humanities, NEA was created in 1965 to support excellence in the arts, both new and established, along with bringing the arts to all Americans and providing leadership in arts education. In the same act of Congress, NEH was established to support research, education, preservation, and public programs in the humanities.

In the 1980s, the objectives of federal support for research, mostly in science fields, were expanded to include major efforts such as the Human Genome Project. Since then, the US research enterprise has continued to blossom, though with challenges to its reputation and value. These include researcher misconduct in fabricating or falsifying results (chapter 10), experimental design that sometimes leads to nonreproducible results (section 4.7), the long time (years to decades) often required for fundamental research to yield outcomes viewed as practical by society, the fact that many published studies are never cited, and violations of agency policy, especially failure to disclose affiliations that might impact national security (section 10.3).

Despite these and other challenges, the public tends to appreciate research having tangible impacts, such as in the medical and technology fields, though has less understanding of how research is performed or the manner in which research *and* teaching are intertwined in higher education. Surveys show that public trust in leaders of research is second only to that of the military (figure 3.2)—a trend that has persisted for approximately two decades. However, the COVID-19 pandemic has impacted public attitudes toward research in ways that are not yet entirely clear. Surveys also show Americans view research as generating opportunities for the next generation, and that the federal government should continue funding basic, discovery-type research.

One key to maintaining taxpayer trust in research and creative activity, among many factors, is anonymous peer/merit review (chapters 6 and 7), in which peers review each other's proposals, journal articles, or other works to ensure high quality and lack of bias (chapter 8). Not to be forgotten are the arts and humanities, which create life-changing introspective development, teach us to engage with ideas critically and independently, and equip us with

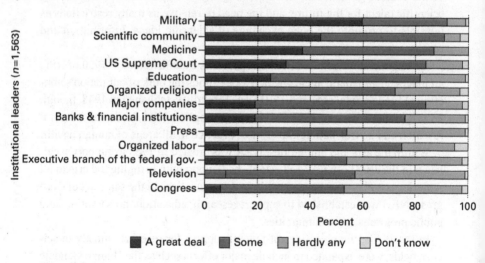

Figure 3.2
Public confidence in institutional leaders, by selected institution, in 2018. *Source*: National Science Board (2020g).

the skills necessary to understand how complex organizations operate and change. They also sustain and preserve the heart and soul of our civilization. Unfortunately, as noted elsewhere in this book, funding for the arts and humanities typically is not given a high priority, when in fact these disciplines reflect the core of our very existence.

Research also has impacts broader than the work itself (chapter 6). Such impacts include teaching and training in K–12 schools, broadening the participation of traditionally underrepresented groups, enhancing public understanding of research through mechanisms such as partnerships with museums and science centers, and commercializing research outcomes to benefit existing companies or start new ones (chapter 12).

3.2   Factors Shaping Public Understanding of Research

How do we develop understanding—about anything? We attend primary and secondary school for twelve years, then possibly go on to college, and then perhaps even earn an advanced degree (master's, doctorate, law degree, medical degree). Such *formal* education is wonderful, but in addition to preparing us for a career, it also prepares us to be lifelong and engaged learners. That is, to have the ability to understand on our own, gather facts and evidence from trusted sources and analyze them, gather opinions and analyze them as well, talk with others, add our own experiences and viewpoints to the mix, and ultimately develop our own assessments.

Historically, once individuals finished their formal education, the bulk of their knowledge and understanding about events shaping their lives came from organized media outlets (radio, newspapers, television), weekly or special publications (e.g., *Time, Newsweek, US News and World Report, Life Magazine*), and conversations with peers. In the late 1980s, the emergence of twenty-four-hour cable news, and later the explosive growth of the Internet and devices that utilize it, transformed the public's ability to gather information, including streaming videos and images.

Numerous studies have been conducted to evaluate the impact of this transformation on public understanding and awareness of national and international affairs, as well as how new "news" elements such as blogs, social media posts, and tweets, have impacted our ability to distinguish between opinion and evidence-supported fact. In the realm of research, leading newspapers once had entire sections dedicated to topics in science, technology, and the arts. Today, science journalism has all but vanished, though one is able to find on the Internet a vast array of resources for learning as much about scholarly activity as one wishes. However, much of this new framework requires *intent* on the part of the reader, and thus only those who already have an interest in or understanding of research and creative activity tend to seek information about them.

Politics and personal ethics also shape public understanding of research, especially for topics such as climate change, genetically modified organisms, and stem cells (discussed further in the next section and in chapter 10). Deeply held beliefs come into play, as do alignments with political platforms and ideologies. Shrinking federal spending on research (figure 2.2), and decreasing funding at the local level, tend to make the arts, fine arts, and humanities targets for funding cuts because they are not seen by many as delivering practical benefits to society.

Consequently, we as researchers must learn how to communicate the results of our work in understandable and relatable ways, and with the proper background and context, to the general public (chapter 11). It also is important to find mechanisms—such as civic organizations, church groups, chambers of commerce, and town councils, to name a few—in which to explain our work and show the importance of it. We need to bring the excitement and substance of our work to the public, not require the public to seek us out.

But in doing so, we should never view our communication as "dumbing down" the work we do, for even experts in one field need clear, straightforward explanations of concepts from another discipline. Far too frequently, researchers become frustrated when others do not appreciate their work, yet they do little to engage them. This is especially true with regard to Congress and others in organizations that determine the course of research itself via the authority they possess to fund it. Our local and national leaders *want* to hear from us, but often we come forward only when it is in our best interest to do so. That is a mistake. Continuous communication is the key.

Many excellent resources exist to help you, as a researcher, communicate your scholarly activities to nonexperts. Doing so can be extremely fulfilling but also exceptionally valuable, and we examine this topic in greater detail in chapter 11.

3.3 Balancing Progress in Research with Belief Systems and Ethics

Should stem cells from human embryos be used in research that might one day cure cancer, blindness, or Alzheimer's disease? Should genetic engineering be used to modify plants and animals, thereby producing organisms more resistant to disease and less expensive for human consumption? Should artificial intelligence and facial recognition technology be used, in the context of a criminal investigation, to identify individuals whose images are captured on public surveillance cameras? Should taxpayer funds be used to study esoteric languages, support the creation of works of art, or study political views on sensitive topics that might endanger funding for the social sciences? How does one reconcile competing views regarding the age of the earth, how humans came to exist, and the possibility of life on other planets?

Because public tax dollars fund the bulk of fundamental research and creative activity via grants awarded by federal agencies, the public, and by virtue of it the Congress, have a lot to say about which areas of research represent national priorities. This is true not only in science, engineering, and medicine, but also in the arts, fine arts, and humanities. Indeed, Congress has the formal role of both authorizing (that is, setting dollar targets) for funding federal agencies that sponsor research, as well as appropriating (that is, actually providing) the money (chapter 2).

With that responsibility comes significant challenges, among them the issue of balancing progress in research with acknowledgment of and respect for belief systems and ethical views held by the public. In that context, two factors are particularly important.

The first concerns fundamental religious, cultural, and personally held beliefs. Stem cell research is a good example of the former, in which some oppose the use of aborted fetuses in research. With regard to cultural beliefs, Native Americans and other people groups sometimes oppose for research purposes the use of lands determined by them to be sacred. Other examples include opposition to the siting of large telescopes or the building of pipelines on certain lands owing to religious or environmental concerns. Questions, such as whether live animals should be used in research, or even euthanized and then used, continue to challenge some sectors of society. In deciding which sorts of research are allowable or ethical—that is, adhere to moral standards established by society—one has to weigh the benefits to be gained against other issues.

The second major factor to be considered concerns political views, which often are intertwined with belief systems. For example, one political party tends to favor fossil energy development while another supports renewable energy and research into public attitudes of our political system. One party may value funding for the arts and culture while the other feels public funding should be directed mostly toward endeavors that lead to outcomes having "much greater" practical benefits for society. These views can have profound impacts on how funding is allocated for research and creative activity. Yet, in the end, progress must be balanced with respect for belief systems and the realization that research does not exist in a vacuum, but rather is part of society itself.

Consequently, as a researcher, it is very important to avoid categorizing a given individual, group, or organization as having one belief versus another because, in reality, a spectrum of belief systems and views exists. Such is the nature of a diverse society. Research rarely identifies immutable truths or contains absolutes in its outcomes. Rather, it builds upon results successively via the continuous gathering, analysis, and refinement of data and evidence—sometimes challenging and even overturning established paradigms—in a continual process of advancing knowledge and understanding.

Additionally, it important that you have a broad view of the academic enterprise and understand inequities that exist regarding public funding for research and creative activity across it. As an example, nearly 50 percent of NSF funding for competitive research grants goes to fifty universities in America (National Science Board 2020b). The remaining hundreds of other colleges and universities, including MSIs (which include HBCUs, TCUs, HSIs, and Asian American, Native American, and Pacific Islander Serving Institutions), as well as ERIs, historically have not been as competitive.

Specific programs have been created to address these challenges and to improve equity within multiple federal agencies, including EPSCoR. Additionally, significant new funding, with strong bipartisan support in Congress, is being proposed for MSIs and ERIs, not only to support research itself, but also to help create the administrative infrastructures required to deal with the associated funding. Only in this manner will all of America's talent have an opportunity to participate in research and creative activity and thus bring benefits to society.

It is axiomatic that research always will have an uneasy coexistence with public belief systems and ethics. Such has been the case for centuries, and the positive value of this construct cannot be overstated. Only if we attempt to eliminate or greatly devalue one or the other will we, as a society, pay a heavy price.

3.4   The Use and Misuse of Research Results in Policy

Each of us has been exposed to policies throughout our lives, sometimes without even noticing. Your parents most likely applied numerous rules and policies as you were growing up, some of which you even followed! How late you could stay out, at what age you could have your own phone or car, when you could take your first job, and when you could begin dating. What guided the creation of their policies? Most likely, practical experience and perhaps a book or two, though ultimately, the desire to *protect* you.

Public policy is very similar. It draws upon the collective wisdom of a diverse array of resources—people, data, and history—to reach a common public goal. It does not involve the creation of new knowledge—which is what we refer to as research and creative activity, but it does involve the wise use of research outcomes. For example, policy governing the storage of nuclear waste, the amount of carbon dioxide that should be released by coal plants, acceptable levels of heavy metals in drinking water, and the manner in which foreign nationals are evaluated for immigration to the US. In these and numerous other examples, research is an extremely important factor in crafting public policy.

Two key points are worth noting about federal government policy, both of which apply to policy concerning research. First, policy is not necessarily law, and in many cases consists of procedures, rules, and processes, promulgated by cabinet departments and their associated federal agencies, which must be followed to avoid negative consequences (chapters 9 and 10). Exceptions include presidential policies such as executive orders, presidential memoranda, and national security presidential memoranda, which have the effect of law for federal agencies. And of course, policy contained in laws passed by Congress and signed by the president indeed are formal laws and carry legal penalties if not followed.

Second, policy is a statement of intent or guidance that is carried out via a series of actions, many of which are outlined in the policy itself but some of which are left ambiguous. A good example is the famous speech by President John F. Kennedy regarding the Cuban missile crisis of October 1962. He said, "It shall be the policy of this nation to regard any nuclear missile launched from Cuba against any nation in the Western Hemisphere as an attack by the Soviet Union on the United States requiring a full retaliatory response upon the Soviet Union" (John F. Kennedy Library n.d.). That policy statement was unambiguous in its intent but, understandably in that situation, conveyed nothing about how the action would be carried out.

OSTP was established by Congress in 1976 (note the combination of science and technology in the title), with a broad mandate to advise the president on the effects of science and technology on domestic and international affairs. It issues policy guidance to federal agencies in the form of memoranda, sometimes in conjunction with other White House organizations such as OMB. OSTP also frames topics and their associated policy implications via reports issued by NSTC and the President's Council of Advisors on Science and Technology (PCAST). Note that numerous federal policies directly impact the academic research enterprise, such as those governing open access to scholarly publications and data (section 11.2), as well as research compliance (chapter 10).

Some cabinet departments in the US government have chief scientists to advise on policy matters (e.g., NASA, NOAA, and even the secretary of state), and many agencies within them do as well. Congress uses the Congressional Research Service (CRS) to provide input on matters of policy and legal issues, and NASEM, the Government Accountability Office, and NSB all support policy creation as well.

Although research is a vitally important ingredient for creating public policy, the research community has, for decades, been extremely careful to avoid being influenced by politics, personal prejudices, or external pressures in performing its work. Academic tenure in fact was created to protect researchers from external political pressures or other factors that could lead to bias (chapter 8) or inappropriate influence in their studies.

The roles played by each sector of society in creating public policy are clear and must be well understood and respected. Scientists discover and communicate evidence and uncertainties in their findings. Policy analysts consider these results in light of values held by various sectors, and they frame the problems to be addressed as well as recommend possible courses of action. Policymakers and lawmakers then make judgments to determine how the information should be applied, and then ultimately create policy. Policy is enforced in a variety of ways, ranging from congressional oversight and federal agency inspectors general to numerous legal mechanisms available to the law enforcement community.

Research has become somewhat of a battleground in the context of policy for topics such as climate change, energy, genetic engineering and gene drives, stem cell research, hydraulic fracturing, and the fundamental value of the arts and humanities. A good example is climate change research. Some wish to see deep funding cuts for research on this topic, despite overwhelming evidence that such work is essential for guiding key areas of society such as food production, construction in coastal zones, and human health. In this manner, research outcomes are not being used effectively, or are being misused and misinterpreted. This is often referred to as the "politicization of science," or "spinning" research outcomes.

Such has been the case in the COVID-19 pandemic, during which the general public became acutely aware that understanding of the novel coronavirus evolved considerably over time, as did the guidance about it provided by public health officials. This, along with poor coordination of messaging, led to considerable confusion regarding actions to be taken by states, communities, and even individuals, with debates about competing ideas and theories—some grounded in science and others not—playing out in the press, on social media, in Congress, and at other venues. The phrase "follow the science" was frequently heard, even though scientific understanding gained through research was unable to provide the desired final answers, and in fact sometimes contained opposing results. This led to the understandable question: "Which science should be followed?" The research enterprise was performing in extraordinary ways, yet the general public had never before been exposed in this manner to its winding paths, intense debates, uncertainties, and stepwise advances.

In addition, a presumption exists on the part of many, not only in the general public but also in the scholarly community, that no daylight should exist between policy prescriptions and scientific findings. However, in reality, science is but one of numerous inputs to policy, as I saw firsthand during my two years at the White House. Other inputs include implications regarding national security, economics, international relations, health and welfare of citizens, demographics, existing laws and policies—and of course, politics. Policymakers must weigh very carefully these and other considerations, thus resulting in policy outcomes that sometimes run counter to expectations of those who view policy through a narrow lens.

An important lesson learned from the pandemic, and one which has long been recognized, is that researchers must stay "pure" in their efforts and not let politics or other similar factors influence the manner in which they perform their work (see chapters 4 and 9). They also must do their best to educate policymakers and lawmakers about research—about how it contains assumptions and uncertainties, how it rarely produces definitive answers to complex questions, and about how freedom to explore ideas using robust techniques always will be in the best interest of society.

OSTP issued a report (National Science and Technology Council 2022b) on the topic of protecting the integrity of government science, and particularly the use of scientific results in policy. It addressed issues not only regarding the scientific process, but also the communication of results and how they are used. Although the report did not formally define the term "government science," it generally is meant to describe scientific research performed by federal government employees. However, the concepts described are equally applicable to research performed in any organization, public or private.

Finally, many researchers are interested in policy, either so they can play a more active and effective role in its formulation and execution, or because a deeper understanding will assist their ability to explain and follow it. I frequently am asked for advice regarding options to engage in federal research policy, and many exist. First, taking one or more courses in public policy lays an excellent foundation. Even if you already are conducting research, say as a postdoctoral scholar or faculty member, you still can sit in on such courses or read books to gain insight into policy.

Second, as a student or practicing scholar, you can volunteer your services to members of Congress, either in their state or district offices or in their Washington, DC offices. You also can seek similar opportunities within staff offices of congressional committees (section 2.2), though I would suggest this route mostly for nonstudents.

Third, numerous professional societies offer policy fellowships, many of which are immersive and involve spending time in Washington, DC, meeting with various federal officials. Examples include the AAAS Policy Fellowship program (http://www.aaas.org/programs/science-technology-policy-fellowships) and American Academy of Arts and Sciences Humanities Policy Fellows program (http://www.amacad.org/about/fellowships).

Finally, the federal government operates a number of policy programs, one of the most prestigious of which is the White House Fellows Program (http://whff.org) for emerging leaders at all stages of their professional career.

3.5 All Academic Disciplines Created Equal?

The various academic departments and programs we are familiar with today—from chemical engineering and architecture to history, English, and atmospheric science—are a relatively new construct in higher education. The University of Paris, which was one of the first educational institutions established outside the church, in 1231 consisted of four so-called faculties: Theology, Medicine, Canon Law and Arts. Educational institutions originally used the term "discipline" to catalog and archive the new and expanding body of information produced by the scientific community.

Most academic disciplines have their roots in the mid- to late nineteenth-century secularization of universities, especially in Germany, when the traditional curricula were supplemented with nonclassical languages and literatures, social sciences, economics, and technology disciplines such as engineering. In the early twentieth century, new academic disciplines, such as education and psychology, were added. Then, in the 1970s and 1980s, an explosion of new academic disciplines occurred, focusing on specific themes such as media studies, women's studies, and African studies. Interdisciplinary scientific fields of study, such as biochemistry and biomedical engineering, gained prominence as well.

At its core, research and creative activity involve the creation and dissemination of new knowledge and understanding for improving the world around us. Nowhere is this better seen than in public and private academic institutions, where dozens of disciplines coexist and interact to both study the world's most interesting and challenging problems as well as create and study works of beauty and culture to enrich the human experience.

Because all such activity requires money (chapters 2 and 6), funding is extremely important to academic disciplines, and to the institutions housing them. During the past few decades, public funding for public research universities has dropped precipitously (though improving recently), with the costs offset by substantial increases in tuition and fees (figure 3.3). Even endowments for private universities have become problematic. Yet, the value of higher education remains mostly undisputed, not only in terms of much greater lifetime earnings for degree earners, but also in creating an educated citizenry that is foundational to our democratic republic.

Government funding for research is, however, extremely varied across disciplines (figure 2.10), reflecting, in part, the perceived "value" of those disciplines but to a larger degree the different costs of actually performing research and creative activity within them. For example, funding for biomedical research dwarfs the nearest discipline (engineering) by a factor of two. Other life sciences and the physical sciences are a factor of two less than engineering, followed by environmental science and computer science. Social science and psychology are smaller yet, with the arts, fine arts, and humanities essentially at the noise level. However, many philanthropic organizations also fund these latter activities, with private companies, overall, funding nearly three-fourths of all research and development in the US, mostly in applied areas (chapter 2).

Often overlooked in disciplinary research funding profiles, and discussions regarding disciplines, is education. This is rather ironic because research and education are inextricably linked. Specifically, research conducted in the

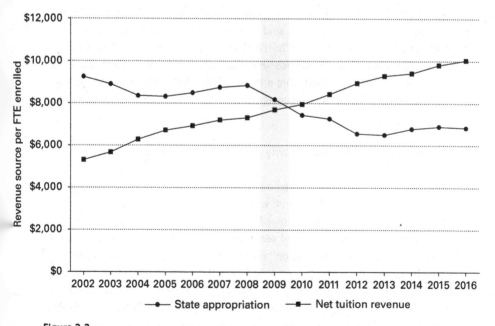

Figure 3.3
Recent trends in state appropriations and net tuition revenue in 2016 dollars per full-time equivalent (FTE) student at public institutions. *Source*: Comrie (2021). Used with permission of Creative Commons License (CC BY 4.0; https://creativecommons.org/licenses/by/4.0/).

discipline of education is foundational to education as a process of learning. Education research results underpin our understanding of how individuals learn. They guide us toward effective pedagogical methodologies and discipline-specific approaches to learning. And they inform education delivery tools (e.g., virtual learning management systems) and analyses describing education progress and factors affecting it (chapter 14).

Conversely, education as a process of learning is foundational to the creation and dissemination of knowledge (i.e., research and creative activity). Next-generation researchers are educated in a wide variety of ways, ranging from standard classroom lectures to active learning environments, individual mentoring by research advisors, independent study, topical-reading and journal clubs, and of course by the research they perform.

Unfortunately, to many, education as a discipline is mistakenly presumed to encompass solely the training of future teachers. In reality, the US government invests considerable funding in education research, mostly through the NSF Directorate for STEM Education (approximately $1 billion per year) and the US Department of Education Institute for Education Sciences (approximately $0.75 billion per year). Numerous other federal agencies also support education research programs, as do private nonprofit foundations.

Society benefits when knowledge advances via research, not only in STEM disciplines but also in the arts, fine arts, and humanities (STEAM, where A represents the arts). It has been said that, during World War II, United Kingdom prime minister Winston Churchill was asked to cut federal funding for the arts in order to direct all possible resources to the war effort. And that Churchill responded, "Then what are we fighting for?" Although the veracity of the attribution is generally accepted as untrue, the response would have been quite appropriate.

3.6 Research and Creative Activity as the Foundation of Innovation

In the early 1950s, when the social compact described in section 3.1 emerged, it was thought fundamental research would yield outcomes for further advancement via applied research, followed by development, followed by commercialization to yield products and services that benefit society. This is known as the "linear model of innovation" for obvious reasons, and it has served very well. In its simplest form, shown in figure 3.4 in the context of academic research, taxes collected by the US Treasury are appropriated by Congress (section 2.2) to federal R&D agencies. These agencies fund both fundamental research as well as applied research and development, in the case of academia usually in response to grant proposals (chapter 6). (Note that other sectors,

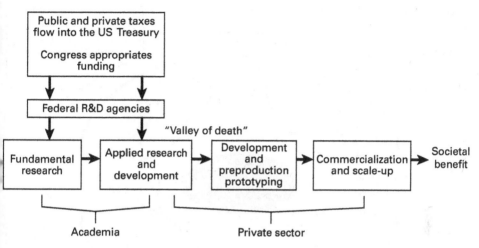

Figure 3.4
Traditional academic linear model of innovation.

including federal agencies, perform applied R&D as well.) Private companies, sometimes in partnership with academia, innovate on these outcomes to commercialize products and services at scale, which yield benefits to society. Sometimes academic institutions have difficulty moving research outcomes from fundamental and applied R&D to the development stage, and in many cases, useful outcomes are never commercialized. This transition therefore is known as the "valley of death" (figure 3.4), with speculative funding in it provided by angel investors, venture capitalists, and other sources (section 12.4).

In reality, the transition from fundamental research to practicable products and services is far more complex, as shown in figure 3.5. Specifically, "innovation" consists not of a set of sequential steps but rather embodies an ecosystem containing multiple, interconnected elements composing an iterative process. Additionally, the starting point often is not fundamental research, but rather innovation itself, namely, the concept behind an interesting idea that requires an integration of multiple components to become reality, including things that already exist. Even when research fails to provide the answer, innovation can fill the gap to make a product, service or public good a reality.

Most public and private colleges and universities are today viewed as engines of innovation and economic development, and most of them have offices to help license inventions to private companies or support faculty who wish to start their own companies (chapters 1 and 12). Students have tremendous opportunities to innovate in so-called maker spaces, where they can rapidly prototype ideas and find support to further develop and even market them. Also,

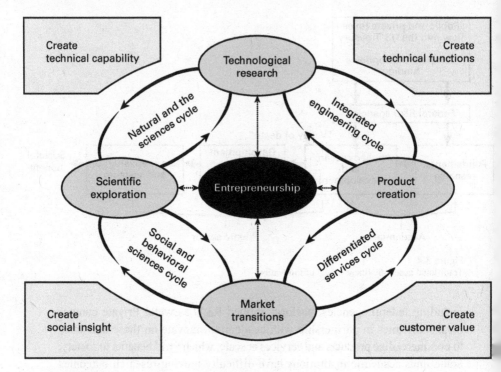

Figure 3.5
Cyclic model of innovation. *Source*: Spill and Mason (2014).

entrepreneurship programs, often housed in colleges of business but engaging all disciplines, including the arts, fine arts, and humanities, have exploded in number and quality and are helping students and faculty be more creative and find ways to make their research ideas and outcomes of practical use to the public.

Some of the more prominent examples of academic innovation include Gatorade, which was invented at the University of Florida, and Warfarin, which is a blood-thinning medicine developed at the University of Wisconsin. You may not have heard of the medicine, but I am certain you've heard of Gatorade. Did you realize it was invented at a research university?

Perhaps the most compelling example of our time is how fundamental research allowed the US and the world to rapidly develop vaccines for COVID-19. Investments in fundamental research made decades ago, which led to rapid genomic sequencing, the utilization of messenger RNA for vaccines, the Internet, and personal computers (which were indispensable for remote learning and work), supercomputers (which proved vitally important for understanding the virus and developing therapeutics and vaccines to combat it), and advanced manufacturing technologies all combined to facilitate an unprecedented response to a global crisis.

Yet, as noted previously and throughout this book, not all academic institutions have sufficient resources to participate in research and creative activity, and thus contribute to innovation and the development of their local and regional communities. In response, creative multi-institutional partnerships and regional hubs of innovation are emerging as partial solutions, along with national programs directing federal funding to specific types of institutions.

Ultimately, research is the "seed corn" of our future—the future of feeding the world, moving people around, communicating with one another, sharing information, remaining secure and healthy, understanding ourselves and our history, and creating beauty that reflects the very best about the human spirit. To compromise support for, and not ensure clear public recognition of the inestimable value of research and creative activity, is to place unnecessary and harmful constraints on our future and that of our children and grandchildren. We, as researchers, own the responsibility of telling the story. Not as we would in some technical journal, but in everyday language, with a context that shows why the work is important, and with humility and gratitude for the public funding that enables it. And we, as researchers, must continue advocating for research funding to the broad array of academic institutions in America so all can contribute and help every student and scholar realize their full potential.

Assess Your Comprehension

1. What is the "social compact" between researchers and taxpayers?
2. Who was Vannevar Bush and what role did he play in shaping America's research enterprise?
3. What factors are key to maintaining trust in America's research enterprise?
4. Describe public confidence in leaders of the scientific community relative to other institutions and sectors in the US.
5. List key factors in shaping public understanding of research and creative activity.
6. Describe the two most important factors in balancing research progress with belief systems and ethical views held by the public.
7. What problems can arise when researchers categorize a given individual or organization in the context of sharing research results?

8. Describe the mission of the Office of Science and Technology Policy (OSTP).

9. List the different roles in setting public policy played by scientists, policy analysts, lobbyists, and lawmakers.

10. In what ways can research outcomes be misused or politicized, and what actions can be taken to prevent this from occurring?

11. Provide a brief timeline of the evolution of academic disciplines.

12. Describe recent trends in state funding for higher education compared to tuition revenues and the reasons for them.

13. Describe the linear model of innovation and its limitations.

14. Describe the cyclic model of innovation and compare it to the linear model.

Exercises to Deepen Your Understanding

Exercise 1: Our views on topics, especially those of a controversial nature, are shaped by a number of factors. Select one or two topics in research and creative activity about which you have clear opinions and describe how your opinions developed over time. What factors or individuals influenced your thinking, including belief systems and ethics, and have your views changed with time? Why or why not? Now explore the views of others on the same topic, either by speaking with individuals or via information from Internet sources and compare and contrast them with your own. Do you see value in examining opposing views? To what extent do politics, belief systems, ethics, religion, race, culture, or other factors impact your answer regarding the views held by others?

Exercise 2: Research results play an important role in the development of policy at the local, regional, and national levels. For this exercise, select a policy issue of personal interest and use the Internet to gather information for evaluating the roles played by research in setting the policy. Examples you may wish to consider include genetically modified foods and plants, immigration, gun control, climate change, safe drinking water, community expansion, poverty, racism, crime, and urban development. You need not draw from this list—the examples are provided merely to stimulate your thinking.

Exercise 3: Research and creative activity are foundational to our health, economic and national security, global competitiveness, and quality of life. Yet, funding is quite varied as a function of discipline, partly because of the associated intrinsic costs, and partly because of the value attached by society and funding organizations to the nature of the work itself. In light of existing relative funding levels, provide a series of arguments for increasing funding in science, health and engineering disciplines at the expense of the arts, fine arts, and humanities, and then perform the reverse exercise. Provide justification and data for your arguments and consider also how funds might be utilized if they are removed from the research enterprise altogether and, for example, redirected to public assistance programs.

Exercise 4: This chapter lists a number of organizations, both public and private, that advise the federal government on research policy. Select three of them, spanning a broad space, and compare and contrast their missions, approaches, political alignments (as are relevant), and positions taken, especially in the form of reports to Congress or the White House. To what extent are these activities grounded in facts and supported by data or hard evidence, and are the facts and data presented in an unbiased, objective manner or grounded more in ideology and perception? Do you find evidence for common ground, and if so, how would you go about persuading the organizations to collaborate productively?

Exercise 5: Tenure is an important feature in most colleges and universities and was established to protect faculty pursuit of research, creative activity, and other scholarly and educational endeavors from undue external influences and pressures. This "academic freedom" ensures that scholars can pursue especially controversial topics without fear of retribution, provided they adhere to principles of honesty, integrity, fairness, objectivity, and so on. Those who secure tenure at an academic institution can only be terminated for cause, and for especially egregious activities as outlined in institutional rules and regulations. Tenure has long been a controversial topic, viewed by some as guaranteeing a job for life and inviting underperformance while viewed by others as essential to the conduct of scholarship. Conduct a review of the origin of academic freedom and tenure and outline arguments for retaining tenure, eliminating it, and modifying it. To what extent do you believe tenure is important for ensuring that research itself remains "pure," as discussed in this chapter? What consequences do you feel might arise if tenure is eliminated?

4

Essential Concepts: Performing Research and Creative Activity

Chapter Overview and Learning Objectives

From the historical and scientific research methods to Indigenous knowledge and lore, research and creative activity are performed using structured frameworks and methodologies so as to ensure quality, integrity, accountability, and reproducibility. This chapter describes the concept of research paradigms and associated methodologies and the extent to which they vary among broad areas of scholarship (e.g., physical science, engineering, and the humanities) as well as individual disciplines. It also discusses how research is conducted by the general public via citizen science, the application of research concepts in daily life, and the importance of reproducibility and replicability of research results. After reading this chapter, you should

- Understand the general framework of research and be able to describe its components;
- Describe the scientific method and how it varies from the historical method;
- Explain the importance of including Indigenous knowledge and lore in research;
- Understand the differences between primary and secondary sources of information;
- Describe citizen science and its role in advancing research;
- Recognize that the process and logic underlying research methods can be applied in everyday life;
- Understand the differences among reproducibility, reliability, and replicability of results and their importance in research; and
- Recognize the roles played in research by serendipity.

4.1   General Framework

Working within a structured framework, adhering to certain principles, and following certain procedures when performing research and creative activity ensure the outcomes have several important properties. Among them, results should be of high quality; they should, when appropriate, be reproducible and replicable as well as reliable; they should reflect thoughtfulness and integrity in design and execution; they should add to and not duplicate the existing body of knowledge; and they should be worthy of the funding and resources used to support them.

Because of the wide array of disciplines in which research and creative activity take place, an equally wide array of methodologies exists. Indeed, many disciplines offer courses in research methods, and entire books (e.g., see Bulmer 2003; Crowther and Lancaster 2008; Wilson 2008; Smith 2012; Groat and Wang 2013; Christensen et al. 2014; Punch and Oancea 2014; Drawson et al. 2017; and Litosseliti 2018 in the references) are devoted to specific methods in education, business, sociology, social work, psychology, law, the arts and fine arts, humanities, science and engineering, and others. Topics covered typically include historical overviews of research in the given field, along with considerable detail regarding research approaches, the collection, analysis, and interpretation of data, hypothesis formulation, sampling, experiment design and execution, and interpretation and presentation of results.

Not surprisingly, terms describing certain aspects of research methodology in one discipline sometimes have a different meaning in other disciplines. Examples include words such as paradigm, approach, method, philosophy, and design. Consequently, given that research methods are almost a discipline in and of themselves, I do not attempt to provide any sort of summary of methods for individual fields of study. Instead, I provide first a somewhat generic overall framework for research and creative activity, borrowing from a number of disciplines and utilizing terms that have the same general meaning across them. I then examine a few specific methods to give you a flavor of their similarities and differences. As a next-generation scholar, you should become intimately familiar with research methods in your own discipline and explore methods in a few others. Doing so not only will facilitate your own work but also prepare you for multidisciplinary collaboration (chapter 13). Additionally, it will allow you to borrow concepts from other disciplines to enhance the application of methods in your own.

In general, research can be divided into three categories (figure 4.1): qualitative, quantitative, and mixed. These terms usually are described as the foundational elements of the research framework, philosophy, scheme, or paradigm.[1]

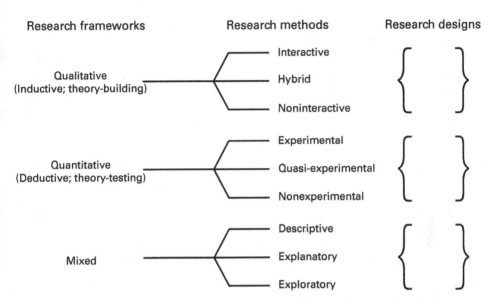

Research frameworks   Research methods   Research designs

Qualitative
(Inductive; theory-building)
    Interactive
    Hybrid
    Noninteractive

Quantitative
(Deductive; theory-testing)
    Experimental
    Quasi-experimental
    Nonexperimental

Mixed
    Descriptive
    Explanatory
    Exploratory

Figure 4.1
A general research framework. *Source*: Adapted from Khaldi (2017, figure 2).

Qualitative methods involve the extraction of meaning via descriptive analyses or interpretation, which makes the results more subjective but nonetheless still valuable as they are determined using a structured approach. Qualitative methods often utilize inductive reasoning, which begins not with a theory, but rather with observations. This "bottom up" approach (figure 4.2) begins with specifics, such as detailed behavior observed regarding some phenomenon or situation. It then proceeds to more general notions by identifying patterns or other structures within observations/data that explain the behavior, resulting in one or more hypotheses and eventually a theory. For this reason, qualitative methods often are referred to as theory-building methods.

Conversely, quantitative methods utilize numerics and frequently involve the use of statistics and the development of computational models. In this regard, the results tend to be objectively determined. Quantitative methods typically utilize deductive reasoning (figure 4.2), which begins with a general concept or theory and then sets out to test one or more associated hypotheses based upon observations or other data collected. This "top-down" approach therefore proceeds from the general to the specific through systematic investigation until reaching a final, specific conclusion. For this reason, quantitative methods often are referred to as "theory-testing" methods.

Another dimension of both qualitative and quantitative research methods is empiricism or the empirical approach. The word "empirical," as applied here,

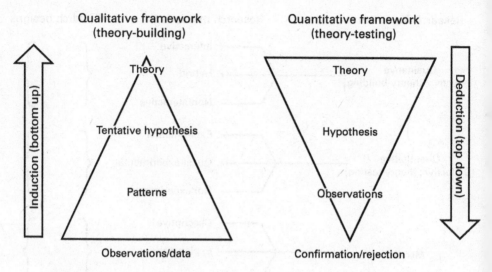

Figure 4.2
Inductive/qualitative and deductive/quantitative research frameworks. *Source*: Adapted from Khaldi (2017, figure 1); Burney and Saleem (2008); Research techniques (2015).

refers to research that can be verified by observation or experiments, as opposed to conjecture, philosophy, or logic. Empiricism involves gathering evidence to answer a question or test a hypothesis (more on hypotheses below). Applied to quantitative research, empiricism might involve collecting and objectively analyzing radar data on a wide array of thunderstorms in an effort to evaluate one or more theories regarding tornado formation. In the context of qualitative research, empiricism might involve assessing interviews from individuals regarding their opinions about a specific historical event. In both cases, the outcomes of the research can be traced directly to verifiable data or information, though using substantially different approaches.

Not surprisingly, numerous research studies do not fit neatly within either the qualitative or quantitative frameworks, giving rise to the application of mixed research methods (figure 4.1). Such hybrid approaches are extremely powerful in that they combine the attributes of both foundational frameworks and thus are particularly well suited for work involving multiple, especially disparate disciplines (chapter 13).

Within the qualitative/quantitative/mixed methods framework just described lies a great deal of complexity. As shown in figure 4.1, qualitative research can involve the application of interactive, hybrid, and noninteractive methods. In the interactive method, the researcher is directly involved with or immersed in the study, such as interviewing a focus group, whereas historians typically utilize the noninteractive method, as when relying upon source material from written documents, recordings, and images produced by individuals who may be deceased. As you will find, additional layers of complexity exist beyond these, extending into specific instruments for gathering and analyzing data, for example. They are indicated by the curly brackets in figure 4.1.

Quantitative research generally is viewed as experimental, quasi-experimental, or nonexperimental. Although these terms have substantially different meanings across disciplines, the word "experiment" generally involves a process or set of processes over which the researcher has complete control, especially in manipulating certain parameters to determine their impact on the end result. The aforementioned example involving the collection of radar observations of thunderstorms is an example of a nonexperimental approach.

All three of the foundational frameworks are used in disciplines ranging from science and engineering to arts, social sciences, and humanities. And each contains numerous possible designs and execution strategies (shown by the empty curly brackets in figure 4.1). Although quantitative research generally is viewed as necessarily reproducible (section 4.7) and yields statistical confidence in or other quantifications of the results, qualitative research generally is not—yet has the advantage of being applicable to situations that are not amenable to quantitative methods.

Finally, research within the general three-part framework can be either independent or directed. In directed research, such as that performed by college undergraduates or students pursuing master's degrees, or amateurs involved in citizen science (section 4.6), the work is overseen by a professional researcher who provides considerable input and directs the work as it proceeds. In contrast, independent research, which is performed by professionals, postdocs, and doctoral students, is for the most part not overly influenced by an advisor, though of course ultimately is judged by peers in publications, performances, exhibits, dissertations, and other forms of presentation (chapter 11).

4.2 The Scientific Method

The foremost example within the deductive/quantitative framework described previously is the scientific method. In fact, is it not a single method but rather, as shown in figure 4.3, a general set of principles, appropriate for a wide array of disciplines, within a flexible procedural structure. That is, multiple starting points exist within the structure, and the ordering of and interaction among steps can vary depending upon discipline or type of study being undertaken. Ultimately, application of this structure leads to understanding of cause-and-effect

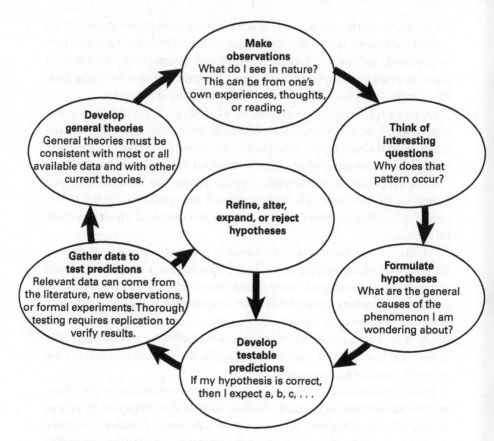

Figure 4.3
The general scientific method as an ongoing process. *Source*: Wikimedia.org. Used with permission of Creative Commons License (CC BY-SA 4.0; https://creativecommons.org/licenses/by-sa/4.0/deed.en).

relationships via experimentation, regarding questions posed by the researcher. The scientific method is based principally upon empirical or measurable evidence though can involve qualitative, nonempirical elements as well.

Application of the scientific method generally begins with a personal awareness of some facet of the world, or some professional interest in a particular phenomenon or process, which leads one to ask questions. How does the SARS 2019 coronavirus mutate? Why does a particular painting or dance evoke such strong emotion? Why did the Roman civilization not persist? Why is a particular form of cancer susceptible to therapy while one very similar is not? Consequently, the "make observations" and "think of questions" balloons in figure 4.3 can be interchanged. That is, informal observations of the world in which we live, leading to questions such as "I wonder why rivers do not flow in a straight line?" are different from observations collected formally as part of a structured research process (figure 4.2). The latter seek to answer questions posed at the outset of the study but also lead to additional questions being posed.

An important consideration in research involves determining whether the question or questions being posed already have been answered. In some cases, such as the examples just provided, the answer is obvious. Indeed, we know exactly why rivers do not flow in a straight line. For other questions, say involving a particular form of cancer, the answer may exist in the form of making incremental progress rather than arriving at a conclusive yes or no.

If the question being posed remains unanswered, or additional knowledge can be gained through further investigation, then becoming more familiar with the topic is important. That is, one needs to review the existing body of knowledge to understand what work has been performed previously and how answering new questions will advance understanding. Once that review has been conducted, the researcher characterizes the subject of inquiry by making formal measurements or observations. And as noted previously, the very process of making measurements or observations can lead to additional questions.

A critical component of the scientific method, once general questions have been formulated based upon observations or other information, involves the generation of hypotheses. A hypothesis is an informed conjecture, or educated guess, that offers a plausible explanation for the observations made or answers to the question(s) being posed. In some cases, hypotheses are formulated mathematically and tested with rigorous statistical analysis—the goal being not to *prove* the hypothesis, but rather to *accept or reject it* based upon measures of statistical significance that address whether the outcome may simply be due to chance. This approach is commonly applied in the social and behavioral sciences.

Well-formulated hypotheses lead to another important element of the scientific method, namely, predictions (figure 4.3). The prediction might involve the presumed outcome of an experiment in a laboratory setting, such as a chemical reaction, or an observation of nature, such as lightning in a thunderstorm. How does one test the prediction? Via experimentation, which is another important step in the scientific method.

It is important to recognize that hypotheses and experiments are not the domain of the sciences alone. In fact, hypotheses often are tested via experimentation in dance studios, on the stage, in art exhibitions, and in the orchestra pit. Experimental results and analyses that support predictions and observations might lead to acceptance of the hypothesis. However, sometimes experiments contain errors in formulation or execution, and observations also can contain errors. For this reason, experiments frequently need to be repeated using different sets of observations (section 4.7). Additionally, as described below, one must not modify hypotheses midstream, or tamper in dubious ways with observations, because doing so—with the purpose of obtaining desired results—would violate principles of research integrity (chapter 9).

Depending upon the outcomes of experiments, additional testing can be performed and other hypotheses evaluated. Ultimately, the work might lead to the verification of a theory, which is an explanation for some phenomenon, behavior, or observation that is still subject to uncertainty and testing. Indeed, theories are not facts or evidence, but rather explanations of them. No theory is ever considered final or complete because new evidence always arises, perhaps not overturning the theory itself but placing it in the context of other, broader theories (as is the case for the structure of the atom). Note that the word "theory," as applied in the scientific method, is quite different from that used in regular conversation. This is one reason why topics such as climate change, which is founded upon theories of how the earth behaves and how humans influence this behavior, often are misunderstood by the general public.

Another important term in scientific research is the word "law." Laws, such as the law of gravity, describe the behavior of a phenomenon in the natural world, and the law always holds true. But the law does not explain *why* the behavior occurs. Theories, on the other hand, explain observations, but can change or be refuted with time as understanding grows or additional observations and understanding become available.

4.3 The Historical Method

The historical method, which is an example of qualitative research (as noted previously, quantitative research methods also are used broadly across the humanities), consists of techniques and guidelines by which historians use primary sources of information (that is, original writings, recordings, interviews, and other materials) to develop their accounts of the past. Of course, they also rely upon other sources, as do all scholars, in building upon the current state of knowledge.

One important aspect of historical research involves the reliability of source material, which is the analog of reliability of observations in the scientific method. When and where the source was produced, by whom, its reliance upon earlier material, its original form, and the credibility of its contents all are critical elements to be considered. Collectively, these are known as *source criticism*. Of course, different sources often contain differing accounts (e.g., the assassination of President Kennedy) or lead to different conclusions, and thus contradiction needs to be considered. Rigorous procedures exist for addressing contradictions in sources, including factors such as degree of authority, eyewitness accounts, source independence, and extent of source disagreement. Anonymous sources require particularly careful vetting.

Once sources have been identified and fully evaluated, hypotheses then are constructed in a manner similar to that used in the scientific method. However, because *quantitative* hypothesis testing usually is not applicable to historical research, other techniques are used to arrive at the best explanation for the hypothesis given.

For example, the hypothesis must be of greater *explanatory scope* than any other incompatible hypothesis about the same subject; that is, it must imply a greater variety of observation statements. The hypothesis must be of greater *explanatory power* than any other incompatible hypothesis about the same subject; that is, it must make more probable than any other hypothesis the observation statements it implies. The hypothesis must be *more plausible* than any other incompatible hypothesis about the same subject; that is, it must be implied to some degree by a greater variety of accepted truths than any other. And so on.

Noted historian C. Behan McCullagh sums up the historical method quite nicely by saying, "if the scope and strength of an explanation are very great, so that it explains a large number and variety of facts, many more than any competing explanation, then it is likely to be true" (McCullagh 1984, 26).

4.4 Indigenous Methods

The research frameworks and methods previously discussed in this chapter were developed within the context of Western civilization. They emerged as study of the natural world became systematized (sections 3.5 and 7.1) and emphasis began to be placed on quantitative/theoretical as opposed to purely descriptive/ phenomenological approaches. Consequently, a vitally important dimension of research and creative activity, *relevant to all areas of inquiry*, became increasingly sidelined—namely, the engagement of Indigenous communities.

Although the very meaning of the terms "Indigenous communities," "Indigenous peoples," and "Indigenous research methods" continues to be debated, one fact is not debatable. Namely, the extent to which traditions, values, perspectives, observations, and knowledge of the world—gathered over thousands of years by Indigenous communities—can enrich not only research, but also *contemporary approaches* to research. Examples of the former include but are not limited to topics such as climate change, variations in ecosystem structure and function, diseases in animals and plants and how they are influenced by the environment, art, evolution of oral and written communication, religious and cultural ceremonies, social and familial structures, community governance, and entertainment. Indeed, the use of cultural burning to manage forests is an important practice of Indigenous Americans, and the federal government now has embraced such Indigenous knowledge in managing the Western US wildfire crisis.

The worldview of Indigenous communities with regard to culture and history differs substantially from that of others, and thus adds tremendous depth to the tapestry of knowledge and approaches available for understanding our world. Nevertheless, this fact frequently is overlooked. All too often, studies are conducted *about* Indigenous communities rather than in authentic *partnership with* them. Consequently, such communities tend to be marginalized in the research process because relationships were not developed, cultural context was not understood, Western approaches to research were presented as the sine qua non, and benefits of research outcomes to participating communities were not delivered. These factors, among many, reinforce notions of colonialism and tokenism, which is especially troubling during a time when diversity, equity, inclusion, and belonging are espoused as high priorities for the academic enterprise.

Although the numerous research methods and approaches in common use today are not incompatible with Indigenous engagement, particularly those of a qualitative nature, they can, because of their Western origin and rules-based frameworks, tend to portray Indigenous populations as subjects having limited power or influence. In their review of Indigenous research methods, Drawson et al. (2017) describe it this way: "One distinction between Western and Indigenous research methods lies in this purpose: research done in collaboration with Indigenous Peoples cannot only reveal knowledge, but also decolonize, rebalance power, and provide healing."

Work by Snow et al. (2016) is useful for further understanding this important notion, and in it they identify six overarching principles for engaging researchers in "practices that privilege the voices and goals of Indigenous populations." They define such populations as "individuals or groups belonging to developing or underdeveloped regions nationally or internationally, as well as those who have been marginalized by Eurocentric values and/or research methodologies." They further note that "Indigenous research recognizes Indigenous communities develop shared ways of knowing guided by how they view the world, themselves, and the connection between the two."

The six principles from Snow et al. (2016) are as follows:

- Indigenous identity development—researchers becoming familiar with Indigenous culture and norms prior to beginning work;

- Indigenous paradigmatic lens—applying research approaches not in isolation from but rather in the context of Indigenous culture and norms;

- Reflexivity and power sharing—building positive relationships among everyone involved and ensuring that individuals other than researchers can bring ideas to the table;

- Critical immersion—complete awareness of self and others in all aspects of the research process;

- Participation and accountability—conducting research according to the highest ethical standards (chapter 9) and empowering all participants to contribute and participate in the entire research process; and

- Methodological flexibility—researchers being willing to modify traditional research processes and frameworks to accommodate Indigenous culture and norms, though always without compromising research integrity.

Even with this brief overview, it should be clear to you that Indigenous research methods implicitly include Indigenous norms, perspectives, and values. I especially like how Wulff (2010, 1290) captures this notion in his review of Indigenous research methods that is informed partly by Wilson's work. Wulff states that "Research is simply another practice or articulation of an Indigenous life, no more, no less." In her book on research methodologies, Smith (1999, 15) notes that "Indigenous methodologies tend to approach cultural protocols, values and behaviours as an integral part of the methodology."

Much insight can be gained into the world in which we live—from how the earth behaves and humans influence it to concepts of self-determination, self-governance, and family and community structure—by conducting research in collaboration with, and not simply on, Indigenous communities. An exercise at the end of this chapter challenges you to identify ways in which your own research could engage Indigenous communities.

4.5 Integrating Research and Education

As described in section 3.5, education and research are inextricably linked. Education is both a discipline within which research is performed, as well as the many-faceted process by which learning takes place as part of research itself. The former is critical for understanding how individuals and groups of individuals learn, and in developing effective methodologies for promoting such learning not only in formal education, but also over the course of one's life.

Yet, education research, like education itself, does not exist in a vacuum. Rather, it is conducted within the context of a wide array of disciplinary communities—ranging from science, engineering, and the life sciences to the humanities and arts. In this regard, education research shares a number of characteristics with Indigenous research discussed in section 4.4.

During the past few decades, a framework known as discipline-based education research (DBER) has emerged. It describes research that "investigates learning and teaching in a discipline using a range of methods with deep grounding in the discipline's priorities, worldview, knowledge, and practices" (National Research Council 2012a). In fact, DBER has fostered the creation of communities (e.g., science and education research community, faculty development research community, higher education research community), recognizing that each has its own culture, norms, practices, tools, perspectives, and indeed, research methods. Do you see the similarities to Indigenous research methods?

Interestingly, DBER is not a research method, but rather a framework of study that utilizes a wide array of methods to answer questions at the intersection of education and specific disciplines. The DBER framework for engineering is shown in figure 4.4.

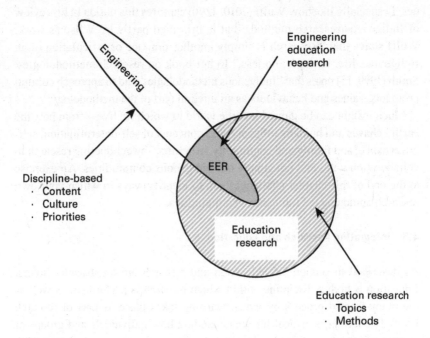

Figure 4.4
An example of DBER in engineering. *Source*: Henderson et al. (2017). Used with permission of Creative Commons License (CC BY 4.0; https://creativecommons.org/licenses/by/4.0/).

Although DBER is geared toward STEM disciplines with the goal of improving science and engineering education, the framework is applicable to all academic fields and thus can utilize all methods for research described previously in this chapter. DBER specifically embraces the flexibility of approach described in section 4.4 for Indigenous methods, and thus is a canonical example of collaborative, multidisciplinary research (chapter 13).

4.6 Broader Application of Research Methods: Citizen Science and Daily Life

Lest you believe research and creative activity are the sole domain of academic scholars, government and private sector researchers, or advanced students, think again! The general public—that is, amateurs, rather than professionals—increasingly are involved in research in what has come to be known as citizen science, crowd science, or crowd-sourced science. Although the terms are relatively new, having been coined in the mid-1990s, citizen involvement in research goes back a long way. In my own field of meteorology, the cooperative weather observer network has been around for decades. In it, volunteers are trained to make regular observations of weather at their homes, businesses, or other locations, and this information is fed into weather forecast models and also used in weather and climate research studies.

Most citizen science involves directed research (section 4.1). In this approach, volunteers engage, with appropriate oversight, in research. They apply elements of the scientific method, and they fulfill their desire of contributing to new knowledge without necessarily holding a degree or even being formally trained. Citizen science is supported in many ways, including by public and private museums, science centers, and even research universities. One of the most famous citizen science efforts is the Search for Extraterrestrial Intelligence (SETI). Now a nonprofit institute dedicated to public education and the advancement of science, SETI is perhaps best known for its SETI@home project, which uses idle time on home computers to analyze vast amounts of radio astronomy and other data in the search for extraterrestrial life.

With the advent of smart mobile devices, the ability of citizens to provide and analyze data has grown exponentially. Smart device apps now allow individuals to report severe weather events, earthquakes, and crimes. And of course, social media itself is an amazing mechanism for gathering information, in real time, regarding virtually anything conceivable that might be happening, including public attitudes toward events that can be studied by social scientists. Not everyone can be or needs to be a researcher, but today, virtually anyone can be involved in research.

Even those not formally involved in research apply research methods in everyday activities. That is, although research methods are designed principally for application to formal scholarly pursuits, their roots trace back to general public interest in the natural world and curiosity about cause and effect. Consequently, the notions underlying logic models and procedures used in all research methods are extremely valuable for nonresearchers as well, particularly in the context of critical thinking skills applied to daily life. In other words, you don't have to be a researcher to apply concepts found in research methods, such as inductive and deductive reasoning, and chances are you already are applying them and may not even know it!

For example, we are bombarded on a daily basis with all manner of news and information about national and world affairs, such as the economy, national security, health care, racism, violence, politics, inequality, bias, and many others. Making informed judgments, and not relying solely upon information fed to us, requires critical thinking skills embodied in research methods. Indeed, the Internet, and new policies in open data access (section 11.2), afford each of us unprecedented opportunity to gather data and information that *we* can independently, and personally, assess. In other words, we can test *our* own ideas and hypotheses, answer questions *we* have, and arrive at our *own* judgments and theories concerning cause and effect in the world around us. And we can do so ethically, factually, and with confidence that our results have been arrived at rigorously, not by quick reaction rooted in emotions or uninformed judgment. However, as noted in section 11.2, open access policies are not without their challenges, as clearly became evident in the COVID-19 pandemic.

4.7   Reproducibility, Reliability, and Replicability of Research Results

Foundational to the scientific method is the notion that research results should be reproducible or independently verifiable. Why? Because research and creative activity are the vital foundation of innovation in areas ranging from health care to aviation, and because most research builds upon work conducted previously. If that prior work cannot be reproduced or replicated—that is, the results verified and trusted—then the starting point for future work becomes problematic. In the case of drug design, for example, the ability of a pharmaceutical company to reproduce results obtained in a university laboratory is absolutely essential for developing commercially available therapies.

Although reproducing research results sounds simple, it is actually quite complex (e.g., see Open Science Collaboration 2015 and National Academies of Science, Engineering and Medicine 2019 in the references). Also, it is not so much a single activity to be performed but rather a continuum of activities and procedures that vary by discipline. Unfortunately, the lack of reproducibility sometimes is conflated with research misconduct (chapter 10), with the mistaken notion that research results which are not reproducible are either flawed or arrived at by unethical means. Such is the case in some circumstances; however, reproducibility does not necessarily imply correctness of the results, and nonreproducibility does not necessarily imply incorrectness of the results.

The National Academies of Science, Engineering and Medicine (2019) provides specific working definitions for reproducibility and replicability and describes the complexity of the concepts and strategies for addressing them. In the context of that report, reproducibility is defined as "obtaining consistent results using the same input data; computational steps, methods and code; and conditions of analysis," while replicability is defined as "obtaining consistent results across studies aimed at answering the same scientific questions, each of which has obtained its own data."

As noted in that report, definitions precisely opposite to that just described exist in the literature. My own view of the two terms, shown in figure 4.5, is that reproducibility and replicability constitute a continuum that must also encompass the situation in which information is obtained only in publications.

At the far left of figure 4.5, it is assumed the person or persons wishing to verify previous results are given access to them, along with the actual or identical tools or methods used. With those assets, the original researcher can try to replicate the results, someone else can try to do so, or someone else can try to do so using similar but not identical tools. Proceeding to the right, verification is attempted by being given access to the original results but using completely different tools, such as different statistical tests or computational models. And then on the far right, one is not given access to the original data or results, but

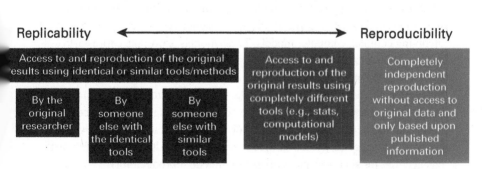

Figure 4.5
One view of the spectrum of replicability and reproducibility. A report by the National Academies of Science, Engineering and Medicine (2019) provides a working definition of each.

instead attempts to reproduce information contained only in a publication using different data and perhaps similar but not identical tools. And even other possibilities exist.

A wide variety of issues can lead to nonreplicability or nonreproducibility of research results. These include but are not limited to improper or ill-conceived experiment design and execution, improper collection and/or quality control of data, errors or misformulations in computer code, lack of documentation as the research is conducted, use of statistics or models that are not suited to the particular problem being studied, and the inherent nature of the problem, such as chaotic systems, where very tiny changes in parameters can lead to dramatically different results. At the present time, although no general methodological framework exists for evaluating reproducibility, community efforts have been launched (e.g., Center for Open Science; https://www.cos.io) that encourage researchers to submit their studies to be reproduced by others. Similar programs exist in the corporate sector.

Additionally, researchers in some disciplines can now "register" their research protocols and procedures, in advance of conducting the work (e.g., Center for Open Science), to demonstrate that no procedural changes were made during the study that might generate overly positive outcomes. In fact, publications from research utilizing such registration are annotated with a seal. Indeed, the federal government is encouraging some of its agencies to promote such practices, including training in study design and statistical analysis. With regard to the arts, fine arts, and humanities, some work has been done in reproducibility and replicability of results, though more is needed.

All of this may lead you to wonder why reproducibility has become such an important issue today and what can be done to address the challenges. First, today's research problems, and the tools used to address them, are increasingly complex, especially efforts involving multiple disciplines. This complexity sometimes makes difficult the ability to reproduce results, especially in cases involving complex computer models. These models, say of the entire earth system, involve dozens to hundreds of parameter settings, few of which are available in formal publications. And even if the actual codes are available, the same code, with the same input data, can produce different results on different computers or even on the same computer using a different compiler. Likewise, data collected via surveys, or in clinical studies, can vary among populations, especially when sample sizes are small. Although research methods account for such variances, they can impede reproducibility.

Second, although the research enterprise is "self-policing" to a large extent via peer review of publications and grant proposals (chapters 6 and 7), it is not always possible, especially in complex studies, for reviewers to spot problems in methodology, or be fully informed about the details of tools and data used, because publications and proposals are necessarily limited in length. Traditionally, a publication had to contain sufficient detail to afford reproducibility, but that simply is not always possible today. Consequently, the open science framework, and related open access policies (chapter 11), are making available all data and related materials, such as computer codes and settings, used in producing results presented in formal publications.

Third, some concern exists that reproducibility can be impacted negatively by the pressures researchers face to publish their findings, and especially to publish only positive results (chapter 8). This has led some scholarly publications to require reproducibility as a criterion for accepting a submitted manuscript. Additionally, in evaluating their scholars, academic institutions are being encouraged to emphasize not the number of articles published but rather the quality and impact of those publications.

Fourth and finally, a notion that has gained traction—including within congressional legislation—is that an inability to reproduce research results somehow suggests the presence of research misconduct. However, as noted previously, such is not necessarily the case.

Given these and other issues, what can be done and what is being done regarding reproducibility of research results? First, all researchers should be formally trained in experiment design and application of research methods. In many disciplines, including my own, such is not the case today. Second, online courses are now available, as are federal resources, to acquaint researchers with the issue of reproducibility of results and steps that can be taken to ensure it is applicable. Third, as noted previously, ready access to data, computer codes, and other aspects of a study, via open access frameworks now being put in place (chapter 11), will help considerably with reproducibility. Fourth, community efforts now exist, in the open science enterprise, to which researchers can submit their results for independent verification. Fifth, an increasing number of publications, especially in certain fields of social and behavioral science, are now requiring a demonstration of reproducibility prior to article publication. Sixth, incentives in academia for publishing are shifting to publishing quality instead of quantity. And finally, many studies are being undertaken to understand why certain research results are not reproducible. Chapter 9 addresses ethical guidelines and best practices that can contribute to the reproducibility of research results, and additional information on reproducibility can be found in the references noted previously.

Ultimately, addressing the issue of reproducibility of research results is a team sport, with many organizations and sectors of the community being involved. Interesting challenges arise in the context of research conducted within industry which, owing to proprietary considerations, usually cannot disclose results broadly (chapter 12). This begs the question as to whether research results produced within industry can be reproduced or replicated by others on the outside. As a result, emphasis on reproducibility is likely to continue for some time. If done thoughtfully, it will strengthen the credibility and increase the value of research in the eyes of all.

4.8 Surprise, Surprise! Serendipity in Research and Creative Activity

Around twenty-five years ago, I served on a multidisciplinary panel to review roughly a dozen research proposals submitted to a federal agency. The proposals were rather special because, with budgets up to $50 million each, they sought to establish major research centers in various topics of science and engineering. In painstakingly discussing each proposal, my review panel colleagues and I came to one that several in the room criticized with notable vigor. Although none of the critics were deep subject matter experts in the work being proposed, they raised insightful and valid concerns. I too had questions but was the lone voice of support for funding the proposal, partly because I had a deeper understanding of the work being proposed, but also because some of the arguments against the proposal were based upon understandably incorrect assumptions made by my fellow nonexpert panel members. As an expert in the field who knew the facts, I was able to explain why the assumptions they made were incorrect. Ultimately, the proposal was funded and the resulting center became a resounding success. The moral to this story has two parts.

The first is that I seemed to have been in the right place at the right time. But more importantly, my participation was a fluke. In reality, I was a last-minute substitute for another reviewer who became ill shortly before the review panel met. The person I replaced, like the other reviewers, was not an expert on the topic of the proposal under consideration. As a result, in all likelihood, the proposal would not have been funded, and the center would not have gone on to do transformative science, had I not been added at the last minute. Serendipity prevailed.

Perhaps you have had similar experiences. Maybe you have found yourself saying, after something positive happened in your life, "What are the odds of *that* occurring?" This begs the question of how one defines serendipity. Generally speaking, it is an unanticipated positive or valuable development. That is, serendipity is something that cannot be predicted or orchestrated.

The word itself was coined in 1754 by Horace Walpole, who was the son of Britain's first de facto prime minister. Walpole described serendipity as "the faculty of making happy and unexpected discoveries by accident"

(Interesting Literature n.d.). As you can see, Walpole viewed serendipity as requiring action on the part of the fortunate recipient via use of the verb "making." He also noted that serendipity leads to inherently positive outcomes. And interestingly, the definition includes the notion of discovery, so it automatically encompasses research and creative activity. Yet, serendipity has much broader application.

For example, serendipity is a popular foundation for movies. In *The Parent Trap*, for example, two identical twins separated early in life attend the same summer camp, completely by chance, and discover they are in fact sisters. After considerable mischief that causes their father's fiancé to run away screaming, they lead their divorced parents to reunite. This example has all the attributes of serendipity; that is, chance, discovery, and a positive outcome. And who can forget the fact that Spiderman's powers came about when an ordinary person, quite by accident, was bitten by an irradiated spider? Those who love the movie *Sleepless in Seattle* will recognize serendipity occurring multiple times throughout the story.

A great deal has been written about the role of serendipity in our lives. How much of what happens to us really does occur by chance? Do *we* play any role, as Walpole would suggest? How do we really know if chance is the explanatory factor? These and many other questions are interesting to ponder and can quickly lead to fascinating and deeply philosophical conversations, even delving into various religious beliefs. Interestingly, you may not be surprised to know—and you can confirm this with a simple web search—that the word "serendipity," apart from referencing a movie having the same name, is associated with discovery research.

As described throughout this book but especially in this chapter, the process of research and creative activity always begins with a purpose; with goals; with a set of questions; and often, with a hypothesis. Frequently, we have a sense of the results in advance, though research methods require that we arrive at findings and conclusions through rigorous processes that may well prove our instincts wrong. And indeed, sometimes things do not turn out as we expect. We obtain negative results. We see unexpected or counterintuitive behavior. Or we stumble onto something truly amazing that could never have been anticipated.

I prefer to conceptualize this notion as a flowing river, the center of which—the fast-moving part—represents the main goals of a research project. They have our attention—they are where our hypothesis lies, and where most of our intellectual energy is expended. However, away from the center of the river, one finds little whirls, sometimes near the shore, that go almost unnoticed. Yet they are fascinating in their own right and would not exist without the fast-flowing water. It is these little whirls I liken to unexpected results or accidental discoveries that potentially are transformative. The trick is knowing whether a little whirl is just an interesting sidelight or something that warrants further exploration. During a lecture at the University of Lille in 1854, Louis Pasteur famously said, "In the fields of observation, chance favors only those minds which are prepared" (Peterson 1954, 473). Not only do our minds need to be prepared for the unexpected, but we need to be willing to take time to explore it.

Many important and surprising discoveries have been made by accident, and they occur in all disciplines. How many discoveries? How often do they occur? Those are difficult questions to answer, but in some respects, surprises occur in every research and creative endeavor. However, those we ascribe to serendipity are of a special type that share three important characteristics: First, they were not planned and could not have been anticipated; second, they ultimately led to something positive or beneficial, usually with broad recognition and utilization by society; and finally, they were not foundational to the original ideas being explored, though could not have occurred without them.

Numerous examples of serendipitous research discoveries exist, and I will examine only a few in detail here. I hope you are sufficiently intrigued to explore others on your own, so for starters, you may wish to explore the origin of aspartame, chaos, saccharin, weather radar, Viagra, radioactivity, the atomic nucleus, X-rays, Post-It notes, microwaves for cooking food, corn flakes, the match, atomic fission, super glue, dynamite, Velcro, the Slinky, vulcanized rubber, and famous, almost priceless paintings that remained hidden for centuries because someone painted over them.

One of the best examples I know is penicillin. Many of us know the story, and today, the word "penicillin" represents a group of both natural and semisynthetic antibiotics that prove very effective at defeating a wide array of staph and strep bacterial infections. Penicillin was discovered by accident in London in September 1928, when Alexander Fleming, a Scottish biologist, was studying staphylococci bacteria. The bacteria had been smeared in several covered petri dishes, after which Fleming left for summer vacation. Upon returning, he noticed that one of the Petri dishes was open to the air and had been contaminated by a blue-green fungal mold called *Penicillium notatum*. Interestingly, no bacteria could be found near the mold—it had been killed by it. Many years and tests later, the drug penicillin was approved for human use and today is termed the "wonder drug," though some bacteria have developed resistance to it owing to its extensive repeated use.

As a meteorologist, my favorite example of serendipity in research concerns chaos, because it is believed to place fundamental limits on our ability to predict weather. The father of modern chaos theory, or at least the rebirth of that theory, as has been noted in recent work, is the late Massachusetts Institute of Technology professor Ed Lorenz—whom I had the extraordinary privilege of meeting. Borrowing from Dizikes (2011), the year is 1961, and it is winter.

Professor Lorenz had developed a highly simplified model of the atmosphere, containing twelve variables such as wind speed and temperature, which he then coded into a computer. As the machine was churning out numbers, Lorenz left to get a cup of coffee. This particular calculation was actually a repeat of one he had performed earlier, but in those days, computers did not have the sorts of storage devices that are commonplace today. Thus, upon returning from his break, Lorenz started the recalculation by typing in numbers from a printout of the earlier one, though in so doing, he chose to round one of the variables to three places instead of six. That is, he typed in 0.506 instead of 0.506127. What he discovered, after the calculation had proceeded for two months of simulated time, was nothing less than astounding.

Specifically, the results were completely different from the previous experiment, when in fact he believed they should have been identical. This led to what we know today as "sensitive dependence to initial conditions," which means a tiny change in the starting point of calculations involving chaotic dynamical systems can lead to dramatically different outcomes.

As a practical example of Lorenz's discovery, the tiny wind fluctuations created when a butterfly flaps its wings could, theoretically, induce changes in global weather patterns two weeks later. This finding—the so-called "butterfly effect," literally transformed the science of mathematics and many other fields, including meteorology. It also has very important implications for the reproducibility of research results, which was addressed earlier in this chapter and also is discussed in chapter 9.

I am sure most of you have had an X-ray at some time in your life, and the discovery of X-rays is a fascinating story. In 1895, German physicist Wilhelm Roentgen was experimenting with cathode ray tubes, like old-style television tubes or the sorts of tubes one finds in an oscilloscope. When the tube was energized, Roentgen observed a glow in a dark office nearby. Realizing radiation was involved, but not knowing the type, Roentgen called the effect X-rays. It was obvious to him the rays were impervious to solid objects, like walls, and Roentgen is said to have taken the first medical X-ray by subjecting his wife's hand to the strange radiation. Today, X-rays and derivatives from them have transformed the fields of medicine, engineering, and astronomy, to name but a few.

Considering these three examples, and others provided in the references (e.g., McClellan 2005; Eisinger 2013; Ward 2015), you will find they meet all three criteria for serendipity mentioned previously; namely, they were discovered by accident, made positive contributions, had wide impact, and were linked to but not foundational to the work originally being performed. As a scholar, I hope you always give place to the possibility and value of serendipity in the work you perform, though being careful to not chase every interesting sidebar that might come your way. Knowing when an unexpected development may be significant is difficult, so as I repeat throughout this book in multiple contexts, if you are uncertain about something, ask! Research and creative activity are team endeavors by virtue of the scholarly community to which you belong, even if you are working mostly on your own. Never hesitate to seek counsel from others. You never know if such a conversation will lead to a serendipitous outcome!

Assess Your Comprehension

1. List key properties of all research outcomes, irrespective of discipline.
2. Describe the two broad categories of research methods.
3. What is empirical research?
4. How does deductive research differ from inductive research?
5. How does independent research differ from directed research?
6. Describe the steps of the scientific method.
7. What is a hypothesis and how is it used in research and creative activity?
8. What is a theory and how does it differ from a law in the context of research?
9. Describe the historical research method.
10. What is source criticism?
11. Describe some of the problematic issues associated with Indigenous research.
12. What are the key principles by which Indigenous research should be performed?
13. What is the difference between explanatory scope and explanatory power?
14. Describe the relationship between education and research.
15. What is discipline-based education research and what tenets does it share with Indigenous research?
16. What is citizen science and how is it applied?
17. What is reproducibility of research results and why is it important?
18. Why has the issue of reproducibility of research results become so important?

19. In what ways do reproducibility, replicability and reliability of research results differ from one another?

20. How can nonreproducibility of research results be mistakenly conflated with research misconduct?

21. What factors can lead to research results being nonreproducible or nonreplicable?

22. What actions can be taken to improve the reproducibility of research results?

23. Define serendipity and the role it plays in research and creative activity.

24. What three criteria are associated with serendipity?

25. List a few examples of innovations that trace their origin to serendipitous outcomes from research.

Exercises to Deepen Your Understanding

Exercise 1: Choose a research problem of interest, perhaps one from a different exercise, and apply the scientific method to frame it. Begin by describing the problem and your motivation for selecting it, form the hypothesis, and then proceed to apply subsequent steps of the scientific method to describe how you would go about testing the hypothesis. Identify road blocks that might occur and ways in which you might be tempted to alter your hypothesis, during the research, to obtain better outcomes—and the negative consequences, including with regard to ethical principles, of doing so.

Exercise 2: Anyone can become involved with research—even nonexperts—via citizen science. For this exercise, choose a research project of interest from the lists provided at the links shown below and put yourself in the position of citizen volunteer. Describe your interest in the project, any specific expertise you bring to it, your reasons for choosing it, and how you would go about providing data or otherwise participating in the project. In some cases, you can actually participate in the project online, and if you choose such a project, describe your experience. Did your views regarding citizen science (e.g., value, effectiveness, rigor) change after completing this exercise?

- https://www.scientificamerican.com/citizen-science/
- https://www.zooniverse.org/projects

Exercise 3: Reproducibility, replicability, and reliability of research results increasingly are important not only in research, but also to other stakeholders, especially when research results are utilized in setting public policy. Identify a few research problems for which the results tend to be reproducible, as well as a few for which they tend to be not reproducible. Describe the reasons for this behavior and potential implications for research itself, the application of research outcomes to policy, and perceptions that nonreproducibility is essentially synonymous with poor experiment design or nefarious behavior on the part of researchers.

Exercise 4: Some of the world's greatest discoveries and technological breakthroughs occurred mostly or exclusively by chance. Identify one or more examples, similar to those provided in the chapter, and trace their evolution, including their impact on society. What other positive or ancillary benefits or developments occurred (sometimes referred to as "spillover") as a result of the serendipitous discovery, and how do they compare to the primary benefits? You also may wish to consider discoveries or research advances that have occurred exclusively as a result of the COVID-19 pandemic and conjecture about their future impacts on society.

Exercise 5: In order to gain deeper insight into methods used by various disciplines in scholarly activities, select three disciplines, all very different from your own, by exploring academic colleges and departments at your institution. For example, if you are a journalism major or scholar, you might select electrical engineering, finance, and geophysics. If you are a physics major, you might select musical theatre, French, and psychology. Develop a single set of questions regarding research methods and conduct interviews of the department chairs in them. Your questions should focus on the key topics described in this chapter—namely, broad research frameworks used, gathering of data or making observations, hypothesis generation as appropriate, analysis or synthesis of data, modeling or testing (for example, dance majors test their hypotheses in studios), synthesis of results, and presentation of new knowledge created. Compare and contrast all three sets of disciplinary approaches, identifying commonalities as well as distinct differences. Do you feel the disciplines would benefit from knowing about and sharing their approaches with one another? If so, what specific elements would be beneficial in doing so, and what benefits would be realized?

Exercise 6: Read the papers by Snow et al. (2016) and Dawson et al. (2017) on Indigenous research methods in the references and describe ways in which your own research could engage Indigenous communities. What community or communities would be most appropriate, and how would you go about learning of their culture, approaching them with your ideas or research questions, building relationships, and engaging them in collaborative work that would both create new knowledge and bring value to them? Describe the value proposition for them as you see it now.

5

Becoming a Detective: Finding What You Need and Using It Effectively

Chapter Overview and Learning Objectives

Similar to a detective, researchers must find appropriate data and other resources to inform their work. Yet, simply obtaining or creating data is only part of the story. This chapter describes the information and evidence-gathering process, from becoming familiar with previous work to identifying sources of information needed (and whether they already exist or have to be created) to validating source material and ensuring its quality and appropriateness for use. It also highlights data analysis, synthesis, and visualization as tools for discovery and understanding. After reading this chapter, you should

- Understand the differences among various sources of data/information for performing research and creative activity, and the importance of becoming familiar with such sources in the context of your own work;
- Be able to explain the differences between primary and secondary sources;
- Understand the importance of source validation, quality assurance and quality control and the differences among them; and
- Have a general understanding of information synthesis and analysis and the different approaches used by various disciplines.

5.1 Becoming Familiar with Previous Work

When my sister and I were little, we loved to pretend we were detectives, searching for clues that would solve some mysterious crime. If you are a fan of detective movies or mysteries, you will love this chapter! Why? Because one of the first things you need to do, after identifying an interesting idea to explore, or a fascinating question you feel needs to be answered, is to piece together facts about work that has been done previously. Often this is referred to as conducting a literature review or landscape analysis, though in contrast to the work of real detectives, the information usually is readily available. In fact, a survey of the literature is *the* first step in research and creative activity, and also in writing a grant proposal (chapter 6), because it accomplishes a number of things.

First and foremost, studying previous work lets you know the extent to which the idea you wish to explore, or the question you wish to answer, already has been studied. It also provides a context for your own work, helps identify gaps in existing knowledge that you may be able to fill, teaches you about previous approaches and techniques as well as information and data sources, and gives you a broad perspective of how knowledge and understanding regarding a particular topic have evolved over time.

Numerous sources exist for building your understanding about previous work, and the most important sources for many disciplines are refereed or so-called archive publications. They bear these names because they have been subjected to rigorous peer and editorial review and are part of the world's repository or archive of our current state of understanding. As discussed below and more extensively in chapter 7, such review does not always guarantee correctness, but rather evaluation and scrutiny by experts which, for the most part, does ensure that mostly original, high-quality scholarship is published. That said, the sources for understanding previous work do not end there. Numerous others exist, including books, oral histories, personal views of researchers you may obtain through conversations, opinion pieces, review articles, conference proceedings, video and audio recordings, diaries, paintings, sculptures, and scripts.

As we all know quite well, accessing information today is relatively easy owing to the Internet. Many previously unavailable documents, images, and audio and visual media are now available at the click of a button. Indeed, digital libraries abound, and open access frameworks (section 11.2) now make scholarly publications widely available (e.g., PubMed Central; http://ncbi.nlm .nih.gov/pmc). However, in our new highly connected, instant-access world, one can quickly become overwhelmed with the sheer volume of information available. Consequently, new tools involving artificial intelligence are becoming widely available to synthesize hundreds to thousands of publications in a matter of seconds (e.g., the CORD-19 data base, described in section 11.2) And, as noted later in this chapter, care must be taken within this universe of material to ensure that sources are trustworthy and of high quality.

How does one deal with all of these challenges?

Most formal publications, such as journal articles and monographs, contain an abstract, an introduction, a description of methods used, findings and an explanation of them, and conclusions, which sometimes include comments about future work. You could literally spend months or years examining all materials relevant to your research topic or question, so a good strategy in the case of journal articles is to begin with a few you feel are most relevant. Read them entirely. You then will quickly realize these papers cite numerous other papers in their bibliographies. All of a sudden, you now have dozens to hundreds of related papers to explore. You may wish to read some of them front to back, but for others, it is best to read only the abstract and conclusions, diving into the rest of the text if the article is especially relevant. This allows you to examine a large body of scholarship in a reasonable amount of time, with deep dives into certain papers that are more relevant to your topic than others.

By virtue of this process, you also will come to know pioneers in the field and which works are viewed as seminal, especially via use of tools such as the h-index (Hirsch 2005) and its variants. Meta-analyses and review articles are excellent places to begin, if they exist for your chosen topic, because they summarize numerous studies over time and contain extensive bibliographies.

One important benefit of studying previous work is setting a context for your own. That context helps both you and others understand which knowledge gaps exist and how your work will help fill them. This contextualization may seem obvious, but I cannot begin to count how many times I have read a grant proposal in which the investigator jumps immediately into their own idea without setting the stage for me. As a result, unless I have deep expertise on the topic at hand, I have little idea whether their approach is novel, if the questions being asked have already been answered, or if their potential contribution will be valuable.

From a practical point of view, when performing literature reviews or other studies of previous scholarly work, you will find it helpful to make notes, including questions and comments. Numerous apps and programs exist to do so, and you can then easily cross-reference and index the material. Knowing the authors, composers, or artists, and the date or dates of the work performed, are especially important and help you recall a particular study when needed, such as in preparing for a thesis defense or a seminar.

One final point regarding becoming familiar with previous work. Unfortunately, published papers and monographs, recordings of performances, or videos of productions show only the end product and not the often-circuitous and difficult path taken to get there—a path that can be fraught with frustrations, dead ends and restarts. Do not simply believe that what you read is the final story, or that a particular piece of music, once played, can never be interpreted by being played in a slightly different manner! Respect previous work, but do not be afraid to challenge it, improve upon it, or use it as a launching pad for a new idea.

5.2   Assessing Your Need, Identifying Sources, and Collecting/Protecting Resources

Once you have completed your review of previous work on the topic you wish to study, and have developed a hypothesis, strategy, and set of tools or procedures for studying it (chapter 4), it is quite likely you will need data, artifacts, records, or other source materials in order to proceed. This is similar to the work of a detective, who needs to gather evidence. Knowing *what* you need may not seem obvious for research, especially if the topic being studied is particularly complex. However, this is where the hypothesis plays a key role because it helps frame, and in fact sets boundaries for, the sorts of resources you likely need. You will see specifically how this works in the exercises associated with this chapter. Not surprisingly, as one proceeds through the research process, the need for additional resources sometimes arises, though how and whether such additions can be used depends upon the topic and research methodology being used. When considering resources, they either exist or they don't. You either go find them or have to create them.

For the situation in which the resources you need already exist and simply need to be obtained, you must determine whether and how you can access then. Such resources typically are divided into two broad categories: primary sources and secondary sources.

A primary source is one that is original or represents a firsthand account and is purely factual. Examples of primary sources include ancient manuscripts in public or private archives, diaries, original or raw data sets from environmental or space observations, data from surveys of people, historical records such as presidential papers and audio recordings, output from computational models, or art objects. Secondary sources, on the other hand, are descriptions, interpretations, or evaluations of primary sources. In other words, they are not firsthand accounts but rather assessments. Examples include articles that review the original work of another person, newspaper and magazine articles, and opinion pieces.

If it turns out that what you need does *not* already exist, then you must collect or create it, and in so doing make a new primary source. For example, you may need to design a survey to evaluate public attitudes toward a particularly important and sensitive issue, such as gun control, or collect water samples from a lake that is infested with a rare form of algae to understand how it became toxic. You may need to create a computer model of the atmosphere on Mars and run simulations to understand how it has changed over the past several million years. You may need to interview a famous artist to understand their creative process and how they have passed it along to protégées. Or you might even need to observe small children in various classroom settings to understand how their uptake of information differs from teacher to teacher or school to school. Some of the information collected by you may be confidential, so you may need to protect the identities of those who provided it, such as in certain types of surveys or clinical trials for experimental drugs. Protocols for such activities are discussed in chapter 10.

Irrespective of the sources and information used for your study, it is extremely important to protect it in other ways as well. If you are dealing with primary sources that you are not allowed to physically possess, then any notes you take, or copies or photos you make of the sources, need to be copied, backed up, and stored in one or more safe locations. This also is true of any and all notes you make or other information you collect as your research proceeds, say in the form of a laboratory notebook,[1] for the following reasons.

First, natural disasters, such as floods or fire, can quickly wipe out massive amounts of work in just a few minutes. Nothing is more devastating to a researcher than to lose critical information that either cannot be recreated or is expensive to recreate. This is why your saved versions should be stored in multiple locations, especially different from where you perform your work. For example, regularly scan your laboratory notebook or daily work summary and save it on a thumb drive in your home as well as office, or in the cloud. Make multiple copies of digital data and do the same with them.

Second, having a complete, archived record of your work—something often referred to as a workflow—is important when organizing your findings for publication or presentation because it is easy to forget seemingly minor but important details. Third, as discussed in section 4.7, the ability to reproduce research results depends upon knowing the steps involved in the process, so it is important to have multiple copies of such records. Fourth, as discussed in chapter 9, if for some reason the ethics and integrity of your work are questioned, having a complete record, with redundant copies, will position you to address concerns raised.

Finally, new open access frameworks (section 11.2) often require that you provide public access to information used in creating a publication. Having backup copies ensures that you can meet this requirement, which allows others to build upon your work as you have built upon theirs.

5.3   Source Validation, Quality Assurance, and Control

If you were a real detective trying to solve a crime, you would want to make sure the evidence you gather is factual before charges are brought and the trial begins. Likewise, regardless of whether you identify and gather information from existing sources, or create completely new information, the associated validity and quality of this information are exceptionally important and must be established at the outset, before research begins. Methods exist, in every area of research and creative activity, for information validation, quality control, and quality assurance, though terminology varies among them. Because space does not permit a comprehensive treatment of validation, particularly because of variations across disciplines, I focus here on the basics. Additional resources may be found in the references (e.g., see Arthur 2017 and US Geological Survey n.d.-b).

In the context of research sources, validation concerns the confirmation or substantiation of the source. As noted in chapter 4, in historical research as well as arts and fine arts scholarship, validation involves addressing issues such as when and where the source was produced, by whom, the reliance of the source upon earlier material, the original form of the source, and the credibility of source contents. In the case of computer codes, such as models of physical, biological, and other phenomena, validation involves various tests to determine whether the code is performing as designed. Note this has nothing to do with the realism of the results produced by the computer model, but rather only that the code was properly constructed based upon its underlying mathematical framework and is working as intended.

Physical instruments used to observe the natural world also undergo validation as well as calibration procedures (sometimes referred to as cal/val). For anything in the digital realm, in this day of computer hacking and other nefarious intrusions, it is especially important to confirm the integrity of sources.

The terms "quality control" (QC) and "quality assurance" (QA) are sometimes used interchangeably, especially in the context of collecting new research data or processing existing data. In fact, QC and QA are quite different. Before examining them, we need to be clear about our use of the term "data," because data exist in every discipline and are foundational to research and creative activity.

Although data can be an elusive concept, I will define them as follows (and note—the term "data" is always considered plural): *Information that provides a quantitative and/or qualitative description or characterization.* This definition is equally applicable to humans, the atmosphere, core samples of ice collected in the Antarctic, an orchestral performance, and a piece of art. Data are not things. Rather, data are descriptive information. And I should mention that output from a computer model, such as a weather forecast model, is called just that—output. The term "data" typically is reserved for information associated with real phenomena, objects, processes, or activities, not those simulated with a computer.

With that preface, the phrase "data quality" is a general term encompassing attributes, both qualitative and quantitative, that characterize a particular data set. Data are said to be of high quality if they accurately represent the phenomenon or state of a system they were intended to portray and are appropriate for the intended use. In that regard, data quality may be subject to interpretation, and because of this, specific values are assigned to quantitative measures, and descriptions assigned to qualitative measures, in specifying data quality.

Data QA represents criteria and processes utilized to prevent problems occurring with data, say as they are being collected. Consequently, QA often is referred to as *defect prevention* because it proactively seeks to ensure that data meet appropriate and agreed-upon quality standards for the problem at hand. Examples of QA in practice include calibrating and siting instruments, say to measure air temperature and wind, so as to avoid false readings caused by nearby buildings and trees, as well as survey questions worded in a neutral manner so as to avoid evoking a desired response.

In contrast to data QA, data QC is the process by which data are subjected to various processes, following collection, to determine whether they meet stated quality goals. For this reason, QC often is referred to as *defect detection*. Examples include the use of automated algorithms to detect missing data, outliers, or suspicious values, and a variety of errors, such as those arising from a faulty measuring instrument (which could be physical device or a survey given to people). QC also addresses whether a given data element is representative of values nearby in space and time, assuming such should be the case.

In some cases, the QC process may determine that, although a data set is quality assured, sufficient issues exist to preclude its use for a particular purpose. That is not to say the QA'd data are unusable if they fail the QC test. In fact, a quality assured data set may be perfectly suited for one application but not for another. Consequently, it is important for you, as a researcher, to know the difference between QA and QC, and to make sure you have a complete understanding of your data or source information, including quality, before using them.

A final but very important point is that, to the extent possible, original or raw data should *never* be destroyed because QA and QC procedures continue to improve with time. A great example, in the context of climate change, is the global temperature record, to which various corrections need to be made to account for how instrument characteristics and placement have changed over decades.

5.4   Analysis and Synthesis

The analysis of data and information are foundational to research and creative activity, more so now than ever before. In fact, thirty to forty years ago, many disciplines were largely experimental in nature, including in the biological and chemical sciences. Today, those same disciplines, though still utilizing theory and experiment, are among the largest generators and users of digital data, ranging from high-throughput genomic sequencing to computer-based molecular modeling to three-dimensional imagery of ancient relics. Likewise, explosive growth in digital humanities, the ability of social and behavioral scientists to capture and study vast amounts of information from online surveys and social media, and the ability of atmospheric scientists to model, with exceptional realism, the entire earth system, have completely transformed the research enterprise. Coupled with open access frameworks (section 11.2) that make vast amounts of data available to anyone at the click of a button, our world—and to be certain, the research enterprise—is literally drowning in data.

Extraordinary potential exists in this sea of information to study entire problems, rather than breaking them into simpler parts (the so-called reductionist method), and to bring to bear all of the relevant disciplines needed to do so (chapter 13). This requires new approaches in data analysis, so much so that specialists in data informatics and analytics, and new tools such as artificial intelligence and machine learning, now dominate the research landscape. In other words, like a detective, you need to bring all of the pieces of evidence together into a coherent picture that tells a story!

As was the case for other topics we have discussed, the general topic of data analysis has its own lexicon, the terms within which differ in their meaning depending upon the discipline or nature of the application. You will find terms such as data synthesis, assimilation, and fusion used to describe the bringing together of data—perhaps of a similar or different type—in a manner that broadens and/or deepens understanding beyond that which otherwise would occur. This is a difficult but particularly powerful process because of the interdependence of information.

For example, atmospheric temperature, relative humidity, and density are related to one another. Consequently, assembling independent data sets of temperature and relative humidity allows one to assess the density without necessarily measuring it directly. As another example, the attitude of an individual responding to a survey on insurance costs may depend upon a recent experience, such as a hailstorm that destroyed the roof of their house. By synthesizing weather data and public survey responses, researchers can better understand what determines personal views and how those views change with time.

Most disciplines, especially in the social, behavioral, biological, and chemical sciences, as well as the humanities, offer entire courses in research methods (chapter 4). They focus on specific tools and approaches for gathering and analyzing data, particularly statistics; methods for constructing and testing hypotheses; underlying factors explaining why data are correlated; and the dangers of making false inferences. Indeed, many disciplines rely upon statistics, and their value lies in the fact that they provide a quantitative basis for estimating whether something likely happened for a reason, usually stated in a hypothesis, or rather likely occurred by chance.

Some interesting examples exist that show amazing statistical correlation without causality (e.g., Woollaston 2014). For example, how the sale of potato chips relates to people dying by falling out of a wheelchair, or how the sale of eggs correlates with the number of people killed in transport accidents. In both cases, no rational cause and effect exists whatsoever between the two quantities being compared. Statistics are incredibly powerful, but they sometimes are used ineffectively or inappropriately by well-intentioned researchers. If, as a detective, you use evidence incorrectly, you could get an innocent person convicted and lose your bar license. As a researcher, if you use statistics inappropriately, you could lose credibility, be subject to charges of research misconduct, or produce results that one day could lead to serious harm or even loss of life.

Statistics also can be intentionally misused to produce favorable results (section 4.7 and chapter 9), which is why a solid understanding of statistics is so important. Advanced tools such as data mining are exceptionally helpful for identifying patterns in data; but once again, causality must be established and the results should be explainable so as to ensure no bias or other problematic issues have arisen.

Another powerful analysis tool is computer visualization. Thirty years ago, visualization tended to be a novelty, used mostly to explain a complex phenomenon to a nonexpert. Today, visualization is used in every field, from classics and architecture to medicine and music. Powerful visualization tools allow researchers to bring many data sets together to understand their complex interrelationships visually, but also quantitatively, through the use of three dimensions, animation, tactile response, stereoscopic viewing, and sound. Ultimately, making sense of the information or data you have gathered, via the testing of your hypothesis through experimentation, is the end game of research. You are incredibly fortunate that more tools and information are available today to achieve this end than ever before.

Assess Your Comprehension

1. Why is placing your planned research in the context of previous work important?

2. What sources of information exist to help frame your research against previous work?

3. What is a primary source of information and how does it differ from a secondary source?

4. Why should you physically protect sources of information for your research and creative activity?

5. In what ways can you physically protect sources of information for your research and creative activity?

6. What is source validation and why is it important?

7. Provide a definition for data.

8. What are data QC and data QA, and how do they differ?

9. How can tools, such as artificial intelligence and machine learning, improve our ability to understand and synthesize data?

Exercises to Deepen Your Understanding

Exercise 1: Select a research topic of interest and perform a literature review or other appropriate analysis of work conducted previously (e.g., video and audio recordings of a performance, imagery if the topic involves art or manuscripts). Summarize your findings and, in so doing, identify important gaps in knowledge and understanding, and limitations of or flaws in previous work, as a means for suggesting future work. Additionally, create several questions you would seek to answer were you to prepare a research proposal on the chosen topic, and from them formulate a hypothesis. Although you may use informal sources, such as Wikipedia, to gain an overall understanding of the topic, your analysis should utilize mostly scholarly, archive sources of sufficient number to make thoughtful, thorough, and persuasive arguments.

Exercise 2: Artificial intelligence/machine learning is dramatically changing the landscape by which researchers can review and synthesize the scholarly record. Exercise 1 involves using the traditional "manual" approach of searching the scholarly record to understand previous work, identify gaps, and pose questions. For the present exercise, explore options for applying artificial intelligence/machine learning to achieve the same ends (you are not asked to apply artificial intelligence, but rather explore capabilities and options). What services exist now, and in what disciplines are they available? Note that artificial intelligence does far more than identify articles relevant to your work, and in fact can synthesize findings across hundreds to thousands of articles, identify knowledge gaps, and even generate hypotheses. Summarize findings from your investigation and also describe capabilities that are on the horizon. How can artificial intelligence impact your own research?

Exercise 3: Data quality control (QC), data quality assurance (QA), and management are critically important in research and must be performed with great care. At https://drive.google.com/file/d/1_E6WfglnCIlUtAFIf6hqi8 A2Uwpv492P/view?usp=sharing, you will find a spreadsheet containing time series data collected from a ground-based weather observing station during the passage of a tornado in Oklahoma. All quantities are labeled, and note that the wind direction is the compass direction from which the wind is blowing—such that a northerly wind is from 360 degrees, an easterly wind is from 90 degrees, a southerly wind is from 180 degrees, and a westerly wind is from 270 degrees. These are "raw" data from the sensors and have not been subjected to quality control processes. Examine the data to see if you can spot anomalies. For example, all values should be positive numbers, and dramatic changes from one time period to the next likely would reflect an error (for example, if the temperature dropped 20 degrees in five seconds with no substantial changes in other quantities at the same time). Also, an observation should be present for each time period shown or else be tagged as "missing data."

If you were developing an automated quality control algorithm, how might you go about identifying and correcting errors, including missing values? What factors might be responsible for creating errors or anomalies in the data? If you are interested in how data quality control and quality assurance are actually applied by the organization supplying the data, visit https://journals.ametsoc.org/view/journals/atot/27/10/2010jtecha1433_1.xml.

Exercise 4: Select a research problem of interest, perhaps from a previous exercise, and describe how you would go about creating (not collecting or finding) data to study it (in this context, data refers to information, physical artifacts, or other resources that support your work). Would you need to build an instrument, conduct interviews, make recordings, and take photographs? How would you go about applying quality control to the data to ensure accuracy and representativeness, and how would you make the data available to other researchers having similar interests? Be specific in your answers and include information about locations or sources where such data could in fact be gathered.

Exercise 5: Describe the tools and methods used in your own research to synthesize data and develop understanding from them. Do you generate the data yourself, depend upon data from other sources, or use a combination of these approaches? What type(s) of data do you utilize (e.g., numerical, textual, graphical, animation, time series)? To what extent are the original data modified in the synthesis process, and what rules or procedures do you employ? If your synthesis/analysis involves multiple steps that produce modified data, which data do you save, and why? If you plan to make your data available to others, say to build upon your research, in what ways will you do so? Do mechanisms exist to archive your data in national repositories?

If you are not yet engaged in research, interview senior researchers and peers in your institution who have collected or are in the process of collecting data, ideally across multiple disciplines, and compare and contrast the approaches used.

6

Diving into the Pool: Research Proposals, Evaluation Processes, and Project Management

Chapter Overview and Learning Objectives

Obtaining funding for research and creative activity almost always involves writing and submitting a grant proposal. This chapter details the steps within the proposal process, from formulating and developing ideas, plans, and budgets to submitting the proposal, obtaining funding, and successfully managing projects once funding has been granted. Additionally, it overviews the proposal evaluation process, discussed in greater detail in chapter 7, along with key considerations to bear in mind for developing competitive grant proposals that adhere to expected standards. After reading this chapter, you should be able to

- Explain the structure and elements of a research grant proposal;
- Know the importance of describing your work in a grant proposal to a technically competent but nonexpert audience;
- Understand how costs of research frequently are shared between funder and recipient;
- Explain facilities and administrative costs (F&A) in comparison to other costs that support research;
- Understand the varied missions, philosophies, and processes of funding organizations;
- Describe the steps involved in peer/merit review of proposals and how they differ among funding sources; and
- Know how to apply best practices for managing a research project once funding has been obtained.

6.1 Structure and Value of the Research Proposal

In chapter 2, we discussed a variety of topics regarding funding for research and creative activity, including the wide array of sources available, how priorities are set, mechanisms available to locate funding, historical trends, and more. Suppose now you have a good idea, a strategy for how you plan to study it, and options for funding. How, then, do you go about actually obtaining funding so you can perform the research and creative activity?

In almost every situation, the process involves something known as a grant proposal. Proposals are formal, written documents created by the individual(s) proposing the work, typically led by a principal investigator (PI). Proposals describe the idea to be explored or the problem to be solved, approaches, methods, and tools to be used, resources available, and the timeline to be followed. Sometimes, alternative approaches are offered in case those proposed do not work as envisioned. Proposals also contextualize the planned work in terms of work performed previously, including that by the PI and others involved, list expected outcomes and impacts, describe costs in a detailed budget (often extending over one to five years), and justify personnel and other resources needed. Because the structure and content of proposals varies substantially across funding organizations, table 6.1 presents a list of generic components typically required in proposals.

Table 6.1
Generic components typically required in research grant proposals (variation exists among funding sources)

Component Description
Project/executive summary
Technical summary of intellectual contributions and significance
Lay summary of intellectual contributions and significance
Summary of broader impacts
Project description (motivation/opportunity, results from prior work, goals, progress to date, research/work plan, methods used, alternative approaches, expected outcomes, relevance and value, congruence with funding organization mission or program requirements, partnerships, collaborators)
Project management plan
Project evaluation plan
Data management plan
Mentoring plan
Sustainability plan
Plan for disseminating products and outcomes
Broader impacts
Qualification of investigators (description and curriculum vitae)
Investigator current and pending support
Investigator conflicts of interest
Facilities, equipment, and other resources required
Budget and justification
References cited

Writing grant proposals is a notably challenging and time-consuming task, and the associated skills and art of communication are best learned through practice.[1] The process requires an ability to convey one's ideas, hypotheses, strategies, and methods of interpretation in clear and compelling ways to those who will be reading the proposal and making recommendations as to whether it should be funded. In some cases, most or all of the proposal reviewers are experts in the field of the investigator(s), and thus jargon and deeply technical explanations are appropriate (section 11.4). In other cases, especially if the proposal topic involves multiple disciplines (chapter 13), say engineering, art history, and law, the challenges in writing a proposal are substantially greater because the material must be understandable to experts in all of these areas. In such cases, one has to strike a balance between technical depth and general notions that allow all reviewers to comprehend what is being proposed and understand the context for it. The moral to the story is to know your audience!

As overviewed in section 6.3 and described more fully in chapter 7, most review of proposals is based upon the merit (intellectual, creative, historical) of the idea being presented. However, other factors do enter the review process, depending upon the funding organization. For example, in the case of some nonprofit foundations, the research track record of the PI, and perhaps the strength of a previous research relationship between the foundation and investigator, are *the* most important factors in determining whether the proposal will be funded. And of course, also vitally important for nonprofit foundations is the extent to which the proposed work aligns with the organizational mission. Although PI track records are important to federal agencies as well, the research relationship between agency personnel and PI or other investigators on the project is less important. In fact, the review process is designed specifically to avoid creating conflicts of interest that might afford an unfair advantage.

Most organizations that seek external funding, especially research universities, have excellent resources to assist with proposal development (chapter 1). However, many do not, especially institutions working to enter or become more active in externally sponsored research and creative activity. This deficiency increasingly is becoming more recognized, as noted in section 1.6, and efforts now are being directed nationally toward providing the administrative resources needed at such institutions to support faculty and student scholarship (section 12.3).

If your institution does not have such resources, speak with your advisor, department chair, dean, or senior research officer about your needs and how the institution can best meet them. One option is for the institution to hire professional consultants to assist with proposal development and project management until such capabilities can be established more permanently. Additionally, you may wish to collaborate with individuals at institutions having such resources, which will allow you to become a local resource for others in your own institution.

Apart from the obvious value of proposals as mechanisms for obtaining resources, the process of developing proposals has additional value. For example, proposals require the PI and others on the project to think through and design a clear plan for the work to be done, including alternative approaches should the chosen strategy prove to not be viable. This is true for all fields, not only STEM disciplines. In some disciplines where hypothesis testing and statistical methods are employed, such as in experimental research within the social and behavioral sciences, proposals document a very specific strategy that can be altered only under certain circumstances as the work proceeds. This helps prevent the implementation of changes, such as making inappropriate alterations to thresholds on statistical significance, which could lead to more desirable results. The issues of reproducibility of research results, and research integrity, are addressed in chapters 4 and 9, respectively.

In fields such as the arts and fine arts, the scholarship to be accomplished sometimes involves creating a work (e.g., painting, sculpture, composition), the pathway toward which may be clear at the outset but may be modified as the research proceeds. In such cases, the modifications are completely appropriate and as valuable to knowledge creation as the work itself, often leading to new lines of creative endeavor.

In addition to the components described above, research proposals typically contain a project summary written specifically for the general public. This document is exceptionally important, especially for federally funded projects, because it conveys the purpose and value of the work to the taxpayers funding it. It also is important for communicating the importance of scholarly activity in nontechnical language, and for educating the public about important advances within all disciplines and their positive impact on society.

Finally, all funding organizations have a mission, and thus you should understand the mission of the agency or foundation relevant to your work prior to submitting a proposal. The term "mission agencies" frequently is used to describe federal government agencies, such as those within DOD and DOE, which typically do not seek to fund research projects based upon curiosity-driven ideas of researchers.[2] Rather, they solicit proposals on specific topics that meet well-defined agency programmatic requirements, such as the development of a certain device, capability, or process. In the terminology discussed in chapter 1, this is known as applied research and development. If the PI does a good job and delivers results as expected, the agency often goes back to them, as a now trusted resource, with additional funding to meet other agency requirements. Funded relationships along these lines can last for years to decades.

Often it is said NSF is not a mission agency in the sense just described. However, it does in fact have a clear mission of funding the bulk of nonclinical/medical fundamental research in the US. As noted in chapter 3, federal agencies such as NEA and NEH also have missions. NEA brings the arts to all Americans and provides leadership in arts education, while NEH supports research, education, preservation, and public programs in the humanities. As noted in chapter 2, all federal agencies and nonprofit foundations have websites describing their mission, the array of programs and funding available, and detailed instructions regarding proposal content, submission, and review processes. Many also provide actual sample proposals from which you can learn.

6.2 Research Project Budget and Sharing the Costs of Research

Although every aspect of a grant proposal is important—especially the project description, intellectual merit of and methods to be used in the work to be performed and impacts broader than direct outcomes from the research itself—the budget, and its associated justification narrative, also are quite important because they detail all of the costs associated with performing the work, as well as the rationale for them. When the proposal is funded and the budget finalized, the approved budget must be followed, though some flexibility exists to transfer money among budget categories so long as the bottom line amount is not exceeded.

Budgets have several components and usually are structured in ways specific to requirements of the funding organization. In the case of federal agencies, efforts are underway to harmonize budget structure so as to avoid unnecessary multiple formats and confusion for researchers. Additionally, instead of detailed budgets, some agencies allow the submission of a simplified budget at the proposal stage. This strategy provides sufficient information to reviewers for assessing whether the budget is appropriately structured and sized relative to the work proposed, while reducing the administrative workload (section 10.6) on the part of the PI and collaborators in developing the proposal. If the proposal is judged to be meritorious during the review process, then a much more detailed budget is submitted.

In the case of private foundations, grant proposal budgets tend to be substantially simpler than those for proposals submitted to federal agencies. Indeed, some foundations require only a relatively brief (two- to five-page) narrative of the rationale for and description of the work to be done, how it aligns with the foundation mission, a consolidated budget specifying the principal costs and justification, and expected outcomes.

The most common components of a grant proposal budget (table 6.2) include the following: salaries and wages, which include those of the PI and other senior or professional researchers, postdoctoral researchers, technicians, programmers, graduate and undergraduate students, and administrative and clerical personnel. For senior personnel, such as faculty, the bulk of their salary typically is paid by their home institution, and thus only a portion is requested in the grant proposal (usually for funding during the summer if they are on a nine-month academic year contract). For the others listed, full salary often is requested. In addition to salaries and wages, fringe benefits—in support of health care and retirement, can be included in grant proposal budgets.

The proposal budget also can include funding for equipment, such as instruments, computers, audio and video recording equipment, and lighting and sound systems, along with national and international travel to support participation of project personnel at professional conferences. Funding also can be requested to collect data or artifacts, and collaborate with researchers at other locations. Finally, the budget can include materials and supplies, costs for publishing journal articles and books, computer software, equipment maintenance contracts, student tuition, and the participation of others who are not part of the core project team.

The determination of what can and cannot be included in a proposal budget is spelled out by detailed federal guidance (2 C.F.R. 200, or Title 2 of the US Code of Federal Regulations, Part 200), created in 2017 by OMB, and by guidelines

Table 6.2
Items for which funding typically is requested in research proposal budgets (variation exists among funding sources)

Item Description
Salaries and wages (principal investigator, coprincipal investigator, other senior personnel, postdoctoral researchers, technicians, and support staff)
Stipends for graduate and undergraduate students
Fringe benefits for all personnel
Materials, supplies, and services
Publication/dissemination costs
Equipment
Consulting services
Special computing services
Domestic and international travel
Special facilities utilization
Subcontracts
Participant support costs (e.g., subjects to be interviewed)
Facilities and administrative costs (F&A)

from the organizations providing and receiving the funding. In cases where some of the work cannot be performed by the organization submitting the proposal, subcontracts are issued to other organizations for meeting the need.

As described previously, research grants provide a benefit to both the funding organization and the organization performing the work—the so-called mutuality of interest principle (recall this is not true for contracts, which provide a benefit principally to the funding organization). Consequently, the costs of research likewise are shared between the organization providing the funding and the organization receiving it. This is known as cost sharing.

Cost sharing has been around for decades and is pertinent to all disciplines, sometimes implicitly, as in the case of prestigious faculty fellowships in the humanities. For example, the Fulbright and American Council of Learned Societies Fellowships (section 2.1) support faculty salaries for a period of time, with the institution paying individuals (e.g., adjunct faculty) to temporarily assume the teaching load of the fellowship recipient. In many cases, full salary is not provided for the fellow, and thus the institution must make up the difference (i.e., as cost sharing) in order to accept the fellowship.

Cost sharing for grant proposals takes many forms and is provided by the organization requesting the funding. It can involve the provision of cash as well as in-kind resources such as space as well as personnel time committed to the project but paid by other resources from the submitting organization. In some cases, funding organizations require a one-to-one cost share. That is, for every dollar provided by the funder, the receiving organization that submitted the proposal must provide a dollar as well, either cash or in-kind.

The problem with this approach is that organizations having relatively limited resources are disadvantaged owing to their associated inability to provide cost sharing, thereby resulting in an unlevel playing field across the research enterprise. This is especially concerning to MSIs and ERIs as they seek to become more active in externally sponsored research and creative activity. NSF, which funds the bulk of nonmedical curiosity-driven research in the US, prohibits cost sharing in all but a few specific programs for which such sharing is foundational to programmatic goals. In this manner, NSF allows all organizations an equal opportunity to seek funding for research. Unfortunately, although it was hoped other agencies would follow NSF's lead, none have.

All of the aforementioned budget items (table 6.2) are lumped into a category known as *direct costs*. That is, they represent costs tied directly to and enumerated specifically within the project being proposed. However, the costs of performing research extend well beyond direct costs.

For example, if the PI on a grant proposal is a faculty member, their position relies on their institution's payroll services and benefits offices. Their institution also supports recruiting and placement services for undergraduate and graduate students, which is extremely important when such individuals are funded on external grants. Additionally, buildings housing research personnel must be maintained, utilities must be paid, the central library must be supported, buildings and equipment must be depreciated, and other administrative services, such as those supporting proposal development and grant management, must be funded.

Because these costs cannot easily be linked to a given project (imagine trying to estimate how much electricity usage to charge to a project that shares space with many other projects), they are called *indirect costs*. The more accurate and appropriate term is *facilities and administrative costs* (referred to as F&A; table 6.3). They represent real costs associated with performing research, and in most cases are charged as a percentage of the total grant proposal budget (see below) irrespective of the nature of the project. The percentage is set by federal agencies—which is an important point I return to below—and reflects an aggregation of sponsored program activities across an institution, updated every few years.

Table 6.3
Breakdown of F&A for academic research assistance awards

Category	Description
Facilities	Building depreciation: expenses associated with university-owned buildings, including the expense associated with federal contributions to those buildings.
	Equipment depreciation: expenses associated with university-owned capital equipment, including federal contributions to such equipment.
	Interest: interest associated with external debt financing of building acquisition and construction or renovation, less interest income earned on debt proceeds.
	Operations and maintenance: utilities, janitorial services, and ongoing repair and maintenance of university-owned and leased buildings.
	Library: operational costs of the university's library system excluding rare books but including staff.
Administration	General administration: payroll, executive and administrative offices, human resources, accounting, etc.
	Sponsored project administration: offices and personnel responsible for administering sponsored project activity.
	Departmental administration: administrative costs for each college and departmental or school.
	Student administration and services: costs associated with supporting students, such as the office of student affairs.

F&A is a somewhat controversial and confusing concept for a variety of reasons, and as a next-generation researcher, it is important for you to understand and be able to defend the F&A concept.

The first point of confusion exists because the costs associated with F&A often are incorrectly equated with profit by analogy to private companies.[3] Such is not the case. F&A represents real costs that must be paid by universities and other organizations receiving grant funding to support the associated research. Unfortunately, some federal agencies set arbitrary limits on how much F&A can be included in a grant proposal, which means the institution receiving the funding has to make up the difference (a form of cost sharing). This is ironic because the federal government determines the F&A percentage allowed to be charged by the institution in the first place. This difference, known as unrecovered F&A, amounts to several billion dollars per year and represents a significant financial burden to institutions, especially because the administrative component of the F&A rate (table 6.3) has been capped since 1991. Although most private foundations do not allow the full amount of F&A to be charged to a grant proposal budget, they utilize other approaches in the budget to account for at least some of the costs.

A second point of confusion regarding F&A concerns how it is applied in a grant proposal budget. Without getting too far into the weeds, which is something you should do as part of the exercises at the end of this chapter, F&A is charged as a percentage of the cumulative costs of a proposal (i.e., the direct costs noted previously). More specifically, the federal government assigns an F&A *rate* to funding recipient institutions, such as a university, every few years. To compute the *total budget* of a grant proposal (direct costs plus F&A), one multiplies the direct costs by the F&A *rate* and adds that sum to the *direct costs* to obtain the *total budget*.

For example, suppose the direct costs[4] of your proposal are $100,000 and the F&A rate at your university is 50 percent. The total budget of the grant proposal therefore is $100,000 + $100,000 × 0.50 = $150,000. Many individuals, especially lawmakers, incorrectly assume that a 50 percent F&A rate means one-half of the total budget is allocated to F&A expenses (table 6.3). Our example clearly shows this is not the case. Rather, a 50 percent F&A rate means that one-third, not one-half, of the total proposal budget is allocated to F&A.

F&A rates at institutions can vary from 25–30 percent to more than 80 percent, depending upon the nature of the institution, its research portfolio, and facilities and other resources. University faculty almost uniformly, and understandably, prefer low F&A rates because this allows them to allocate more money in a proposal budget to supporting direct project costs (e.g., students, equipment, travel, supplies).

116 Chapter 6

When a grant proposal is funded, it becomes an award issued to the organization that submitted it—and that award can take many forms, such as a grant or contract. This leads to a final confusing point about F&A.

When research on an award begins and money is expended, the award recipient, such as a university, actually pays F&A up front, out of its own coffers. When award money is sent to the university by the funding organization, the F&A is thus reimbursed to the university. Consequently, this reimbursement can be used for items such as equipment, personnel, faculty start-up funding, internal incentive programs, and buildings, provided appropriate policies and laws are followed. Yet some, especially lawmakers and policymakers, have the mistaken impression this reimbursement has to be used directly to pay for items composing F&A, such as the library, building depreciation and maintenance, and personnel services. Such is not the case. Although this topic seems a bit esoteric, it is extremely important, and because of it, billions of dollars are at stake.

To illustrate the confusion, suppose you wreck your car and your insurance company agrees to buy you a new one. You purchase a new car using money from your savings account, and then a few weeks later, a check arrives in the mail, from your insurance company, in the amount of the car you just purchased. Instead of depositing this check in your savings account to replace the money you withdrew to purchase the car, you take a cruise with it instead. Have you defrauded the insurance company? Of course not! The insurance company simply reimbursed you for costs you already paid, and you therefore are free to use that reimbursement for anything you wish, so long as you don't break the law in doing so. F&A reimbursement works in exactly the same manner.

6.3 Proposal Submission and Evaluation Processes

When all components of a grant proposal (table 6.1) are complete—which, in addition to the aforementioned items, often includes documentation by the submitting organization of institutional conflicts of interest (section 10.2), lobbying certification, drug-free workplace policies, and a research security (section 10.3) program as appropriate—the proposal package is formally submitted. In almost all cases, the submission is performed electronically, with a variety of automated checks to ensure completeness. Only a limited number of individuals at academic institutions are allowed to submit proposals, usually the senior research officer or their designees, because doing so formally obligates the institution, and thus its governing board (section 1.6), to the terms and conditions of the funding organization.

Exceptions do of course exist, especially for faculty, graduate student, and postdoctoral fellowships, where the grant funding is provided directly to the individual and not the institution. A good example is the Fulbright Fellowship. However, most institutions encourage researchers to process such submissions through the office of sponsored programs so the academic unit of the submitter is aware of the activity. This is important because, in some cases, cost sharing will be required, and as noted previously, deans and department chairs do not appreciate being surprised when asked to provide such funding without prior notification or approval!

Once a grant proposal arrives at the funding organization, what happens to it? Irrespective of whether the organization is a federal agency, a nonprofit foundation, a private company, or some other entity, the proposal is evaluated, often against others of a similar nature in competition with one another. The process of evaluation depends upon a number of factors, including but not limited to the nature and structure of the funding organization and the specific announcement of opportunity or solicitation. In almost all cases, the merit of the work being proposed is judged against very specific criteria, and thus the process is known as peer/merit review (chapter 7). As noted previously, curiosity-driven research tends to be evaluated principally on the creativity or intellectual merit of the idea and the broader impacts of the work (discussed below), whereas applied research and development are evaluated not only on the idea and approach, but also the manner in which the work meets specific programmatic or mission requirements of the organization requesting or funding the work.

For most US federal agencies, impacts broader than those associated with the work being proposed are included as a review criterion, and therefore are known as broader impacts. This includes but is not limited to promoting teaching, training, and public education, broadening the participation of traditionally underrepresented and underserved populations, and enhancing infrastructure for research and education.

The review process itself also is highly variable (chapter 7), including the time elapsed from proposal submission to funding organization decision. In some federal agencies, such as NSF and NIH, review involving peer researchers is utilized. In this so-called peer review, researchers anonymously evaluate each other's proposals, either individually or in panels, and make recommendations to the funding organization. Ranking often is involved.

At NSF, a five-part scale is used, with program officers having considerable discretion in funding proposals based upon peer reviewer guidance. This discretion is valuable because, for some research which potentially is transformative and could overturn established paradigms and knowledge, great skepticism may exist on the part of the reviewers. Yet, funding such proposals is a necessary part of research to ensure that even seemingly far-fetched ideas are given a chance, especially if the outcomes could have a significant societal impact.

NIH uses a quantitative system of scoring in which agency program officers have comparatively less discretion. The "payline" of reviewed submissions separates proposals to be funded from those that will not, and usually is applied quite stringently. This too is an appropriate strategy.

The review process at NEA follows a similar process (see chapter 7 for details), except that once the panel review is complete, its recommendations are forwarded to the National Council on the Arts, which then reviews the recommendations in a session open to the public. The chairman of NEA makes the final decision. Although NSF functions in a similar manner through the panel stage, all reviews remain confidential unless released by the PI, and all associated discussions bearing on the decision likewise are confidential (though as noted in chapter 7, the process is periodically reviewed by outside experts to ensure integrity exists throughout the entire process). The processes of other organizations, public and private, may be found on their respective websites.

Although the US proposal merit review system is the gold standard of the world, it contains inherent challenges because it relies on personal and professional judgment. One important challenge is reviewer bias. Various studies have shown that bias, even unconscious bias, exists in the merit review process. Sometimes it is manifest as gender bias while in other cases, it is based upon the names of investigators or even the size and name of their institution. Fortunately, training is available to mitigate many forms of bias, and organizations that fund research and creative activity increasingly are employing it. Yet, more needs to be understood before bias is minimized or eliminated completely. Bias is discussed in greater detail in chapter 8.

The merit review process necessarily considers the proposal budget as a means for determining whether sufficient funding (or too much) has been requested to complete the work proposed. However, the budget itself rarely makes or breaks the final funding decision, which as we have seen is based principally upon intellectual merit or meeting the needs of the funding organization. Once merit has been evaluated, the funding organization may request changes in the budget. If such changes are sufficiently large in terms of reductions (rarely is the budget requested to be increased), the project may need to be reduced in scope to accommodate the smaller funding level.

If the reviews of a proposal are less than stellar and the proposal is not selected for funding, one should not despair! The success rates of competitive research grant proposals range from the single digits in some parts of federal agencies to around 25 or 30 percent in others. Percentages also vary widely for private companies and foundations. This means one needs to keep trying, using reviewer comments to improve the proposal (see chapter 7) so that, in the process, the PI and others involved become better at developing their ideas and communicating them effectively in proposals. First-time investigators may need to submit a proposal multiple times, or submit multiple proposals on different topics, to be funded. Once an award is made and the work produces important outcomes, a track record is established that will improve one's competitiveness next time. Perseverance is the name of the game!

6.4 Managing a Research Project

If you are fortunate enough to receive funding for a grant proposal as the PI, you now enter a new realm of responsibility as the project director (PD). In this role, you not only are responsible for making sure the entire project succeeds (e.g., that research is proceeding as planned, communication is effective, collaborations are healthy, students are being advised and mentored appropriately, outcomes are being communicated, and the overall research environment is diverse, inclusive, welcoming, and free from bias and harassment), but you also are legally responsible for making sure all applicable rules and laws are followed. This includes rules for spending money, hiring and evaluating personnel, making purchases, and reporting progress to the funder and perhaps your own institution. It also includes following rules related to involving human subjects and animals in research, the use of select agents, carcinogenic chemicals, and certain strains of bacteria, and the use of items that cannot be accessed by certain persons, or removed from the country, without appropriate licenses owing to export control rules and regulations (chapter 10). See Burroughs Wellcome Fund & Howard Hughes Medical Institute (2006) for practical guidance. It is important to keep in mind that, although funding usually does not go to the PI directly—in the case of a university, for example, it goes to the institution—the PI is *personally responsible*, from a legal standpoint, for all aspects of the project.

Fortunately, most institutions have resources to assist with virtually all of the compliance topics just mentioned, and then some. For those which do not, options exist for needs to be met and it is up to the researcher to identify and take advantage of them.

On the brighter side, research projects yield a wide array of outcomes in the form of reports, refereed publications, performances, exhibitions, technologies, processes, algorithms, software, lectures, and engagements with K–12 education and the public that are both very important and personally fulfilling. Indeed, the main purpose of research and creative activity, as noted in chapter 1, is to add to the body of existing knowledge. As also noted in chapter 1, fundamental or curiosity-driven research results may not yield practical benefits for years or decades, yet they nevertheless are important as the foundation for future research and innovation and improving quality of life.

As a researcher, it also is important for you to convey the purpose and value of your work beyond formal mechanisms within the research community; that is, to nonexpert audiences (chapter 11). Doing so is not an easy task because of the highly specialized nature and distinctive attributes of today's disciplines, and their use of terminology unique to the work within them. Numerous resources are available to assist you (e.g., those at the Alan Alda Center for Communicating Science [http://aldacenter.org]) in learning how to explain your work to nonexperts in venues such as public lectures, TED (Technology, Entertainment and Design) talks, interviews, social media, visits with lawmakers, and presentations to civic organizations. Such outreach is extremely important so those not involved in research, or in your area of expertise, understand its value and appreciate the need to support it.

For most individuals having a career in research, landing a grant or contract is only the beginning. In the midst of an existing project, it is important to look over the horizon and begin thinking about the next proposal or set of proposals. Most grants and contracts last only a few years, and that time frame usually is insufficient for answering all of the questions associated with a problem you wish to solve or an idea you wish to explore. And in most cases, it is not sufficient to fund a graduate student through their entire degree program.

Thus, even before one grant is finished, work needs to begin on new proposals either to continue or extend the work now underway, or to explore new ideas. Those funded entirely on research projects cannot, of course, plan their lives on a two- or three-year cycle of known salary, and thus continuity is important to keep a research program going and in fact to grow it over time. Consequently, it is important for you, as a researcher, to focus not only on the next grant or contract, but also on the long view of what you wish to accomplish, say over a period of ten to twenty years. In that manner, proposals serve as mechanisms to achieve intermediate goals without losing sight of one's overall dreams to understand the world in which we live.

Assess Your Comprehension

1. What is a principal investigator on a grant proposal?
2. Writing a grant proposal is valuable for a number of reasons. List and describe several of them.
3. List and describe several components of a research proposal budget.
4. What is the mutuality of interest principle and what is its relevance to grant proposals versus contracts?

5. Describe cost sharing and the forms it can take in grant proposals.

6. How can cost sharing create inequity in the research enterprise?

7. What are facilities and administrative costs (F&A) in a grant proposal?

8. List the two categories of F&A and some of the items contained within them.

9. Why is F&A controversial and often misunderstood?

10. What is peer review?

11. What should you do if your research grant proposal is not funded the first time?

12. What are some of the key responsibilities of a project director in overseeing a grant proposal once it is funded?

Exercises to Deepen Your Understanding

Exercise 1: Using the https://www.grants.gov website, compare and contrast proposal structure and submission requirements in calls for proposals—in your field of study or fields of interest to you—for any of the following federal agencies: National Science Foundation (NSF), National Institutes of Health (NIH), National Endowment for the Arts (NEA), and National Endowment for the Humanities (NEH). Discuss the range of requirements with regard to content, format, and merit review process and criteria, and suggest ways in which these funding organizations might modify their requirements to improve their processes and reduce administrative workload of principal investigators.

Exercise 2: Follow the instructions in exercise 1, though now applied to a few private nonprofit foundations. Also, describe the manner in which such foundations differ from federal agencies in all of the attributes noted above. Lists of foundations can be found online, and one particularly useful source is the Open Education Database (https://oedb.org/ilibrarian/100_places_to _find_funding_your_research/).

Exercise 3: Using the https://www.grants.gov website, compare and contrast cost-sharing requirements in calls for proposals—in your field of study or fields of interest to you—for any of the following federal agencies: NSF, National Aeronautics and Space Administration (NASA), NIH, US Department of Energy (DOE) Office of Science, National Institute of Standards and Technology (NIST), NEA, and NEH. Discuss the range of cost-sharing requirements and the extent to which you feel such sharing may limit or disincentivize participation by certain organizations and individuals, (e.g., institutions having smaller budgets and less flexibility in discretionary funding). What policies might you suggest to create a more level playing field?

Exercise 4: In the link below, you will find a research project description and associated budget and budget justification for an NSF Early Career proposal, courtesy of Professor Ankur Desai at the University of Wisconsin-Madison. Using this material as an example from which to learn, develop a budget and associated justification for the project you outlined in exercise 4 of chapter 2. Include items in all relevant budget categories and assume the F&A rate is 60 percent of modified total direct costs. Once you complete the form, answer the following questions:

- How does the bottom-line budget figure change if the facilities and administrative costs (F&A) rate is only 50 percent? 10 percent?

- Do you understand why some agencies limit the F&A rate?

- Do you understand why some researchers protest F&A, or want substantially lower rates, even though it is a legitimate and necessary cost for performing research?

- Suppose you are told by the funding organization that you must reduce your budget by 30 percent. Where will you impose cuts, and how did you make those decisions? What impacts will those cuts have on the project goals/scope?

    Project summary: https://mitp-content-server.mit.edu/books/content /sectbyfn/books_pres_0/14740/Career-Summary.pdf

    Project budget and justification: https://mitp-content-server.mit.edu /books/content/sectbyfn/books_pres_0/14740/Career-Budget.pdf

Exercise 5: F&A is not well understood by many people, ranging from faculty to members of Congress. As a result, every few years, proposals are put forward to modify how F&A is computed, cap it, or restructure the reimbursement system entirely. For this exercise, examine the history of F&A and identify key points of controversy around it. Utilize congressional hearings, reports, and media to form your own opinion about the role of F&A in America's research enterprise and steps that might be taken to clear up the confusion around it. In your search for references, note that F&A also is known as overhead and indirect costs.

Exercise 6: Contact your office of sponsored programs, which typically resides within the office of the vice president for research or vice chancellor for research, and tell them you wish to experience the process associated with submitting a fictitious grant proposal to a federal funding agency as a means for preparing yourself to submit an actual proposal in the future. If your university has no such office, speak to your advisor, department chair, or dean to determine the appropriate office to engage. Select a federal agency relative to your area of research or creative activity, visit their website to evaluate procedures for submitting a proposal, and then develop a blank, mock proposal containing the necessary sections and work your way through the process used at your institution. Be certain to ask your office of sponsored programs about available training aids, such as videos or short courses, to assist your learning about institutional and agency processes. What surprised you the most about the overall experience? Did you find helpful the assistance provided by your institution? What changes would you suggest to improve the experience?

Exercise 7: Working with a faculty mentor, select an appropriate external funding source for your research and develop a sample proposal by following the guidelines on the source's website. This is a considerable task for which you should allocate several weeks of time. You may wish to complete only parts of the required sections (e.g., project summary, project description, budget, budget justification, facilities required, qualifications of the investigator[s]) to get a flavor of what is required and the writing style to be used. Note that many funding organizations provide sample proposals from which you can learn.

7

The Give-and-Take of Criticism: Subjecting Research to Scrutiny via Peer/Merit Review

Chapter Overview and Learning Objectives

As is true for many aspects of our lives, research and creative activity are subject to scrutiny, particularly via the peer/merit review process.[1] By identifying not only problems or flaws but also new ideas and approaches, such review can aid in ensuring that rigor, quality, validity, significance, and originality are present in the work. This chapter describes the purpose and importance of peer/merit review as well as foundational principles and the steps involved in the processes. It also discusses strengths and weaknesses in review processes, variations arising from them, and methods for effectively using professional criticism. After reading this chapter, you should

- Understand the importance of and mechanisms for scrutinizing research proposals, methods and outcomes;
- Be able to define peer/merit review and describe the associated principles and processes for both publications and proposals;
- Be aware that principles of peer review are applicable to scholarly activities other than traditional publications, including performances, exhibits, and scores;
- Be able to explain the strengths and weaknesses of traditional peer/merit review and alternative methods being explored; and
- Understand the nature of professional critique and be able to apply it effectively to your work.

7.1 Importance, History, and Forms of Scrutinizing Research and Creative Activity

Throughout our lives, virtually everything we do is subject to scrutiny—that is, to critical evaluation for the purpose of learning, improving, and achieving the highest standards of excellence. As children, our school work was scrutinized for errors, and we learned by receiving guidance and correction. Our performance in sports and in our jobs, our tax forms and bank accounts, and our posts on social media all come under scrutiny. Receiving criticism from scrutiny often is not enjoyable, nor is learning from it always easy. However, scrutiny is an essential and extremely valuable part of our lives, and research and creative activity are no exception.

In that context, scrutiny helps ensure that rigor, quality, validity, significance, and originality are present in research, and that the work performed meets the intended purpose. Scrutiny helps identify problems, flaws in concepts and approaches, and misconduct such as fraud and plagiarism (chapter 9). By its very nature in evaluating and challenging processes and outcomes, scrutiny sometimes leads researchers to identify new approaches and ideas, helps train researchers to improve over time, ensures public trust and confidence, and lends prestige to the entire enterprise. Never lose sight of the fact that someone is funding your research and creative activity, and wherever money is expended, high expectations and accountability understandably also are present!

However, we also must remember a very important point that argues strongly in favor of scrutiny—namely, that the stakes regarding research are extremely high. That is, our work as scholars is critically important to ensuring the health and vitality of all living beings, the sustainability of our environment, our personal as well as national security and prosperity, and the celebration and enrichment of our humanity. That is an enormous responsibility and is why we need to scrutinize the research process itself, along with grant proposals, journal articles, books, exhibits, performances, presentations, interviews, blog posts, and more.

Scrutiny of research and creative activity began long before today's process-oriented methods came into existence (chapter 4). Those who developed astrological, astronomical, and other bases of knowledge in prehistoric times no doubt debated one another's viewpoints, though we have little direct evidence given that the spoken word was at that time the only form of communication. Early Greek philosophers, who focused on understanding the natural world from non-supernatural viewpoints, probably marked the beginning of organized scrutiny of research—or as it was known then, natural philosophy.

Plato and Aristotle, who lived in the late fourth and early third centuries BC, respectively, are familiar names and are credited with systematizing inquiry into the natural world. In so doing, the scrutiny of one another's ideas and writings in their day became more formal. Because space does not permit a thorough examination here of the history of research scrutiny, several references are provided (e.g., Moran 2010; Cohen and Lloyd 2014; Moore 2019; McElreavy et al. n.d.). However, we should not overlook the consequences of disagreement among scholars during the formative period of intellectual inquiry, with one of the most fascinating examples being the trial of Galileo in 1633. Galileo was accused by the pope of heresy for advocating heliocentrism, or that the earth revolves around the sun. Galileo ultimately spent the rest of his life under house arrest for his beliefs and writings, which like those of Copernicus, turned out to be correct!

In modern times, as research methods and academic disciplines became more formalized, scrutiny of research and creative activity likewise took on a more formal structure. Many forms of scrutiny now exist, including the review of progress reports by funders of research; congressional hearings on specific topics of interest to lawmakers; work by inspectors general at federal agencies to ensure appropriate laws and processes are being followed and that waste, fraud and abuse are not occurring in research; and the ability for the general public to comment on proposed government policies via the Federal Register.

The form of scrutiny that you, as a researcher, will encounter most often is known as peer review, which most trace to seventeenth-century Europe and the founding of the Royal Society of London in 1662 and the Academie Royale des Sciences of Paris in 1699. Both societies began publishing their own journals, and the first formal instance of peer review, in that context, is thought to be the *Philosophical Transactions of the Royal Society* and the French *Journal des Scavans*, more than three hundred years ago.

We will formally define and examine peer review in great detail in subsequent sections of this chapter, but for now, as the name implies, it is sufficient to know that peer review involves the evaluation, by peers, of grant proposals, journal and book manuscripts, performances, exhibits, data sets, and course materials. And of course, the book you are now reading! As you might imagine, peer review varies in its application across disciplines and circumstances, and also has its strengths as well as weaknesses—both of which we examine in subsequent sections. Yet, despite thoughtful efforts to improve peer review and even devise other strategies in place of it, peer review remains the global de facto form of scrutiny applied to research and creative activity.

7.2 Definition and Purpose of Peer/Merit Review

Scholarly peer review is the process by which research and creative activity are evaluated, according to specified criteria, principally by peer experts in the same or similar fields for the purpose of rendering some sort of decision. Note that merit is one criterion upon which review by peers can be based, usually for grant or other types of proposals. Consequently, peer and merit review are different, with the latter being one possible component of the former. For simplicity, unless otherwise noted, henceforth I will use the term "peer review." Although the definition of peer review is seemingly straightforward, it is rich in content and worthy of being unpacked.

The first point to note is that peer review is a process, built upon a foundation of core principles (section 7.3), which involves proceeding through a series of steps that depend upon the particular situation at hand. For example, the peer review process applied to a grant proposal tends to be somewhat different than that applied to a journal or book manuscript, and varies across funding organizations and publishers, respectively. Issues such as conflicts of interest, confidentiality, and bias (chapter 8) are key considerations of the process, irrespective of where and how it is applied.

Second, the phrase "research and creative activity" in our definition can refer to a proposal, concept, or strategy, but also to an outcome or communication of results. The latter includes but is not limited to journal and book manuscripts, performances, exhibits, inventions, computer codes, data sets, processes, sculptures and other physical objects, course materials, and so on.

The third component of our definition concerns "evaluation according to specified criteria." The evaluation of research and creative activity is intended to emphasize a thorough assessment of motivation, questions or hypotheses put forward, methodological approach, information utilized, analyses conducted, and so on. And this evaluation is made relative to specific criteria, which can vary markedly among funding organizations, publishers, and disciplines and include the aforementioned items but also the fundamental intellectual merit of the activity; its potential impact on the scholarly field and/or society; the degree to which the work improves education and the engagement of others, especially those from traditionally underserved, underrepresented or marginalized populations; the creativity and innovativeness exhibited by the researchers; and the relevance of the work to the mission of the organization funding or publishing it.

Fourth is the notion of a "peer." Traditionally, this term referred to experts in the field or fields closely related to the research or creative activity being scrutinized. For example, cosmologists peer reviewing a journal manuscript on black holes, or a musical theorist reviewing an orchestral score. Today, the notion of a reviewer can be broader, sometimes including individuals in the general public who are knowledgeable about a topic but not formally degreed or credentialed (section 4.6).

The fifth and final component of our definition of peer review involves the "purpose of rendering of a decision." This is more complex than it sounds because, embodied in this phrase are the words "purpose" and "rendering a decision." Although we already have defined peer review, its actual purpose, somewhat surprisingly, is a topic of debate. For the most part, in the context of making decisions such as selecting proposals for funding, papers and books for publication, and scripts for performance, peer review is intended to lead to the selection of the "best" among alternatives. But against what do we measure in defining "best," and would we always arrive as the same outcome if we used different peers?

Interestingly, peer review most frequently informs the decision being made but does not directly determine it. For example, a journal or publishing house uses editors to assess responses provided by peer reviewers of a particular submission, such as a journal or book manuscript. Quite often, the reviews exhibit widely varying views of the work and frequently require clarification and/or revision of the work by the researcher. Ultimately, the editor is responsible for considering all reviews, including his or her own, and rendering the final decision regarding acceptance for publication. The same holds true for federal agency program officers charged with selecting proposals for funding, though as noted previously, differences in process exist among funding organizations.

7.3 Principles and Processes of Peer/Merit Review

The process and components of peer review vary depending upon the circumstances in which they are applied. However, peer review is grounded in certain foundational principles that transcend the nuances of its application, though in a few cases, this is changing.

The first principle of peer review is *evaluation* by individuals other than those who produced or are proposing to conduct the work. The second principle is *objectivity*, guided by criteria utilized for the evaluation. The third principle is *impartiality* and absence of bias (chapters 8 and 9), which is managed by conflict of interest disclosure and other means. The fourth principle is *confidentiality* on the part of those reviewing and passing judgment on the work, though as we will see, in some situations, more open processes are now being tested. The fifth principle is *honesty and integrity*, with the peer review process free from political and other non-scholarly external influences. The sixth and final principle is *accountability*—to those funding the work, including but not limited to taxpayers, and to the research enterprise itself. Important to accountability are independent assessments of peer review itself, including how decisions based upon it are rendered, to ensure the processes are operating at the highest levels of professional integrity.

At the end of the day, as in so many aspects of our lives, the peer review process relies on trust—trust among reviewers, between author and editor, between researcher and agency program officer, and between the public and the research enterprise itself.

The best way to become familiar with the peer review process is to walk through the detailed steps involved in its application. Not surprisingly, each federal R&D funding agency, each nongovernmental funding organization (e.g., a private foundation), and each journal or publisher has its own set of rules, procedures, and criteria for evaluating submissions. Although one could examine several in detail, a more effective approach is to equip you with an understanding of the foundational elements of peer review by studying four specific examples: peer review of a research grant proposal submitted to NSF, NIH, and NEA, and peer review of a manuscript submitted to a generic archive journal. One might refer to these as examples of "classical peer review," upon which many variations have been developed (section 7.5). Once you understand these examples, others will be easier to grasp (US Government Accountability Office 2014, figure 1 provides an excellent generic life-cycle workflow for federal grants). Other examples and applications (e.g., juried performances and exhibits) are described in the references (e.g., Hunter and Russ 1996; Lerch et al. 2020).

For the first example, assume you have written a research grant proposal, as described in chapter 6, to study tornadoes and have submitted it to NSF via the electronic system at https://www.grants.gov. Upon receiving it (figure 7.1), and after the automated system has determined the proposal meets all agency requirements for format and completeness of information provided, NSF assigns the proposal to the appropriate program for review, in this case the Physical and Dynamic Meteorology Program within the Division of Atmospheric and Geospace Sciences. Although the overall process is supervised by the division director, a specific program officer is given responsibility for stewarding most of the peer review steps. Note that, for some federal agencies and programs and even some private foundations, proposals are reviewed internally, by organization personnel only, without involvement of outside subject matter experts.

The NSF merit review[2] process (figure 7.1) proceeds with the selection of reviewers who are familiar with the subject area as determined by personal knowledge of the program officer, reference to reviewer work in the proposal itself, reviewers recommended by the principal investigator, and databases that list researcher expertise. In considering possible reviewers, the program officer checks for conflicts of interest, which might take the form of familial relationships, prior or current collaborations, institutional affiliation, or significant

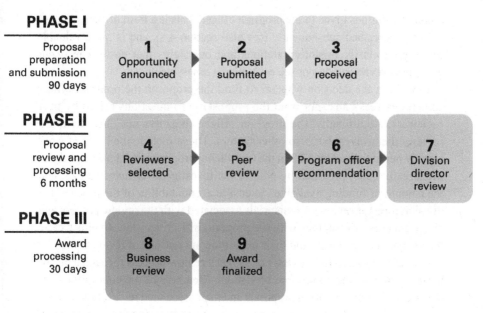

PHASE I

Proposal
preparation
and submission
90 days

1 Opportunity announced
2 Proposal submitted
3 Proposal received

PHASE II

Proposal
review and
processing
6 months

4 Reviewers selected
5 Peer review
6 Program officer recommendation
7 Division director review

PHASE III

Award
processing
30 days

8 Business review
9 Award finalized

Figure 7.1
Merit review process for grant proposals submitted to the National Science Foundation. *Source*:
National Science Foundation (n.d.-b).

financial interest such as ownership of stock by the principal investigator in a
corporation led by a reviewer. We address these and related compliance issues
in chapter 10.

Once reviewers have been selected, the proposal is provided to them for
review. Although reviewers know the identity of the investigators proposing
the work, the investigators do not know the identity of the reviewers unless
the reviewers choose to make their identity known. This is known as the *single-
blind model* of review. NSF requires reviewers to maintain strict confidentiality of their reviews within the process being utilized. It also requires that
reviewers not take ideas from the proposal for their own use nor share the proposal with others, and that they destroy or return the proposal when the
review is completed.

NSF utilizes two criteria for merit review, the first involving the intellectual merit of the work being proposed and the second involving broader
impacts. Detailed guidance is provided to reviewers regarding how to assess
these criteria, and once reviews are received, the program officer evaluates
them to render a decision regarding funding. Sometimes, panels of experts
are utilized to review a group of proposals, and in the process, they meet,
either in person or virtually, to share their reviews and arrive at consensus

recommendations given to the program officer. This is a form of "consultative review," described subsequently (see also section 4.8), and is quite valuable for helping clarify misinterpretations and oversights that easily can occur when peer reviewers do not see each other's assessments.

In making the decision whether to fund the proposal, the program officer sometimes seeks answers from the proposer(s) to questions raised by peer reviewers. Additionally, the program officer considers not only the merit reviews themselves, but also other factors. These include the body of work already being funded by NSF in the topic being proposed, the amount of funding already being provided by NSF to the investigator or investigators, and the amount of funding available. To ensure accountability of the process, the division director reviews all materials associated with the review process and either concurs or disagrees with the program officer decision. In either case, the principal investigator and their institution are notified of the outcome.

NSF conducts external reviews of its merit review process through a mechanism known as the committee of visitors. Members of the committee conduct periodic assessments of proposals and their associated reviews and agency decisions drawn at random from those that were both funded and rejected. Additionally, they examine other aspects of the review process, and make recommendations for change, to ensure that the peer review system is operating at the highest levels of integrity.

With the NSF example now in hand, it is useful to briefly examine the overall characteristics of procedures used by two other key federal agencies.

The NIH review process (National Institutes of Health n.d.-c) shares some features of that used by NSF, though notable differences exist. They occur in part because NIH itself consists of a number of centers and institutes, each of which performs research (known as intramural research) and has its own variations upon the foundational NIH review process. (NSF itself does not perform research or operate facilities, and although its directorates operate a wide array of programs, all reviews utilize the aforementioned two criteria.)

Generally, a research proposal submitted by an academic scholar to NIH is assigned to a study section, which comprises expert reviewers who conduct the initial peer review. If the proposal has institute-specific features, the relevant institute coordinates the review. Numerous criteria are considered in the review process (e.g., significance, innovation, approach, capabilities of the investigators), and the outcome of the first review is expressed as an overall impact score, with the scores for a given study section ranked into percentiles. Additionally, reviewer comments and a summary statement are prepared.

The second level of review is performed by NIH institute or center councils or boards which, in addition to subject matter experts, include other individuals having expertise in health and disease. In many cases, a payline then is determined based upon funding available, the number and quality of submissions, and other factors. Submissions falling within the payline generally are funded, though exceptions can be made.

In the case of NEA, the peer review process is less elaborate but nonetheless rigorous (National Endowment for the Arts n.d.). As for NSF and NIH, proposals submitted are first evaluated to ensure they conform to stated formats and timelines. NEA staff then review the submissions for eligibility and completeness and assign proposals to an appropriate review panel of subject matter experts. Typically, a panel consists of six experts who handle up to forty submissions in a given review cycle. In this first level of review, each panelist assesses every submission and provides each proposal with a rating, according to NEA criteria. The panel meets as a group in closed session to discuss the ratings, which may be changed based upon that discussion.

In the second level of review, the National Council on the Arts (NCA) assesses the panel recommendations and considers available funding to arrive at a final recommendation for each proposal. These recommendations are forwarded to the Chairman of the Council, who renders the final decision.

This second level of review is quite similar to that for exceptionally large or otherwise special proposals that come before NSB, which is the governing body of NSF. However, instead of recommending to the NSF director which proposals should be funded, NSB makes the final decision and formally authorizes the director to make the award. Interestingly, both NSB and NCA members are presidential appointees serving six-year terms.

Research grant proposal review procedures used by other federal agencies are similar to those described here, though for many mission agencies (section 6.1), only internal agency review or limited external review is utilized. Additionally, some mission agencies require only brief statements of work and budgets for continued funding, or for proposals that address specific mission requirements.

Turning now to the review of a manuscript submitted to a generic archive journal, the process is quite similar to that just described for a proposal submitted to NSF, though with some important variances. Of course, in reality, the process varies by journal, discipline, and type of publication.

As shown in figure 7.2, the principal author submits the article to a chief editor or editor. The submission undergoes a compliance check to ensure it meets criteria for topical relevance and is properly formatted according to journal policies. If the article fails the compliance check, it is returned to the author. Otherwise, it is assigned to an editor or associate editor who identifies appropriate reviewers using much the same process as described for an NSF proposal. As always, conflicts of interest (chapter 10) are managed appropriately. The

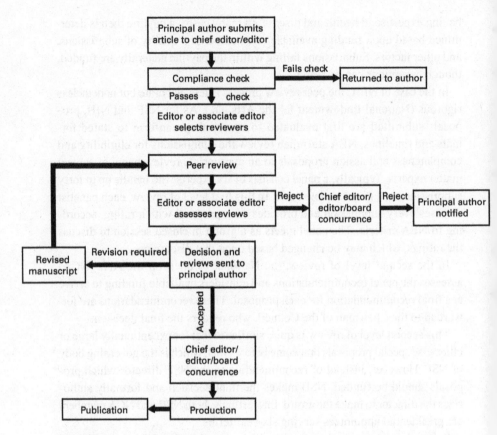

Figure 7.2
Generalized peer review process for archive journal publications. The actual process depends upon the publisher and type of publication.

reviewers are provided with the manuscript, along with guidelines, and submit their review to the assigned editor. Typically, publishers apply the single-blind model.

The editor then evaluates the reviews and renders a decision, which usually is provided to the chief editor or editorial board. This decision can include (figure 7.2) outright rejection, whereby the manuscript is returned to the author, acceptance with minor revision that requires no additional review apart from that of the assigned editor, or provisional acceptance subject to revision and possibly multiple rounds of assessment by the original reviewers. If the manuscript eventually is accepted by the assigned editor, it usually is passed to the chief editor or editorial board for concurrence, and then to the publisher for production and then publication.

7.4   Strengths and Weaknesses of Peer/Merit Review

Although peer review has stood the test of time and frequently is referred to as the "gold standard" for scrutinizing scholarly activity, it is not without its limitations and critics, especially those involved in the process itself. Studies of peer review, though not numerous by traditional measures or involving huge amounts of data, have been quite valuable in identifying challenges and recommending improvements (section 7.5). Thus, we examine both the strengths and limitations of peer review as a natural preface for considering the value of possible improvements. What follows is generally applicable to all disciplines.

Starting with the strengths of peer review, many exist. First, as classically applied, peer review involves the use of highly knowledgeable subject matter experts who comment on and independently verify or validate results, spot problems with design and interpretation, identify fraud or plagiarism, clarify vague explanations, interpret expression, assess performance skill, identify and suggest ways of removing bias (chapter 8), and provide insight into omissions and missed opportunities for more effectively achieving the goals of the work. For grant proposals, peer review also provides an assessment of researcher capability, an evaluation of the history of collaboration, if appropriate, data and project management plans, and the availability of necessary resources, including facilities, for performing the work.

Second, peer review traditionally has involved maintaining anonymity of reviewers, which allows them to comment openly and honestly (though in some cases, overly harshly and even vindictively). Additionally, the material being reviewed traditionally is required to be held in confidence, with reviewers bound to not disclose or use it to their advantage. In this regard, as in so many aspects of the research enterprise, trust is foundational to the effective application of peer review. We will see in the next section that some of these traditions now are being modified in favor of new approaches that seek to enhance the review process as well as its transparency and accountability.

The third strength of peer review is that those receiving the reviews gain insight into how others think and approach problems. This not only improves the research itself but also educates researchers and broadens their own views. In fact, it is not unusual for a new idea to be birthed, or a better approach to be identified, as a result of the peer review process. Researchers also gain value by serving as peer reviewers, not only in understanding how to conduct reviews, but also in assessing how their own research might be reviewed—thereby improving its quality prior to submission.

Fourth and finally, in the context of grant proposals, peer review is an important mechanism for ensuring that proposed budgets align with the work to be performed, that the research is consistent with the mission or goals of the organization providing the funding, and that protocols—such as those involving human and animal research (chapter 10)—have been appropriately structured, thoroughly evaluated and effectively are integrated into the work plan. This scrutiny is important for ensuring public trust, both in the expenditure of taxpayer dollars as well as in the outcomes of the research itself. It also creates a sense of prestige for projects chosen for funding.

Turning now to challenges associated with peer review, you may not be surprised to learn that some are the obverse of the strengths just mentioned. First, by its very nature of thoroughness and involving subject matter experts from around the world, peer review is a slow process. The time elapsed from submission of a grant proposal to final decision can be six months or more. Journal manuscript processes generally are somewhat faster, though books often require up to a year for review. The evaluation of performances and exhibits generally occurs more quickly, though with no less degree of intensity.

Second, although peer review represents a measure of quality control, papers containing errors, flaws, plagiarism, and fraud sometimes do get published, though they are relatively rare among the more than one million papers published, and tens of thousands of grant proposals funded, every year. New technologies exist to help identify plagiarism and other issues, and as discussed in section 4.7, mechanisms are available in some disciplines to attempt the reproduction of research results prior to publication.[3] Additionally, several studies have examined the ability of peer review to identify an array of problems and can be found in the references (e.g., Jefferson et al. 2002; Nature 2006; Smith 2006; Ware 2008).

Unfortunately, given the heavy research and teaching workloads of most college and university faculty and the number of documents they are called upon to review, not every paper or proposal receives the sort of in-depth analysis for which peer assessment was designed. Also, for large national-scale activities involving dozens or hundreds of researchers, especially in one or a few disciplines, finding experienced peer reviewers who are not conflicted is sometimes difficult.

A third limitation of peer review, transparency and openness, is related to one of its traditional foundational principles, namely, confidentiality. The traditionally closed nature of peer review makes it subject to speculation regarding things that may or may not be happening "behind the curtain." For example, making certain that all processes are clearly articulated to authors or researchers submitting proposals; that reviewers are not conflicted and are free from bias, including partiality for or against the researchers involved; that reviewers truly understand how to utilize the criteria provided; that the process is consistently applied; and that decisions rendered are supported by written material that adequately explains the reasoning involved. These points are important not only for the research enterprise, but also for the general public. One solution for the transparency challenge, known as open peer review, is discussed in the next section.

A fourth limitation of peer review is its admittedly subjective nature, which has led some to question whether the outcomes it produces are better than flipping a coin. Most researchers certainly believe peer review is the better option, though quantifying the ability of peer review to identify the "best" among many, as noted previously, can be problematic. This has led to calls for developing quantitative measures of peer review and applying science to assess its value.

A fifth limitation that exists in peer review, but in other aspects of our lives as well, is bias. So important is this topic that chapter 8 is devoted to it.

Sixth, peer reviewers sometimes find difficult the task of judging inter- or multidisciplinary work; that is, research and creative activity involving scholars from more than one discipline (chapter 13). This issue occurs in both evaluating proposals as well as outcomes of research. Although finding subject matter experts is not difficult, the challenge they face involves understanding and passing judgment on the contributions and relevance to the work of disciplines other than their own.

For example, the study of an ancient language might involve anthropologists, linguists, computer scientists, mathematical modelers, and historians—all of whom have different disciplinary lexicons, research methods, and views of the project. Coming to a consensus view of a grant proposal, for example, by integrating these dimensions is a challenge indeed, though one that increasingly is the norm in the research enterprise.

Finally, as noted in chapter 1, research generally advances by relatively small increments of progress. However, big ideas sometimes lead to breakthroughs that result in transformational capabilities for society. Examples include the transistor, LASER, nuclear reactor, and blood thinner, Warfarin. Unfortunately, peer review, especially for grant proposals submitted to federal agencies and those reviewed by panels, tends to "regress to the mean," which means that particularly big, potentially transformative ideas often are viewed as too risky to be funded. Indeed, it is generally the case today that, in order to obtain federal funding for research, one must have sufficient results in hand to convince reviewers that the outcomes are fairly certain. Why? Because federal research budgets are extremely stressed and the competitive demand for funding is huge and continues to grow.

Additionally, overturning established paradigms[4] can be difficult when some of the individuals responsible for creating them are reviewing your proposal!

Combined, these factors have the effect of suppressing even the submission of the most creative, potentially transformative ideas. Researchers simply don't bother. And that is a problem for our nation because it means we risk losing the creative spirt that led the US to become the world leader in research and creative activity. You can learn more about potentially transformative research in National Science Board (2007).

7.5 Variations on Classical Peer/Merit Review

It is the very nature of researchers to search for ways of building upon and improving existing knowledge and capabilities. Also true is that advances in technology, especially the Internet, open doors to new capabilities. Peer review is no exception to both of these realities. As a result, numerous variations on the classical peer review model described in the preceding sections are being developed and evaluated. The goal is not to create the perfect model, for we know this is impossible owing to the diversity of circumstances to which peer review is applied, the multiple dimensions of its purpose, and its inherently human-based subjective nature. Rather, the goal is to address known limitations of peer review to maximize its utility for the situation at hand. One of the most important contributors to this goal involves training reviewers to understand the review process and be effective in applying it.

Space does not allow for a comprehensive assessment of every alternative model or possible improvement, so I provide here information about those receiving the most attention.

The simplest variation on the classical model of peer review involves whether the identities of both researchers and reviewers are mutually disclosed. We have examined the single-blind model, which means the identity of the author or investigator is made known to the reviewer, but the identity of the reviewer remains confidential. In the *double-blind model*, the identities of both the reviewer and researcher or author are held in confidence. This strategy is motivated in part by studies showing the presence of bias in reviews (chapter 8) owing to the author or researcher's sex, institutional affiliation, race, or nationality (as might be determined by a web search or simply one's name). As you might imagine, it is difficult to truly double-blind the review process because, in many papers and proposals, authors describe their previous work and build upon it.

On the other hand, the most complex variation on the classical model takes exactly the opposite approach to double-blind review; namely, an open process in which everyone's identity is disclosed, and in the extreme case, where proposals, manuscripts, and other items are made available on the Internet for public input. Known generally as *open peer review*, this framework seeks to enhance transparency and accountability, in some situations accelerate the review process, and improve the quality of assessments provided, including reducing bias.

Consider two specific versions of open peer review, the first of which is referred to as "consultative" peer review. This process involves all participants in the review process—authors and editors in the case of publications, and researchers and program officers in the case of grant proposals—working together, sharing information and exchanging reviews and responses. The collaborative nature of the process helps resolve conflicting statements made among reviewers as well as uncertainty regarding their understanding of the work. It also helps reduce calls for unnecessary or redundant additional work on the part of authors or grant proposal investigators and increases transparency of the process. Ironically, although consultative review was envisioned as a more efficient strategy than confidential review, it can in fact lengthen the process.

In the more elaborate form of open peer review, manuscripts or proposals are submitted as usual and assigned to editors and reviewers. However, the submissions also are posted on the web for public comment, and input from those comments, which usually cannot be submitted anonymously, is added to those from subject matter experts, with the consultative mechanism previously described used to arrive at a final decision. The advantages of this approach are the same as for consultative peer review, though by making the work as well as all reviews and reviewer identities public, it is believed reviewers will be more tactful and constructive in their comments and more likely to be thorough.

Additionally, efforts to suppress a manuscript from being published, or prevent a proposal from being funded (section 10.3), are arguably more difficult to undertake in the open peer review framework, thereby enhancing accountability of the process. Allowing the public to comment challenges the notion of a subject matter expert and posits that someone with considerable knowledge, though lacking formal credentials, can still contribute to scholarly research and creative activity (section 4.6).

Nevertheless, fully open peer review has an important drawback for grant proposals. Namely, by placing proposals on the web, one loses the ability to prevent misappropriation of the ideas and methods being proposed. That is, stealing ideas from proposals—which is explicitly prohibited in classical peer review, as discussed previously—becomes very easy. Few things are as important to scholars as their ideas and proposed research, and fully open review places those things in jeopardy. Although proposals posted on the web for open review obviously do not contain classified information, they could include information considered to be "dual use" (that is, applicable to both civilian and military purposes). This is a particularly important issue for certain topics of national importance, such as artificial intelligence, quantum information science, advanced manufacturing, microelectronics, and biotechnology. Additionally, in the increasingly globally competitive research enterprise and the intentional subversion of America's research enterprise by some governments (section 10.3), extra care must be taken to balance openness against protection, intentional collaboration against illicit competition.

Interestingly, the open peer review model is used by the federal government to allow the public to comment on proposed changes to policies and rules, including those governing research. The document being reviewed in this case is known as a Notice of Proposed Rulemaking (NPRM), and they are posted almost continuously in the Federal Register. The main disadvantage of open peer review is that it can cause reviewers to be less forthcoming or critical, especially if they are critiquing someone well known in the field. Additionally, rebuttals of reviews, or other mechanisms for conveying how the reviewer comments were or were not included, generally are not part of the open process owing in large part to the sheer magnitude of the input typically received.

Other models of peer review exist, including hybrid review, *a posteriori* review, and *a priori* review. With all of that, as you might expect, considerable debate exists regarding the value of the various alternative methods of peer review, and references are provided so you can further explore these issues (e.g., DeCoursey 2006; Kelly, Sadeghieh, & Adeli 2014; King 2017; Tennant 2018).

One thing seems certain, however. For all its shortcomings, no one has yet found a better approach to scrutinizing scholarly research and creative activity than peer review.

7.6 Using Criticism Effectively

I want you to be completely honest in answering the following question: Do you enjoy being criticized, even if you know it is coming? Say, on a term project, thesis, dissertation, journal manuscript, performance, or exhibition? Do you find criticism valuable? Do you *actively* use criticism to your advantage? That is, do you think carefully about the critique, determine whether it is valid, and then seek to improve your work from it?

The influential French Renaissance philosopher Michel de Montaigne said the following: "We need very strong ears to hear ourselves judged frankly, and because there are few who can endure frank criticism without being stung by it, those who venture to criticize us perform a remarkable act of friendship, for to undertake to wound or offend a man for his own good is to have a healthy love for him" (Montaigne 1958). In the context of this book, I would modify that last sentence to read "is to have a healthy love for the research enterprise."

In the present chapter and in chapter 6, we addressed the importance of scrutinizing scholarship, especially via peer review. How, then, does one actually utilize critique effectively and, as de Montaigne states, not be stung by it but rather see it as a favor done for you? Here is some important and generally accepted guidance about using criticism effectively. It does not address the issue of how one *provides* effective criticism because, in the context of research, it varies widely among disciplines and circumstances. However, I believe you will gain insight into this aspect of critique by understanding how to handle it yourself, thus preparing you to provide it to others.

First, realize that critical assessment of your work is foundational to the research process, and that irrespective of the feedback provided—be it highly critical or even something with which you disagree—you can always learn from it. Once you accept this fact, criticism won't be a hard pill to swallow. As M. Scott Peck famously said in his classic work *The Road Less Traveled* (Peck 1978, 15), "Once we truly know that life is difficult—once we truly understand and accept it—then life is no longer difficult. Because once it is accepted, the fact that life is difficult no longer matters." I therefore urge you to be positive about criticism and accept and embrace it!

Second, carefully review critiques of your work to fully understand what each reviewer is trying to convey. Our human tendency is to react to criticism by defending ourselves rather than being open minded and accepting that we might learn from it. This often causes us to miss the message which, in research, could lead to a proposal or paper being rejected, or an opportunity to exhibit being denied.

Third, judge the criticism carefully to discern which comments are factual and which are patently false. Although all critique has value, some feedback may obviously be wrong and should be dismissed out of hand.

Fourth, take time to process the critique and do not prepare your responses immediately. This is especially important if your initial reaction to the critique is one of indignity. Remember, research inherently involves debate and disagreement, and being able to handle criticism is an important and necessary skill you will develop over time.

Fifth, never take critiques personally. In other words, the critique is of your work and not of your personality or value as an individual.

Finally, be calm and measured in your response if one is required. Use data and facts to bolster your arguments, and if possible, have others review them prior to submission. Focus on the points raised and not the tone of the critique, which sometimes can be quite harsh. Also, avoid negative or emotionally driven responses. Simply respond to the critique, point by point to avoid ambiguity, and make your responses as easy as possible for reviewers to digest, especially if they are measuring your responses against enumerated criteria.

In some of the courses I teach in meteorology, students undertake term projects and prepare conference-style papers which they then review—as peers—via the single-blind process. I find it fascinating that students are very adroit in identifying shortcomings in the work of their classmates, while making *exactly* the same mistakes in their own papers! This is why peer review is valuable, and why we, as scholars, must rely upon and *trust* one another to thoughtfully critique each other's work. In this way, we help ensure the research enterprise operates with maximum quality and integrity.

Assess Your Comprehension

1. What are some of the foundational benefits to subjecting research and creative activity to critical evaluation and scrutiny?

2. Define peer review and explain its core components. How does it relate to merit review?

3. Explain the foundational principles of peer review.

4. To what forms of scholarship can peer review be applied?

5. Outline the process of peer review utilized by the National Science Foundation (NSF).

6. Describe the two review criteria used by NSF to assess research grant proposals.

7. List a few ways in which the proposal review processes conducted by the National Institutes of Health (NIH) and the National Endowment for the Arts (NEA) differ from those of NSF.

8. What is a committee of visitors at NSF?

9. Outline the generic process of peer review applied by journals.

10. Describe key strengths and weaknesses of classical peer review.

11. Compare and contrast single-blind and double-blind peer review and list strengths and weaknesses of both.

12. What is meant by open peer review, and how does it differ from the classical model?

13. Describe other variations on classical peer review and ways in which they are formulated to improve upon the traditional process.

14. List several ways to most effectively interpret and utilize critical evaluation of your work.

15. What things should you carefully avoid doing when responding to critical evaluation of your work?

Exercises to Deepen Your Understanding

Exercise 1: This chapter described a number of strengths and weaknesses associated with peer review and also presented several alternative models now being explored. Using that information plus references provided, devise a new, never-before tried method of peer review and describe your rationale for it. Note that your new method can be a variation upon an existing method but must be different from what now exists. What problems or limitations does your method seek to address? Why do you feel your method improves upon existing methods? How might you suggest conducting a pilot project to evaluate your method in a head-to-head competition against existing methods?

Exercise 2: Describe a situation in which you, or your work, were evaluated either by a peer or a mentor or teacher. Consider sports, presentations, performances, a paper or proposal, and so on. What form did the evaluation take, and did it utilize specified criteria? How did you react initially to the evaluation, and ultimately, how did you utilize it? Did you find it helpful? Now turn the tables and describe a situation in which you evaluated the work of someone else. Were you reluctant to be critical? Was your identity known to the one being evaluated? How did they respond to your evaluation, and did you have an opportunity to discuss it with them? To your knowledge, did they benefit from it? If so, how?

Exercise 3: The merit review principles and criteria used by the National Science Foundation (NSF) may be found at the following link (see the table of contents): https://www.nsf.gov/pubs/policydocs/pappg22_1/nsf22_1.pdf. Read them carefully and provide a critical analysis of their strengths and weaknesses. What recommendations would you make to NSF to improve both the principles and the criteria, and how might such changes, if implemented, be viewed by the research community? Also, comment on how your recommended changes might impact public perception about the effective use of taxpayer dollars to fund basic research.

Exercise 4: Select two federal agencies (other than NSF) and two nonprofit foundations that provide funding for research and compare and contrast their criteria for evaluating grant proposals. A list of federal agencies is located at https://www.grants.gov/learn-grants/grant-making-agencies.html, and a list of several private foundations that fund science is located at https://sciencephilanthropyalliance.org/. Additional foundations may be found at https://oedb.org/ilibrarian/100_places_to_find_funding_your_research/. The reader can locate other foundations in nonscience/STEM fields via an Internet search. What are the greatest similarities and differences? How could both federal agencies and nonprofit foundations benefit from using certain elements of each other's procedures and criteria, and why did you select those procedures and criteria as mechanisms of improvement?

Exercise 5: Over the past several years, Congress has entered the debate about merit review, in some cases with a specific desire to improve transparency and accountability. This includes ensuring that the "good old boy" system, in which those traditionally receiving high marks continue to receive them, does not prevent entry of investigators who are in earlier stages of their career, and that the work being funded by the federal government indeed is worthy of taxpayer dollars. Proposed actions have included publicly disclosing, on federal funding agency web sites prior to a decision being made by program officers, full proposals as submitted, complete reviews of proposals including reviewer names and affiliations, and full responses to reviews. Describe the potential benefits and drawbacks to these proposed actions, taking the point of view of investigators, funding agencies, academic institutions, taxpayers, national security interests, and the science enterprise broadly. Do you feel, on balance, that such actions would be beneficial or harmful, and why?

8

We See the World Differently: Bias and Differing Views

Chapter Overview and Learning Objectives

Whether we realize it or not, everyone has biases. In many cases, they are manifested as behavior impacting our decisions or recommendations, often leading to undesirable outcomes. Although bias is not inherently negative, it can have a profound effect on society, including the research enterprise. Indeed, bias appears in a variety of forms in research and creative activity, ranging from how reviewers are influenced by the names, institutions, races, and quality of writing in grant proposals, books, and journal manuscripts, to how researchers gather and interpret content from interviews or performances. Education regarding the nature and forms of bias, and the ability to identify and mitigate it, are critically important for research and creative activity to operate with integrity and flourish.

This chapter describes the fundamental concept of bias, the types of bias present in the research enterprise and their associated impacts, and strategies for mitigating bias in various forms. It also provides perspectives regarding bias in peer review across a wide range of stakeholders. After reading this chapter, you should

- Understand the concepts of bias and discrimination;
- Understand the differences between conscious and unconscious bias;
- Be able to describe the types of bias occurring in research and creative activity and understand their associated impacts;
- Understand and be able to apply actions for mitigating bias, and know how to access associated resources for doing so; and
- Understand the differing views of bias among key stakeholders and the factors giving rise to them.

8.1   Defining and Understanding Bias

What comes to mind when you hear the word "bias"? Most likely, something negative, such as bias against a particular race, political party, or media outlet. On the heels of that thought, you may reflect that you hold no such biases but know individuals who do. Take a moment to think about biases in your life and the extent to which they are either positive or negative. Also, consider whether such biases impact your behavior, or simply are beliefs upon which you never act.

A word closely related to bias is discrimination, which today has an almost purely negative connotation. Yet, bias and discrimination are not always pejorative. You can, for example, have discriminating taste in food or clothing, the type of car you choose to drive, or in art and music. Funding agency program officers must discriminate among a wide range of comments in selecting which proposal is worthy of support. They also sometimes have to apply measures to ensure geographic, disciplinary, or other types of balance in their funding portfolios. If done ethically, none of these actions or their outcomes is improper.

An interesting fact about discrimination and bias is that they are related, and both can occur quite intentionally or completely subconsciously. In this book, we are concerned with the intentional and unintentional application of bias, with the former being addressed largely by oversight and peer assessment mechanisms described previously (chapters 6 and 7) and in chapter 10. It is the latter—unconscious, negative, and potentially harmful bias—that is more challenging to understand and address and is the subject of the current chapter.

At its very core, bias is the tendency to *think or reason* in a particular way and is a shortcut of sorts for how we process and retain information. Bias is not behavior per se, but it is a partial determinant of behavior. According to the *Oxford English Dictionary*, bias is a "Tendency to favour or dislike a person or thing, especially as a result of a preconceived opinion; partiality, prejudice" (Bias n.d.-b). The *Cambridge English Dictionary* defines bias as "The action of supporting or opposing a particular person or thing in an unfair way, because of allowing personal opinions to influence your judgment" (Bias n.d.-a). Note that both definitions portray bias in a negative light which, as I just explained, is not always the case. Note also how the latter definition involves action, not simply a point of view.

With regard to our focus on scrutinizing research and creative activity, say using peer review, bias generally is viewed as violating the principle of impartiality (chapter 7). What is impartiality? Quoting from Lee et al. (2013, 4), it is "the ability for any reviewer to interpret and apply evaluative criteria in the same way in the assessment of a submission." In other words, ideally—and that is an important word—any reviewer who holds no bias would apply the criteria in exactly the same manner and arrive at the same result, completely independent from "the author's and reviewer's social identities and also the reviewer's theoretical biases and tolerance for risk." The identities being spoken of include but are not limited to one's sex, race, ethnicity, institutional affiliation, current and/or previous positions or titles, professional expertise, publication record, awards received, and so on. In today's social media culture, identity also can be a function of what one posts or tweets, including comments made on items posted by others.

Bias comes to our attention, and to the attention of others, when it actively, even unconsciously, influences our behavior. As a result, we make decisions that end up being flawed or narrow. When a given bias is established based upon information not grounded in fact or agreed-upon truth—for example, all people with blue eyes are smarter than people with brown eyes—its influence may result in decisions and behaviors that are in opposition to fact and truth. By this description, bias has influenced behavior. However, without the behavior, the bias may or may not be known to self or others.

We use observations of behavior to gain insight into our own or another person's thinking. When behavior suggests thinking is biased in opposition to fact or truth, what should we attempt to do? Change the behavior, change the thinking, or both?

Training on conscious and unconscious bias, described below, addresses both types of potential change but also the impacts upon patterns of thought. And, if the influences on thinking are unconscious—that is, the thinker is unaware of the influence—then it becomes difficult to address changes in thinking. One first has to assist the thinker in becoming aware of these influences, followed by them understanding and accepting that bias indeed influenced their behavior.

Bias has been and continues to be studied extensively. As you might imagine, a wide range of views exists regarding the extent to which bias present in our subconscious mind actually influences our behavior. What is not questioned is the fundamental existence of unconscious bias, and the fact that bias clearly is present in research and creative activity.

8.2 Types of Bias and Their Impacts: The Research Process

Before examining various classifications and types of bias, it is useful to formally define it in the context of research and creative activity. Definitions, and their interpretation and application, depend somewhat upon the nature of the research being performed (e.g., qualitative, quantitative, clinical). In general, however, bias in research and creative activity occurs when prejudiced, unfair, or tainted practices intentionally or unintentionally affect the planning, structure, execution, and outcomes of the work. Because bias ultimately leads to conclusions that deviate from the actual outcomes, it violates the fundamental tenets of scholarly conduct (section 9.2 and chapter 10).

The broad universe of research bias can be placed within two buckets: implicit, unintentional, or unconscious bias, and explicit, intentional, and conscious bias. Although the terminology largely is self-explanatory, a closer look is valuable.

Implicit bias occurs when we act out our views and beliefs—including prejudices, stereotypes, and attitudes—without awareness or intent. Common examples include giving higher scores to job applicants if their names sound Caucasian or European or providing greater weight to advice given by a male colleague—in both cases "without even thinking." Explicit bias is just the opposite; namely, when actions are intentional and based upon biased views inconsistent with known facts.

Within these two broad categories, bias can occur within the research process itself (i.e., as part of project planning, design, data collection, execution, analysis, and presentation of results), and within peer/merit review (e.g., of grant proposals, journal manuscripts, performances, and exhibitions). Because research can, in general, be classified as qualitative, quantitative, or mixed (section 4.1), various types of bias sometimes exist within all three categories, with bias in clinical trials often classified separately. To avoid confusion, given that some types of bias are common to multiple research frameworks, I simply describe the more common biases in both the research process as well as peer review, providing examples of their occurrence and impact. Numerous references are provided if you wish to explore bias in greater depth (e.g., Pannucci and Wilkins 2010; Lee et al. 2013; Ioannidis et al. 2014; Sarniak 2015; Batterbee 2017; Tricco et al. 2017; Nosek et al. 2018; Mehta 2019; Roper 2019; Bradley et al. 2020).

Beginning with the first steps of the research process, *design bias* occurs when the structure, methodologies, and processes used to conduct research are based not upon objectively determined or previously successful approaches, but rather upon your own preferences or other subjective determinations. You may, for example, be attracted by the simplicity of a particular method, its shallow learning curve, or the ready availability or low cost of needed software. As described in section 4.7, poor experiment design, whether done intentionally or unintentionally, is one of the leading causes of irreproducible or flawed results. If you believe your research methodologies are not firmly grounded, seek guidance from others, especially if you are employing methods, such as certain statistics, with which you are not completely familiar.

As described in chapter 5, the collection of data for research—in the form of observations, measurements, population samples, documents, recordings, or videos—is foundational to the research process. Not surprisingly, bias can occur during these activities and is known as *data collection/sampling/measurement bias*. In the case of physical instruments, bias can occur as a result of improper calibration or use. Observations can be biased if not collected in ways that account for outliers, bad data points, or are taken during times and in locations that fail to accurately portray reality (e.g., a video showing a small protest being portrayed as if it is taking place over a huge area). Bias in population samples—such as surveys of public opinion—can occur if the samples do not reflect the make-up of the population, if only certain dimensions of sampling are considered (e.g., sampling from users of a particular social media platform as a proxy for all of society), or if a particular part of the population is systematically excluded. The latter example is illustrative of *selection/participant bias*. Fortunately, sampling bias is well understood, and consequently a variety of approaches exist to address it.

Historical bias is an issue in social and behavioral science research and can be manifest in surveys as changes in participant responses owing to the occurrence of a particular event. For example, scholars conduct surveys nationally to determine the extent to which the general population is aware of certain weather patterns, events, and climate change. A response can be skewed if, for example, someone was impacted personally by a recent storm or wildfire. Similarly, statistics of particular events, such as tornadoes, protests, and homelessness, have been greatly impacted by the proliferation of mobile phones and social media. Is the number of tornadoes really increasing, or are more simply being reported and documented as a result of technology? In this case, historical and observation bias converge!

In section 4.4, we examined Indigenous research methods and described the importance of culture not only as a research topic, but also as part of the research process itself. Challenges exist when conducting research through a particular cultural lens, which can lead to *cultural bias*. More specifically, cultural bias occurs when researchers employ their own cultural norms, values, and standards to the study of other people, groups, or communities that do not subscribe to them. The evaluation of island tribal families from the viewpoint of Western familial structures is an example. This type of bias can result in misleading or incorrect conclusions, and even harm the community being studied (section 4.4).

Procedural bias, as the name implies, takes place when procedures used in research are constrained artificially and thus negatively affect the outcome. In the context of social and behavioral sciences research, this type of bias occurs if survey technology requires the interpretation of color and thus creates different responses for those who are colorblind (assuming color differentiation is not the topic of the study), if insufficient time is allocated for survey completion, or if the survey is conducted at times and locations that preclude certain individuals from participating.

The analysis of data is a key component of the research process (chapters 4 and 5), and thus awareness of *analysis bias* is critical for obtaining unbiased outcomes. This type of bias occurs when a researcher is influenced by his or her own desired outcomes, and then takes steps in the analysis process to steer the results toward them. Two of the "big three" forms of research misconduct (chapter 9) rear their heads at this point. That is, researchers can fabricate data by simply creating information that was not collected, and they can falsify data by excluding or modifying certain values to improve the results. Fortunately, efforts to ensure reproducibility (section 4.7) are aiding in the identification of this nefarious bias.

Closely related to analysis bias is *confirmation bias*, which involves seeking evidence, interpreting data or other information, and storing and recalling facts in a way that confirms existing beliefs or expected outcomes. This well-known bias manifests in everyday life when, for example, we read news articles, or watch news programs, that align with and thus reinforce our political or cultural worldviews. In the context of research, confirmation bias is a "tunnel vision" of sorts that can greatly limit one's ability to explore new avenues or utilize the work of others. In extreme cases, it can lead to analysis and interpretation bias. As noted in the next section, confirmation bias is particularly problematic in peer/merit review, where the reviewer assesses a proposal, manuscript, or performance through their own perspectives or work rather than a broad context of previous work.

Anchoring bias occurs when a researcher is overly influenced by one theory or study (the anchor, which sometimes is their own work), or by the first impression they had on a given topic, thus leading them to ignore other sources. Strongly held views often are difficult to overcome and can lead to "blind spots" that hinder consideration of other perspectives. In a similar vein, the *halo effect* occurs when our overall impression of an individual influences our views toward other dimensions of their personality or character, even if we do not know them personally. For example, a researcher may seek to collaborate with a world-renowned scholar, presuming that because they are brilliant and successful, they also will be an effective collaborator (chapter 13).

Another important bias is *publication bias*, which concerns the tendency for journals to avoid publishing negative results; that is, research in which results opposite those expected were obtained despite sound experiment design and data analysis. One such example concerns a study (Mehta 2019) in which a gene-editing tool was used in an attempt to render a particular tropical plant—one that is a staple of the diets of a billion people—resistant to a viral disease. The results obtained showed that the genetic intervention not only failed to create immunity, as originally envisioned based upon previous work, but actually led to greater vulnerability to disease. Although the paper describing these results was in fact published, many researchers do not even bother submitting papers regarding negative results, thereby influencing statistics regarding trends in scholarly topics and outcomes and depriving other researchers of knowing the negative outcomes.

Although some consider publication bias synonymous with *citation bias*, I prefer to view citation bias as including the tendency for researchers to cite their own prior work over the work of others. This type of bias gives readers an inappropriately narrow impression and can be especially harmful to early-career scholars. The correct approach is of course to cite all relevant literature even if the outcomes of other studies, or the views of other scholars, are inconsistent with your own.

8.3   Types of Bias and Their Impacts: Peer/Merit Review

Bias in peer/merit review—irrespective of the discipline and form in which such review occurs—is an exceptionally important issue. Why? Because subjecting scholarly work to scrutiny (chapters 6 and 7) helps ensure its outcomes are consistent with scholarly values (chapter 9).

In virtually all situations, peer review involves three participants: the scholar(s) and their work, the reviewer(s), and the sponsor or publisher. Here, I presume the sponsor or publisher is operating with integrity, is broadly inclusive in selecting reviewers, addresses conflicts of interest, and only applies bias in an appropriate manner. Likewise, I assume the scholar(s) evidence little or no bias of the types described in the previous section, leaving us to focus on bias associated with the reviewer(s) and review process.

The first type of bias concerns how reviewers interpret scholar characteristics. Reviewers may be biased, in a positive or negative manner, by the *institutional affiliation* of the scholar. For example, if the scholar is employed by a highly prestigious institution, the reviewer might not conduct as thorough a review, presuming the work to be solid (this is an example of *prestige bias*—see below). Or, the reviewer might not be favorably inclined toward the work, irrespective of its quality, if they applied for but were not selected for a position at the same institution ("sour grapes"). *Affiliation bias* also can occur if the scholar and reviewer are personal friends. Although professional interactions of scholars are now required to be disclosed by virtually every funding organization, the review process usually does not address personal scholar-reviewer interactions.

Another example of prestige bias is reflected in the familiar saying, "the rich get richer." That is, scholars from prestigious institutions may tend to be funded more frequently, and receive more funding, than those at other institutions. Data show that roughly half of NSF funding for research goes to fifty universities in the US (National Science Board 2021a). However, one also must recognize that such institutions tend to have outstanding facilities, highly accomplished faculty, vast research administrative support structures, and funding to incentivize and support research and creative activity. Additionally, as noted in section 7.3, major federal funding organizations, such as NSF, undergo periodic review of the review process itself to help ensure it is unbiased. Consequently, I would characterize the "rich get richer" bias as equity bias, not prestige bias.

Race, gender, and nationality bias occur when reviewers presume these characteristics based upon the scholar's name. Numerous studies have been conducted on these topics, and the results are not entirely clear (e.g., Ginther et al. 2011; Kaiser 2018; National Institutes of Health n.d.-d). In general, owing to research comparing double-blind and single-blind reviews (chapter 7), gender bias appears to be less an issue than originally thought. Racial and nationality bias, with the latter often manifest as publications favoring authors located in the same country, does appear to occur more readily, and of course, world events sometimes impact these issues (e.g., relations between the US and China).

Finally, *language bias* occurs when the scholar's native language is not the same as that of the reviewer. This can make difficult the reviewer's ability to understand and assess the content of the proposal or article, leading to frustration on the part of the reviewer and thus a negative evaluation. Many years ago, a reviewer usually could decline to review a submission if the writing was deemed substandard or a barrier to assessment. However, more recently, funding organizations have attempted to address language bias by urging reviewers to proceed even if they find a language barrier to be problematic.

Turning now to reviewer assessment of submission content, *content bias* can occur regarding anything associated with the work (goals, structure, execution, analysis, etc.). Confirmation bias, described in the preceding section, is an important consideration for peer review, as is *bias against interdisciplinary work*.

With regard to the latter, historically, the single-authored publication and single-investigator grant proposal (section 1.4) were viewed as most prestigious, especially prior to the establishment of integrative disciplines such as biomedical engineering and entrepreneurship. Indeed, some scholars prefer deep dives in a single discipline while others lean more toward boundary-spanning activities. This can lead to biases in reviews, though of course one also has to consider possible impacts of the ability of funding organizations and publishers to facilitate review of submissions involving multiple disciplines.

One of the topics I worked on as a member of NSB (National Science Board 2007) was the inherently conservative nature of peer review (especially when conducted in panel form) and the tendency for reviewers to dismiss or overlook potentially transformative research that might overturn established paradigms (section 7.4). This characteristic is known as *conservatism bias* and is something I addressed while serving at the White House. Specifically, I argued to Congress that failure to consistently fund potentially transformative research would impact America's competitiveness, and that eventually, scholars would stop submitting such proposals and ultimately even stop having big ideas!

All peer/merit reviews are conducted using evaluation criteria supplied by the sponsor or publisher (chapter 7). They vary from methodological and technical issues—such as goals, design, approaches used, data, quality of analyses, and logic of conclusions—to project justification, effectiveness of presentation, and potential impact on the scholarly record. Such criteria usually are well explained and, in some cases, involve numerical ratings. However, they differ considerably in their nature, and possibly in their relative importance in the eyes of the reviewer. Ultimately, reviewers must synthesize assessments across this broad space and arrive at a single numerical rating or conclusion: accept, reject, fund, decline, and so on. *Commensuration bias* is a term used to describe how some criteria are prioritized by reviewers over others, which can lead to problematic decisions that are inconsistent with the intent of the sponsor or publisher.

8.4   Approaches for Mitigating Bias

It is unrealistic to believe bias can be eliminated completely in the manner conflicts of interest can be eliminated or managed (chapters 9 and 10). Rather, the goal for you, as a next-generation scholar, is to understand various types of bias and how it is manifested, and to use this understanding to reduce your own biases and their impact on the research enterprise.

Consequently, the first and most important step to bias mitigation in research and creative activity is education and training. Numerous resources exist, ranging from those offered at academic institutions—often as part of compliance training regarding bias and discrimination in the workplace—or as formal courses on research methods. Additional training is available via in-person and online courses, seminars offered by professional societies, and guidance provided by federal agencies and publishers. If your institution does not provide training in research compliance that includes the topic of bias, consult your advisor or senior research officer to learn about options available to you.

A variety of specific actions exist for reducing bias in both research and peer/merit review. Those that span multiple types of bias include registering experiments and reports in advance (section 4.7), attempting to replicate research results (section 4.7)—a process facilitated by open access to data (section 11.2)—use of double-blind or open peer review (section 7.5), rigorous management of conflicts of interest (sections 10.2 and 10.3), and improving diversity among reviewers.

Confirmation bias, the halo effect, and cultural bias all can be reduced by challenging your own thinking and presumptions regarding the work of others, the characteristics and culture of the people you study, and the viewpoints you hold. Try to formulate alternative views and seek peers or those senior to you to discuss your thoughts and approaches. You might be surprised at how quickly such discussions expose biases of which you were unaware, and lead to specific steps you can take to address them. Strategies for mitigating other types of bias can be found in the literature, including the references noted previously.

Although the existence of bias in the research enterprise is well established, additional research is needed to fully understand its manifestation, frequency of occurrence, the nature and depth of its impacts both short and long term, and the effectiveness of mitigation measures.

The bottom line with regard to bias—and something I hope you internalize from this chapter—is that in the research enterprise, bias exists, its influence can be positive but usually is quite negative and limiting, it is a very complex topic that needs more attention, and mechanisms exist to reduce its influence even as we continue to learn more about it.

8.5 Differing Points of View: Agencies, Publishers, the Research Community, the Public, and Law/Policy Makers

In chapter 7, we examined the role, process, and value of peer/merit review in research and creative activity. We also noted that, although peer review is not perfect, with variations always being explored, the foundational concepts of peer review continue to serve well the research enterprise and society more broadly. Indeed, no radically new approach has arisen to replace it on a large scale. Despite these facts, and in some sense because of them, multiple perspectives exist regarding peer review among audiences such as the general public, law and policy makers, and private corporations.

Considering first the general public, their trust in the research enterprise is quite high, second only to the military (chapter 3). It therefore is not surprising that, in the eyes of the public, the rigorous processes associated with peer review lead to trust and the assurance of quality. The public is not aware, nor should we expect it be, of realities such as differences in quality and rigor among journals, inherent limitations of the peer review process (including its inability to identify all fraud or other misconduct), and of course, bias.

However, public awareness regarding research is probably higher now than at any previous time owing in no small part to the COVID-19 pandemic. This is a very positive development. Consequently, now is a good time for researchers to dialogue with the public about the scrutiny of research outcomes, and how our understanding based upon research evolves over time mostly via incremental advances and rigorous debate and disagreement. Researchers also need to make clear their recognition of, and desire to continue addressing, important issues such as bias, the protection of research assets from malign foreign government interference (section 10.3), and research misconduct (chapter 9). It is not up to the public to seek us out! The greater the transparency, accountability, and trust between researchers and taxpayers, the more effective the research enterprise.

Turning to private companies, especially those in the pharmaceutical arena, they understandably are cautious about subjecting their internal research to broad scrutiny as their competitive edge depends upon maintaining confidentiality, and because of the high monetary stakes involved. Yet, such lack of transparency and accountability naturally leads to suspicions that unfavorable findings may be suppressed or that rigorous methods are not being employed. And some reason exists for these fears based upon past revelations, including most recently in the automobile industry (e.g., Mehrotra and Welch 2017), where test results regarding emissions were modified and later uncovered. Of course, we must avoid painting the entire private sector with a broad brush because the majority of companies most likely operate with integrity and are subject to other forms of evaluation and compliance.

Finally, policy and law makers have widely differing views of the peer review process and, in some cases, about the integrity of the research enterprise as a whole. Perhaps most prominent among the skeptics was US senator William Proxmire, who in the mid-1970s established the Golden Fleece Award to highlight examples of what he considered wasteful federal spending on procurements, research, and programs (Wisconsin Historical Society n.d.). As you might imagine, not everyone agreed with the senator's assessments. And indeed, a counterpart award, known as the Golden Goose Award (http:// goldengooseaward.org), was established in 2012 to recognize scientists whose federally funded basic research has substantially impacted society in notably positive ways.

Yet, the Golden Fleece theme survives. Senators now publish a yearly *Wastebook* and *Federal Fumbles* (Flake 2015, 2017; Lankford 2017) to highlight what they consider wasteful and unnecessary activities, including specific research projects funded with taxpayer dollars. And indeed, I do myself wonder how a small number of projects get funded. Additionally, some politicians have questioned peer review at federal agencies and especially the criteria by which decisions are made.

Although it may be easy, as current- and next-generation scholars, to become frustrated with viewpoints and strategies that do not align with our own, we must never forget—as described in the next section—that the opinions of others are useful if we choose to respect, understand, and as appropriate take time to act upon them.

For example, NSF now formally responds to the *Federal Fumbles* publication (National Science Foundation n.d.-c, n.d.-d). In so doing, NSF provides itself an opportunity to reflect more deeply upon the work it funds and perhaps modify the manner in which descriptions of it are conveyed to general audiences. The originator of *Federal Fumbles* has an opportunity to better understand the true value of research that was criticized and perhaps not effectively portrayed by NSF, and the overall exchange helps the general public continue knowing that open, thoughtful, and well-intentioned debate still occurs, thus leading to an even more robust and trustworthy research enterprise.

Assess Your Comprehension

1. Define bias in the context of research and creative activity and compare and contrast it with discrimination.
2. Do bias and discrimination always constitute negative behaviors?
3. Does bias always determine behavior?
4. What are the principal differences between conscious and unconscious bias?
5. Compare and contrast the key types of bias that occur in the research enterprise.

6. In what ways is bias manifested differently in publications, peer review, and various stages of the research process?

7. What types of bias do you believe are potentially most damaging to research?

8. What mechanisms exist to address bias?

9. Compare and contrast the views toward peer review by the public and private sectors.

10. What is the Golden Fleece Award?

11. What can federal agencies and the research enterprise more broadly learn by carefully considering the Golden Fleece Award, *Federal Fumbles*, and similar assessments?

12. In what ways can bias impact potentially transformative ideas and proposals to pursue them?

13. Why should researchers not dismiss public opinion about their work?

14. What resources exist for you to learn more about bias?

15. Without painting groups with a broad brush, compare and contrast the views toward bias generally held by researchers, publishers, law and policy makers, funding organizations, and the general public. Discuss the reasons for any differences that exist.

Exercises to Deepen Your Understanding

Exercise 1: Whether we realize it or not, all of us have inherent biases on a wide range of topics or issues, and in many cases these biases impact decisions we make or actions we recommend. In fact, researchers from Harvard University, the University of Virginia, and the University of Washington have created "Project Implicit," which includes tests to measure our unconscious biases. For this exercise, utilize the Project Implicit evaluation framework (https://implicit.harvard.edu/implicit/) to learn about your own biases. After completing the tests, reflect on the results and summarize them. Were you surprised? Do you think the results will impact your behavior or views in the future?

Exercise 2: As noted in this chapter, a wide array of bias types exists in the context of scholarly activity. Select a half dozen or so biases and compare and contrast them (a comprehensive list of biases, with examples and impacts, can be found at https://catalogofbias.org/biases/). What common features do you find among them, and how specifically do they differ? Place them in the context of your own research or creative activity and describe how such biases might be manifest, as well as their possible impacts.

Exercise 3: Bias is an issue principally when manifest as behavior, and in the world today, bias is a popular topic of discussion from politics to science, from race to immigration. Select two to three such topics and expound upon them in light of the biases you perceive to exist, using information from this chapter, and supplementary resources, to guide your analysis. Do you find yourself frequently noticing bias in society? If so, in what ways do you believe it is harmful in the context in which it occurs? How might it be reduced?

Exercise 4: A recent study (cited at https://psyarxiv.com/r2xvb/) finds no race or gender bias in the peer review of US National Institutes of Health (NIH) grant proposals, which contradicts earlier published findings cited at https://www.nature.com/articles/news.2008.988. Yet many are convinced bias in peer review is pervasive and serious. Considering this issue, study the two articles provided and use the Internet to identify other sources. How would you frame the argument of bias in peer review and explain the situation to a member of Congress?

Exercise 5: Contact the office of sponsored programs at your institution (typically housed within the office of the vice president or vice chancellor for research) to determine what types of bias training are available to faculty, staff researchers, and graduate and undergraduate students (if your institution has no such office, contact your advisor, department chair, or dean to determine how you can complete training in bias related to research). If you have never completed such training, do so now and comment on its breadth and depth. How do the issues raised apply to your own research or creative activity, and do you feel you have exhibited bias in your scholarly work, either consciously or unconsciously? If so, elaborate.

9

Honesty Is the Best Policy: Ethical Conduct and Research Integrity

Chapter Overview and Learning Objectives

From promoting moral or social values when collaborating with others to building and maintaining public support and accountability, adhering to ethical standards is a critical element of the research process. This chapter describes responsible conduct of research, how ethics is applied in a research context, and the increasing importance of ethical conduct in research today. Additionally, it provides insight into research misconduct behaviors, their associated consequences, and strategies for creating and maintaining an ethical program of scholarship. After reading this chapter, you should

- Have a strong appreciation for the importance of ethical conduct in research and how upholding values and ethical standards is foundational to the research process;
- Understand the difference between ethics and morality and how to apply ethical principles in research;
- Understand the "big three" types of research misconduct: plagiarism, fabrication, and falsification;
- Be able to identify research misconduct and understand the consequences associated with it;
- Understand the importance of integrity in federal and other government science and how political influence can undermine the use of scientific results;
- Know where to find resources and training materials about responsible conduct of research; and
- Know how to create and maintain an ethical program of scholarship.

9.1   Importance of Responsible Conduct of Research

It is impossible these days to turn on the television or radio, or read a newspaper or online news publication, without learning of the latest scandal or example of bad behavior. Not necessarily a violation of law, but some act that clearly is deemed unacceptable by society: from power and greed in the corporate world that can bring down entire organizations to doping in sports, sexual misconduct in the workplace—even in Congress and the ministry—to covering up indiscretions that might have occurred long ago. Unethical and immoral behaviors seemingly surround us. Perhaps some of us even experienced this firsthand by cheating in school to get that better grade so we could land a scholarship or play on the varsity team. Or maybe we told the truth but with the intent to deceive by withholding some of the facts when confronted by an authority.

We humans obviously have shortcomings, yet humans are at the center of the research enterprise. This begs the question of how morals and ethical behavior figure into that enterprise. Are most researchers honest in how they devise and conduct their experiments? Analyze their data? Present their findings? If research misconduct occurs, what forms does it take, and what motivates people to behave badly? And then what happens if one gets caught? What are the penalties? How high are the stakes? We consider these and other questions in the current chapter, which is among the most important in the entire book. For without responsible and ethical behavior in research, everything else is irrelevant.

Ethical conduct in research, also referred to as responsible conduct of research (RCR) or responsible and ethical conduct of research (RECR), is part of a broader topic known as research compliance. Ultimately, the goal of research compliance, which comprises rules, regulations, laws, and norms involving numerous topics—including ethical norms—is to drive human behavior in certain directions that are deemed essential for ensuring high standards of research practice, personal conduct, and professional accountability. Chapter 10 is devoted to research compliance topics, and in it you will learn about protocols for research involving human and animal subjects, chemical and laboratory safety, conflict of interest, use of controlled substances, clinical trials, research security, the effective handling of restricted or sensitive information, and more.

Before addressing ethics more deeply in the next section, consider first the importance of RECR. Many reasons exist for ethical conduct, but I like how NIH explains it (National Institutes of Health n.d.-a). First, as you know by now from preceding chapters, research involves a variety of methods and procedures, with notable variations among disciplines (chapter 4). Research also involves perspectives. A physical scientist studying climate change, for example, may have a perspective different from that of a philosopher or historian studying the same topic—and both will use very different approaches for asking and analyzing questions. Disciplines have their own standards for behavior that link to their approaches and goals, which helps scholars to trust one another and the public to trust scholars. Additionally, these standards promote the aims of research, such as developing new knowledge, sticking to the truth in what is uncovered, and avoiding errors. In short, ethical norms play a key role in being able to trust research outcomes.

Second, as we will discuss in chapter 13, research frequently involves collaboration within disciplines and also across them. Ethical standards promote values, and lead to trust, mutual respect, and equitable treatment, all of which are critical elements of working with other people. This especially comes into play when determining how much credit to assign team members as coauthors on a paper, or in an invention disclosure or patent filing. Third—and we touched on this earlier—ethical norms help ensure accountability to those funding the research which, in many cases, is the taxpayer. We address this issue further in chapter 10.

Fourth, ethical norms help build public support for research. If the public knows research is being performed with integrity, taxpayers will have greater comfort in providing funding. (Recall from chapter 3 that public trust in research leaders is second only to that for the military.) Fifth, ethical standards evidenced in research demonstrate more broadly the importance of moral and social values, including human rights, for example. Indeed, as noted at the beginning of this chapter, it is difficult to find examples in society today where ethical standards are uniformly high and conduct is beyond reproach. The research enterprise is without question an important beacon for such behavior, and it does not go unnoticed.

Finally, as noted in section 3.4, the conduct of research itself must be kept free from political or other influence so that results are obtained following accepted practices with the highest integrity. This is true irrespective of the type of organization in which the work is performed, as noted in a report by the National Science and Technology Council (2022b) regarding protecting the integrity of government science—particularly the use of scientific results in policy. Some in the scientific community even have called for the creation of a government-operated research policy board (Gunsalis et al. 2019) to focus on research robustness and quality.

9.2 Ethics and Morality and Applying Ethical Behavior to Research

The words "ethics" and "morality" often are used interchangeably, but in fact are different. Most would agree that ethics is best reflected by the Golden Rule, which states, "Do unto others as you would have them do unto you." You probably heard this as a child. I know I did, though I rarely applied it! In this context, and others such as the physician's Hippocratic Oath, ethics is our road map or set of norms for distinguishing right from wrong—acceptable from unacceptable behavior. Actually, to be precise, ethics is a branch of scholarship involving the study of morality, but we will use the terms interchangeably here. So, what is morality? It is a foundational set of behavioral norms to which we adhere. Who gets to determine what is moral or immoral? For the most part, society does. For example, that murder is immoral and thus unacceptable in most cultures.

We become aware of morals from a variety of influences throughout our life—such as parents, places of worship, school, friends, television, and now social media. And these morals are what shape our values, which are our personal beliefs and application of morals. One of my favorite quotes is "Early in life we shape our values, and thereafter our values shape us." Another one, from Roy E. Disney, is "When your values are clear to you, making decisions becomes easier" (Roy E. Disney Quotes n.d.). I would add that, in my view, morals are what we believe, and ethics is what we do with them—how we act out our moral principles. We will return to this point shortly because, although it may seem as though ethics mostly involve common sense principles, people interpret them differently based upon their own life experiences.

If not apparent already, you soon will discover that bright lines do not always exist between ethical and unethical or marginally ethical conduct in research. Why? Because choices and judgments involving ethics must be made, and interpretations vary about what is acceptable and unacceptable in a given situation. However, one hard truth is that responsible conduct, and following all rules of compliance, is up to *individual* researchers. No excuses can be made for failure to understand rules and ethical norms, or for ignoring them. The consequences of failing in this regard do not fall on our institutions or mentors, but rather they fall squarely on us—the researcher—personally and professionally.

With that preface, it is important to recognize that moral norms are related to, but different than, formal laws. This distinction is important in research because in some situations unethical behavior is not formally illegal. And one could argue the reverse more broadly in society—namely, that some behavior that is formally illegal can in fact be ethical. Immigration is an excellent example. Entering the US without following the proper procedures is formally illegal. However, for those who entered illegally, say twenty years ago and have been model citizens, some believe it would be immoral or unethical to now deport them.

So, what does the research ethics road map look like? What are the rules? Again, to some extent this depends upon disciplines. However, a foundational moral or ethical code for research does exist, and once again, NIH provides excellent information. First and foremost is *honesty*, which means being truthful in all aspects of research. Never fabricate, falsify, or misrepresent data (more on these topics in the next section), deceive colleagues, research sponsors, or the public, or tell the truth with the intent to deceive. On the heels of honesty comes *integrity*, which means acting with sincerity and consistency. Closely related is *objectivity*, which means avoiding bias (chapter 8) in all aspects of the research process where being objective—which is the hallmark of research—is required.

Be diligent and thoughtful in all you do, keeping excellent records and reviewing results multiple times to ensure their correctness. If you find yourself hurrying to meet a deadline, you may be tempted to skirt the rules or not check facts. Never allow that to happen! As noted in chapter 10, you, as the researcher, have grave responsibility for managing information, money, relationships, and processes that require following strict rules. If you make a practice of doing the right things for the right reasons, and also seek the advice of others if you are uncertain about a particular situation, you will successfully uphold the moral code that underpins the research enterprise.

9.3 Research Misconduct and Associated Consequences

Having examined the concepts of ethics and morality and the role they play in the research enterprise, let us flip the coin and examine circumstances under which ethical breaches occur in research. This is known as research misconduct.

Following adoption of a federal policy on research misconduct in 2000 by OSTP, the Office of Research Integrity (ORI; http://ori.hhs.gov) of the US Department of Health and Human Services (DHHS; http://hhs.gov) defines research misconduct as "fabrication, falsification, or plagiarism in proposing, performing, or reviewing research, or in reporting research results" (Office of Research Integrity n.d.-a). I like to refer to fabrication, falsification, and plagiarism the "big three." According to ORI, this policy also sets the legal threshold for proving charges of misconduct. To be considered research misconduct, actions must do the following three things: first, represent a "significant departure from accepted practices"; second, have been "committed intentionally, or knowingly, or recklessly"; and third, be "proven by a preponderance of evidence." These further stipulations limit the federal government's role in research misconduct to well-documented, serious departures from accepted research practices.

Let us unpack the "big three" terms, again quoting federal government policy. *Fabrication* involves "making up data or results and recording or reporting them." *Falsification* involves "manipulating research materials, equipment, or processes, or changing or omitting data or results such that the research is not accurately represented in the research record." Finally, *plagiarism* involves "the appropriation of another person's ideas, processes, results, or words without giving appropriate credit." Note that research misconduct does not include honest error or differences of opinion. It also is important to note these government definitions are adopted by most public and private institutions, including research academic institutions, and were arrived at through discussions with researchers and administrators from those same institutions.

Although fabrication, falsification, and plagiarism are the foundational components of research misconduct, so-called other deviations from accepted practices are important as well and increasingly included in institutional policies. Examples of these other behaviors include publishing the same data or results in more than one publication; inappropriately assigning author credit in publications; withholding details of methodology or results in proposals; using inadequate or inappropriate experiment designs; deleting observations or data points from analyses without rigorous justification; inadequate record-keeping; failing to present data that contradict one's own findings; unauthorized use of someone else's data; changing the design of an experiment in the middle of a study; and failure to report conflicts of interest.

With all of these things in play, you might wonder how frequently research misconduct actually occurs. Although it is impossible to know for certain, studies have shown that outright fraud in the form of the "big three" is relatively rare (e.g., Steneck 2006; Bormann 2013). However, when it comes to some of the "other deviations from accepted practice," the statistics are a bit more concerning (e.g., Kalichman 2020). In various studies involving large populations of researchers, approximately 10 percent of those surveyed indicated they had done things such as dropped data points or failed to present results that contradicted their own prior research.

Because research is a human endeavor, one might believe common sense prevails in making most decisions regarding ethical conduct. However, the path to be taken when confronted with an ethical dilemma sometimes is far from clear. Even well-intentioned people make the wrong call, and often this occurs owing to pressures in research—pressures to publish and garner grants and contracts in order to secure tenure at an academic institution, pressure to perform in private industry so as to improve the corporate bottom line or get the next product to market, a desire for fame, or because of poor oversight by a superior. This is known as the "imperfect environment" theory of research misconduct because the environment in which one is embedded influences behavior.

The other theory, known as the "bad apple" theory, recognizes that bad actors can be found in virtually any human endeavor. Fortunately, as noted previously, such individuals represent a small fraction of all researchers, though sometimes their actions as so egregious as to garner a great deal of public attention. Unfortunately, this causes certain elements of society, such as members of Congress, to begin painting the research enterprise with a broad brush, believing research misconduct is widespread when in fact it is not. It also leads to unwarranted inherent conflation of certain topics, such as reproducibility of research results (section 4.7) with research misconduct.

The consequences of research misconduct can be severe, ranging from the destruction of one's reputation owing to debarment, which means prohibition from submitting grant proposals or publishing papers, to the most severe penalty of incarceration. In some situations, however, few options exist for punishment of the offender or restitution to those harmed. For example, if an academic researcher conducts experiments in one country and then steals the results and moves to an institution in another country, where the findings are published, the first institution has essentially no legal recourse. One can attempt to convince the journal involved to issue a statement or perhaps retraction, though journals tend to avoid involvement in such disputes unless the published results are demonstrably flawed.

Given the significant time and effort involved in establishing a professional reputation, the horrible outcomes associated with research misconduct tend to be sufficient to keep most researchers on the straight and narrow path of ethical behavior. Indeed, audits, the peer review process, accreditation, program review, software that identifies plagiarized material, and other factors help ensure the research enterprise operates with integrity. Collectively, these and other preventative measures lead many to characterize the research enterprise as "self-policing." Additionally, institutions, and especially academic research institutions, have strict policies for dealing with research misconduct, and they also teach faculty and students how to identify as well as report it. In fact, training in RECR is a requirement for recipients of funding from most federal agencies, which includes faculty, graduate and undergraduate students, and postdoctoral researchers. In the references you will find examples of research misconduct, including some especially famous ones (e.g., Mintz 2012; DuBois et al. 2013; Cantu n.d.).

9.4   Creating and Maintaining an Ethical Program of Scholarship

The most important and effective strategy for creating and maintaining an ethical program of scholarship is to understand the associated issues and requirements, and then obviously, to follow the rules. As noted at the end of the previous section, most academic institutions offer RECR training, and numerous resources are available online as well. If you begin your research career by committing firmly to never stray from the ethical pathway, and to consult those with more experience if you encounter a situation involving an ethical dilemma that is beyond your ability to resolve, you will never regret it.

Both NIH and NSF provide excellent resources for RECR education and training. Quoting from NIH (National Institutes of Health n.d.-e), the goals of such education and training are to:

- Develop, foster, and maintain a culture of integrity in science;
- Discourage and prevent unethical conduct;
- Empower researchers to hold themselves and others accountable to high ethical standards;
- Increase knowledge of, and sensitivity to, ethical issues surrounding the conduct of research by researchers with diverse backgrounds;
- Improve the ability to make responsible choices when faced with ethical dilemmas involving research;
- Provide an appreciation for the range of accepted scientific practices for conducting research;
- Inform scientists and research trainees about the regulations, policies, statutes, and guidelines that govern the conduct of US Public Health Service-funded research and promote compliance with the same; and
- Promote a career-long positive attitude toward research ethics and the responsible conduct of research.

Topics covered include the following, and most or all of these can be found in the numerous programs referenced on federal agency websites (e.g., National Science Foundation n.d.-e). Note that virtually all of these are covered in this book.

- Research misconduct and questionable research practices;
- Data management (i.e., data acquisition, record-keeping, retention, ownership, analysis, interpretation, and sharing);
- Scientific rigor and reproducibility;

- Responsible authorship and publication;
- Peer review;
- Conflicts of interest in research;
- Mentor/mentee responsibilities and relationships;
- Collaborative science;
- Civility issues in research environments, including but not limited to, harassment, bullying, and inappropriate behavior;
- Policies regarding laboratory safety, biosafety, and human and animal research subjects;
- Views about scientists as responsible members of society;
- Social and environmental impacts of research; and
- Contemporary ethical issues in biomedical research.

Although resources exist containing various rules and practices for ethical research encompassing all of the aforementioned topics, with several listed in the references (e.g., Steneck 2006; Kligyte et al. 2007; National Academy of Sciences, National Academy of Engineering, and Institute of Medicine 2009; Bornmann 2013; Shamoo and Resnik 2015), I wish to highlight one topic in particular in the set above that frequently is overlooked, but which is becoming ever more important in the context of responsible authorship and publication: predatory journals.

In general, predatory journals are publications that portray themselves as legitimate, scholarly resources for communicating research and maintaining the historical scholarly record. In reality, just the opposite is true. As noted by Elmore and Weston (2020), predatory journal practices include "falsely claiming to provide peer review, hiding information about article processing charges (APCs), misrepresenting members of the journal's editorial board, and other violations of copyright or scholarly ethics." As a scholar, you must avoid the temptation of publishing in journals that provide a lower bar of entry—which might seem attractive as a means for producing a greater number of publications in a shorter period of time—and instead focus on publishing in highly respected journals that rigorously assess submissions and adhere to the highest standards of integrity. Measures of quality, such as the journal impact factor—which measures the frequency with which articles in a journal have been cited over time and thus indicates the impact of a journal on scholarly work—will assist you in doing so, as will discussions with more senior colleagues.

If you already are conducting research and, by virtue of this book or other means, now realize you have done something unethical or questionable, fear not.

Whatever you do, do *not* continue without addressing the problem. Contact your institutional ethics official or supervisor, discuss the situation, and then work to remedy it. The worst thing you can do is keep it a secret. Secrets are distracting, and previous misconduct, if not addressed, could make you more comfortable breeching ethical standards again. A clear conscience, obtained by exposing your misstep to those capable of assisting you, will make you feel good and be a weight off your shoulders, perhaps setting the stage for additional training to ensure you uphold ethical standards going forward. Additionally, you may be especially effective in training others owing to personal lessons learned.

When you become the leader of a research group or organization, you have an added responsibility of ensuring that everyone in the group is both properly trained in ethical behavior and practices it. You also have, as do all researchers, the responsibility of modeling ethical behavior each and every day. One of the easiest and surest ways to ensure effectiveness is to apply the LAM model, which I have used for many years:

- Learn it—make sure you and others in your charge have completed appropriate training in RECR, whether required or not;

- Apply it—put your RECR training into practice daily to benefit you and your work, but also to model ethical behavior to others; and

- Monitor it—ensure that you, and everyone in your direct charge, are behaving ethically by periodically reviewing your compliance with institutional and other policies. Integrate discussions of RECR into the research process itself and examine scenarios where misconduct might arise. Individuals tend to better internalize concepts such as RECR when discussing and being given the opportunity to explain it to others.

The environments in which research and creative activity are performed are an important factor in setting the proper tone for appropriate conduct. Making sure the environment in your charge is one of high integrity, welcomes questions, and encourages individuals to report possible misconduct, does *not* have a chilling effect on research. Rather, it does just the opposite—it promotes the values and behaviors that are foundational to the conduct of research, and indeed the trust placed by stakeholders in researchers themselves.

Assess Your Comprehension

1. What is the goal of research compliance?
2. List several reasons why responsible and ethical conduct of research (RECR) is so important.

3. What is the difference between ethics and morality?

4. Why do "bright lines" not always exist between ethical and unethical conduct in research?

5. In what ways do moral norms for research differ from formal laws?

6. The moral code for ethical conduct in research consists of a number of principles. List and briefly describe them.

7. What is the formal definition of research misconduct?

8. Compare and contrast the three pillars of research misconduct.

9. What is the "imperfect environment" theory of research misconduct?

10. What is the "bad apple" theory of research misconduct?

11. List some consequences of research misconduct and their potential impacts on one's career as well as the scholarly enterprise more broadly.

12. What mechanisms are in place to help prevent research misconduct?

13. List several actions that you, as a researcher, can take to ensure you are behaving ethically, and that you can take to ensure ethical behavior if you oversee a group of scholars.

Exercises to Deepen Your Understanding

Exercise 1: The US Department and Health and Human Services' (DHHS) Office of Research Integrity makes available a number of case studies for training in responsible and ethical conduct of research (RECR) (https://ori .hhs.gov/rcr-casebook-stories-about-researchers-worth-discussing). Select one case each from two of the categories shown on the website (see the list below) and answer all questions at the end of the exercise:

- Authorship and Publication
- Research Misconduct
- Data Acquisition and Management
- Conflicts of Interest
- Social Responsibility

If you have completed chapter 7, you may wish to select a case from the Peer Review category. If you have completed chapter 13, you may wish to select a case from the Collaboration category.

Exercise 2: Most organizations, public and private, operate with specific "codes of conduct" to which their employees or affiliates must adhere. Often these are cast as institutional values, and in some cases, they are contained in formal employee contracts. Violation of certain elements may lead to severe penalties, including dismissal or even legal action. For this exercise, use the Internet to identify codes of conduct or formally articulated values for a few organizations in the federal, nonprofit, and for-profit sectors, including educational institutions. Compare and contrast them, and also evaluate the consequences of failure to adhere to the policies. What elements are common to all? How do nonlegal penalties vary among the types of organizations? Provide one example of a recent, high-profile case in which failure to adhere to institutional values or code of conduct resulted in dismissal.

Exercise 3: A number of actual, high-profile research misconduct cases have been reported in the media during the past several decades, and you can find them via an online search for the phrase "research misconduct cases." Search the universe of cases and select one you find particularly interesting. Summarize the circumstances behind the case, identify specific areas of ethical behavior that were violated, and use what you learned from the chapter to determine how such misconduct could have been avoided. For the latter, consider issues such as policies, physical safeguards (e.g., locks, passwords, cameras), and so on.

Exercise 4: Some actions or behaviors can be unethical even if they are not illegal, with the reverse also being true. Identify a specific topic or situation, different from the one provided in the chapter (i.e., on immigration), and explain the ethical and legal dimensions and how they differ from one another. To what extent might laws or policies be changed to address the situation you describe? Do you believe laws and ethical norms are applied equitably, and if not, how could they or their associated processes be modified to do so?

Exercise 5: Suppose you have been selected to lead a team of two hundred researchers in the study of a topic of great national significance. Ethical behavior is of course critical to the project, yet you cannot possibly personally oversee the activities of every individual on the team. Devise an RECR plan for the group. Discuss the various elements of the plan, the way in which you will present the plan to the group to ensure that all elements are clearly understood, and mechanisms for monitoring behavior to ensure compliance by all members of the group.

10

Better Safe than Sorry: Research Compliance

Chapter Overview and Learning Objectives

Analogous to the rules, policies, and laws governing our everyday lives, various laws, guidelines, and policies govern research and creative activity in a broad subject area known as research compliance. Because severe consequences can occur when research and creative activity are conducted inappropriately, research compliance rules and regulations exist to maintain the integrity of work as well as stakeholder trust in researchers. Failure to adhere to such rules and regulations can result in stiff penalties to the researcher, damage to one's reputation, and of course harm resulting from the research itself and to the research enterprise more broadly.

This chapter highlights various categories of research compliance and the history, importance and enforcement of each. It also discusses the roles played by researchers in understanding and complying with rules and regulations, and participating in the development and modification of compliance requirements. After reading this chapter, you should

- Understand the history and importance of research compliance and your roles in both ensuring compliance in your own research and participating in the broader creation of compliance rules and regulations;

- Be able to describe the key categories of research compliance and the most important elements within them;

- Know how research compliance rules and regulations are enforced and the consequences for violating them; and

- Understand efforts now underway to streamline and reduce the burden associated with unnecessary or ineffective research compliance rules and regulations.

10.1 History and Purpose of Research Compliance

In chapter 9, we addressed the importance of ethical conduct of research and discussed the exceptionally harmful consequences to researchers, their institutions, and the research enterprise more broadly that arise when research results are fabricated, falsified, or plagiarized. We also discussed how other deviations from accepted practice can be equally damaging, and the keen responsibility you have, as a researcher, for making decisions and conducting yourself in an ethically responsible manner.

Actually, ethical conduct is part of a broader topic known as research compliance, which encompasses an extremely complex and diverse set of laws, rules, regulations, and policies governing research and creative activity. In this sense, research compliance is not unlike other rules we encounter in our daily lives—such as automobile speed limits, procedures for filing our taxes, and keeping our dogs on leashes. Ultimately, these and other forms of compliance, just like research compliance, are designed to achieve one principal goal: to drive human behavior in desired directions, usually via the imposition of stiff penalties, to ensure that we act with the highest standards of ethics, integrity, safety, and security.

In the context of research, the penalties (section 10.4) must be stiff because so much is at stake. For example, human subjects involved in clinical trials of experimental drugs; the use of biological agents in understanding and curing diseases; the development of materials and devices having dual use in both civilian and military applications, which therefore could harm national security if not adequately protected; and the expenditure of billions of taxpayer dollars each year to fund most of the fundamental or discovery research conducted in the US (chapter 2).

Although research compliance as we know it today emerged only over the past eighty years or so, the Hippocratic Oath, dating from the fifth to the third centuries BC, perhaps is the first known example in which ethical conduct was formalized—in that case for the healing arts. Perhaps not surprisingly, human subjects were the focus of research compliance in its early modern years.

For example, the Federal Food, Drug, and Cosmetic Act, passed into law in 1938, required drugs to be shown safe prior to marketing, which resulted in the need for testing using human subjects. Not long before, a fifty-year study, started in 1932 and known as the Tuskegee Syphilis Study (Gray 1998), was sponsored by the US Department of Health to evaluate the impacts of syphilis on African American males. Unfortunately, the subjects of the study were not told of their disease, nor were they offered penicillin, which was a proven cure.

Many subjects died, and this atrocity led to the National Research Act in 1974, which focused on the protection of human subjects in biomedical research.

Ironically, it was World War II that contributed substantially toward an effective research compliance framework owing to an American military tribunal, convened in late 1946, that brought criminal charges against twenty-three German physicians and others for conducting experiments on concentration camp prisoners without their consent. Many prisoners died or were permanently disabled, and in 1948, the Nuremburg Code (e.g., Shuster 1997) was created as a result. Among its ten stipulations, the Code states, first and foremost, that "The voluntary consent of the human subject is absolutely essential." It goes on to state that benefits of the research must outweigh the risks; that experiments must be scientifically necessary and conducted by qualified personnel; that animal studies should precede experiments involving humans; and that, during the course of the experiment, the human subject, or the scientist in charge, must be free to bring it to an end. These same issues were addressed in the 1964 Declaration of Helsinki, in which the World Medical Association provided guidance for human subjects research. The Declaration has since been revised many times and serves as the foundation for good clinical practice.

A watershed report, which set the course for modern research compliance involving human subjects, was the Belmont Report, issued in 1979 by the National Commission for the Protection of Human Subjects of Biomedical and Behavioral Research (US Department of Health, Education and Welfare 1979). It laid out the following three fundamental ethical principles: Respect for persons. Beneficence. And Justice. From this report, and subsequent reports and discussions, came in 1981 the "Common Rule" (and subsequent modifications) governing research involving human subjects, discussed in the next section. Numerous other laws and policies subsequently have been enacted, and lists can be found in the references (e.g., Resnik 2015; Resnik n.d.).

10.2 The Universe of Research Compliance

Although research involving human subjects dominated the compliance landscape for several decades and continues to be vitally important today, other types of research compliance began to emerge following World War II, owing in large part to dramatic increases in federal government funding for nonmedical fundamental research. Today, research compliance can be divided into seven broad categories.

The first category of research compliance involves the *use of human and animal subjects*. With regard to humans, the most well-known example concerns clinical trials of experimental medical therapies, devices, or other interventions as a means for demonstrating their effectiveness and safety. These steps are part of the process needed to gain government approval for actual use. Such trials are carefully designed and monitored and consist of five phases, ranging from testing on small populations using limited doses, in the case of drugs, to tests involving several thousand subjects just prior to commercialization. Any research study involving human subjects is required to develop a set of protocols, or specific rules and steps by which the work will be conducted, and submit them for approval to what is known as an Institutional Review Board (IRB).

An IRB is a committee, consisting of peer experts, that reviews proposed research methods to ensure they are ethical. It also approves and monitors all activities associated with research involving human subjects. In the US, IRBs are governed by federal law and are regulated by the Office for Human Research Protections (http://hhs.gov/ohrp/index.html) within DHHS (http://hhs.gov). At academic institutions, IRBs usually are coordinated out of the office of the senior research officer (section 1.6), such as the vice president or vice chancellor for research.

The foundation for IRBs is the Common Rule (Office of Human Research Protections n.d.). It establishes the ethical principles for research involving human subjects and consists of three requirements: First, assuring that research institutions comply; second, obtaining and documenting informed consent; and third, guidelines for IRBs. Most federal research funding agencies have signed onto the Common Rule, and most academic institutions conducting research involving human subjects enforce it even when the research being performed is funded internally or by a nonfederal source. Note that private companies, nonprofit research institutions, and even Native American tribes have IRBs if they conduct research involving human subjects.

It is important to recognize that research involving human subjects is not confined to the medical arena, but extends to areas such as history, sociology, political science, psychology, art, anthropology, language, and other disciplines. In such cases, human subjects can be involved via participation in surveys, focus groups, interviews, or even as subjects being observed in particular settings, such as students in a classroom. The Common Rule provides a variety of protections for certain populations such as prisoners, pregnant women, and children, to ensure informed consent is obtained. This is to avoid the sorts of abuses that occurred in the early and middle part of the twentieth century, as described in the preceding section.

Turning now to the use of animals in research, the associated protocols are not governed by the IRB and the Common Rule, but rather by a parallel construct known as the Institutional Animal Care and Use Committee (IACUC). Here, the word "animal" has broad meaning, ranging from fish, frogs, rats, and mice to chimpanzees, baboons, cats, and dogs. As is the case for IRBs, any institution, public or private, that conducts research involving animals must have an IACUC. Policies for the IACUC, which were formally established in 1986, are developed by NIH's Office of Laboratory Animal Welfare (http://olaw.nih.gov/home.htm). The IACUC itself comprises no less than five individuals appointed by the chief executive of the institution, with all members being able to judge whether rules are being followed. Some are expert researchers, but at least one must be a nonscientist. Additionally, law requires that a veterinarian, who has experience conducting research with animals, serve on the IACUC.

Rules governing the use of animals in research are quite specific and emphasize solid experiment design, avoiding discomfort and distress to the animal, provision of care and appropriate living conditions, and so on. Every few years, the National Research Council issues a guide regarding the use of animals in research (see National Research Council 2011). It is important to note that some individuals and organizations are adamantly opposed, on ethical grounds, to the use of any type of animal in any type of research. One study indicates a statistically significant increase, over a fifteen-year period, in the use of vertebrate animals—principally mice—in research funded by NIH (Goodman et al. 2015). Yet, overall trends are difficult to assess owing to the complexity of issues involved.

The second category of research compliance involves the *research environment* itself, particularly safety in laboratories, studios, and field sites. Many academic institutions have an Environmental Health and Safety Office (EHSO), which collaborates across numerous organizations to ensure a safe and healthy work environment for the campus as a whole, including research but also education, recreation, and other activities. Of particular importance in this context is safety in laboratories that support the use of hazardous chemicals, dangerous gases, or devices that pose a significant threat to life and property if not used in the manner intended.

Given the wide variation of characteristics among facilities, the EHSO works with researchers to develop specific protocols for training, facility access, use and storage of materials, and facility organization and management. The value of such protocols was highlighted in a report (Association for Public & Land-grant Universities 2016) that emphasizes the importance of a culture of safety in academic research laboratories. It provides a fascinating overview of accidents that motivate the need for continuous improvement of laboratory safety, as well as tools and resources available for ensuring a safe environment.

The third broad category of research compliance concerns *materials used in research*, including but not limited to radioactive isotopes, select biological agents such as highly virulent strains of bacteria, and other toxins that might pose a severe threat to public health and safety, or to animals and plants or their products. The use of radioactive materials typically is governed by a campus radiation safety office or committee based upon an array of federal rules and regulations. The use of biological agents is governed by an Institutional Biosafety Committee (IBC). Similar to the IRB and the IACUC, the IBC comprises research experts who review and approve all research activities and protocols involving items such as recombinant DNA, synthetic nucleic acid molecules, microorganisms, viruses, and biological toxins. They also sometimes review research involving bloodborne pathogens, stem cells, dual use activities, and nanotechnology. IBCs are overseen by the National Institutes of Health Office of Biotechnology Activities, and as for IACUCs, IBCs consist of at least five individuals with appropriate expertise, two of whom are not affiliated with the home institution.

The fourth broad category of research compliance involves *research grant proposals, contracts, and other instruments related to funding*, including their associated terms and conditions. Although, as mentioned in previous chapters, individual researchers have a personal obligation to understand their roles and responsibilities associated with the receipt of grants and contracts, the breadth and complexity of laws, policies and rules involved has led to the creation of entire offices (section 1.6) devoted to such matters, especially at research universities. They deal with rules that include but are not limited to grant and contract provisions, reporting of results, cost accounting, lobbying certification, audits, and many others.

OMB, which is the largest executive branch organization, has so-called circulars that contain key rules and regulations governing these and other topics. Consult the office of sponsored programs or the grants and contracts office of your institution for assistance in all matters related to this dimension of compliance. If your institution has no such office, speak with your advisor or research supervisor to determine how your needs can be met. As noted previously, in many cases, underresourced institutions sometimes partner with nearby larger institutions on matters of compliance using a shared-services model that is quite effective.

The fifth broad category of research compliance concerns the *reporting* and/or public posting of information and data related to a research project, including progress and final reports, information about project participants, use of funding, and data used in publications. Most of the guidance is contained in the terms and conditions of grant and contract awards and varies by agency or funding source. However, I want to highlight one point in particular, which is discussed further in section 11.2, that is having a transformative impact on research and creative activity. Namely, a 2013 policy (updated in 2022) from OSTP requiring that publications resulting from most federally funded research be made available free of charge, in a publicly accessible online repository (Office of Science and Technology Policy 2013, 2022). The same is true of all data used in a given publication. Open access publishing (section 11.2) and OSTP guidance on public access are very effective means of ensuring that scholars and the general public have ready access to publications resulting from taxpayer- or philanthropically funded research and creative activity.

The sixth general category of research compliance concerns *conflicts of interest and commitment*. In general, a conflict of interest (COI) exists if one cannot be impartial or objective in carrying out a specific task, such as making decisions, owing to personal benefits they may derive in doing so. Additionally, a COI can exist owing to inherent incompatibility between the role of one individual and that of another person or persons, say by virtue of their position or relationship. Conflicts of interest can be both real and perceived.

As an example of the former, suppose a researcher is working to create a cure for diabetes and the research is being funded by a company in which the researcher owns stock. In this case, the researcher would stand to benefit personally by finding the cure and thus a financial COI exists. Likewise, if the researcher did not personally own stock in the company, but rather her husband was employed by the company as the individual who determines which research the company funds, a familial COI would exist. Both of these examples are real COIs.

In some cases, a COI does not formally exist, though the appearance of one does. Such would be the case if the husband noted above simply worked in the company funding his wife's research but had no formal role over the funding decision.

The existence of conflicts of interest does not necessarily preclude the associated activity from proceeding, and in many cases, conflicts can be managed. In the aforementioned example, the husband making the corporate funding decision could recuse himself from all activities in which his wife was involved, with another individual in the company serving in his place. The use of such a "substitute" individual, usually having a positional rank higher than the one conflicted, is standard practice for managing conflicts of interest. Yet, in some cases, management is impossible and the conflict needs to be eliminated.

Conflicts of interest also can occur at the institutional level. For example, a university receiving a large donation from a private company for a new building would be in a potentially conflicted position if it also accepted money from the same company to conduct research on a topic for which the company could receive a financial windfall, or which might involve changing federal regulations that would be disadvantageous to the company. Because of these and many other situations, federal research funding agencies, private foundations, and even journals have strict policies whereby researchers and institutions are required to publicly disclose financial and other information to ensure integrity of the research enterprise.

Conflicts of commitment involve dedicating time to organizations or activities in ways that interfere or are inconsistent with one's primary employer and stated duties. Examples include a professor who spends more time consulting for a private company than her academic institution allows, a researcher who is affiliated with and is compensated by either domestic or foreign institutions without disclosing such information as required on grant applications, and a faculty member who commits more time to federally funded projects than they have available.

The final category of research compliance involves the *protection of sensitive information, processes, devices, activities, or other things* that might pose a threat to personal, economic, or national security if disclosed. The most familiar and extreme example is classified information, which contains multiple levels of security and operates with very clear and strict rules regarding access and handling.

A more recent innovation in security and access is export controls, which started in the late 1970s and involves, quoting from the federal government (US Department of State n.d.), "the control of exports of sensitive equipment, software and technology as a means to promote national security interest and foreign policy objectives." Three federal agencies are involved in the current export control system: the Department of State, the Department of Commerce, and the US Treasury.

Exports can be either real, which means material actually leaving the US, or deemed, which means something is deemed to have been exported if it is viewed or accessed by an unauthorized individual while in the US. In contrast to rules for classified research, rules regarding export controls have long been in a state of flux and are in many cases ambiguous. One important consideration for academic research institutions is an exemption from export controls for research that is determined to be fundamental or curiosity driven. However, an increasingly large body of fundamental research is deemed to be of dual use; that is, applicable to both civilian and military applications, and thus subject to export control restrictions. An interesting dilemma exists when research that was originally fundamental in character (and thus open according to export control rules) progresses to the point where it becomes dual use or even needs to be classified. Such is the complexity of today's research enterprise in an increasingly challenging global context.

Other types of sensitive information exist and must be protected via appropriate measures, such as Controlled Unclassified Information (CUI). Overseen by the National Archives and Records Administration, this control formally began in 2010 and is still evolving. CUI is government-owned information that is of a sensitive nature and which, if disclosed, could have negative consequences. Examples of CUI include personally identifiable information (e.g., social security numbers), confidential employment records, federal agency information about principal investigators, and proprietary business information provided to the federal government, say in a grant proposal application.

Perhaps the most important example of managing sensitive data, outside national security and related issues, is that associated with research involving human subjects. When humans are involved in clinical trials and certain other types of studies, they provide what is known as personalized health information (PHI). This might include a good deal of their medical history as well as other information, and obviously such information must be protected. Certain strategies exist for deidentifying PHI data, such as removing names, addresses, and birth dates. However, in situations where the number of research subjects is small, specific individuals are more easily identified. Special measures are employed in such cases. Key data privacy and security provisions for safeguarding medical information in the US are governed by the Health Insurance Portability and Accountability Act of 1996, otherwise known as HIPAA.

10.3 Research Security: A Balancing Act between Promotion and Protection

An increasingly significant challenge facing America's research enterprise involves striking an appropriate balance between two goals that often are viewed as competing with one another but which, as described below, I view as complementary: protecting America's research assets against malign foreign government interference and promoting the openness of America's research enterprise—as both a domestic and international endeavor—which is so critical for scholarly work to flourish.

Apart from the categories of restricted research and data described in section 10.2, the American research enterprise has been very open since the end of World War II. Specifically, guided by National Security Decision Directive (NSDD)-189 (National Archives and Records Administration n.d.), issued in 1985, fundamental research remains unrestricted to the extent possible. Additionally, individuals from other nations who come to study and conduct research at US colleges and universities generally have unrestricted access to libraries, collaborators, support staff, facilities, data, equipment, and instruments. This also is true for many government laboratories and facilities. Unfortunately, reciprocity is not provided by certain other countries to American researchers studying abroad, and in some cases, the restrictions imposed are severe. Even worse, the presence of malign foreign government interference has been documented at many US universities, large and small, thus representing a serious and systemic threat to America's research enterprise and indeed, that of the world. More importantly, the theft by some foreign governments of America's research ideas, plans, outcomes, and intellectual property is well documented (e.g., National Research Council 2009; Hannas et al. 2013; Federal Bureau of Investigation 2019; Stark and Tiffert 2021) and has profound implications for America's economic and national security.

For these and other reasons, the issue of research security has become a topic of great interest within all three branches of the federal government, as well as in academia and private industry. Not surprisingly, research security and research integrity often are mentioned together in policy and practice. Although they overlap to some extent, they are different. Specifically, the National Science and Technology Council (2022a) defines research integrity as "The use of honest and verifiable methods in proposing, performing, and evaluating research; reporting research results with particular attention to adherence to rules, regulations and guidelines; and following commonly accepted professional norms." It defines research security as "Safeguarding the research enterprise against the misappropriation of research and development to the detriment of national or economic security, related violations of research integrity, and foreign government interference."

During the past several years, numerous reports have been written about existential threats to US research (see references above), as well as the dangers of restricting academic research in any manner. Moreover, given that some foreign governments pose a greater threat than others, issues concerning possible racial and ethnic profiling have been raised, leading to concerns that some categories of foreign nationals currently in the US are being persecuted as well as targeted inappropriately by federal officials for presumed illegal activity. And of course, this notion has a chilling effect for those looking to come to the US to pursue their education and research interests.

These and many other issues in the research security domain are difficult indeed, requiring careful analysis of data, open dialog among all stakeholders, and thoughtful policy. I was on the front lines of research security during my time as director at OSTP and can speak to the challenges directly.

Specifically, while at OSTP, I had the privilege of taking part in the research security policy effort within the Executive Office of the President, where we created the Joint Committee on the Research Environment (JCORE) within the NSTC. With membership drawn from all federal agencies that fund research or have research policy responsibilities, JCORE collaborated with academia, private industry, nonprofit organizations, and the National Security Council (NSC) to develop two important documents, both issued in 2021.

The first is National Security Presidential Memorandum 33 (NSPM-33) (White House 2021) on securing America's research assets. It emphasizes, among many things, the disclosure of activities and affiliations by researchers that might compromise personal and research integrity and thus imperil personal or national/economic security. Basically, the policy simply seeks to ensure that everyone involved in American research—irrespective of discipline, organization, or country of origin—plays by the rules. In this regard, JCORE took a "behavior-based" approach to research security, for as noted previously, research compliance is the personal responsibility of every researcher. The NSTC issued a follow-on document (National Science and Technology Council 2022a) regarding federal agency implementation of NSPM-33, and work continues.

The second document is an NSTC report (National Science and Technology Council 2021), developed in close collaboration with the academic community, which offers recommendations "research organizations (e.g., academic institutions, private companies, independent research institutes) can take to better protect the security and integrity of America's research enterprise." One of the most important aspects of the document is that it lays out a set of foundational principles and values for research, which it notes are consistent with American values:

- Openness and transparency enable productive collaboration and help ensure appropriate disclosure of potential conflicts of interest and conflicts of commitment.
- Accountability and honesty help acknowledge errors and correct behaviors that can hamper progress.
- Impartiality and objectivity protect against improper influence and distortion of scientific knowledge.
- Respect helps create an environment where all can be heard and contribute.
- Freedom of inquiry allows individual curiosity to guide scientific discovery.
- Reciprocity ensures that scientists and institutions exchange materials, knowledge, data, access to facilities and natural sites, and training in a way that benefits all collaborating partners.

- Merit-based competition helps ensure a level playing field where the best ideas and innovations can advance.

I mentioned previously that I view openness of America's research enterprise and the protection of its assets to be complementary. The research values listed above are the reason why. The performance of research, as noted in chapters 4 and 9, is founded upon integrity, openness, accountability, trust, and respect. Research simply cannot exist without them. Fortunately, and not surprisingly, these same research values comport with our American values—namely, the freedom to discover and create; the freedom to respectfully debate, challenge, and speak freely; the freedom to share; a free-market system to transition research outcomes into practice for the benefit of humanity; and the freedom to pursue our own pathways and dreams while adhering to policies and laws.

Some individuals coming to study and perform research in America did not learn these values in their home country, at least not in the manner we interpret and apply them. Consequently, research security affords an opportunity for those of us in America to lead with our values. That is, to ensure that individuals coming to America understand these values as scholars, know how to put them into practice, are aware of the consequences of failing to uphold the values, and know where to turn if they have questions. Values determine decisions and decisions determine direction. Research security is not about country of origin, ethnicity, race, or any other attribute. It is about playing by the rules, period.

When I was at the White House working with JCORE and meeting with hundreds of researchers across America, not a single one—not one—told me they wanted someone in their studio, laboratory, or group who knowingly breaks the rules. Research security—which importantly represents a *working partnership* among academic and other research institutions, funding organizations, the intelligence community, and law enforcement—is about behavior, and also about leading with our American values. In doing so, the research enterprise remains open and accountable, welcoming to all, and mindful of the risks we face in today's world. Failure on our part to take a balanced approach to research security could result in notably negative consequences, ranging from limiting foreign collaborations to halting completely the immigration of foreign nationals who seek to study and perform research at US colleges and universities. In those cases, everyone loses.

10.4 Creation and Enforcement of Research Rules and Regulations

As is the case with laws and policies governing our everyday lives, it is important to understand and to actively participate in the processes by which research compliance rules and regulations are created and enforced. In fact, active involvement by the research community is essential because we, as researchers, are the experts in knowing how rules and regulations are likely to impact the research enterprise. Thus, we are best suited to helping others determine whether the rules and regulations will in fact meet their intended purpose.

You probably won't be surprised to hear that multiple processes and organizations are involved in creating and enforcing research compliance regulations at multiple levels—ranging from research institutions themselves to individual states to the federal government, not to mention private corporations and nonprofit foundations. It is lot to keep track of, and as described in the final section of this chapter, efforts are underway to streamline and harmonize compliance requirements, and to eliminate those which are known to be ineffective, so as to reduce unnecessary administrative work and maximize researcher productivity.

Consider first how compliance requirements are created. Quite often, the need for a new rule or regulation comes about by virtue of a negative consequence. For example, an accident in a research laboratory, fraud uncovered during an audit, the theft of intellectual property, or—as was the case in the Tuskegee Syphilis Study described previously—the eventual realization that research subjects were being severely mistreated.

Rules and regulations also come about when a need is recognized and is deemed to be in the public interest, such as providing free and open access to data used in government-funded publications, the public posting of researcher COI information, and the submission to funding agencies of research progress reports to ensure full accountability and transparency of how taxpayer dollars are used.

Congress frequently promulgates research compliance rules and regulations, as was the case in the 2007 America COMPETES (Creating Opportunities to Meaningfully Promote Excellence in Technology, Education, and Science) Act, where responsible conduct of research (chapter 9) training was mandated for all students and postdoctoral researchers funded by NSF grants. Likewise, OSTP creates research compliance rules, though it is not formally a directive agency. Such was the case with the aforementioned public access policy for publications and data created with federal funding.

Individual grant funding agencies also have their own array of compliance policies, such as NSF which, in contrast to other agencies, prohibits those seeking funding from making their proposals more attractive by providing cost sharing (section 6.2) or matching support (a few exceptions exist). OMB has broad responsibility for establishing and enforcing financial accounting, auditing, and related research compliance rules and regulations. Its Office of

Information and Regulatory Affairs (OIRA; http://whitehouse.gov/omb/in formation-regulatory-affairs) is where much of that work takes place. In the case of human health research compliance, the Office of Research Integrity (ORI) oversees and directs activities on behalf of the Secretary of Health and Human Services, with the exception of the regulatory research integrity activities of the Food and Drug Administration (http://fda.gov).

When a new rule or regulation, or a change to an existing rule or regulation, is being considered by an agency of the US government, the law requires that an NPRM be placed in the Federal Register (http://federalregister.gov) to solicit public input. Information gathered is used to develop the actual policy, which sometimes is issued as an interim rule or interim guidance until the final version is completed. In the case of academic research compliance, comments to Federal Register notices frequently are provided by academic institutions themselves, or by consortia that represent the interests of a collection of institutions.

One such organization, which is extremely effective in this role, is COGR (http://cogr.edu). As a national, nonprofit consortium of research universities, affiliated medical centers, and independent research institutes, COGR is an important partner with the federal government that helps ensure research compliance is appropriately conceived and structured, effectively implemented, and that it meets the intended purpose with known impacts. COGR often partners with professional associations to work on behalf of the broader academic research enterprise, especially the Association of Public and Land-grant Universities (APLU), the Association of American Universities (AAU), the Association of American Medical Colleges (AAMC; http://aamc.org), and the American Council on Education (ACE; http://acenet.edu).

With regard to enforcement of research compliance rules and regulations, the mechanisms are as varied as the rules themselves. At the institutional level, most research colleges and universities have senior research officers, such as a vice president or vice chancellor for research, who help coordinate research compliance activities (section 1.6). They often are aided by other offices, such as those of legal counsel and the provost, and are a wonderful resource for both learning about compliance as well as making sure you indeed are following the rules. If your institution does not have a senior research officer, consult your advisor or research supervisor to learn how compliance is managed and the resources available to you.

Clear processes exist for dealing with possible rule violations, and sometimes violations are uncovered through audits conducted periodically by federal agencies or institutions themselves. In some cases, such as research involving human and animal subjects, institutions go through a periodic accreditation process to ensure all required administrative and other structures are in place. Accrediting organizations include AAHRPP, which stands for Association for the Accreditation of Human Research Protection Programs (http://aahrpp.org), and AAALAC, which stands for Association for Assessment and Accreditation of Laboratory Animal Care International (http://aaalac.org). At the federal level, inspectors general (IGs) serve in agencies as an independent mechanism to determine whether the agency is following all required rules, laws, and procedures. In some cases, IG offices become involved in research misconduct cases, and in severe cases they work with law enforcement on prosecution.

Although the research compliance landscape is highly complex, a variety of excellent resources exists to ensure your understanding of and ability to follow the rules, as described in the next section.

10.5 Your Role in Understanding and Meeting Compliance Rules and Regulations

As mentioned many times throughout this book, you, as the researcher, ultimately are responsible for knowing about, understanding, and following all rules, procedures, and processes associated with the performance of research and creative activity. Fortunately, a wide array of resources exists to assist you in this rather daunting task, and the institution where you are performing research, such as a research university or even a private company, has in many cases a legal responsibility to make resources available to you.

One of the most effective ways to become familiar with research compliance rules and regulations is to attend workshops and seminars. They are offered not only by research institutions themselves, usually through the senior research officer and involving experienced faculty and administrators, but also by private companies that specialize in researcher training. The workshop format provides an opportunity for you to interact with others as you learn together, and to work through sample scenarios that will be of practical use in your own research. You can learn more by visiting the research website of your institution, or by searching the web for research compliance workshops and seminars, many of which are free.

Not surprisingly, a variety of online training options also exist, one of the most well-known of which is the Collaborative Institutional Training Initiative (CITI; http://citiprogram.org). Founded in 2000, CITI is "dedicated to promoting the public's trust in the research enterprise by providing high quality, peer-reviewed, web-based educational courses in research, ethics, regulatory oversight, responsible conduct of research, research administration, and other topics pertinent to the interests of member organizations and individual learners." Many institutions use CITI-based training as an eligibility requirement for IRB-based and other forms of research, and topics offered by CITI include animal care and use, COI, good laboratory practice, responsible conduct of research, and biosafety and biosecurity. If your institution has a membership in CITI, the training likely is free to you. If it does not, consult your advisor or research supervisor regarding options for obtaining such training.

Despite this wide array of resources and after years of practical experience, you still may find yourself in a situation of having failed to comply with research rules and regulations. What then? The consequences depend upon the situation, of course, so here are a few examples.

If you fail to complete a progress report to a federal agency funding your work, the agency may withhold additional funding or not allow you to submit another proposal until you are current with all pending reports. If you fail to disclose a financial or organizational conflict of interest or commitment to a federal agency funding your research, the agency may terminate your research grant and perhaps require that your institution return all funds expended. If you are not properly trained in the use of laboratory equipment or the handling of toxic materials, you may cause injury to yourself or others. If you violate protocols for experiments involving human subjects, your research may be suspended or terminated and, if the violation was egregious, you may not be allowed to perform research again for up to several years. If you allow unauthorized individuals to access materials, data, or equipment that is subject to an export control restriction, you may be prosecuted, and even jailed, if the violation is deemed to be sufficiently severe.

These are not extreme examples, though only the more extreme ones tend to appear in the media. All inspectors general are required to submit semiannual reports to Congress, and in them you can find a variety of examples in which research compliance rules and regulations were violated. The bottom line for you as researcher is this: be aware of the rules, understand the rules, and follow the rules. When in doubt, ask. Never forget that the goal of research compliance is to drive human behavior in desired directions, not destroy careers or cause harm to the research enterprise.

10.6   Recent Reforms: Ensuring Effective Compliance without Undue Burden

I hope it is clear from the preceding sections of this chapter that research compliance is an extremely important element of our Nation's research enterprise—important to those funding the research, performing the research, and using outcomes from the research. Compliance rules and regulations ensure that research and creative activity are performed with safety, integrity, sensitivity, transparency, and accountability. All of these attributes are foundational to maintaining the trust and confidence placed by taxpayers and others in our research enterprise, and thus in ensuring that the US maintains its role as a world leader in research and innovation.

Yet, compliance has another dimension to it. During the past thirty years or so, research compliance has grown dramatically in scope and complexity. This is due in part to the increasingly complicated nature of research itself, but also as a result of increasingly limited federal research budgets and heightened national security, which has led to increased scrutiny and restrictions on broad classes of activities.

Since 1991, as shown in figure 10.1, the number of new research compliance regulations impacting US universities has increased dramatically. Ironically, that same year, the percentage of funding available to universities from research grants and contracts to support such compliance was capped (i.e., the administrative or A component of the F&A rate, described in section 6.2, was capped at 26 percent). As a result, compliance costs have been shifted to other sources, including tuition.

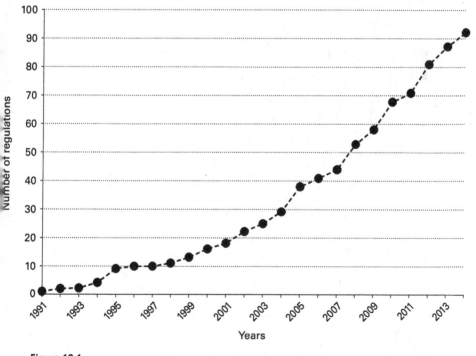

Figure 10.1
Cumulative number of federal regulatory changes, applicable to research institutions, in the US from 1991 to 2014. *Source*: National Academies of Science, Engineering and Medicine (2016).

Another important indicator of how research compliance regulations have increased is a national survey, first conducted in 2005, by the Federal Demonstration Partnership (FDP). It showed that, for research projects funded by the federal government, university principal investigators spent 42 percent of their time *not* performing research, but rather working on research compliance and proposal preparation activities (Rockwell 2009). Remarkably, when the survey was given seven years later, in 2012, this same figure of 42 percent was obtained (Federal Demonstration Project 2014). And even more remarkably, when the survey was given yet again in 2018, the workload had risen to slightly over 44 percent (Schneider 2020).

Looking more closely at the workload data (figure 10.2), one can see a number of the compliance topics discussed in this chapter. For example, COI; IRB; chemical safety; HIPAA and IACUC; export controls; and select agents. In some cases, the workload is substantial (figure 10.3), and thus an obvious question to ask is: What is the *appropriate* workload? No one really knows, but 42

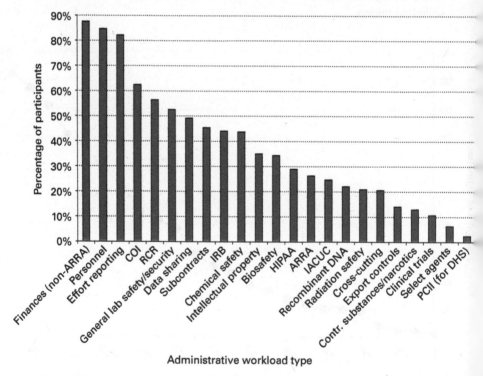

Administrative workload type

Figure 10.2
Prevalence of twenty-three administrative responsibilities associated with federally funded research, among principal investigators in American universities, from the 2012 Federal Demonstration Partnership Survey. *Source*: Federal Demonstration Partnership (2014).

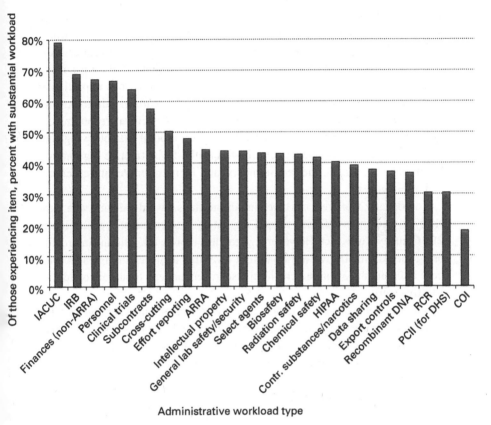

Figure 10.3
For participants in the 2012 Federal Demonstration Partnership Survey of university principal investigators who experience a given type of workload, the percentage reporting substantial (some to very much) time taken by that responsibility. *Source:* Federal Demonstration Partnership (2014).

percent is, on its face, probably far too large. Is 20 percent right? 25 percent? Instead of trying to answer that question, let me turn to a final point.

In light of the dramatic and sustained increase in compliance regulations and associated costs, efforts have been underway for many years to reform the research compliance framework. Leading the way are professional research societies, university associations, and organizations representing independent research institutes. Recognizing the value of compliance in research, as noted previously, emphasis in these efforts has been placed on the following key actions (Smith et al. 2011): "Eliminate outright or exempt universities from the regulation; Harmonize the regulation across agencies to avoid duplication and redundancy; Tier the regulation to levels of risk rather than assuming that one size fits all; Refocus the regulation on performance-based goals rather than on process; Adjust the regulation to better fit the academic research environment."

Numerous reports have been written along these lines (e.g., Leshner 2008; National Academies of Science, Engineering and Medicine 2016; Association of American Universities n.d.). I was privileged to work on one in particular (National Science Board 2014), which examined researcher administrative workload on federally funded grants and framed its several recommendations for NSF, as well as other federal agencies, around the following four actions: Focus on the science, eliminate or modify ineffective regulations, harmonize and streamline requirements, and increase university efficiency and effectiveness.

Additionally, Congress has taken important steps toward reducing what generally is known as research-related regulatory burden, most recently in the 21st Century Cures Act. However, a great deal more work remains in order to bring the administrative workload to a level that achieves the intended purpose of compliance without crushing researchers under a mountain of administrative work.

In the end, it is important to note that research compliance is important and generally is viewed by researchers as necessary and valuable. It also is important to recognize that compliance regulations need to be thoughtfully conceived, appropriately structured and implemented, shown to be achieving the intended purpose, and funded in ways consistent with the social compact upon which our research enterprise so critically depends.

Assess Your Comprehension

1. Define research compliance.
2. Describe how research compliance has evolved over the past several decades.
3. What is the Nuremburg Code and why is it important?
4. List the principal categories of research compliance.
5. What is an Institutional Review Board (IRB) and what roles does it play in research?
6. What is the Common Rule and how is it applied?
7. What is an Institutional Animal Care and Use Committee (IACUC) and what roles does it play in research?
8. What is the role of an Environmental Health and Safety Office (EHSO) in supporting research and creative activity?

9. What types of materials might pose a threat to researchers if not used and stored properly?

10. What is an Institutional Biosafety Committee (IBC) and what roles does it play in research and creative activity?

11. What are "terms and conditions" of grants and contracts and what roles do principal investigators have in ensuring they are met?

12. What is a conflict of interest and why is it important?

13. How do real and perceived conflicts of interest differ from one another?

14. What mechanisms exist to address conflicts of interest?

15. What is an institutional conflict of interest, and how does it differ from an individual conflict of interest?

16. What are export controls and how are they applied in research and creative activity?

17. What is a deemed export?

18. What is personalized health information (PHI)?

19. Why is it important for researchers to disclose affiliations and other required information to organizations to which they are applying for funding?

20. What is National Security Decision Directive 189 (NSDD-189) and what are its principal elements?

21. What is National Security Presidential Memorandum 33 (NSPM-33) and what are its principal elements?

22. How does NSPM-33 differ from NSDD-189?

23. What factors or events stimulate the creation of research compliance rules and regulations?

24. List organizations in the research enterprise that have and enforce compliance rules and regulations.

25. What is the Federal Register, and how is it used in the compliance process?

26. What mechanisms exist for you, as a researcher, to learn about compliance rules and regulations?

27. What mechanisms exist to address violations of compliance rules and regulations?

28. List the penalties that may arise if you fail to comply with compliance rules and regulations.

29. What percentage of time, on average, is spent by university principal investigators in America on compliance activities associated with federally funded research?

30. What administrative compliance rules and regulations tend to dominate the time of federally funded principal investigators in America?

31. What key principles and values underpin America's research enterprise?

32. Describe the importance of research security and balancing the openness of the research enterprise with protecting its assets.

33. Why is streamlining compliance rules and regulations important to the research enterprise?

34. How can you, as a researcher, participate in developing or changing compliance rules and regulations?

Exercises to Deepen Your Understanding

Exercise 1: It is likely you have seen one or more media reports describing unethical behavior or other inappropriate conduct in the context of academic, government, or industry research. As you have learned, however, these situations sometimes happen to those having no ill intent. For this exercise, find and summarize a recent news article or set of articles concerning violation of research compliance rules and regulations (e.g., conflict of interest, inappropriate protocols in human/animal subjects, etc.). Discuss what resources the researcher(s) could and should have drawn upon to avoid the associated negative consequences. Additionally, discuss any factors that may have led the researcher(s) to make their decisions.

Exercise 2: Select a research topic of interest that involves the use of human subjects. As noted in this chapter, such studies range from the testing of medicinal therapies to focus groups on key topics of national concern to individual interviews to the observation of children in the classroom. Using information found at https://files.eric.ed.gov/fulltext/EJ1136504.pdf, create a framework for an Institutional Review Board (IRB) protocol. In performing this exercise, briefly describe what surprised you about the process, and what you found to be particularly useful.

Exercise 3: Identify those compliance topics in this chapter that apply to your own research and describe training you have taken relative to them, as well as actions you are now taking to ensure that you follow all appropriate rules and regulations. How much time do you spend on compliance-related activities relative to the research you actually perform, and do you undergo periodic assessment or review to ensure you remain compliant? Note that compliance can include—for students, postdoctoral and staff researchers— submitting to their supervisor or institution periodic reports on research progress.

Exercise 4: Research compliance is an extremely important and valuable element of the research enterprise. However, some compliance requirements are either ill-suited for application to academic institutions, are not appropriately structured to achieve their goals, or simply are out of date. This has led, as noted in this chapter, to significant efforts to reform the compliance framework. Using information in this chapter, supplementary information provided, and references found on your own, identify a particular compliance rule that is viewed as problematic and describe why this view exists. Also, discuss alternatives being considered and make recommendations as to how you would modify the rule or perhaps replace it with something more effective.

Exercise 5: Interview your institution's senior research officer to determine how much his or her position involves dealing with research compliance-related activities (athletic compliance is another very important and complex topic for academic institutions but resides outside the domain of research compliance). Seek to determine how staffing levels related to research compliance have changed at your institution over the past twenty years, and the sources of funding used to support those changes. What specific positions have been added, modified, or eliminated, and what changes are on the horizon? Ask your senior research officer whether compliance with research rules and regulations, in terms of researcher behavior, has changed during the past twenty years, and the extent to which these changes have mirrored investments in compliance staffing.

11

Show Time: Making Your Work Known to Multiple Audiences

Chapter Overview and Learning Objectives

Research and creative activity involve not only the generation of new knowledge but also the dissemination of associated outcomes. Without the latter, the value of the former is greatly diminished, in some cases to the point of irrelevance. This chapter discusses the importance of communicating research outcomes and highlights innovations, such as open access, for improving dissemination. It also provides insight on key strategies for communicating research outcomes with both general and expert audiences. After reading this chapter, you should

- Have a strong appreciation for the importance of communicating research outcomes and impacts to multiple audiences;
- Be able to explain the open access method of publication and the various options within it;
- Understand the broader concept of open science/open scholarship;
- Be aware of repositories for accessing federally funded research and creative activity and know which apply to your work; and
- Understand how to most effectively communicate your work to both expert and general audiences and the resources available to assist you.

11.1 Importance of Communicating Scholarly Outcomes

We generally describe research and creative activity as the generation *and* dissemination of new knowledge. In previous chapters, we discussed the generation component; that is, identifying sources of funding and problems to be studied, writing a grant proposal, collecting data and other information, and applying research methods across multiple disciplines. The other key component—namely, dissemination—is extremely important as well because research and creative activity obviously are of limited value if the associated outcomes are not made known to others.

Communicating research outcomes is important for several reasons. First, it allows those performing the research, including students, to receive appropriate credit for their contributions and to build national and international reputations as scholars. Second, it ensures that other researchers, as well as practitioners, have access to previous work upon which to build. Third, private companies depend upon the outcomes of basic or discovery research to innovate new products and services. Thus, access to results is critically important to their mission and to maintaining US competitiveness in a global society. Fourth, dissemination of outcomes from publicly funded research ensures that taxpayers remain informed about how their dollars are used and the value of important discoveries being made. Fifth, dissemination, especially to the general public, inspires others—especially students, but also the general public—to become involved in research and creative activity. And last but certainly not least, dissemination enriches our lives directly, especially in the humanities, arts and fine arts, via exhibitions, books, and performances.

11.2 Traditional and Open Access Frameworks

Among the most frequently used forms of communication across all disciplines are journals (sometimes called archive journals), books, and monographs. Other forms exist, of course, including works of art, scripts and scores, performances, lectures, and exhibitions. I focus here principally on journals because they are the most common, and because books and monographs have notably different business models.

Individuals and organizations access journal publications in hard copy or digital form via subscription, purchase or loan. Researchers producing the content typically pay publishers to typeset manuscripts, prepare tables and refine images, and distribute the final versions to libraries and individual subscribers or buyers. However, researchers themselves are not paid for their articles; that is, they receive no royalties from them. Publishers also manage the review process as well as the volunteer scholars who donate time to serve as unpaid reviewers. Both for-profit and nonprofit publishers operate in this space, with the former generally on large margins and the latter often as part of professional societies that use some of the publication revenues to support member education and other professional development programs. This framework, though serving the research enterprise well for decades, suffers from a number of limitations in today's digital era.

First, institutional and even individual subscriptions often are expensive (particularly from for-profit publishers) and thus prevent some scholars, especially in certain disciplines and institutions (e.g., MSIs, ERIs, institutions that are resource-limited), from accessing content. Even books have become extraordinarily expensive, thus contributing to college costs and student debt.

Second, for research funded by the federal government, say NSF or NIH, users of research products end up paying for them twice—once as taxpayers who fund the research agency, and then as individuals or institutions who also pay, via subscription, to access results from the work their colleagues reviewed for free.

Third, removing barriers to access is seen as accelerating the progress of research, as described below with an example from the COVID-19 pandemic. Fourth, removing access barriers also stimulates inter/cross/multidisciplinary research (chapter 13)—for example, by allowing a researcher in biomedical engineering, or her institutional library, to easily access relevant journals in material science, medicine, physics, and mechanics. Finally, in many disciplines, scholars have to assign copyright (chapter 12) of their articles to publishers, both public and private, thus limiting or removing their ability to share freely with colleagues, especially online.

All of these factors have led the scholarly community to begin transitioning to a so-called *open access framework* for publications and data, and you should consult the references (e.g., Willinsky 2006; Royster 2016; Jhangiani et al. 2018; National Academies of Science, Engineering and Medicine 2018; Rabesandratana 2019; Science Europe 2022) to learn more about the history and details of open access, including the European model known as Plan-S. In it, products of research, such as individual articles, journals, monographs, and books, are made freely available online, for use without restriction and at no charge to the user. Costs for such access are assessed in various ways, as described below.

In science and engineering, open access is part of a broader concept known as *open science*. The National Academies of Science, Engineering and Medicine (2018, 18) lay out a vision for open science, which for the purposes of that study define it as follows: "As public access (i.e., no charge for access beyond the cost of an Internet connection) to scholarly articles resulting from research projects, the data that support the results contained in those articles, computer code, algorithms, and other digital products of publicly funded scientific research, so that the products of this research are findable, accessible, interoperable, and reusable (FAIR), with limited exceptions for privacy, proprietary business claims, and national security." More broadly, the open science concept can include innovative open models of peer/merit review (chapter 7), collaboration (chapter 13), and facility sharing.

Although many for-profit and nonprofit publishers already offer various open access options (see below) in addition to more traditional ones and are moving in the direction of even greater open access, most private foundations that fund research already require full open access to publications and data, either immediately upon formal publication or within a specified period of time following it.

The concept of open access to *publications*, though notionally straightforward, actually is rather complicated in practice and contains a great deal of nuance in principles and practices owing to the array of stakeholders involved and their differing views and priorities (e.g., public and private publishers, funding organizations, academic libraries, college and university administrators and faculty, students, and the general public). Additional complexity arises owing to the considerable variation among disciplines regarding the manner in which scholarly outcomes are communicated, and the broad spectrum of open access now in existence.

A variety of open access publication options exists from which authors can choose. In the *gold open access* paradigm, which often is viewed by researchers as the most desirable model, a publisher, say of an open access journal, provides everyone free access to articles and associated content on the publisher website. For most open access journals, this is a one-step process that mimics traditional subscription journals. Namely, the article proceeds through the review process (chapter 7) and is posted when it is published.

Some gold open access journals offer other options, such as a two-step process in which the publisher first posts the final accepted manuscript on a so-called preprint or early release server. In the second step, the formally typeset version—which sometimes can take months to produce—is posted. This strategy dramatically reduces waiting time for access to content yet results in the creation of a formal archive version. Under gold access, authors are free to share (known as reuse) their manuscript and final typeset version without restriction via various types of open access licenses. Example licenses can be found on the Creative Commons website (https://creativecommons.org/about /cclicenses).

Obviously, someone has to pay for gold open access articles given they are shared free of charge. These costs are born by the author, their institution, or sometimes the organization funding the research and are known as article processing charges (APCs). In contrast to traditional publishing, in which the user pays for access via subscription (user-pull model), APCs shift the entirety of the payment responsibility to the author, or to the author's institution or grant funding source (user-push model). In reality, for many disciplines including my own (meteorology), authors have always had to pay charges for articles to be typeset, tables to be constructed, and images or photos to be rendered. Consequently, APCs are not a fundamentally new or disruptive concept. Indeed, many federal funding agencies allow "page charges" to be included in proposal budgets (see chapter 6), though now the shift is toward APCs.

The next type of open access is *green*. In contrast to gold open access, in which the journal itself is known as an open access journal, green open access applies to any type of publication. In it, authors are given permission by a publisher to post or distribute near-final or accepted versions of their articles on their own or institutional websites, or place them in central repositories such as those operated by federal agencies (e.g., PubMedCentral [http://www.ncbi.nlm.nih.gov/pmc] in the case of the National Library of Medicine). This is known as self-archiving. The journal also posts the final typeset article on its website, though it is usually available only via subscription. A major advantage of this model is that authors do not pay APCs, though charges sometimes are levied.

In the *hybrid open access model*, publishers offer both open and restricted access options to authors depending upon their willingness or ability to pay APCs, or their strategy in utilizing the article.

Other models exist, such as *bronze, black and diamond*. The *diamond model* (sometimes also referred to as platinum), which is relatively new, is similar to the gold model with the exception that no fees are assessed to the author, their grants, or their institution. Consequently, neither reader nor author pays anything and access is immediate upon publication. Of course, costs still need to be paid, and thus diamond journals generate revenue from other sources, such as grants from federal government funding agencies, philanthropy, advertising, professional societies, and even academic institutions or consortia.

In some disciplines, preprint servers are used to post submitted articles which have not yet been peer reviewed (e.g., medRxiv). This practice is well known and sometimes valuable, but it became problematic during the COVID-19 pandemic as some articles, on the virus or associated disease, that appeared on centralized preprint servers ultimately were rejected for publication—though only after their results were discussed in the press, sometimes with fanfare, leading to belief of validity and causing understandable and unnecessary confusion for the general public.

Open access to *data* is vastly more complicated in light of the many steps through which data often pass (chapter 5). This leads to several questions. Does one keep only the raw data, the quality-controlled data, or data from various steps in between? Additional complexity arises owing to the wide array of formats in which data reside, storage and access frameworks, security, and policies for protecting privacy and propriety. And of course, what responsibility falls to the researcher to assist those who wish to use the data but are having difficulty doing so?

Despite these and numerous other challenges, the community has developed a simple but profoundly important set of principles governing open data. Comprising the acronym FAIR (https://www.go-fair.org/fair-principles/), they consist of *findability* (data must be easily locatable by humans or machines), *accessibility* (ease of access including processes for dealing with sensitive or protected data), *interoperability* (defined in a broad sense to include ease of use with other data sets, different computers and archival systems, and other data formats), and *reuse* (as the word implies, easily recreated for a wide array of purposes, particularly with regard to reproducibility and replicability, discussed in section 4.7) of digital assets. These principles have helped guide the deployment of resources that are of great value to research and creative activity, as described in the next section.

11.3 Publicly Accessible Publications and Data

As noted in chapter 10, the White House in 2013 announced a new policy (Office of Science and Technology Policy 2013) that requires publications resulting from most federally funded research to be made available free of charge, in a publicly accessible online repository, within a specified period of time, usually a year following publication. The same is true of all data used in a given publication. The rationale is that research funded by the federal government (i.e., taxpayers) is a public good and should be made freely available to everyone, without restriction, after an appropriate interval that allows publishers to recoup their costs and authors to file patents and other protections (chapter 12). Although most federal agencies have implemented this policy for publications with some work remaining, they have been notably slow in addressing open access to data, for the reasons mentioned above.

In late summer of 2022, the White House issued guidance (Office of Science and Technology Policy 2022) requiring federal R&D agencies to update their public access policies. Efforts toward this rather landmark change were actually begun several years ago and were underway when I became director of OSTP. With the new policy, the White House is requiring that "all peer-reviewed scholarly publications, authored or co-authored by individuals or institutions resulting from federally funded research, [be] made freely available and publicly accessible by default in agency-designated repositories without any embargo or delay after publication." The new agency plans are to be completed by the end of calendar year 2024 and be fully implemented within a year. Scientific data underlying the publications likewise are to be made freely available. This extraordinary public access policy will dramatically improve access to scholarly publications in STEM fields and have a particularly positive impact on institutions which are financially constrained.

An excellent example demonstrating the value of public access to publications and their associated data can be found in actions taken at the start of the COVID-19 pandemic. At that time, I was serving as director of OSTP and convened a group of science ministers and senior science advisors from some 17 nations around the world. The purpose was to share, in an informal manner, information about scientific questions, challenges, and potential solutions for addressing the pandemic. For example, we discussed progress in testing protocols for disease detection, strategies for accelerating funding for research, and joint research projects and clinical trials. Other participants included representatives from relevant government agencies in each country, including the US Department of State. Although the group was informal, it did make one formal request of the global research enterprise: that both public and private publishers of articles relevant to the pandemic remove all distribution restrictions and make both articles and the underlying data freely available to all, immediately upon publication, in machine readable format for a finite but unspecified period of time. The latter point, known more generally as digital reuse, is an important benefit of open access, as illustrated in the example below.

Many publishers did so, and a parallel effort was undertaken in the US—the COVID-19 Open Research Dataset (CORD-19; http://allenai.org/data/cord-19) —to assemble the publications in repositories and make available to users globally, again free of charge, artificial intelligence and machine learning tools for analyzing digitally the thousands of publications being produced every month. Such analysis was critical owing to the fact that the traditional method of reading articles would have been far too slow and thus would have greatly inhibited progress. Both the publisher response to the international call, and the creation of CORD-19, are viewed has having greatly accelerated research progress and thus are a testament to the value of open and public access. A variety of information regarding open access articles, data, and their impacts is available at http://sparcopen.org/why-open-matters.

In the case of private companies funding research, rather than the federal government, the situation is somewhat different. Research performed at academic institutions, but funded by private corporations, typically is published or otherwise disseminated openly as well, though sometimes with delays of sixty to ninety days to allow for patent filings or other protection of the results (chapter 12). Such protection is of course very important if a company wishes to commercialize research outcomes. In some situations, proprietary data may be withheld from a publication if doing so does not materially impact presentation of the findings. Most academic institutions will not accept private sector funding for research if publication is prohibited entirely, or if the embargo period for intellectual property protection extends beyond ninety days, because doing so can delay student graduation and also runs counter to the philosophy of open sharing of knowledge that is foundational to the academic research enterprise.

On the more extreme end of the scale is classified research. Although the majority of US academic institutions do not perform classified or otherwise highly restricted research, some do—including research involving export-controlled activities (chapter 10). It often is the case that such research results can be published in standard ways, though only if the classified or otherwise restricted elements are withheld.

A wide array of publicly accessible, online repositories exists—in virtually every academic discipline—for both accessing and contributing to large-scale data sets. The US Federal Data Strategy (http://strategy.data.gov) created a federal open data framework (http://data.gov) that contains "data, tools, and resources to conduct research, develop web and mobile applications, design visualizations, and more." Specific examples of open data repositories include, in the life sciences, GenBank (http://ncbi.nlm.nih.gov/genbank), operated by the National Library of Medicine. GenBank is an online annotated collection of DNA sequences that can be applied to a huge array of research problems. In biology, the Global Plants database (http://plants.jstor.org) is a collection of nearly three million plant specimens. NOAA's National Centers for Environmental Information (http://ncei.noaa.gov) is one of the world's largest archives of atmospheric, coastal, geophysical, and oceanic research. And the Inventories of American Painting and Sculpture (http://americanart.si.edu/research/inventories) document more than 400,000 artworks in public and private collections worldwide. Countless other databases exist, several of which are operated by nonprofit organizations and focus on very specific topics (e.g., the Egyptian pyramids).

11.4 Communicating with Expert Audiences

Although the importance of disseminating outcomes from research and creative activity is fairly obvious, less clear is the issue of *when* such results are actually ready to be communicated. Virtually every researcher will tell you that identifying the completion point of a project is difficult. Additional questions always remain to be answered. Additional experiments always can be run. Tweaks and improvements always are possible. Yet, at some point in the research process, one must declare an outcome ready for publication, performance, exhibition, or other means of dissemination.

Moving too quickly toward dissemination, without sufficient evidence for a given result or enough time spent developing the work, can be embarrassing, damaging to one's career, and deleterious to the scholarly enterprise. Such issues typically are identified and addressed during the peer review process (chapter 7). Also, sharing results in a public forum, formally or informally, can sometimes lead archive publications to decline the submission of a manuscript, or the United States Patent and Trademark Office (USPTO; http://uspto.gov) from issuing a patent (chapter 12). Consequently, one must be extremely careful in assessing *when* the time is right to share research results and also ensure that the results are of the highest quality, are produced with integrity, and represent the work of those involved.

Assuming your research results are in fact ready to be communicated, it is clear we, as a society, have available to us more options for communicating with one another—instantaneously and on a global scale—than ever before in human history. From social media to digital archives to real time streaming video, we are able not only to personally send information to vast numbers of people, but also receive feedback from them and even dialogue with numerous individuals simultaneously. It is within this massive and rapidly evolving ecosystem of communication mechanisms that dissemination of outcomes from scholarly research and creative activity takes place. Yet, in addition to the mechanism or mechanisms used, the communication must consider the audience, the goals of the communication, and ways in which the information being communicated likely will be used. Let us consider these elements separately.

As a researcher, your primary concern usually involves communicating outcomes of your work to peers, that is, to other scholars in your field of expertise, including students. The principal goal is to inform them of your work so they can use or build upon it, and also to identify yourself as having contributed to the existing body of knowledge. Such communication usually takes the form of refereed or archive journal publications, monographs, books, and juried performances or exhibits. The process by which scholarly research is evaluated for publication, presentation or exhibition varies across disciplines, but in general follows the peer/merit review model for grant proposals described in chapter 7. A great deal of communication also occurs at professional conferences, which involve both oral and written forms of dissemination as well as informal conversations.

The content being communicated in all of these examples tends to be deeply intellectual, utilizing terminology, diagrams, and other forms of expression that, for the most part, are understood by experts. Such audiences are found at academic institutions, private corporations, private foundations, conservatories, and at federal government agencies and laboratories. These experts learn of new research results by perusing journals, receiving automated notifications from publishers, and scanning social media posts. Additionally, most organizations, including those which both fund and perform research, issue formal press releases about new research projects and outcomes, and these releases lead to articles in print, online posts, and televised media.

Note that some of today's most challenging and interesting research problems reside not within a given discipline, but at the boundaries of multiple disciplines (chapter 13). A good example is biomedical engineering, which encompasses biology, engineering, medicine, physics, mathematics, and chemistry. This raises the question of how an expert in biology, for example, most effectively communicates her research results to an engineer. This is not an easy task, and not until engineers and biologists have worked together for a while can a biologist pick up a journal of engineering and understand how a particular set of results relate to biology.

The solution, apart from journals that publish research performed at the boundaries of disciplines, such as biomedical engineering, is for researchers to learn how to communicate their discipline-specific research results in ways researchers from other disciplines can discover, view as being relevant, and also understand. You can learn more about methods for doing so in the exercises associated with this chapter. We discuss the issue of team and collaborative research in chapter 13.

11.5   Communicating with General Audiences

The communication of research outcomes to experts in one's field, and even to scholars in other fields, has been occurring for centuries and is a relatively straightforward activity. By analogy, if you love football, talking to a friend who also loves football and is informed about the game is both easy and fun. However, talking about football, and the excitement you have for it, with someone who has little or no knowledge of the game and perhaps limited interest in it, is an entirely different matter, especially if your goal is to help them *become* interested and appreciate it the way you do! The same is true for communicating research outcomes to another very important audience—nonexperts. This includes but is not limited to the general public, special organizations such as think tanks and topical special interest groups, formal or traditional media outlets, popular media, lawmakers and policymakers, political lobbyists, students, informal educators, and K–12 teachers.

Perhaps not surprisingly, this is an area where researchers often fall short because our world consists mostly of working with other experts—a world filled with jargon, methods, and resources that are mysterious and unfamiliar to those on the outside. Yet, the nonexpert audience is one of the most critical because, as described in chapter 3, the social compact for much of the research and creative activity performed exists between experts and the nonexpert taxpayer. Also, many researchers fall into the trap of using the "deficit model" of communication. In it, one sees general audiences as simply uninformed about a particular research outcome. Thus, all a researcher needs to do is explain the outcome and voilà—problem solved! Of course, life is not that simple!

Consequently, the first and most important rule in communicating with a nonexpert audience is to actually know that audience. Note that I said and have been saying "*with* your audience" and not "*to* your audience" because communication to nonexpert audiences should be a dialogue, not a monologue. In fact, I cannot tell you how many times I have seen an excellent researcher stand before a general audience and give their latest highly technical conference presentation with virtually no interaction whatsoever or recognition that they lost the audience after the first sentence. The result was a lot of blank stares and disappointed people, and the situation clearly demonstrated that the researcher did not take time to think about the audience and how to best convey scholarly information to them.

In that context, one should *never* view communicating with a general audience as needing to "dumb down the results." I have had Nobel laureates ask me questions about my field of weather that were surprisingly simplistic—to me because I am an expert, but not to them because they are not. Please do not ever "look down upon" those to whom you are presenting if they are nonexperts. Remember, everyone is an expert in something!

With that preface, I strongly encourage you to actively seek opportunities to present your scholarship to nonexpert audiences. Give presentations or performances to the local Kiwanis and Rotary Clubs, the local Chamber of Commerce and Business Roundtable, or other civic and service organizations. Give presentations or performances at nursing homes, churches, and social clubs. Sign up with a local speaker bureau that helps organizations to identify speakers. You will find that numerous general audience venues exist, and that gratitude and personal fulfillment are high when you to take time to engage with them.

Once you know your audience, think about how you can best interest them in your work by finding points of intersection between your research and their interests or lives. For example, a Chamber of Commerce might be interested to know how your work might help grow the local economy, while a civic fine arts organization might be interested to know how your sculpture is being interpreted by various audiences. When engaging with such general audiences, be sure to avoid using discipline-specific jargon or other expressions with which they are likely to be unfamiliar. This is easier said than done, and developing this skill takes practice.

In the exercises provided with this chapter, you will find the Alan Alda Center for Communicating Science at Stony Brook University. As an actor, Alda shows researchers how to use improvisation, and other acting-based approaches, to help general audiences understand complex topics. Another excellent resource is the Technology, Entertainment and Design (TED; http:// www.ted.com) series of presentations, available on the web. TED presenters are extraordinary and provide some of the best examples of communication with general audiences.

Also, when communicating with a general audience, have specific goals in mind. What points are you trying to get across and what do you want them to remember? You should never make more than three key points. If at all possible, use narratives, give common examples, employ analogies and metaphors, and tell stories that make your topic relatable. Engaging the audience directly is another excellent strategy. Surprise them by asking them a question right at the start and letting several people contribute answers. Make them a character in your story, even if that character is a planet, a molecule, or an animal. Have fun and make jokes, though being careful to avoid doing so in an offensive manner. Quite honestly, many presentations are dry and methodical. Switch things up by injecting humor and telling stories about yourself and the silly mistakes you made on the journey to the results you are presenting. Your audience will love you for that and remember much more of what you say in the process!

Of course, as you are well aware, we live in a world in which certain topics have become lightning rods for violent disagreement, protest, and even murder. Gun control. Abortion. Evolution. Immigration. Climate change. Sexuality. Please think carefully about the following.

The *scholarly study* of these or *any* other topics is extremely important and valuable. Discussion of research outcomes—which hardly ever are the final word on any given topic—*discussion* in a civil and respectful manner—is the hallmark of the research enterprise. We as a society cannot advance if we forget how to communicate or are unwilling to do so in a civil, respectful manner. Spirited debate and disagreement are foundational to research and creative activity, and they can and must occur without *ad hominem* attacks. It is up to you and me—as participants in the research enterprise—to reinforce these notions at every turn. Diversity, equity, and inclusion are extremely important, as discussed throughout this book, and it is our high task to ensure they are authentic. That is, they must not place arbitrary limits on the topic to be discussed, the politics of those involved, or competing theories being addressed.

One final but very important point about communicating on notably divisive topics with general audiences, particularly involving one individual or a small group. If you know up front that the audience or individual disagrees with your position or results, you should not go into the conversation or presentation with the goal of converting them. Studies have shown that even researchers with the best of intentions, and employing the gentlest of approaches, tend to widen the gap of disagreement with their audience if they have even an implicit goal of showing why the audience is wrong. Few people enjoy being shown or told they are wrong, especially if moral or religious issues are at play.

Instead, you, as a researcher, should begin not by speaking, but rather by listening. Also, develop your presentation in a way that respects the views of others, even if you disagree with them, and use the opportunity to begin a conversation. Learning is a road that goes both ways, and building trust with those who disagree with you takes time and patience—and it rarely can be done via social media. So, do not use social media for meaningful debate about scholarly research. At the end of day, you have an obligation to serve as a role model by listening carefully and presenting your results in a manner that respects and considers the views, emotions, and values of others. In doing so you will not compromise your scholarship, but rather offer it in ways that others can understand and appreciate. And indeed, you may well learn to interpret your findings in new and interesting ways that lead you to become both a better scholar and communicator.

11.6 Special Circumstances and Other Helpful Hints

Although it is impossible to cover every possible situation in which communication of research results occurs or is important, I describe here a few of the more common and important ones.

First, when speaking with the press, be very careful and precise with your words. Things you say "off the cuff" and informally can still be "on the record" and thus may find their way into an article. Be careful. Also, realize journalists often are looking to highlight controversial or divisive issues or write an article with a particular edge that attracts readers and garners clicks. Ask to see the article before it is published to ensure accuracy of contents, especially direct quotes. Usually you will be denied, but ask anyway.

Second, learn the so-called elevator speech. In other words, be able to describe the essence of your findings, and their relevance, in plain language in the time it takes to ride an elevator between a few floors, say while speaking with a member of Congress. This practice is being taught in academia via the "three-minute thesis."

Third, if your results are to be communicated via publication in an archive journal, or by a particular press, learn which journals and presses are most appropriate for your topic, most prestigious, or have the widest reach and respect. Measures now exist, imperfect though they are, for assisting you with this task. They include journal impact factors as well as more qualitative, historical measures of prestige and accessibility, especially in the latter for traditionally underrepresented populations.

Fourth, you can track the extent to which your work is being used or formally cited by others using a variety of online tools. Such citation indexes (e.g., the h-index; Hirsch 2005) and other measures, though again imperfect but improving constantly, help assess the impact of your scholarly contributions in specific ways. Similar measures exist for patents, licensed inventions, and other products.

Fifth, if making an oral presentation involving visuals to expert or general audiences alike, make certain the images are relatively simple and can be seen clearly in the back of the room when projected. Clearly define terms that may be unclear, keep text to a minimum, and focus on making a maximum of three points. Additionally, be very careful to give attribution to figures and text that have been taken from previous work, whether formally published or not. A good rule of thumb is that a figure should be understandable on its own, without any explanation or accompanying text.

Sixth and finally, if giving a presentation, performance or exhibit, be certain all audio and lighting are properly configured. Testing of these and other elements is common practice and usually done quite well. However, as the scholar, you have the final responsibility of making certain everything is as it should be so that your work shines as brightly as it can. Nothing is as frustrating as losing time, especially if it is limited, owing to technical difficulties.

Assess Your Comprehension

1. List several reasons demonstrating the importance of effectively communicating research outcomes.
2. Define open access in the context of research and creative activity. Compare and contrast it with public access.
3. List and describe several limitations of traditional publishing and ways in which open access seeks to address them.

4. Describe, and compare and contrast, various models of open access publishing (e.g., gold, green, hybrid).

5. Describe challenges associated with open access to data.

6. Describe the four principles associated with FAIR access to data: findable, accessible, interoperable, and reusable.

7. What is the current federal policy, developed by the White House Office of Science and Technology Policy (OSTP), for open access to publications and data?

8. In what ways is research, funded by private companies, handled differently, with regard to publication of results in comparison to that funded by the federal government?

9. What factors should you consider in determining whether your research results are ready for presentation?

10. What issues should you consider when communicating your research results to peers?

11. What issues should you consider, and what things should you avoid, when communicating your research results to general, nonexpert audiences?

12. List opportunities to communicate research results to nonexpert audiences.

13. How can you, as a researcher, most effectively communicate your research results if they pertain to topics that are politically or socially sensitive?

14. List important things to remember when communicating with the press.

15. Why is a brief (e.g., three-minute) summary of your research, for a general audience, valuable, and when might you use it?

16. What tools exist for you to judge the quality of professional journals and the impact of your research on your or other fields of scholarship?

Exercises to Deepen Your Understanding

Exercise 1: Suppose a member of Congress representing your district will be casting his or her vote on a new bill regarding a controversial issue or topic about which you are passionate. Currently, this member is undecided as to which way he or she will vote. You have been given an opportunity to deliver a three-minute presentation to this member, the day before the vote, to share your thoughts about the topic. For this exercise, write a script for a three-minute presentation you believe would best convince your member to seriously consider your point of view.

Exercise 2: The concept of open access publications generally is accepted as valuable for accelerating progress in research, particularly because it empowers individuals and organizations that historically have been unable to access the literature. However, differing viewpoints exist on a variety of key issues depending upon one's role in the scholarly research enterprise (e.g., researcher, student, head of an academic library, university provost, university vice president/vice chancellor for research, large for-profit publisher, large nonprofit publisher, professional society publisher, and the general public). For this exercise, use the literature and other information available to compare and contrast the positions on open access of several of the aforementioned groups. What federal government policies would you recommend to accelerate open access, and what implications would they have on the groups you selected?

Exercise 3: Communicating effectively with a nonexpert on a complicated topic is a challenge, though one that increasingly is important to the research enterprise. Select a topic that most interests you, perhaps from an earlier exercise (for example, the one for which you have performed a literature review), and prepare a two- or three-minute video overview of the topic using your smartphone. Use graphics as you see fit and invite someone to operate the camera for you. Now, watch the videos linked at https://vimeo .com/253144273 from the Alan Alda Center for Communicating Science (http://aldacenter.org). Note how the removal of jargon greatly improves the ability of people to understand your work! Re-record your video presentation after following instructions in the Alda Center videos and compare it with your original version. Which do you feel is more effective, and why? Although the Alda Center videos speak to issues in science, the concepts are applicable to all disciplines.

Exercise 4: A wide variety of venues exist in which to communicate the outcomes and impacts of research and creative activity. They include but are not limited to church and civic organizations, nursing homes, college dorms, coffee shops, bars, and private companies. Given the sorts of topics in research and creative activity that most interest you, which venues would you select for communicating your work to nonexpert audiences, and why? Would you use different approaches based upon the organization or venue? How might you use social media to achieve the same goals, and what specific approaches do you believe would be most appropriate for different social media venues (e.g., Facebook, Twitter, Instagram, LinkedIn, etc.)?

Exercise 5: As described in this chapter, preprint servers increasingly are being utilized to publicly post scholarly articles prior to their formal review or prior to a decision regarding such review. This strategy brings benefits to the research enterprise but also has shortcomings. Investigate the use of pre-print servers by multiple publishing outlets, both traditional and open access, and explore how such servers have impacted research and public opinion regarding the COVID-19 pandemic. Note in particular preprint server papers on the topics of COVID-19 and SARS-CoV-2 that have been discussed in the press, only to be withdrawn or discredited. What consequences resulted from such situations, and what recommendations would you offer to improve the use of preprint servers?

12

Yours, Mine, and Ours: Ownership of Research Outcomes

Chapter Overview and Learning Objectives

As research and creative activity proceed and scholars give thought to disseminating the associated work products (chapter 11), they also must consider ownership rights and protections of those products, also known as intellectual property (IP). This chapter provides a foundation for understanding IP, the policies and laws governing its ownership, how it is protected, methods of disposition, and benefits accruing to the owner/inventor, his or her institution, and society more broadly. Additionally, it discusses challenges associated with IP in the context of multisector R&D partnerships. After reading this chapter, you should

- Be able to define and explain IP and the important role it plays in research and innovation;
- Explain federal policies and laws governing IP ownership;
- Differentiate among the various types of IP protection and know how to access and apply them;
- Understand how the academic enterprise supports researchers in IP commercialization and the various mechanisms available for the disposition of IP; and
- Be able to describe the value to society of IP.

12.1 Context, Definition, and Importance of Intellectual Property

In chapters 1 and 3, we discussed how research and creative activity follow naturally from our innate human curiosity about, and our desire to improve, the world in which we live. We also discussed the spectrum of research, from so-called basic/fundamental/discovery research—which does not necessarily have a practical end in mind but is the seed corn of innovation—to use-inspired, applied research and development, which frequently builds upon fundamental research and seeks to create practical, implementable solutions to specific problems. Yet, as noted in chapter 11, research outcomes only have *value* (monetary and otherwise) if they are made known to others. This is where the topic of the present chapter becomes relevant. That is, the valuation of research outcomes. Not surprisingly, this leads to the related question of who owns those outcomes and thus who can benefit from them, especially financially. In this context, research outcomes are referred to as intellectual property (IP).

To understand the importance of IP and the role of academic institutions in its creation and disposition, it is useful to briefly review how universities evolved during the past 150 years. One of the most important developments was establishment of the land-grant university by the Morrill Land-grant Act, signed by President Lincoln in 1862. The Act required each state to set aside roughly thirty thousand acres of public land, per member of the state's congressional delegation, based upon the 1860 census. Proceeds from the sale of this land funded public colleges and universities, with emphasis on those specializing in the agricultural and mechanical arts. This specialization is where the acronym A&M came from, as in Texas A&M University.

Subsequent acts were passed, and the development of extension services became a core part of the land-grant model. With typically one extension office in every county of a land-grant state, these "extensions of the university" provide services and new capabilities to citizens, mostly to agricultural interests, which is a form of economic development and technology transfer. Today, the role of extension offices continues to evolve, consistent with our move from an industrial and agrarian economy to one based upon knowledge, data and information.

Up to the time of World War II, university research was funded principally by private foundations and philanthropy. Very little federal government funding was involved, though that changed rapidly after the war. Given that university researchers helped develop the atomic bomb and other innovations, such as radar, which led to the Allied victory, the federal government not only began funding university research on a much grander scale, but also helped set public and private expectations for research universities, including land-grant institutions. We discussed this "social compact" in chapter 3.

With federal government—that is, taxpayer—funding for research at universities came the notion that everyone should have equal access to research outcomes. In other words, what the public paid for, the public should be able to access. This seems logical unless you are an entrepreneur or a private company looking for a competitive advantage. If you invest money commercializing an outcome from academic IP, but everyone else has access to the same IP, what is your leverage against the competition?

In 1980, Congress passed the Bayh-Dole Act, which allows academic institutions to protect the assets of federally funded innovations and control their disposition, subject to a few caveats. We dive more deeply into the Bayh-Dole Act in the next section, but for now, consider academic institutions themselves and how they have changed in the age of IP commercialization.

Traditionally, quoting Hill (2012, slides 14 and 15), modern research universities have served as: "a place for teaching and learning; a codifier of, and repository for, old knowledge and understanding; a generator of new knowledge and understanding; a community for personal growth; a transmitter of values and builder of citizens; a neutral space for debate; a home for criticism of society; and an organizer of entertainments." However, in the past few decades, public expectations of research universities have changed markedly. The role of research universities today encompasses most of the elements just mentioned, but also includes universities serving as "a generator of new technologies; a prime source of new ideas; a founder of new companies; a solver of practical problems; a partner in economic development; a bridge to the world; a venue for political presentation; a critical contributor to economic growth; and a source of specialist leadership." Notice the components of technology development, company creation, economic development, and economic growth. All of these connect directly to and rely upon IP. So, let us now define it.

The World Intellectual Property Organization (2020) (http://wipo.int/portal/en/) defines IP as "creations of the mind," which includes "everything from works of art to inventions, computer programs to trademarks and other commercial signs." Another good definition (van Dusen 2013) sees IP as "products of the human intellect that are unique, new and innovative, have some value in the marketplace, and are the creation of a single person or team." Some mistakenly refer to IP as patents, copyrights, trademarks, and trade secrets. Those items are *not* IP but rather are mechanisms for *protecting* IP and those who utilize it.

Some of the most well-known examples of research-based university IP that resulted in hugely successful products and services are shown below:

- Google, invented at Stanford University
- Rocket fuel, invented at Clark University
- Insulin and the electron microscope, invented at the University of Toronto
- Penicillin, discovered at Oxford University
- The heart-lung machine, invented at the University of Minnesota

- Gatorade, invented at the University of Florida
- Magnetic resonance imaging, developed at the State University of New York
- The time release capsule, developed at the University of Kansas
- The blood thinning agent Warfarin, invented at the University of Wisconsin

Not only did these and other inventions, discoveries, and contributions bring vast benefits to society on a global scale, but they also led to substantial financial windfalls for the inventors *and* their institutions.

For example, according to the sports network ESPN (Rovell 2015), those who developed Gatorade some five decades ago, and their families and friends, have made more than $1 billion in royalties from the widely used drink product. The University of Florida, where the work was performed, has made nearly $300 million in royalties. Although success stories of this magnitude are, not surprisingly, somewhat rare, the commercialization of academic IP continues to grow and yield tremendous benefits for the inventors, their institutions, and society. We examine more closely national and global statistics in subsequent sections of this chapter, as well as the challenges faced by colleges and universities, their faculty, and students in IP commercialization.

Based on the examples just presented, it may appear as though IP is relevant only to technological inventions and discoveries. Such is not the case. From your favorite books you read as a child to the songs you listen to in the car to the latest TV show or movie you watched, a great deal of IP exists in forms of scholarship including but not limited to: novels and poems, films, music scores, plays, ballets, dances, paintings, and sculptures. This is why you, as a next-generation scholar, need to understand what IP is *and* is not, how to protect it and yourself, and how to utilize IP effectively.

Unfortunately, many students go through college without ever hearing about or understanding IP, and as a result, they pay a price upon entering the workforce. For example, if you invent something valuable and do not patent it, you may miss a huge opportunity to see it put into practice, or even worse, watch helplessly as someone else takes your idea and becomes very wealthy from it. If you do not understand the notion of copyright, you could end up creating major problems for your employer or miss an opportunity to receive royalties from a brilliant musical composition, computer code, or piece of courseware that might see broad use nationally or internationally. So, you see, IP is not solely the domain of scientists and technology inventors, attorneys and contract negotiators, but rather is something every scholar, within *every* discipline, needs to understand.

Numerous organizations within the academic enterprise focus on IP and related topics such as technology commercialization, including the Association of American Universities (AAU; http://aau.edu), the Association of Public and Land-grant Universities (APLU; http://aplu.org), the Government-University-Industry Research Roundtable (GUIRR; http://nationalacademies.org/guirr /government-university-industry-research-roundtable), the Association of University Technology Managers (AUTM; https://autm.net), the Federal Demonstration Partnership (FDP; http://thefdp.org), and the University-Industry Demonstration Partnership (UIDP; http://uidp.org). And a new report by COGR (Council on Governmental Relations 2022) dispels various myths about technology transfer in US universities. You should consult these and other sources if you wish to dive even deeper into the topics of IP, technology commercialization, and entrepreneurship.

Finally, it is important to remember that not every piece of IP can be protected everywhere on earth, and indeed, circumstances may exist in which "creations of the mind" can have utility without being disclosed generally. We refer to this IP as "know-how." Indeed, the intellectual capacity of faculty and students in our colleges and universities is an enormously powerful and valuable asset that sometimes is overlooked in the context of IP. Quite frequently, private companies wish to tap this know-how to help solve problems or address challenges without ever performing research or creating an outcome that could be considered IP in the classic sense. Such capability is one of the innumerable benefits of colleges and universities, as discussed in chapter 3 and described further in section 13.7.

12.2 Types of Intellectual Property Protection

In everyday life, we have certain rights, including rights to privacy, liberty, and property. In the case of IP, certain legally enforceable rights can be granted because the US and other nations recognize the rights of individuals and corporations to own and use the assets that result from intellectual endeavors— that is, research and creative activity. More specifically, as in other types of rights, IP rights represent a form of protection—for the inventor or creator of IP, as well as for the user or investor who wishes to innovate with it to provide benefit to society. The type of protection utilized depends in large part on the nature of the innovation and its novelty, and four principal types exist: *copyright*, *patent*, *trademark*, and *trade secret*. We consider them individually and then later describe circumstances under which these protections are most effectively applied as part of the research and IP commercialization processes. The type of protection also depends upon the intended use of the IP. An excellent and succinct summary of the four types of IP protection may be found in Blakeslee (2004).

Beginning with *copyright*, US Code (17 USC § 102) defines it as a protection for "original works of authorship fixed in any tangible medium of expression." Whew! Let us unpack this important sentence point by point.

First, the term "work" refers to any intellectual creation, which might be a book, musical score, painting, film, data base, choreography, poem, computer program, technical drawing, recording, photograph, set of processes, and so on. Second, this work must have an "author," which might be one or multiple individuals. We will see below that determining the amount of credit assigned among multiple authors can be a challenge. Third, a medium of expression must exist, and it must be "tangible"; that is, exist in a physical, fixed form. The examples I just gave fit this requirement. Finally, and not actually mentioned formally in our definition, the work must be "original," which is consistent with our earlier concept of research as original contributions to knowledge.

Many scholars are surprised to learn that a copyright is established for a given work as soon as the work is created in a tangible, fixed form. Even a blog post you write is automatically copyrighted once you create it. No action is needed on your part. That said, one can *register* a copyright with the US Copyright Office. Although doing so is optional, the value of registration includes proof of ownership and the ability to enforce use standards of your work.

Because some people devote their entire careers to copyright law and policy, it is not surprising that copyright contains numerous complexities and nuances. You can explore these and other topics by consulting works in the references (e.g., Blakeslee 2004; Van Dusen 2013). Ultimately, copyright affords the author protections such as clearly assigning credit and recognition for having created the work and also provides the author control over the reproduction, publication, performance, or translation of the work into other languages. Copyright also incentivizes scholarship by providing a means for authors to receive a financial reward, say via royalties for a music score, thus stimulating additional research and creative activity for the benefit of society.

The second type of protection is the *patent*, which confers on the patent holder "only the right to exclude others from making, selling, or using the patent holder's invention" (US Patent and Trademark Office n.d.). Some mistakenly believe patents confer a right or are required to utilize or market IP, but such is not the case. As you will see in the next section, the IP license fulfills that role. Three types of patents exist: utility patents, design patents, and plant patents.

Utility patents are the most common and cover items you would expect; that is, devices, processes, molecular formulations, and so on. Design patents relate to designs for something that can be manufactured, though the design itself is only ornamental, not functional (which would fall under utility patents). The third type of patent is the plant patent which, as the name implies, is granted to inventors of certain types of plants. If any work is seen as having potentially significant financial or societal value, then patent protection usually is sought.

Drilling down now on the most common patent, the utility patent, it is granted if the discovery is novel, useful, and nonobvious. Novelty is determined by patent searching for published evidence of the invention, called "prior art," to ensure that an item to be patented has in fact not already been patented or disclosed publicly. Patents only can be obtained via a very formal process in which a series of application steps is made to the USPTO. Because the patenting process can be quite expensive, especially if substantial legal background work is required, considerable thought must be given as to whether a patent is really necessary.

A provisional patent is the easiest first step because it is relatively informal and requires only a modest filing fee. It establishes an early effective filing date but requires the inventor to make formal application within one year. No examination is required of the work—the filing is simply a place holder. It is extremely important to recognize that patents are granted not to those who are first to *create* the work, but those who are first to *file*. In the US, one has only a year to file a patent from the time the work is first made public. For example, if you present your work at a national conference and then, two years later, decide to file a patent on that same work—well, you are out of luck! And finally, patents are valid twenty years from the date of filing, and both US and international patents may be obtained depending upon the potential market for the product or service.

The third type of IP protection is the *trademark*. I am sure you have seen the capital TM symbol on logos, but what really is a trademark? Basically, it is an identifier for a "word, name, symbol, device or combination of these things to distinguish one's goods, products or services from those of another." One of the most famous is the Nike "swoosh." As another example, the logo of the University of Oklahoma is an interlocking O and U. Whenever you see it, say on clothing or the website or brochures, you will see either the symbol TM or an R within a circle, the latter of which means the trademark has been registered with the USPTO and thus cannot be used without the university's permission. Sometimes that permission is given in return for monetary or other considerations.

The final type of IP protection is the *trade secret* or "know-how." It is defined in 18 USC § 1839(3) as "All forms and types of financial, business, scientific, technical, economic, or engineering information, including patterns, plans, compilations, program devices, formulas, designs, prototypes, methods, techniques, processes, procedures, programs, or codes, whether tangible or intangible, and whether or how stored, compiled, or memorialized physically, electronically, graphically, photographically, or in writing if: (a) the owner thereof has taken reasonable measures to keep such information secret; and (b) the information derives independent economic value, actual or potential, from not being generally known to, and not being readily ascertainable through proper means by, another person who can obtain economic value from the disclosure or use of the information."

Perhaps the best example is the highly secret and well-guarded formula for Coca-Cola. Federal law makes the theft of trade secrets a crime. If, however, a soft drink company were to replicate the Coca-Cola taste and even the formula on its own, without having actually accessed the real formula directly, they would be free to produce their drink and could not be sued for patent infringement. In other words, legal protection of trade secrets is limited to situations only in which the secret was improperly obtained.

12.3   Policies, Procedures, and Challenges in the Academic Enterprise

In light of the role played by academic institutions in today's economic and technology development ecosystem, many of them, and especially research universities, now have offices of technology development, economic development, technology commercialization, and/or IP licensing (section 1.6). Not only do these offices lead the creation and enforcement of institutional policies governing IP, but they also serve as institutional focal points for moving research outcomes into practice for societal and institutional benefit. In so doing, they provide a wide array of services to faculty, staff, and student researchers in navigating the many complexities associated with IP. Most importantly, the technology transfer or licensing office can help you evaluate the protectable elements of your IP and develop a strategy for transitioning your innovation to the public domain in a way that complements your research efforts.

However, many academic institutions do not have such resources, especially MSIs and ERIs. It is vitally important that everyone in America's postsecondary research and education enterprise has access to the resources needed to be successful, including those involving IP. Fortunately, Congress, and the National Science Foundation in particular, are addressing this compelling need through a series of financial investments and programmatic innovations, one of which is NSF's GRANTED (Growing Research Access for Nationally Transformative Equity and Diversity) program. Remember, research outcomes are the end product of the research process and consequently have great intellectual and other value. Do not be discouraged if your institution lacks the resources needed to protect those outcomes and bring their benefits to society in tangible ways. Suggestions are provided throughout this chapter regarding how you can obtain the assistance needed to manage your IP.

An important question facing all researchers, and especially those in the academic enterprise, involves knowing *when* an outcome of research or creative activity becomes IP. You may recall from chapter 11 the difficulty researchers sometimes face in knowing when research results are ready to be communicated, say in publications, recitals, or exhibitions. The same is true in filing protections for IP. The answer, as noted in the previous section, is clear for copyrights, trademarks, and trade secrets. However, patents are another matter altogether. In addition, each institution, be it a university, private company, nonprofit organization, or state or federal agency, has its own internal processes for seeking patent protection. Given the focus of this book on academic research, I will discuss processes most common to academic research institutions and use the utility patent as the example of protection being sought.

At some point in the research process, one realizes the work performed is sufficiently mature or complete, and may have enough potential value in the marketplace, to warrant consideration of being patented (note that market value isn't always a strong consideration). For example, suppose an academic researcher develops a new type of battery that charges in seconds, is extremely small, but has massive storage capacity. Laboratory experiments may have been performed using only a crude model of the device and a limited number of application scenarios under highly controlled conditions. Yet, the results are unmistakably positive and perhaps revolutionary. Although additional work certainly will need to be performed prior to the battery becoming a commercial product, the researcher judges the results so potentially significant that exploring IP protection seems warranted.

To ascertain whether a patent is, in fact, appropriate, the researcher files a formal IP disclosure with their institution, usually one of the offices noted previously. This disclosure is a formal document containing a detailed description of the IP, a list of all inventors and the proportional contributions of each, background information on existing and possibly competing IP, how the disclosed IP advances the current state of the art, potential markets, how the work was funded, whether any existing commercial products are part of the IP, whether and when the IP was presented in the public domain, and sometimes other information. The office then works with the researcher and other institutional officials to determine whether to file a patent. In so doing, the institution usually pays the filing cost, though sometimes it can be recouped if the IP is licensed.

Regarding the latter point, as described in the next section, IP is made available for practice via the issuing of a license, with a portion of the revenues from associated products and services usually reverting back to the developers and their institution. The percentages governing revenue splits are set by the academic institution and usually are designed to incentivize researchers and the institution to pursue activities that lead to more IP.

If your institution does not have an IP or technology commercialization office, speak with your advisor, department chair, or dean to learn about whether and how the institution deals with IP. If they or the institution have little or no experience doing so, opportunities exist to partner with nearby institutions which do (usually requiring some sort of payment), or utilize legal firms on retainer which specialize in IP law. Also, national organizations can be helpful, and one in particular is the APLU Office of Economic Development and Community Engagement. Although APLU does not provide IP services per se, it can be helpful in identifying partners and connecting those institutions that have needs to those that have resources.

Although the creation and disposition of IP are now common practices in many academic institutions, certain challenges exist. For example, applied research and development tend to yield more patentable outcomes, and often fewer opportunities to publish in the scholarly literature, than fundamental or discovery research. Yet, the reward system for faculty tenure and promotion still tends to place greater value on fundamental research, even though academic institutions are placing ever greater emphasis on solving practical problems, commercializing IP, and contributing to economic development.

These competing forces, which include fears about academic research being directed more toward the applied end of the spectrum (chapter 1) based upon budgetary trends of funding sources and institutional roles, lead to tensions which today are only partly resolved. Fortunately, things are improving. About a decade ago, the National Academy of Inventors (http://academyofinventors .org) was established to bring appropriate recognition to researchers at academic institutions and nonprofit research institutes. This move highlights the importance of inventions and the roles played by these institutions in economic development. The Academy also serves as an important force in modifying the academic reward system to give greater weight to the generation of IP in performance evaluations.

Another challenge concerns ownership of IP and the distribution of royalties from it. At most academic institutions, IP is owned by the institution or its governing board. This makes sense because, in the context of research, creative activity, or the development of educational materials, the work is performed by employees of the institution, using institutional resources. However, as you might imagine, some researchers believe they should own the IP because the idea and work originated with them, irrespective of where the work was performed. In the case of students, the situation is a bit murky because at some institutions, students—especially graduate students—are considered employees while at others, they are not.

Some academic institutions have agreed to waive their right of IP ownership, either completely or in certain situations, thereby allowing researchers to deal with it on their own. Although this can be valuable, all of the responsibility and cost, say for patenting and commercialization, rests with the researcher. The tradeoff is that researchers taking on these additional responsibilities tend to be drawn away from their work, spending considerable time on IP-related activities rather than on the research that gave rise to the IP in the first place. The bottom line is that, prior to becoming an employee of any organization, you should carefully evaluate all IP policies and ask for explanations of any that are unclear to you.

Finally, as described previously, research results are valuable only if they are made known to and used by others. This presents a bit of a dilemma in academia because, on the one hand, academic institutions are founded upon the notion of unfettered distribution of scholarly outcomes, while on the other hand, economic engagement increasingly is a foundational mission, and innovation may require protection for the effective use by a commercial partner. Finding the right balance between openness and protection can be difficult, though general agreement exists about the value of both elements in the academic research ecosystem. The best thing to do is contact your institution's technology transfer or licensing office personnel before publishing your work. They can provide advice on the protectable aspects of your innovation and do the heavy lifting with respect to filing for protection domestically and internationally to ensure you receive attribution and retain control over how your discoveries are used in the public domain.

12.4 Disposition of Intellectual Property

Once IP has been identified and formally disclosed, what happens to it? Three principal options exist when considering disposition of IP: first, licensing the IP to an existing company or other entity, such as a nonprofit organization; second, starting a new company or entity; and third, doing nothing with the IP.

Consider first the option of doing nothing, which in fact was the norm for the US government until the Bayh-Dole Act, formally known as the Government Patent Policy Act (US House of Representatives n.d.), was signed into law in 1980 and expanded in 1983. Prior to passage of this law, the federal government held title to any invention created using federal funding. That is, the federal government owned it all. The government also controlled patents and would not grant exclusive licenses to IP. Consequently, little incentive existed on the part of private companies to license government IP because their competitors could do exactly the same thing.

As a result, in 1978, the federal government owned more than 28,000 patents, yet quite remarkably and not surprisingly, it had licensed less than 5 percent of them (US General Accounting Office 1978). And inventions reported to the government actually began to decline even though a boom in federal funding for research was underway. Lawmakers recognized this problem, and the Bayh-Dole Act was the result.

Bayh-Dole allows institutions performing government-sponsored research, including academic institutions, to hold title and right to the IP resulting from the research, and to be able to license it, including exclusively, to anyone they wish.[1] As you might imagine, Bayh-Dole quickly incentivized colleges and universities to commercialize their IP, thus bringing the benefits of their research to the public in more tangible ways while also generating royalties to support additional work. It also incentivized more colleges and universities to spin out companies and, in many cases, hold equity in them. In the last section of this chapter, you will see the fruit of Bayh-Dole, which you may find quite impressive.

With the Bayh-Dole Act in place, the licensing process took center stage in the academic IP world. An IP license, known as a license agreement, is a formal, legally binding contract, issued by the owner of the IP, such as a university or its contracting agent, which conveys upon the recipient certain rights related to the practice of IP. Thus, instead of doing nothing with IP, an institution may choose to license it to an existing company or entity, which is the second overall option for disposition.

Although many types of licenses exist, numerous elements are common among them. First, the license enumerates the parties involved, provides a rationale for creation of the license, and defines various terms used. Second, the license very clearly defines the IP in question, be it patented or not, and lays out certain conditions for commercialization. One of the most important of these is due diligence, especially for exclusive licenses. That is, the university issuing the license wants to ensure the IP is acted upon and not left sitting on the shelf. Consequently, a specified period of time is agreed to in which the company obtaining the license must act in good faith to commercialize the IP. If such commercialization is unsuccessful, the license describes the consequences.

Third, the license sometimes specifies the domain or domains in which the IP may be practiced (for example, in a certain component of an industry, such as the exploration of oil in deep water only), and whether the license is exclusive or nonexclusive. An exclusive license is exactly what it sounds like, and in exercising this option, academic institutions must carefully weigh the tradeoff of engaging with a single entity only, which may not succeed, against the freedom to engage with many others, thereby increasing the opportunity for success. Usually, even in the case of exclusive licenses, the academic institution owning the IP maintains a right to utilize it in research and education, which of course is in the interest of the licensee.

Fourth, the license agreement lays out terms of the license, such as recouping fees paid by the college or university (or its licensing agent) for patenting, as well as royalties that will be paid to the academic institution or licensing agent by the company licensing the IP. This latter point often is challenging because the value of the IP in the commercial marketplace usually is unknown at the start. This is because, as noted previously, academic research leads to outcomes but not to products and services that are immediately commercializable. Most of the time, additional work is needed to innovate on research outcomes and turn them into products.

The gap between research outcome, which usually was funded by the government, and innovated product, which usually is produced and funded by a company, is referred to colloquially as the "valley of death" (figure 3.4). Why? Because non-research (i.e., development) funding—usually from private foundations, venture capitalists, angel investors, or other sources—is needed to bridge this gap and translate research outcomes into practicable products and services. Even if a product is forthcoming, it may not be competitive or may have been overtaken by a development elsewhere. Thus, the valley of death is the valley of big bets and big uncertainty.

Finally, the license agreement covers other topics such as options for sublicensing, indemnification, insurance, termination, publicity, use of logos, and the manner in which disputes will be litigated.

In many cases, the IP to be commercialized does not yet exist, but is developed via a partnership between a company and an academic institution (chapter 13). The partnership often takes the form of a sponsored research agreement, whereby the company funds academic researchers to study a particular topic of interest. Such agreements, also legally binding, lay out IP provisions prior to the work being undertaken. In most cases, existing IP brought to a project by an academic institution continues to be owned by it, and vice versa for the company. Any IP developed jointly by company and academic researchers is jointly owned, with each party usually having undivided, nonexclusive rights to the invention. Most colleges and universities also retain a nonexclusive right to practice the IP for educational and research purposes. To that point, they typically will not agree to perform any work that involves restrictions on publication of results, especially for student theses and dissertations, though a delay of two or three months, prior to publication, often is allowed for the company or university to evaluate the IP and file for patent protection if deemed appropriate.

The research agreement typically grants the sponsoring company a right of first refusal to negotiate a license once the IP has been disclosed. This can be a major sticking point for many companies that fund academic research because, in spite of such investments—which can be substantial in some cases—they understandably view their only return as an option to negotiate access to something that they already funded. Adding to their discomfort is the fact that the value of the IP is not known in advance, even though the terms of the license agreement usually must be finalized before work begins. In reality, academic institutions that perform corporate-sponsored research do in fact bring a great deal to the table, including buildings, equipment, services, personnel and their expertise, and reputation—none of which the company paid for directly. Thus, the private company is leveraging extraordinary assets, which unfortunately is a point lost during many academic-corporate negotiations. The important point to bear in mind is that academic-corporate interactions represent a partnership in which all participants invest and in which all participants reap benefits.

The third option for the disposition of IP is to start a company. This form of technology commercialization exploded across the academic enterprise after passage of the Bayh-Dole Act. Although incorporating a for-profit company is relatively simple and inexpensive, the process that follows can be quite laborious. We hear of stories, such as for Apple and Facebook, where a company was started in a garage and dorm room, respectively, with a brilliant idea and a few collaborators. That still occurs! When a college or university, however, is involved with starting a company based on IP developed by its researchers, its staff sometimes help prepare the business plan, identify capital, identify and assemble the leadership team, and perhaps even house the start-up in incubator space. And of course, the academic institution usually has a vested interest in its start-ups via holding an equity stake and receiving revenues from IP licensed to them.

In fact, the meteoric rise of maker spaces, coworking spaces for start-ups, regional innovation hubs, and multidisciplinary entrepreneurship programs that engage faculty, students and existing companies in developing business plans attests to the great interest in, and value placed by academic institutions—and the communities in which they are located—in starting new companies. The principal down side to academic start-ups is that the developers of the IP—the researchers—are the de facto subject matter experts and thus usually are heavily involved with starting the company. Care therefore must be taken by the institution to fully support researchers in creating the company so they are able to continue their research and manage conflicts of interest. Fortunately, numerous federal funding programs exist to support the creation and growth of small companies, especially in collaboration with academic institutions. Among them are the Small Business Innovation Research (SBIR), Small Business Technology Transfer (STTR), and I-Corps (Innovation Corps) programs.

12.5   The Value to Society of Academic Intellectual Property

A number of excellent sources exist for information regarding the impact to society of academic IP commercialization. Most notable among them are the Association of University Technology Managers (AUTM), NSB's biennial Science and Engineering Indicators (the gold standard for global data on the science and engineering research and education enterprise), and the World Intellectual Property Organization. I highlight here only some of the key measures and show how the US fares in the globally competitive environment in which we now live.

According to AUTM (Association of University Technology Managers n.d.-b), during the twenty-year period from 1996 to 2017, IP commercialization and technology transfer in the US academic enterprise contributed $865 billion to the US gross domestic product and supported 5.9 million jobs. More than 480,000 invention disclosures were filed by, and more than 117,000 patents were issued to, universities. Some 15,000 start-up companies were created, and 68 percent of IP to start-ups and small companies was licensed from universities. In 2020 alone, universities submitted over 27,000 invention disclosures (compared to only 10,800 in 1998), filed 17,738 patent applications, were issued 8,706 US patents, executed 10,050 licenses and options, were responsible for creating more than 900 new products, and launched 1,117 start-up companies. And the research institutions received equity from almost half of the start-ups. As one might expect, the number of invention disclosures in the US correlates directly with total US research expenditures, as shown in figure 12.1. This underscores the importance of healthy federal, corporate, and nonprofit organization funding in the nation's research enterprise.

Considering now how the US compares globally, data from NSF show that the share of patents issued in the US steadily declined from 2012 through 2016 (figure 12.2), now representing less than 50 percent of all patents issued globally. The only country showing a steady increase during this same period is China, which still issues less than 5 percent of all patents. It is interesting to see the breakdown of US patents by manufacturing and nonmanufacturing

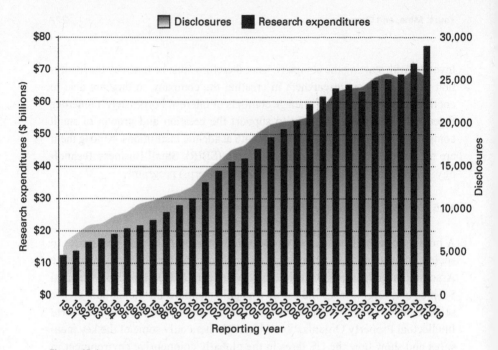

Figure 12.1
Total US research expenditures and number of invention disclosures received from 1991 through 2015. *Source*: Association of University Technology Managers (n.d.-a).

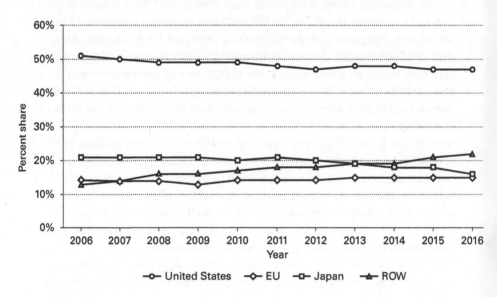

Figure 12.2
Percent share of patents granted by the US Patent and Trademark Office by region/country/ economy of inventor during the period from 2006 to 2016. ROW denotes the rest of the world. *Source*: National Science Board (2018a).

industries (figure 12.3), and not surprisingly, the numbers are largest for computer and information-related technologies and services.

Consider now the degree to which a country is active in a given area of technology patented. The so-called patent activity index measures this attribute and is computed as the ratio of a country's share of a technology area to its share of all patents in that area. Thus, a ratio or patent activity index greater than one, in a given area, shows that the country is more active in that area.

Figure 12.4 shows the patent activity index for the US, the European Union (EU), and Japan. One remarkable feature is that the US has an index of one or greater in all but three of the technology areas listed, with clear emphasis on information technology and related device activities. With optics as a major focal point for decades, both in cameras and instruments, Japan continues to dominate this technology domain.

As noted previously, venture capital (VC)—which is money provided by investors, at considerable risk, to start-up companies that are believed to have long-term growth potential—is a critical component of academic IP commercialization. The degree of VC investment made is an indicator of the availability of IP, its quality, and the extent to which it is viewed as viable in the marketplace.

Figure 12.5 illustrates VC investment in the US relative to the rest of the world (ROW). Although the amount invested in the US has remained relatively steady during the period shown and has been larger than for ROW, the graph suggests significant changes are occurring. These changes are driven principally by the continued rapid rise of China and its massive investments in education, universities, and research infrastructure, as indicated in figure 12.6, which shows the breakdown of ROW among key contributing countries. Although the US celebrates the rise of other nations, especially developing countries, in the research, education, and technology commercialization enterprises, it is critical for the US to continue investing. Doing so will allow us to maintain our global leadership position and thus continue generating the benefits associated with that position to the nation and world.

Assess Your Comprehension

1. Describe the Morrill Land-grant Act and its significance in the American education and research enterprise.
2. Who had access to federally funded research outcomes prior to 1980?
3. What are the fundamental tenets of the Bayh-Dole Act?

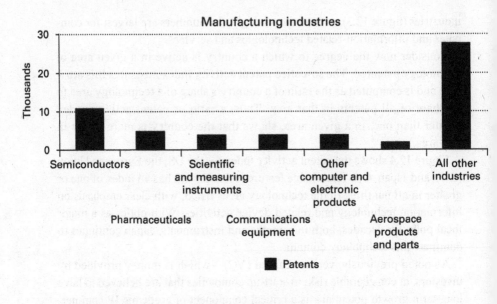

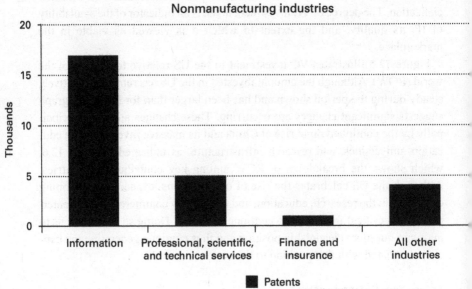

Figure 12.3
Patents granted by the US Patent and Trademark Office by manufacturing and nonmanufacturing industries for 2012. *Source*: National Science Board (2016c).

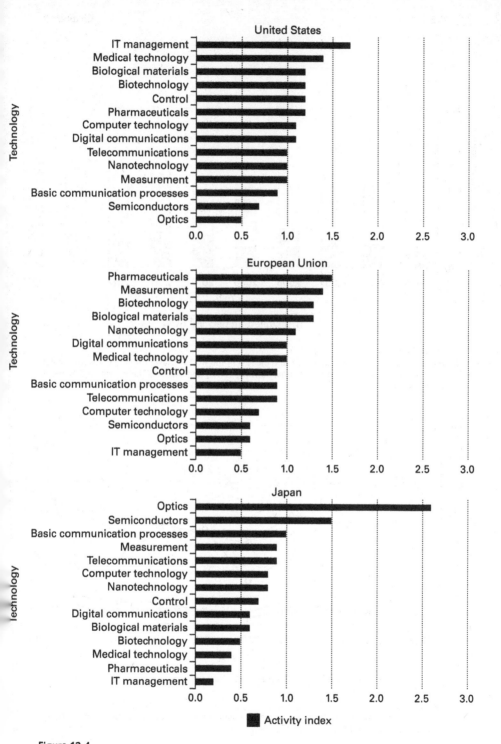

Figure 12.4
Patent activity index of selected technologies for the US, the EU, and Japan for the period from 2012 to 2014. *Source*: National Science Board (2016a).

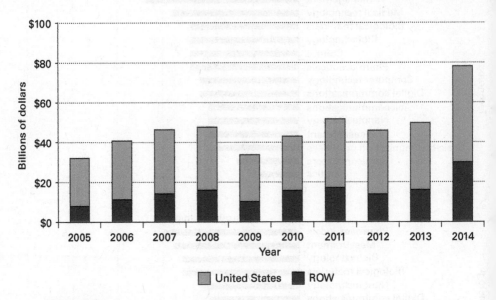

Figure 12.5
Venture capital investment in the US and the rest of the world (ROW) for the period from 2005 to 2014. ROW includes Canada, China, Europe, India, and Israel. *Source*: National Science Board (2016e).

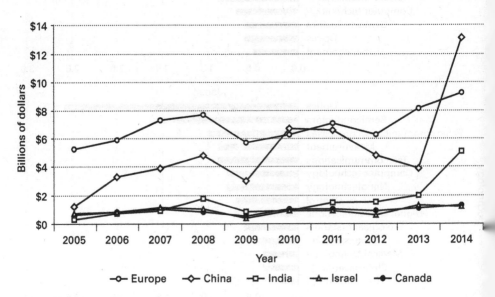

Figure 12.6
Venture capital investment by selected region/country/economy for the period from 2005 to 2014. *Source*: National Science Board (2016d).

4. How have the roles of research universities changed over the past few decades with regard to intellectual property (IP), technology commercialization, and economic development?

5. How does the World Intellectual Property Organization (WIPO) define IP?

6. Give some examples of IP developed outside the areas of science, engineering, and technology.

7. How does "know-how" differ from traditional IP?

8. List the principal types of IP protection.

9. How does US law define copyright?

10. Briefly describe the meaning of the key terms in the US definition of copyright.

11. At what point in the creation of a work is copyright formally established?

12. How does US law define a patent?

13. What are the principal types of patents in the US?

14. What are the key characteristics of a utility patent?

15. What is a provisional patent?

16. How long does one have to file a patent in the US, and when does the "clock start ticking?"

17. To whom are patents in the US granted? First to file or first to create?

18. What is a trademark and how does it differ from a patent and copyright?

19. What is a trade secret and how does it differ from other types of IP protection?

20. How do colleges and universities support their researchers in IP identification and protection?

21. What is an invention disclosure and what role does it play in IP?

22. How are colleges and universities, and the research enterprise more broadly, providing increased recognition to those who develop and act upon IP?

23. At most academic research institutions, who or what entity owns the IP?

24. Describe some advantages and disadvantages to faculty or other university researchers in engaging in IP-related activities, such as starting companies.

25. What is an IP license?

26. What attributes are common to most IP license agreements?

27. What are the most commonly used options for commercializing IP?

28. What is the "valley of death" in the context of research and technology commercialization?

29. Why are academic institutions sometimes reluctant to perform research funded by private companies?

30. What IP challenges do private companies face in collaborating on research projects with academic institutions?

31. How is the US performing in IP generation and utilization relative to other nations?

32. What is venture capital (VC), and what role does it play in IP and technology commercialization?

Exercises to Deepen Your Understanding

Exercise 1: Research and creative activity naturally tend to produce things: a process or method for accomplishing a task, a piece of software, an invention, a composition, a sculpture or piece of art, a script, and so on. Given your interests, select an outcome of research and creative activity that you have performed, or may perform in the future, and describe it. Then, discuss which mechanisms of intellectual property (IP) protection are most appropriate for your outcome, and why. How will that protection, or those protections, be useful should you wish to commercialize your outcome? What restrictions might you face by having such protection, and how might you trade them off?

Exercise 2: The US Patent and Trademark Office (USPTO) is responsible for handling all patent and trademark activities in the US. Using the USPTO website, describe the process involved in filing a US patent and then compare and contrast it with the process for filing an international patent. How do the protections offered differ from one another? What services are offered by your institution to assist you in filing a patent, including training sessions and advice, and does your institution pay associated legal and other fees?

Exercise 3: The Bayh-Dole Act of 1980 is the foundation for commercialization by colleges and universities of IP developed with federal funding. Today, the Act is being modified to increase its effectiveness. Describe the nature of and rationale for these modifications and the benefits expected from them. Then, compare the benefits to society of IP commercialized in the US, under the Bayh-Dole Act, with the benefits achieved under the commercialization policies of Canada. How do the policies differ, and to what extent are they responsible for the differences in societal benefits?

Exercise 4: As noted in this chapter, most large colleges, and virtually all research universities, have offices of technology commercialization or transfer to assist faculty and other researchers in dealing with IP. Contact the office or offices at your institution to learn of recent patent or trademark filings. Identify two or three researchers, from different disciplines, who made such filings and have them describe their experience so you can compare and contrast them. Ask these individuals to recommend improvements to the system, and to provide specific lessons learned that will help you in your own future filing. If your institution has no such office, contact your advisor, department chair, or dean to determine how to access such services.

Exercise 5: Use the Internet to identify a high-profile case involving a legal dispute over IP (e.g., patent, trademark, trade secret). Describe the nature of the dispute and the legal basis for it, referencing material presented in this chapter. Do you believe the dispute is justified? Why or why not? How might it have been avoided? Describe the outcome of the dispute and provide your thoughts about whether justice was served.

13

I Need You and You Need Me: Collaboration, Multidisciplinary Inquiry, and Academic-Corporate Partnerships

Chapter Overview and Learning Objectives

Because many of today's most intellectually stimulating, societally important, and personally rewarding challenges lie at the boundaries of multiple disciplines, collaboration among researchers increasingly is important, even to the point of having its own descriptor—*convergent research*. Such collaborations come with unique challenges that must be recognized and addressed if team-oriented and multidisciplinary research are to succeed. Additionally, collaboration extends beyond the academic realm to engage other sectors (e.g., private industry, nonprofit organizations, government organizations), and numerous funding programs exist, across all disciplines, to stimulate such collaborations via the creation of professional networks, public-private partnerships, research centers and regional hubs, and other mechanisms emphasizing regional economic development and community transformation.

This chapter highlights the purpose and importance of research and creative activities that engage multiple individuals within a given discipline, multiple disciplines, and multiple sectors of the research and innovation enterprise. It also addresses challenges in tackling boundary-spanning problems as well as key characteristics of successful research teams and strategies for creating and managing them. After reading this chapter, you should

- Understand the history and importance of research collaboration and the various ways in which multiple disciplines can work together to solve problems residing at disciplinary boundaries;
- Understand and be able to distinguish among the modalities of research involving one or more disciplines;
- Be able to explain barriers to collaborative research;
- Understand the characteristics of successful research teams and be able to apply those characteristics to your own work as appropriate;

- Be aware of funding opportunities and other resources that support building collaborative networks, centers, and hubs both within academia and with other sectors;
- Understand the importance and basic tenets of multisector collaboration and the factors which tend to inhibit it;
- Understand ways in which to initiate collaborations and partnerships with nonacademic organizations; and
- Be familiar with ways in which academia and corporations can partner beyond sponsored research activities.

13.1   Lexicon, Challenges, and Opportunities of Collaboration

In the earliest days of intellectual inquiry, philosophers, many of whom also were theologians, generally worked alone, focusing on their individual views and theories regarding spirituality, philosophy, the human experience, and the natural world, though of course corresponding with others in doing so. The names of pioneers are familiar: Aristotle, Socrates, and Plato. A millennium later, this same modality remained dominant with the likes of Galileo, Kepler, and Newton, who published principally as sole authors, though building upon previous works in advancing knowledge. In fact, paying homage to those who paved the way for him, Sir Isaac Newton said the following about his own work: "If I have seen a little further, it is by standing on the shoulders of giants" (Newton and Hooke 1675).

We focus in the present chapter on two important and related topics: collaboration within and beyond academia, and inquiry involving more than one academic discipline. In its broadest interpretation, collaboration—which in the context of science is known as team science—involves two or more individuals working together to achieve a common goal or set of goals, stimulated by the fact that each brings something unique or valuable to the effort.

For example, hundreds of physicists can collaborate to understand the nature of exotic particles generated in billion-dollar atom smashers, such as the Large Hadron Collider in Europe, while three or four musicians can collaborate to create a score for a musical. In these cases, most or all participants are in the same general discipline, though likely having different areas of expertise and perspectives. On the other hand, inquiry involving scholars from multiple disciplines is another form of collaboration, which again brings together researchers working to achieve a common goal. An example is civil and structural engineers, social scientists, urban planners, and architects all working together to study and make recommendations about how to reduce the impacts of severe flooding within a city.

As detailed in section 13.5, collaboration does not reside exclusively within the walls of academia, but rather can involve organizations in other sectors, such as private companies. For decades, faculty and other academic researchers have collaborated with industry, in some cases via formal partnerships, resulting in research outcomes supporting the development and marketing of new technologies and even the creation of new private companies. Such partnerships sometimes bear other fruit, including endowments to academic institutions for buildings, facilities and professorships. It is important to recognize that private companies are not banks to which academic researchers can turn for funding. Rather, they exist and survive by making a profit, keeping shareholders happy, and being competitive in the marketplace of ideas and products viewed as valuable by consumers. Consequently, academic-corporate partnerships must be pursued with proper motivation and a full understanding of the value proposition for all involved.

Not surprisingly, the lexicon of collaboration is a bit more nuanced than just portrayed, irrespective of the disciplines or types of organizations involved. When everyone on a collaborative team is from the same discipline, the term *intradisciplinary* or *unidisciplinary* collaboration applies. The aforementioned music example fits this definition. At the other end of the spectrum, if members of the team are from different disciplines but draw only upon their disciplinary expertise in the collaborative work, the term *multidisciplinary* applies. The aforementioned flooding example fits this definition.

Cross-disciplinary collaboration occurs when researchers view their work through the lens of other disciplines. For example, a physicist working on the fundamental properties of matter at the atomic scale seeing her work from the perspective of a private sector engineer who develops synthetic materials arising from it. In such cases, the dependence of one field upon the other yields important insight regarding approaches and ultimate goals.

Interdisciplinary collaboration, on the other hand, involves integrating and synthesizing perspectives from multiple disciplines. A good example is the development of new weather forecast guidance by integrating the expertise of federal government and private sector operational meteorologists with those of academic communication and behavioral scientists who know how forecast information can best be organized, communicated to, and interpreted by the public.

Finally, *transdisciplinary* collaboration takes place when disciplinary perspectives are combined to create a new, unified framework of theories, models, and approaches. A fun example here, for those of you who are foodies, is fusion cuisine, which is cuisine that combines elements of different culinary traditions to arrive at something new and different. An example more relevant to research is biomedical engineering, which now is its own discipline and represents a true fusion of chemical engineering, material science, biochemistry, physics, mathematics, and computer science.

Recently, the term "convergence" has been used to give specific meaning to transdisciplinary collaboration. The National Research Council (2014) defines convergence as "an approach to problem solving that integrates expertise from life sciences with physical, mathematical, and computational sciences, medicine, and engineering to form comprehensive synthetic frameworks that merge areas of knowledge from multiple fields to address specific challenges." The report goes on to note that "Convergence builds upon fundamental progress made within individual disciplines, but represents a way of thinking about the process of research and the types of strategies that enable it, as emerging scientific and societal challenges cut across disciplinary boundaries in these fields."

For now, it is important to recognize that collaborative research, no matter the specific form it takes or the types of organizations involved, is challenging and involves addressing a number of important questions at the outset. How do I know if I need collaborators? Where do I find them, especially if they are in another discipline or located at another institution? How do I know if someone will work with me? What are the characteristics of a good collaborator or set of collaborators? How do I learn to work with someone or several individuals from a completely different discipline, where words I use in my own work have different meaning to them, and where each of us uses completely different methodologies for solving problems?

Though collaboration can be challenging, it also is extremely valuable as well as rewarding. Why? First and foremost, because it allows you to tackle problems beyond your particular area of expertise, and even pursue problems outside your discipline. And second, it brings other important resources to the table that you otherwise would not have. Facilities. Ideas. Funding. Reputation of collaborators or their organization. Linkages to others and their networks. Collaboration expands our horizons. It also challenges us, and provides opportunities for us, to go beyond our own ideas and ways of thinking.

In fact, some of today's most interesting, challenging, and societally relevant problems require collaboration because they reside not within a particular discipline—though such problems obviously do exist—but rather at boundaries among multiple disciplines. Examples include tissue engineering, which combines medicine, chemical engineering, biology, mathematics, and computer science; digital humanities, which combines computer science, classics, history, library science, and anthropology; and environmental impacts on food production, which combines atmospheric science, agriculture, plant biology, microbiology, social science, and hydrology.

Figure 13.1 underscores the importance of collaborative research, showing that the percentage of publications involving more than one author has been increasing over the past sixty years. Additional detail can be found in figure 13.2, which provides a breakdown of publications by number of authors. Incredibly, some papers have more than 1,000 authors!

13.2 Disciplinary Research and Education in a Multidisciplinary World

Not surprisingly, and quite obviously, multi/cross/inter/transdisciplinary research is impossible without individual disciplines. Yet, one of the greatest barriers to academic scholarship involving more than one discipline is the irony that most colleges, universities, and even funding agencies are organized around disciplines! For example, most universities have within them colleges of arts and sciences, engineering, humanities, business, education, and fine arts, to name a few. More recently, discipline-spanning colleges have emerged, such as in biomedical engineering, environmental science and sustainability,

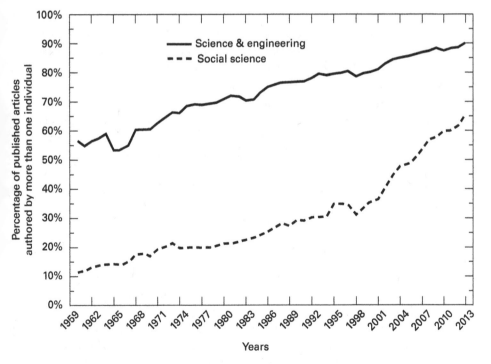

Figure 13.1
Percentage of publications authored by more than one individual during the period from 1960 to 2013. *Source*: National Research Council (2015).

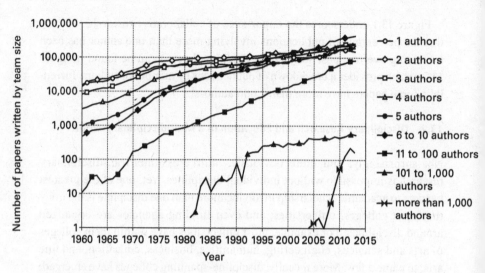

Figure 13.2
Frequency of author team sizes in science and engineering during the period from 1960 to 2013.
Source: National Research Council (2015).

and data science. Within such colleges are housed individual departments containing specific disciplines, such as physics, mathematics, psychology, sociology, art history, sculpture, modern dance, and electrical engineering. This structure has been with us for quite some time.

Indeed, as noted in the preceding section and in chapter 3, academic disciplines arose over several centuries, though during the eighteenth century, greater emphasis was placed on topics such as history, geography, geometry, algebra, modern languages, and astronomy. Additional emphasis on biology and physical science led to an increasingly complex intellectual and societal landscape, and then in the late nineteenth and early twentieth centuries, the disciplines of sociology, psychology, anthropology, economics, and others emerged in support of agriculture and the mechanical arts, especially at land-grant institutions. Students seeking higher education degrees in the first two-thirds or so of the twentieth century tended to focus mostly on their chosen discipline, such as physics, chemistry, engineering, or mathematics, with electives and areas of emphasis outside the discipline becoming ever more popular.

Today, in addition to a degree in a given discipline, one can obtain a variety of formal credentials in areas other than one's chosen academic major, such as minors, areas of concentration, certificates, and badges. One also can obtain multiple degrees in different disciplines, a degree with multiple majors, or even a customized degree that combines courses from multiple disciplines, such as law, physical and behavioral science.

In this environment of increasingly rich opportunity and intellectual vitality, which includes the study of discipline-spanning problems, comes several interesting challenges. First, the administrative college and departmental structure of academic institutions today—sometimes referred to as disciplinary "stove pipes"—can create barriers to collaboration because different disciplines, and the academic programs that house them, have different philosophies by which they operate. They also tend to have different and often conflicting reward structures.

For example, one discipline might not value the publication of research outcomes in the journal of another discipline, and thereby the associated incentives for researchers to pursue multidisciplinary work are diminished. Also, although colleges and universities have improved the manner in which they recognize and reward collaborative research, the academy remains centered largely around measuring outcomes at the level of individual researchers. For example, how many papers *you* published, how many performances *you* gave, how many exhibitions at which *your* work was presented, and how many grants *you* received.

For this reason, most colleges and universities allow faculty to create or pursue funding to establish multidisciplinary centers and institutes. This construct allows multiple faculty and researchers from across an institution, perhaps working with colleagues from other institutions, to collaborate effectively and establish their own management and reward structures apart from traditional university colleges and academic departments. Though such frameworks face their own sets of challenges, they have proved to be an effective mechanism for tackling boundary-spanning problems. More information about them can be found in the references (e.g., Kezar and Lester 2009; Lyall et al. 2011; Bennett and Gadlin 2012; Lyall and Meagher 2012).

Second, with regard to funding agencies and private foundations, most continue to be organized in a manner similar to colleges and departments in academia. That is, they are structured around traditional disciplines such as mathematics, life sciences, physical sciences, engineering, social and behavioral sciences, and so on. Although this sometimes makes difficult the review of grant proposals involving multiple disciplines, the situation has improved markedly over the past twenty years. In the same manner that many academic institutions now house multidisciplinary research centers and institutes outside of discipline-based academic departments, funding agencies and also private foundations have a plethora of cross-cutting programs that bring many disciplines together and offer mechanisms for attacking boundary-spanning problems.

Ultimately, it is wise, in obtaining a degree or multiple degrees, to garner some level of expertise outside of one's core discipline, via the mechanisms described previously. Why? Doing so enables you to tackle boundary-spanning problems. Also, it no longer is the case for most people that one obtains a degree in a particular discipline and then works in that discipline for the rest of their lives. In fact, one must today be able to reinvent themselves, usually multiple times, over the course of a career to adapt to rapidly changing technology, challenges, and opportunities. Obtaining formal expertise outside your chosen discipline is wonderful preparation for lifelong learning and gives you the ability to adapt and respond to opportunities in the future.

Yet, a word of caution is in order along these lines with an important caveat that depends upon the pathway you wish to follow in your career. One must be mindful, in obtaining formal expertise outside a core discipline, to avoid in some career paths becoming so broad as to not have a clear identity. As an example in which having multiple areas of formal credentialing does *not* pose an identity problem, many engineers today, in addition to obtaining a degree in engineering, also have a law degree or a master of business administration. The market for such individuals is competitive, and the value placed on such combinations of credentials is quite high.

On the other hand, if one has a double major in computer science and fine arts, with another degree in journalism and a minor in French, it becomes difficult to attach an identity to this individual. Although identities can be either very useful or very problematic, they do in fact exist, and careful thought needs to be given to them during one's formal postsecondary education.

At the end of the day, you simply need to recognize that we live in a world where problems to be solved increasingly involve collaboration among multiple disciplines. The better equipped you are to function in that world, the more successful you likely will be.

13.3 Characteristics of Successful Teams

Turning now to the very practical topic of actually developing and working in teams, I apply the word "team" to describe collaborations ranging from a few scholars working together on a small project to large, multi-institution, multi-disciplinary, and even multinational centers involving dozens to hundreds of researchers. Most of the points made below apply across this entire spectrum, though appropriately modified when the number of collaborators is relatively small.

The most obvious question to ask regarding working in teams is the following: What makes for a successful team? This is important if you want to create and manage a team as well as consider being part of one. Of course, the answer depends to some extent upon how one defines success, so let us assume that success relates to outcomes that reflect achievement of project goals via a productive and collegial working environment for team members.

First and foremost, successful teams need an effective leader. Leadership is a somewhat elusive concept for many people as it tends to suggest someone being in charge, making all of the decisions, or having a specific title or role. Although true, leadership involves much more. First and foremost, a true leader understands and empowers others. When you are a true leader, your work no longer focuses exclusively on your individual success, but rather also on helping others succeed, including members of a collaborative team.

Additionally, the leader clarifies goals, helps build trust among those involved, creates a comfortable, safe, and productive work environment that ensures all views are encouraged and welcome, and then manages this environment effectively, providing resources and removing barriers so those involved can do their work effectively. I have seen teams of exceptional, willing, and able scholars literally fall apart owing to the *absence* of leadership, and teams of people who are marginally interested at the outset come together and do great things *because* of great leadership. Numerous excellent resources exist on the topic of leadership, and I find the following to be particularly valuable (Heifetz 1998; Heifetz, Grashow, and Linsky 2009; Heifetz and Linsky 2017).

The second characteristic of a successful team is diversity, inclusion, and belonging. Though we hear the term "diversity" used frequently and in many contexts, here it means involving individuals on a team who are different from one another—in every way you might imagine. Views, approaches to tackling problems, race, ethnicity, sex, gender identity, religion, nationality, birthplace, military service, age, and academic discipline. Building a diverse team—even if within a single discipline—weaves a tapestry of richness into the entire scholarly process of creating and disseminating new knowledge, yielding innumerable benefits. Yet, it does not stop with diversity. Those on the team need to be included, which is the job not only of the leader but of everyone on the team. All voices are important, all views should be welcome. And, being made not only to *feel* as though one belongs, but actually *does* belong by virtue of active engagement and respect, is foundational to each and every team.

The third characteristic of a successful team is the development and clear understanding, by all participants, of a shared vision for the work to be done, along with a clear sense of each individual's role in it. In my own experience, I have explained this as analogous to the rays of light passing through a lens and converging on the focal point (figure 13.3). Each ray represents a project participant and the lens the project framework that brings participants together such that they contribute to the project goal (focal point) while seeing their own

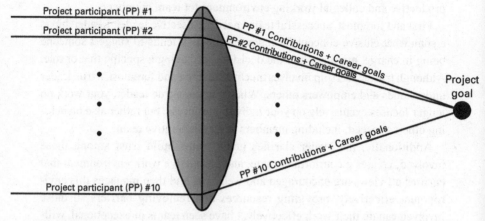

Figure 13.3
Conceptual depiction showing how the framework of a collaborative project (lens) allows individual project participants (rays) to contribute to the project goal (focal point) while simultaneously advancing their own career goals. For simplicity, only a few rays are shown converging on the project goal whereas, in reality, all do.

careers and interests advance in the process. I'll touch on this point a bit more in the next section, where we examine constructing a team.

The fourth characteristic of a successful team, and one which develops over time but must explicitly be pursued, is trust. Expecting you to devote a portion of your time to a project involving others means putting a part of your career in their hands. It also means giving up some of the power or authority you would have if you managed a project or pursued activities on your own. The reverse of course is true for others if you are leading a team. Trust arises via building relationships and ensuring a work environment that promotes open, frank and collegial discussion and welcomes dissenting views. Trust also comes about via the sharing of ideas, no matter how unconventional they may seem initially, and via a collaborative approach to achieving consensus on important decisions. Trust, mutual respect, and effective, open communication go hand in hand and are foundational to successful collaborative endeavors.

The fifth characteristic of a successful team, and one that often is the most difficult to achieve, is developing an appreciation and understanding of the terminology and methodologies used by others, especially if they are from academic disciplines different than your own. Initially, this can be frustrating because terms you have used without thinking likely have an entirely different meaning to others. I experienced this firsthand as a meteorologist when I began working with social scientists. You see, I use computer models of the atmosphere to study severe storms, yet the word "model" meant something entirely different to my colleague social scientists.

Specifically, in the context of our work, to my social science colleagues "model" meant a theoretical framework for testing a specific hypothesis. Not a computer code. Not a bunch of equations to be solved. But rather, a conceptual framework. Although we struggled at first and even became frustrated because such a simple notion created a significant barrier to regular conversation about our topic, we soon learned to communicate effectively and, in the process, learned a great deal from one another about our own approaches and thought processes.

The sixth characteristic of a successful team is an agreed upon approach for assigning credit and recognition, including the following: authorship of papers and the ordering of authors; involvement in promotional and public relations materials as well as press releases, interviews, and media inquiries; quantification of involvement for the purposes of intellectual property disposition (chapter 12); and strategies for resolving disagreements or disputes should they occur.

The seventh characteristic of a successful team, and the role of the team leader, involves developing leaders. Although the team may consist of individuals across many career stages, each is on their own pathway or trajectory of professional growth. As the leader, you have the daunting but exhilarating responsibility of developing the capabilities of others, empowering, challenging, and resourcing them to grow in the many and often unique ways that are possible when working in teams. Learn about their career goals and ambitions and make sure the project is advancing them. Never treat project participants as "worker bees," and make certain everyone—from undergraduate student to senior researcher—understands the purpose and goals of the project and their unique contributions to it.

Finally, and most importantly in my view, you must *have fun* when working with other people! You may not particularly like everyone, but I am quite certain you can have a genuine appreciation for their work and the contributions they make to the project. Remember, a bright light at the focal point of the lens requires all of the individual rays to do their part while not interfering destructively with other rays!

13.4 Developing Teams and Engaging Boundary-Spanning Problems

Having laid the foundation regarding the characteristics of successful collaborative research teams, the obvious and most important requirement moving forward is to have a research problem that requires a team approach. That is, the problem should be of such a nature that it lies beyond the capabilities or scope of an individual researcher and his or her research group, or requires expertise from more than a single discipline or type of organization.

Quite often, the problem to be tackled is identified by one or more people, but ideally and optimally, one person—one person—steps forward to actually lead the effort, both intellectually—as the visionary and subject matter expert—and administratively. And I want to stress that the leader must actually embrace all of the challenges as well as opportunities that come with team-oriented research. This includes addressing all of the items noted in the preceding section that make for successful teams. But it also includes the fact that teams consist of diverse individuals representing different ages, institutions, stages in career, races, nationalities, ethnicities, gender identities, cultures, and religions. Managing a group with such diversity can be challenging, yet it is precisely this diversity that brings multiple perspectives that are of such great value to team-based collaboration.

Given the tremendous value of collaborative research, numerous resources have been developed for creating collaborations and building teams (including those with international partners, as noted below, though with due consideration given to issues of research security, as discussed in section 10.3). One example is the National Science Foundation's Research Coordination Networks (RCN) program (http://nsf.gov/pubs/2015/nsf15527/nsf15527.htm), the goal of which is to "advance a field or create new directions in research or education by supporting groups of investigators to communicate and coordinate their research, training and educational activities across disciplinary, organizational, geographic and international boundaries. The RCN program provides opportunities to foster new collaborations, including international partnerships, and address interdisciplinary topics. Innovative ideas for implementing novel networking strategies, collaborative technologies, training, broadening participation, and development of community standards for data and meta-data are especially encouraged. RCN awards are not meant to support existing networks; nor are they meant to support the activities of established collaborations." Note the focus on both domestic and international teams, and that the program supports both large and small teams. Similar examples exist in other federal agencies, not only in the sciences, but also in the arts, fine arts, and humanities.

When building the research team, a number of important points must be considered. A potential team member must have the appropriate expertise and be interested in the project. In recruiting team members, it is the responsibility of the leader to articulate how a particular individual's capabilities fit the project, and how their expertise will contribute to the overall goal. You may wonder how this is possible for teams involving several disciplines, but such is the unique role of the visionary leader. That is, the leader may not be able to fully articulate all details of each person's role at the outset, but he or she can provide each participant with a general idea of their role and excite them about the innovative nature of the project. As the project proceeds, each participant gains deeper understanding of their role, eventually becoming the expert in explaining it to others, including the leader!

Numerous funding opportunities, especially within federal grant agencies, exist to pursue team-oriented research, largely in science and engineering. NSF, NIH, and DOE—to name a few—all offer funding for major ($5 million or more per year) research centers, institutes, and regional hubs. Some are focused on specific topics, such as artificial intelligence and quantum computing, while others allow researchers to pitch their own ideas. Examples are shown below.

- National Science Foundation
  - Big Data Regional Innovation Hubs
  - Centers for Chemical Innovation
  - Engineering Research Centers
  - I-Corps Hubs
  - Industry/University Cooperative Research Centers
  - Major Research Equipment and Facilities Construction Program
  - Major Research Instrumentation Program
  - Materials Research Science and Engineering Centers
  - Mid-Scale Research Infrastructure Program
  - Nanoscale Science and Engineering Centers
  - National Artificial Intelligence Research Institutes
  - Physics Frontier Centers
  - Regional Innovations Engines Program
  - Science and Technology Centers

- National Institutes of Health
  - Centers of Biomedical Research Excellence
  - Clinical and Translational Science Award
  - IDeA Networks of Biomedical Research Excellence
  - P30 Center Core Grants
  - P50 Specialized Centers

- US Department of Energy
  - Energy Frontier Research Centers
  - Energy Innovation Hubs
  - National Quantum Information Science Research Centers
  - Regional Clean Hydrogen Hubs

Although NEH and NEA generally do not offer funding programs to create centers for scholarly activity, NEH operates a residential National Humanities Center (http://neh.gov/divisions/research/fellowship/national-humanities-center) "for advanced study in art history, classics, history, languages and literature, musicology, philosophy, and other fields of the humanities." NEA supports state and regional organizations and alliances that fund projects in the arts and fine arts.

Many opportunities also exist for large training and equipment grants, mostly in the areas of scientific research. Increasingly, regional research hubs are being funded to place additional focus on economic development and community transformation in the form of job creation, and on reskilling and upskilling, especially within economically disadvantaged communities. Multiagency federal programs, such as the Established Program to Stimulate Competitive Research (EPSCoR; sections 2.3 and 3.3), bring together multiple disciplines across several institutions within a given state/jurisdiction to address major research challenges and enhance competitiveness.

International collaborations, large and small, have been and continue to be vitally important to advance the progress of scholarship in all disciplines, from high energy physics and meteorology to art, drama, and musical theater. The development of major facilities is very much an international or multinational endeavor owing to their enormous cost and broad international user base. Examples include the Large Hadron Collider (http://home.cern/science/accelerators/large-hadron-collider) in Switzerland, the Atacama Large Millimeter Array (http://www.almaobservatory.org) telescope in Chile, and the Event Horizon Telescope (http://eventhorizontelescope.org), the last of which is a series of radio telescopes around the world that were brought together in a major collaboration that gave the world its first image of a black hole shadow. International collaborations and partnerships not only advance scholarly activities but they also promote international relations, cultural understanding, diversity, and serve as tools of diplomacy.

Yet, working in teams is not for everyone, and thus attention needs to be given to attitude and interpersonal skills when selecting team members. Team members need to enjoy working with others and be willing to share credit and assume a greater workload when health or other challenges take team members out of the game. They must be openminded and willing to learn from others and to try unfamiliar approaches. Bias and prejudice (chapter 8), if manifest as behavior, are absolutely toxic to research teams, as are people who tend to build alliances within the team to gain advantage over others. Frequently, it is difficult to know how someone who has *not* participated in team research will behave until they actually *join* a team. This is why significant attention needs to be paid to creating an environment for the project that encourages open dialogue and the sharing of issues and concerns, so they do not become problems.

In executing the project once the team has been assembled, careful attention needs to be given to developing the shared vision and goals, and to identifying the roles and responsibilities of all team members. In especially large projects, such as multi-institution and/or multisector centers, an overall project manager, different from the project leader, may be given the responsibility of ensuring effective communication of all members by holding regular meetings, or video conference sessions if the team is geographically distributed. Small group sessions built around subthemes of the project often are helpful, and if the project is divided into thrusts largely involving single disciplines, it is important that cross-cutting activities be created to ensure that the various strands of disciplinary work eventually flow together.

Social and team-building activities, which can be done both within and outside the work environment, are especially valuable for building relationships and trust, though care must be taken to ensure all team members are able to participate. That is, if some on the team do not drink alcohol, for example, activities not involving alcohol should be offered. An example where team building proves valuable is a situation in which new ideas arise as the project proceeds and the team needs to decide how to respond. Good teams are able to redirect resources to pursue them, if deemed appropriate, without harming overall core goals.

I have had the privilege of leading research teams involving multiple disciplines and institutions for nearly four decades. In some cases, the team consisted of more than one hundred people from nearly a dozen different institutions. I also have been a participant in small team collaborations. Although leading teams and working in them certainly requires more effort than for other types of projects, the team research with which I have been involved provided the most intellectually exhilarating and rewarding experiences of my career.

13.5 Multisector Collaborations and Academic-Corporate Partnerships

Lest you have the impression collaborations of various flavors exist only among colleagues in academia, such is far from the case. Indeed, collaborations and partnerships—formal and informal, large and small, national and international—occur across all sectors of the research enterprise and involve academia, government, private industry, nonprofit companies, and other nongovernmental organizations. Activities range from significant corporate engagement in large research centers and institutes to individual academic scholars working with their counterparts in the private sector. Even federal agencies partner with one another, and with the private sector, on a variety of programs to enhance America's research and education enterprise.

Early in my professional career, I learned that the word "partnership" has a very specific legal meaning, such as in a limited liability partnership or public-private partnership. Consequently, I was counseled to be mindful of the situation in which the word was being applied. In academia, the words "partnership" and "collaboration" often are used interchangeably and somewhat loosely, and I will follow that practice here. However, if you find yourself in a situation of uncertainty about which term is most appropriate, I encourage you to obtain legal guidance.

With that preface, let us begin by asking obvious and important questions: What motivates the creation of partnerships between academia and other sectors, especially private industry, and what forms do they take? Recall some of the expectations placed by society on today's academic institutions, as enumerated by Hill (2012, slide 15) and described in section 12.1: "a generator of new technologies; a prime source of new ideas; a founder of new companies; a solver of practical problems; a partner in economic development; a bridge to the world; a venue for political presentation; a critical contributor to economic growth; and a source of specialist leadership." Although research is a foundation of many postsecondary institutions, most of the items listed above are recent developments related directly to academic-corporate partnerships.

To answer our questions, consider the fundamentals of private companies: what they are, why they exist, how they operate, what they need to be successful, and how their foundational characteristics align with those of the academic research enterprise. Because space does not allow for a comprehensive treatment of all types of partnerships, I focus here on those between academic institutions and for-profit private companies.

The fundamental purpose of private for-profit companies is to provide various goods and services of value to society as a means for profit (understanding and appreciating the profit motive is important when creating academic-corporate partnerships, as described below). Companies innovate and are driven by a free-market economy to build wealth. If successful, companies remain in business, expand, redefine themselves over time, merge, and are acquired. To achieve this success, apart from the value of specific offerings, companies need, first and foremost, a capable and reliable workforce. They also need capital, space and facilities, raw materials in the case of manufacturing, effective marketing strategies, and new approaches, technologies, and products to remain competitive. Additionally, companies seek tax and other incentives to identify optimal siting, are proponents of corporate-friendly policies and laws to lower costs and maximize profits, and often locate in communities having convenient transportation infrastructure (especially airports), high quality of life for employees, appropriate housing, and opportunities for expansion.

Turning now to colleges and universities, their fundamental purpose (sections 12.1 and 14.3) is to educate individuals as a public and private good, serve as a codifier of and repository for knowledge and understanding, and in the case of institutions performing research, generate and disseminate new knowledge. They also provide a community for personal and professional growth, serve as a space for thoughtful debate, and help prepare individuals to productively participate in and serve society.

What do such institutions need to be successful? First and foremost, jobs for their graduates. Indeed, academia plays a significant role in providing workforce to private companies, not only in terms of individuals who receive formal degrees, but also in the skilled technical workforce created by career and vocational technical schools, as well as via certificates and badges offered by institutions of higher learning and other organizations (e.g., in cyber security, information technology, data analytics). The provision of workforce does not require any sort of formal relationship between industry and academia owing to the fact that, at least for public institutions, corporate tax dollars fund some portion of higher education. Thus, apart from the salaries of individuals hired, companies need make no formal investment in an institution in order to benefit from the students it educates.

Colleges and universities also require internships and service learning opportunities for their students, funding for research and pathways toward practical uses for its outcomes, philanthropic support, and the ability to show a clear return on investment to a wide array of stakeholders including governing boards, parents, students, and lawmakers.

Historically, research interactions between academia and the private sector have been structured around individual projects (including federally funded centers), motivated by mutual need and value and framed by a supplier-consumer model. In this model, private industry, the principal consumer, provides funding to academic institutions to undertake research and development projects of specific interest to the company, or agrees to participate as a team member in a research center or consortium. In a manner similar to funding provided by federal agencies to support academic research (chapters 2 and 6), funding provided by private industry typically supports personnel (faculty, graduate student, and postdoctoral scholar salaries and fringe benefits), equipment, travel, and possibly publication costs (if industry is a partner in a center, their support may not involve direct funding but rather be provided in-kind; e.g., use of corporate facilities or donation of personnel time for collaboration).

In return, private industry obtains access to the associated research outcomes and intellectual property (chapter 12). In many cases, students working on private sector-funded research later are hired by the supporting company because of their familiarity with company activities, and because of their proven capabilities (which both reduces risk on the part of the company and spin-up time for a new employee).

In many cases, research relationships between industry and academia, though having humble beginnings, blossom into partnerships bearing all manner of fruit. For example, many academic institutions now have research campuses, research parks, or corporate parks where private companies can establish facilities. This allows the company and institution to interact in a deeper, more continuous manner, sometimes leading companies to co-brand their products and services with their academic landlord.

Although academic-corporate partnerships increasingly are important in today's research enterprise, they can be challenging to establish and manage because, as noted above, private companies and academic institutions were created for entirely different purposes and thus operate with different philosophies, structures, and vocabularies. One of the biggest barriers to academic-corporate partnerships is intellectual property (IP; chapter 12) and the extensive legal and other negotiations that occur regarding ownership, rights of usage, and confidentiality. For institutions unfamiliar with or lacking the resources to engage in such negotiations, IP can be an insurmountable brick wall. Misperceptions by academia and industry about how each other operates (e.g., Council on Governmental Relations 2022), and their perceived lack of willingness and ability to work together, especially regarding IP, also hamper partnership creation.

A second challenge to academic-corporate partnerships involves managing conflicts of interest (chapters 9 and 10), especially in the context of graduate students and postdoctoral scholars working on projects funded by private industry. Importantly, such work must be performed without any undue influence by the private company sponsor, and conflicts of interest must be managed effectively (for example, if the faculty member overseeing a project owns stock in the company funding the work). If the company funding the work is in fact *owned* by the faculty member or their family, as often occurs in federal STTR and SBIR awards (sections 2.3 and 12.4), and if this same faculty member is the advisor of the students working on the project, care must be taken to ensure that the students' work is directly related to the project and that the faculty member is not utilizing them for other activities that benefit the company.

Third, most private companies understandably want to specify a set of deliverables for academic research projects they fund, using the contract rather than grant funding vehicle (section 2.3). Although some colleges and universities are willing to accept deliverables and thus "guarantee" their completion, most are not. This is because academic research is focused, in some cases with legal implications, on delivering "best effort," without the ability to guarantee outcomes.

Finally, as noted in section 13.1, it is important for researchers and academic institutions to not view private companies as banks, but rather as organizations that make decisions principally to ensure their profitability. This especially comes into play when colleges and universities seek to increase their research portfolios—in some cases dramatically so (e.g., genuinely doubling expenditures in five years)—which leads them to sometimes unrealistically view private companies as an avenue for significant funding solely in light of the uncertain and highly competitive nature of federal funding (section 2.1 and chapter 14). Private companies indeed can be excellent partners, but they always should be approached with the true spirit of a partnership in mind.

13.6   Establishing an Academic-Corporate Partnership

I have been fortunate to participate in many academic-corporate partnerships, starting from my first days as a university faculty member. Not surprisingly, I found that no single recipe or set of steps exists for creating them or guaranteeing their success because the factors involved are many and complex: discipline(s) involved, nature and size of the company, type of work to be performed, availability of students and other researchers to perform the work, personalities of all involved, philosophy of the participating academic institutions regarding corporate-sponsored research and mechanisms available to support it, local and state laws, and economic conditions. Imagine how this complexity increases if multiple companies are involved, say in a consortium associated with a major academic research center!

Consequently, I provide here four foundational principles for academic-corporate partnerships, along with a personal example of how modest initial interactions with private industry can blossom into major partnerships. Also, I wish to note that America is blessed with several excellent organizations that focus on the philosophy, creation, nurturing, and expansion of academic-corporate partnerships. They include the University-Industry Demonstration Partnership (UIDP), Government-University-Industry Research Roundtable (GUIRR), Association of Public and Land-grant Universities (APLU) Commission on Economic and Community Engagement, and several Association of American Universities (AAU) programs on technology transfer and intellectual property.

The first of the four foundational principles is *mutual need*. In a partnership, individuals or organizations come together because they need one another and cannot achieve their desired goals alone. Although this may appear self-serving, and in some sense is, partnerships should yield *mutual benefits*, which is the second point. However, the benefits need not be distributed equally among all players, though all involved should see value for them or their organization as well as for other participants. Third, as noted previously, partnerships are built upon *mutual trust*. Without it, partnerships simply cannot thrive and, in many cases, dissolve. Finally, *effective leadership and management* are needed to ensure partnership success. I have seen many partnerships begin with great possibility and excitement, only to see them wither on the vine owing to the lack of effective stewardship.

With those points in mind, my first taste of interacting with private industry came one year after becoming a university professor. Specifically, I received an NSF Presidential Young Investigator (PYI) award, which provided $25,000 per year for five years, and another $37,500 in matching support per year if I were able to obtain $37,500 per year from other sources, such as private industry. Given that my research involved computer simulations of thunderstorms, I reached out to several private computer manufacturers as obvious partners. In so doing, I quickly learned that I needed to express my work in general terms (which wasn't that difficult because everyone experiences weather and has their favorite weather story to share), describe how it related to the company, and enumerate how the company might benefit by supporting me. Because NSF provided matching funds, the argument of leveraging corporate funding against federal funding was quite compelling to potential partners and remains so today. I note that, at the time, my university had no corporate engagement office or intellectual property support structure, so I simply struck out on my own. I return to that point below.

A year later, I began writing a proposal with a very esteemed colleague to establish a research center focused on predicting individual thunderstorms with computer models—something most people, and prevailing theory, said was impossible. Ironically, the proposal not only built upon my PYI work (and of course the pioneering work of my senior colleague), but also required the engagement of corporate partners that, fortuitously, turned out to be exactly the ones with which I had built a working relationship two years earlier! To our great surprise, our proposal was one of eleven funded out of 323 submissions; and thus, in 1989 NSF established the Science and Technology Center for Analysis and Prediction of Storms (CAPS).

As our work began to show evidence of success, I reached out to the manager of weather services at American Airlines (AA), whom I met by virtue of my work in aviation weather, and also owing to funding my university was receiving from the Federal Aviation Administration. With his strong support, I was able to convince AA's executive vice president, and ultimately its chairman, Robert Crandall, that our novel CAPS weather technology could potentially provide value to AA's hub operations in Dallas, Texas and thus throughout its system. Project Hub-CAPS was born.

That three-year effort brought $1 million to my university, along with the first research supercomputer in the state. Based upon the difficulty faced in negotiating terms of an agreement with AA, this project also spurred the creation in my university of an intellectual property office. In addition, AA endowed a professorship in my home department—which certainly was not an initial goal or expectation but reflected the reality of a genuine, successful partnership.

As Hub-CAPS was winding down, AA expressed a desire to continue using its products for actual operations. Because such capability is beyond the scope of a research university, I decided to launch a private company—which was an expectation, or at least a hope, for NSF centers such as CAPS. I thus cofounded Weather Decision Technologies (eventually acquired by DTN), and it assumed responsibility for providing operational products to AA. In so doing, it obtained an exclusive IP license (chapter 12) to the CAPS technology and also funded continuing research associated with it at my university.

Around that same time, a major energy company—Williams Energy Marketing and Trading—expressed interest in our ever-maturing weather prediction technology, and thus I approached them, through a student at my university who was one of their key employees, about a possible partnership. A year and eleven contracts later, the $10.6 million partnership was consummated. It was showing notable success when the Enron scandal brought down the entire energy marketing and trading enterprise, thus shuttering the project. However, the Williams Companies funded an endowed chair in my home department and contributed significantly to establishing a supercomputing center at my institution.

I wish to note that, in establishing both the Hub-CAPS and Williams projects, then University of Oklahoma president and former US senator David L. Boren was instrumental by virtue of his strong support and personal and professional interactions with both AA and Williams.

Two other major projects, one involving significant corporate engagement, emerged from CAPS and its associated activities: The NSF Engineering Research Center for Collaborative Adaptive Sensing of the Atmosphere and the NSF Large Information Technology Research project titled Linked

Environments for Atmospheric Discovery. More detail about how these and other activities emerged from CAPS can be found in an article prepared by NSF (National Science Foundation 2013a).

In reflecting upon these strongly connected events—which are not unique in the world of academic-corporate partnerships—I continue to be amazed at how one phone call, one introduction, can lead to a cascade of successes that transform institutions and establish careers.

With those examples as a hopefully motivating force, I suggest you do the following if you wish to explore creating a collaboration or partnership with a private company, being sure your institution is aware of your activities. First, learn as much as you can about the company and define very specifically the value they might obtain by working with you. Second, formulate a research plan and learn how to describe it to both expert and general audiences (chapter 11) because eventually, your idea will be pitched, by you or someone within the company, to senior corporate leaders who likely will not be deep subject matter experts.

Third, recognize that, in most cases, your first contact with a company will be someone you know, or at least someone who is familiar with your work. Their preexisting relationship with you, mutual colleagues, or even your institution (e.g., if they or their relatives are alumni) is helpful in "breaking the ice" for next steps. In the absence of these relationships, do not be shy about "cold calling" the company to introduce yourself and determine how to best begin engaging them. Some companies have specific mechanisms for external engagement, but many do not. You should not be discouraged if your initial overtures fail to gain traction. However, the most important thing to remember is to go in prepared!

Fourth, if you reach the point of making a formal pitch to the company or preparing a written proposal, do not approach those activities as if you were dealing with a federal funding agency. Although details of the proposed research obviously are important and must be addressed, a company's greatest interest usually lies in how the work will translate into profit—either through enhancement of existing corporate activities or the creation of new ones. Coordinate with your corporate contacts to ensure you are addressing issues of direct relevance to the company and are "speaking their language," rather than the language of an academic scholar.

Finally, many academic research institutions house sponsored programs and corporate engagement offices to assist you. However, many do not, and this especially is true for ERIs and MSIs. If you find yourself in this situation, contact your advisor or senior research officer for advice. Also, contact the aforementioned national organizations, which can provide wise counsel. You should be encouraged by the fact that, as noted in section 12.3, federal agencies now are working to provide administrative infrastructure support to academic institutions for proposal development, project execution, intellectual property disposition, and corporate engagement, in addition to funding for research. In so doing, those institutions that historically have not been able to participate in academic-corporate partnerships now will be empowered to do so.

13.7 Beyond Research in Academic-Corporate Partnerships

While serving as Oklahoma Cabinet Secretary of Science and Technology, and based upon my personal experiences as a researcher, private company cofounder, participant in many projects with industry, and university vice president for research, I developed a framework for academic-corporate partnerships founded not upon a consumer-supplier model, but rather on a peer-to-peer partnership model in which academia and industry interact at deeper, broader levels and leverage their strengths and differences for maximum mutual benefit. The need for a broader approach was stimulated by the fact that many companies do not wish to enter into sponsored research agreements with academic institutions which, as noted previously, can be complex and difficult to create. Additionally, companies often do not wish to license existing intellectual property or work jointly to develop new capabilities. Rather, they want access to other resources provided by colleges and universities. Most of the elements of the framework are activities already underway at many colleges and universities, and my strategy was to organize and make them more visible and readily available.

A final motivation for the new framework is the fact that, during the past few decades, the percentage of R&D funding provided to academic institutions by private industry (figure 2.5) has been nearly constant. Although funding is a single, imperfect measure of partnerships (additional ones are presented in chapter 14), these data suggest that industry is not taking full advantage of the extraordinary capabilities and assets of America's colleges and universities, and conversely, academic institutions are not reaping the full benefits of partnering with the private sector. My multicomponent framework is designed to help address this issue.

Because space does not allow a full description of all aspects of the framework, I summarize here a few of them.

- **Consulting:** Private companies frequently need access to subject matter experts in a variety of disciplines, and most colleges and universities allow their faculty to consult for a certain percentage of their time. The company benefits by obtaining needed expertise, and this especially is true for small and medium sized businesses, which have relatively few personnel and cannot afford to hire experts in every area of need. The faculty member benefits not only financially, but also by gaining experience and perspectives beyond academia to enhance their own teaching and research. As a result, students benefit as well.

To promote this concept, academic institutions can seek volunteer faculty consultants from across the institution and advertise their capabilities broadly, thereby heightening institutional visibility and its service to society. Additionally, the funding to consultants can be routed through the academic institution, thereby removing the burden of faculty having to develop their own consulting companies and ensuring legal use of institutional facilities, as necessary. Finally, consulting, even if performed at a small level, serves to begin building a relationship between the sponsoring company and the academic institution, leading to enhanced trust with time and possibly larger projects in the future.

- **Data sets and data analysis:** Data, and sophisticated analyses of them, are the coin of the realm in today's knowledge economy. From online shopping patterns to medical diagnoses to legal analyses to understanding and predicting the behavior of competitors, the mountains of data being collected and analyzed today are improving efficiencies and enabling entirely new industries. Academic institutions not only are repositories of historical data and knowledge in their libraries, now rapidly being digitized, but also are home to sophisticated techniques for synthesizing, fusing, and assimilating vast types and quantities of data for a virtually unlimited array of uses.

  In this component of the partnership framework, private companies engage with colleges and universities to use extant data held by the institution, analyze proprietary data owned by the company, collect new data that is of interest to the company, and assist in developing algorithms for use by the company. Such activities could be performed by faculty, as consultants (see above), or by undergraduate or graduate students as a component of, or a supplement to, their formal educational activities. The sponsoring company benefits in obvious ways (e.g., streamlining operations, improved understanding of customer needs, more efficient supply chains, market differentiation factors), and the experiences gained by faculty and students working with real data, in real corporate settings, likewise is extremely valuable.

- **Facilities and equipment:** Many academic institutions are blessed with a wide array of facilities and equipment for conducting research, ranging from clean rooms, wet laboratories, machine shops, greenhouses, powerful microscopes, and specialized equipment such as lasers to theatrical production facilities and equipment. Many of these resources are notably expensive and sometimes unique. Although larger companies likewise have specialized equipment, typically at a scale much larger than what one finds in academia, small- and medium-sized businesses typically do not. More importantly, many small- and medium-sized businesses were not even created because such capabilities were beyond their budgetary constraints. Yet, small- and medium-sized businesses represent the majority of private sector revenue in the US.

This component of the framework involves private companies using academic facilities and equipment to enhance their commercial success and promote local economic development. Academic institutions can legally charge fees for such usage and involve students and faculty on associated projects to ensure educational benefit. Such interactions can be aligned with the strategic directions of the academic institution and company, and as in many of the components of this framework, such collaboration—even though perhaps not involving research at the beginning—can lead to deeper interactions in the future, including sponsored research, internships, and so on.

- **Internships/apprenticeships:** Internships and apprenticeships are an excellent and long-standing mechanism by which private companies engage with academic institutions to develop talent, bring corporate experience to the educational process, stimulate new ideas and ways of thinking within a company, and "test drive" potential future employees. Such programs benefit academic institutions by providing practical experience for their students, professional relationships, monetary support, and often a discriminating advantage when applying for positions.

- **Restricted funding opportunities:** Quite frequently, private companies wish to pursue grant/contract funding or other opportunities but cannot do so by themselves because the solicitation requires that a nonprofit or academic institution serve as the lead organization or "prime." Conversely, certain funding opportunities available only to academic institutions require the participation of private companies. Developing such relationships, as noted previously in this chapter, can be difficult, time consuming, and require years to mature. Yet, those having strong and long-standing academic-corporate partnerships tend to have a distinct advantage in such situations.

This particular component of the framework highlights the importance of academic-corporate partnerships in research and creative activity in seeking external funding for mutual benefit. As noted above, the relationship need not begin with research in mind, but rather can start with an internship, use of a data set or facility, or even a bit of consulting by faculty. The most important point is that researchers and their institutions should plan ahead and consider which types of partner-based funding opportunities (e.g., the NSF Engineering Research Center) they might wish to pursue. Initiating a partnership at the same time one decides to pursue an opportunity is not a useful strategy. This is because most peer evaluations (chapters 6 and 7) of academic-corporate interaction consider the nature and history of collaboration. If the period has been relatively brief, and compelling evidence of meaningful collaboration is lacking, reviewers likely will doubt the probability of success.

Finally, motivated by many of the challenges to multisector partnerships described in this chapter, the White House issued a report (President's Council of Advisors on Science and Technology 2021) outlining a possible new framework for future partnerships. Although the application area was industries of the futures (e.g., artificial intelligence, quantum computing, biotechnology), the structure is applicable to any set of problems involving multiple disciplines and sectors of the research enterprise.

Assess Your Comprehension

1. Compare and contrast the following types of scholarship: intradisciplinary, interdisciplinary, cross-disciplinary, and transdisciplinary.

2. What are the principal benefits of and drawbacks to collaboration?

3. What is "convergence" in the context of research and creative activity?

4. What principal factors motivate collaboration?

5. What key questions should you ask yourself if you are considering forming a collaborative team?

6. How have trends in collaborative research changed over the past several decades?

7. How and when did the current array of disciplines in academia come into existence?

8. What options exist today for obtaining formal credentialing in areas other than one's core discipline of study?

9. What barriers exist to collaboration involving more than one discipline? Consider researchers, funding sources, communication mechanisms, and other factors.

10. Why is having an identity as a scholar important even in a multidisciplinary world?

11. What are the key characteristics of a successful collaborative team?

12. Describe the importance of diversity, in the broadest interpretation of the word, in collaborative teams.

13. What characteristics are most important when considering individuals to join a collaborative team?

14. What resources exist to support the creation of collaborative teams and networks?

15. What actions can be taken to ensure the success of a collaborative team once it has been formed?

16. What can be problematic about the term "partnership" in the context of academic-corporate collaborations?

17. What are the fundamental characteristics of private companies and what do they need to be successful?

18. What are the fundamental characteristics of academic institutions and, in the context of research, what do they need to be successful?

19. Describe some key barriers to academic-corporate partnerships.

20. Why should academic institutions not consider private companies as banks in the context of research partnerships?

21. What are the four foundational principles of academic-corporate partnerships?

22. What steps should you take in preparing to develop a partnership with a private company?

Exercises to Deepen Your Understanding

Exercise 1: Some of the most complex and intellectually stimulating problems now are being tackled through the work of multidisciplinary teams. For this exercise, create the framework of a plan to study a large-scale societal issue. In doing so, however, you must take a multidisciplinary approach that assembles at least two different disciplines, one from the sciences and one from the arts (you may use more but these two are the minimum required). As you are creating your framework, here are a few things to consider:

• Why is the problem you chose important and what are the driving intellectual questions?

- What value exists in studying the problem?
- What disciplines will be involved and why did you choose them?
- What different perspectives does each discipline bring to the project?
- What challenges do you foresee in assembling individuals from these various backgrounds and perspectives together to function as a coherent team?

Exercise 2: Most federal agencies that fund research, and most academic institutions, are organized along traditional disciplinary lines yet strongly promote multidisciplinary research and creative activity. How would you go about reorganizing or otherwise modifying the structure of such institutions so they support strong discipline-based research as well as multidisciplinary activities? In the case of academia, where performance evaluations are strongly linked to individual achievement (e.g., number of papers published, proposals funded, students mentored), what changes would you suggest in order to adequately recognize and reward the work of teams? And how would you ensure that one discipline recognizes value and legitimacy in the engagement of another, given often strong differences in culture, even with regard to mechanisms for formally placing research outcomes in the scholarly archive?

Exercise 3: If you are a graduate student, postdoctoral scholar, or faculty member at any career stage, what actions might you take to maximize your ability to work on problems that span multiple disciplines, or pivot in your career to achieve the same end? For example, in the case of students, this might include taking courses, pursuing minors of areas of concentration, or obtaining certificates and badges outside your major discipline. Which areas would you choose, and why? In the case of postdoctoral scholars or faculty, this might include attending seminars and arranging for special mentoring, taking courses to broaden your expertise, or taking a sabbatical to gain knowledge in a discipline different from your own.

Exercise 4: How would you characterize your own research in the spectrum of unidisciplinary to transdisciplinary scholarship? If it leans more toward unidisciplinary, describe ways in which you could expand the scope of your research topic or expertise to include other disciplines and thereby tackle a broader range of problems. What value would be wrought in such expansion, both from an intellectual point of view as well as with regard to societal benefit? How would you go about creating such an expansion, and can you identify researchers today who you would invite to join you as collaborators?

Exercise 5: Diversity in scholarly activities is important for a wide array of reasons, as described in this chapter and throughout the book. How would you, as a leader, go about assembling a diverse team of collaborators to tackle an especially important and intellectually stimulating problem? What factors regarding diversity—in its broadest possible interpretation—would you consider, and what steps would you take to also ensure equity, inclusion, and a sense of belonging and participation?

Exercise 6: Identify one or more real for-profit private companies you could approach to develop a collaborative research partnership. Describe in detail why they are best suited for the partnership, the research you would propose to them, the manner in which they would collaborate with you (if appropriate), and the expected outcomes and benefits to both you and them. Discuss any previous or existing connections you have with the company and the manner in which you would utilize them in approaching the company. What specific issues or challenges might you expect to encounter? If your institution contains offices that support corporate engagement, involve them in the process and describe particular experiences, both positive and negative, that surprised you. If not, seek assistance from your advisor, your department chair, dean, or senior research officer regarding options to obtain such assistance externally.

14

A Glass Half Empty or Half Full: Challenges and Opportunities for the US Academic Research Enterprise

Chapter Overview and Learning Objectives

From its world-class research institutions to its production of world-renowned inventions, the US is a global leader in research and innovation. Yet, certain challenges must be addressed in order to maintain this position in an increasingly globally competitive environment—an environment in which other nations are investing heavily in R&D and related education, and in which some governments are interfering with and actively undermining our research and innovation enterprise.

This chapter describes past trends, possible future directions, and emerging opportunities in the US research enterprise and presents a variety of comparisons between the US and other nations. After reading this chapter, you should

- Be able to compare and contrast the state of research investment, productivity, and other related measures of the US and the rest of the world;
- Understand the importance of a strong education system for the future of research and technology development;
- Understand the trends of participation of various demographic groups in STEM education and careers;
- Understand the importance of diversity, equity, and inclusion in ensuring American leadership in science and technology; and
- Identify various challenges faced by the US academic research enterprise and actions that can be taken to meet them.

14.1 Comparisons between the US and Other Nations

In this final chapter, it is appropriate to step back and consider the challenges, and also the opportunities, within the US academic research enterprise. Let us begin by looking at the current situation and underpin our assessment with hard data.

The US has long been a world leader in research and innovation, especially fundamental research conducted at academic institutions. Of the top ten universities in the world, five or more are located in the US according to multiple assessments. Of the top twenty, roughly half are located in the US.

The US has produced three times as many Nobel laureates as its nearest competitor, and the number of innovations that have sprung from research conducted in the US literally boggles the mind. The transistor. The digital computer. The Internet. The global positioning system (GPS). Chemotherapy. The LASER. The LED. Computer-based weather forecast models. And the list goes on and on. The US boasts a massive number of private foundations that fund research and creative activity, in addition to twenty-six federal agencies and untold private companies. In fact, the US now expends well over half a trillion dollars each year on research and development.

Let us put this in context with the rest of the world, particularly with regard to trends across a number of key research and related metrics. The gold standard source of information regarding such metrics is NSB's biennial (published in even years) Science and Engineering Indicators (SEI), which is a comprehensive set of data on the state of science and engineering research and education in the world. Now fully available online, SEI contains only data, trends, and analyses, not predictions, and by statute it offers no policy recommendations. Given the dependence of SEI upon surveys and other data that require considerable time to collect and analyze, many of the measures are lagging indicators and are two or three years old when published. However, most such measures do not change appreciably during that time.

Figure 14.1 shows gross domestic R&D expenditures in billions of purchasing power parity (PPP[1]) dollars, by country, over the period from 1990 to 2017. Although the US and the EU are growing at roughly the same rate of 4 to 5 percent per year after 2010, the most striking feature is the rapid growth of expenditures by China—at approximately three times that of the US and the EU. As a result, the US share of global R&D dropped from 37 percent in 2000 to 25 percent in 2017. Although increases in the research output of other nations is to be celebrated given that research is a global enterprise, it is important for the US to continue increasing its investments as well.

Another way to portray government investment is via R&D expenditures relative to a country's GDP.[2] This ratio is important because it shows the fraction invested in R&D of a nation's total value of goods and services produced. Shown in figure 14.2, the R&D-to-GDP ratio of the US has been roughly constant since 2008, consistent with that of most other nations. The exceptions

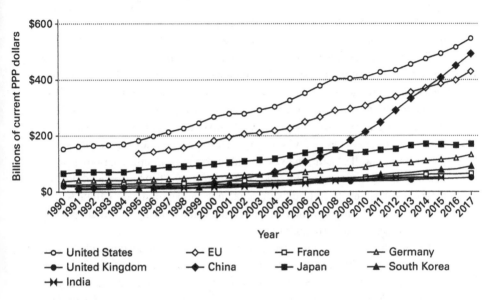

Figure 14.1
Gross domestic expenditures on research and development, in purchasing power parity dollars, by selected region, country, or economy, 1990–2017. *Source*: National Science Board (2020d).

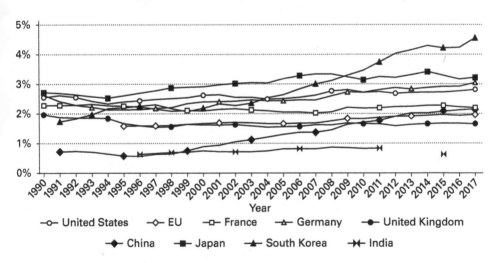

Figure 14.2
Gross domestic expenditures on R&D as a share of gross domestic product, by the US, the EU, and selected other countries, 1990–2017. *Source*: National Science Board (2020e).

are China and South Korea, both of which exhibit steady increases for two decades or more, with South Korea increasing sharply.

Turning to measures other than dollars, scholarly publications represent the end product of research (especially fundamental research) and are a valuable measure of productivity. Figure 14.3 shows science and engineering articles produced, by global share of selected region, from 1996 through 2018. Note the US share has steadily declined and now is well below 20 percent, while China surpassed the US a few years ago, with other developing countries now increasing as well. Again, the rise in publications from other nations is a net positive, though it is important the US remain strong. Total patents granted by national office in 2021 (https://wipo.int; not shown) indicate China with a more than 2 to 1 lead over the US, though the value of many of China's patents remains questionable (He 2021).

The production of college degrees is an extremely important indicator of workforce capability and capacity and thus future research and development. Figures 14.4 and 14.5 capture this information for baccalaureate (first) as well as doctoral degrees in science and engineering fields. In the case of baccalaureate degrees, the US and the EU have grown at roughly the same rate, though both exhibit a flattening during the past few years. China began exhibiting rapid growth starting in 2002 and the trend continues unchanged, though as

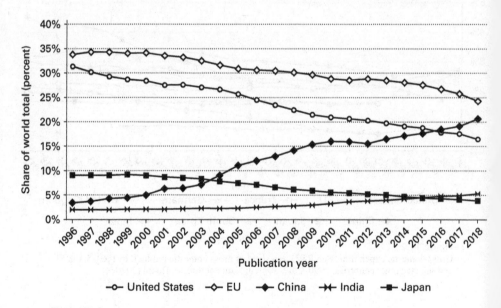

Figure 14.3
Science and engineering articles, by global share of selected region, country, or economy, 1996–2018. *Source*: National Science Board (2020c).

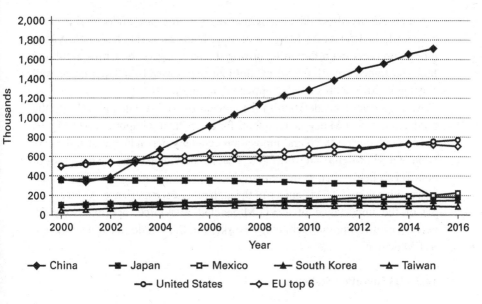

Figure 14.4
First university degrees in science and engineering, by selected region, country, or economy, 2000–2016. The EU top six includes France, Germany, Italy, Poland, Spain, and the United Kingdom. *Source*: National Science Board (2020h).

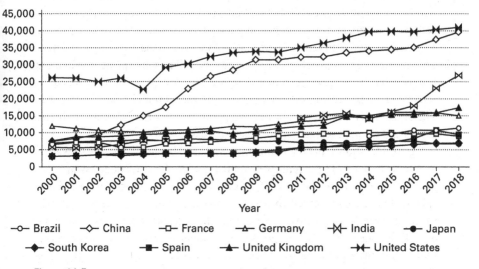

Figure 14.5
Doctoral degrees in science and engineering, by selected region, country, or economy, 2000–2018. *Source*: National Science Board (2022a).

noted previously, these data lag by five years. In the case of doctoral degrees produced, the US and the EU grew at roughly the same rate for several years, though both exhibit a flattening during the past few years. China exhibited rapid, sustained growth from 2002 until 2010, followed by a flattening as well starting in 2013, with a notable uptick beginning in 2016.

An important consideration in the context of STEM fields is not only the production of STEM degree recipients for the critically important STEM jobs upon which our research and innovation economy depends, but also the creation of a STEM-enabled workforce. That is, individuals who have degrees in non-STEM fields, such as the humanities, but who possess some STEM capabilities via taking STEM courses or through practical experience. As an example of the importance of a STEM-enabled workforce, approximately 25 percent of information technology workers in the US do not in fact have a STEM degree.

14.2 US Education Statistics

I am sure you are aware that demographics in the US are changing dramatically. According to the US Census Bureau, the US increasingly is pluralistic, meaning no race or ethnic group will have a share of more than half the total population. In fact, the Census Bureau projects that 32 percent of Americans will be a race other than White by 2060. As a result, in order for the research enterprise to remain robust, enhancing the participation of traditionally underrepresented, underserved, or marginalized individuals is critically important. This is true in terms of college accessibility as well as subsequent employment. Progress has been slow, as shown in figure 14.6, which depicts the receipt of science and engineering master's degrees by race, ethnicity, and citizenship. The situation is a bit better for baccalaureate degrees (not shown), with Hispanics and Latinos seeing the greatest progress.

Figure 14.7 shows that the percentage of STEM bachelor's degrees awarded to Asian students (33 percent) was almost double the percentage awarded to students overall from 2015 to 2016. In contrast, the percentages of STEM baccalaureate degrees awarded to Black, American Indian/Alaska Native, Hispanic, and Pacific Islander were lower than the percentage awarded to students overall. Because of the disproportionate number of women and underrepresented minorities pursuing STEM careers, particularly within academia, agencies such as the National Science Foundation have begun initiatives such as the ADVANCE (Increasing the Participation and Advancement of Women in Academic Science and Engineering Careers) program, which is designed to increase participation and advance diversity in academic STEM careers.

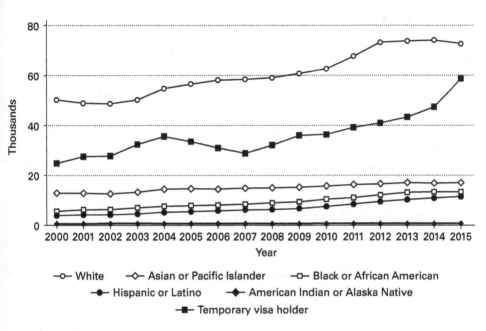

Figure 14.6
Science and engineering master's degrees, by race, ethnicity, and citizenship, 2000–2015.
Source: National Science Board (2018c).

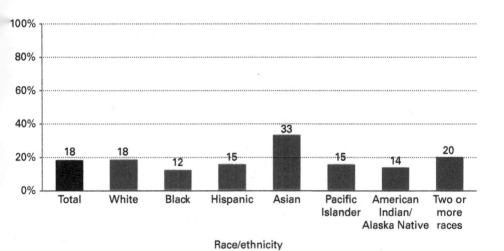

Figure 14.7
STEM bachelor's degrees as a percentage of total bachelor's degrees conferred by postsecondary institutions, by race/ethnicity, for the academic year 2015–2016. *Source*: National Center for Education Statistics (2019).

Looking a bit more closely at measures for women, figure 14.8 shows women's share of science and engineering degrees, by degree level and field, in 2017. In all fields combined, women dominate at all levels, driven mostly by dominance in psychology and the biological sciences and at the doctoral level in the social sciences. Clearly, more progress is needed for women in computer science and engineering.

Figure 14.9 shows trends for women bachelor's degrees from 2000 through 2015. Since 1982, women have outnumbered men in undergraduate education. And, since the late 1990s, women have earned about 57 percent of all bachelor's degrees and half of all science and engineering bachelor's degrees. The curves since 2000 for women are basically flat, except for computer science, which exhibited a drop of 10 percent during this time.

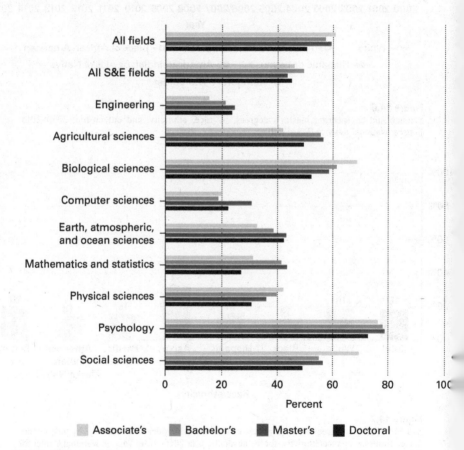

Figure 14.8
Science and engineering degrees awarded to women, by degree level and field, 2017. *Source*: National Science Board (2019a).

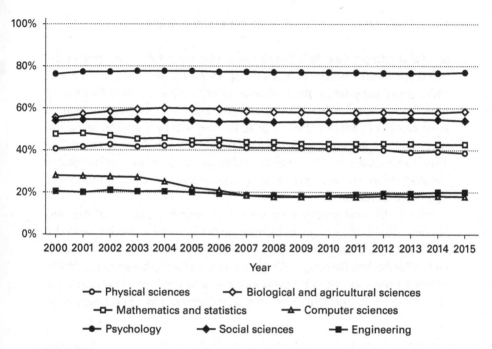

Figure 14.9
Women's share of science and engineering bachelor's degrees, by field, from 2000 through 2015. *Source*: National Science Board (2018b).

Of course, college readiness and success depend upon adequate preparation in grades K–12, and the NSB science and engineering data contain a wide array of measures on K–12 performance in the US compared to other countries. Space does not allow for a comprehensive treatment of this important topic, so here are a few key points from the 2018 edition of SEI.:

- Less than half of fourth, eighth, and twelfth grade students achieved a level of proficiency, defined as "solid academic performance" or higher, on standardized mathematics and science assessments in 2015.

- Performance disparities in mathematics and science were evident in 2015 among different demographic groups at all grade levels, beginning as early as kindergarten and persisting through subsequent school years.

- For the latest data available, US average mathematics assessment scores were well below the average scores of the top-performing education systems in the world. And the US performs better internationally in science literacy than it does in mathematics literacy.

14.3   Challenges Facing the US Academic Research Enterprise

Several challenges face the US academic research enterprise, and here I mention those which I believe to be most important. The first concerns the level and, equally importantly, the predictability of funding available for research from federal agencies. Establishing and growing a research program requires some degree of certainty that adequate funding will be available. Just as the stock market hates uncertainty, so do researchers when it comes to funding. This is particularly true for federal funding directed toward fundamental or curiosity-driven research, and several recent reports have called for sustained, significant increases.

Among the most notable documents is American Academy of Arts and Sciences (2014), which proposes increases in fundamental research support that would put the US back on a trajectory similar to that which existed from the mid-1970s through the early 1990s (figure 14.10). During that period, inflation-adjusted annual growth for federal investment in fundamental research was approximately 4.4 percent. Since then, investments have fluctuated, never

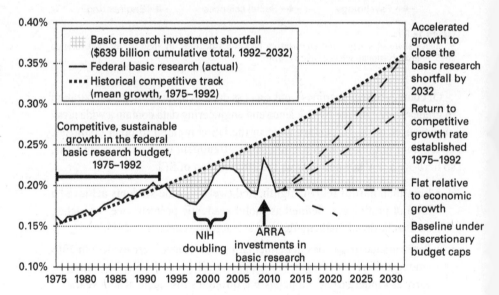

Figure 14.10
US federal basic (fundamental) research investment, in current dollars, as a share of gross domestic product. The dotted line is a least-squares fit of federal obligations for basic research during the period from 1975 to 1992 and is projected out to 2032. The hatched region shows the difference between this curve and a budget that is flat relative to economic growth. The shallow dashed line shows the rate of investment needed to equal the long-term projection by 2032, and the steep dashed line shows the rate of investment needed to close the funding gap by 2032. *Source*: American Academy of Arts and Sciences (2014).

recovering in a sustained manner to previous levels. The report provides recommendations to address this and other challenges.

Second, as noted in chapter 10, the number of research compliance rules and regulations has grown dramatically during the past thirty years and in many cases is hampering research without meaningfully driving behavior in desired directions. This is an especially acute problem for MSIs, ERIs, and institutions that focus primarily on instruction but seek to become more active in research. As Congress increases funding for research at such institutions, it must recognize that such increases require concomitant scaling of administrative frameworks (section 12.3), and that additional research activity can fundamentally change institutional culture. Although good progress is being made to address these issues, including reducing researcher administrative workload (section 10.6), more needs to be done.

Third, especially in times of tight research budgets, the degree of patience exhibited by Congress and others regarding practical outcomes from research investments tends to diminish. Yet, as noted in this book, the time taken for fundamental research results to manifest themselves in ways seen as practical can be quite long, even a few decades. It is important for the US to have a balanced portfolio among all funding sources such that the entire research ecosystem, which as we saw in chapter 3 is highly intertwined, can be successful.

Fourth, as noted previously, increasing the diversity of the scholarly enterprise, particularly in STEM fields, is critically important to the future of research and creative activity. Here, I interpret diversity in the broadest possible manner to include attributes of race, ethnicity, gender, sexual orientation, geography, military service, age, religion, political affiliation, viewpoints, and country of origin. To be successful and serve as a beacon of values through practice, not merely words, the American research enterprise not only must welcome all potential participants, but also take steps to ensure that everyone who wishes to become involved has the opportunity to do so.

Fifth, we must never forsake the arts, fine arts, and humanities in seeking to cure cancer or build the next transformative invention. Our humanity, in its many dimensions of richness and expression, is as important to our future as the next technological discovery. Scholarly pursuits in all areas are essential to our future and must continue.

Finally, this book has addressed the academic research enterprise. Consequently, its future depends upon that of the academy itself; that is, on the health and well-being of our system of postsecondary education. Colleges and universities are in the midst of significant challenges for a number of reasons. They include the value of a college degree relative to its cost, associated with which has been a loss of the fundamental notion of higher education as a public good;

the need to be more inclusive while maintaining high standards; a diminution of universities as the place where divergent viewpoints are welcome and thoughtful debate occurs without fear of retribution; uncertain federal support for tuition aid; continued increases in regulation; and online education, which is of great value for many reasons but could fundamentally alter the financial structure upon which institutions have always operated.

It is well documented, as shown in figure 3.3, that funding for public research universities dropped significantly following the Great Recession in 2008/2009. Although the trend is now reversing, appropriated funding for public colleges and universities remains well below that of a decade ago in real spending power—and thus tuition costs have risen as a means to offset a large part of the difference.

14.4 Looking Ahead

Despite many challenges, some of which are significant and have no simple solutions, I remain very optimistic about the future of the US research enterprise, as described in the afterword. And I know most of my colleagues share that view. Although we cannot ignore and are not ignoring those challenges, our nation is better positioned than ever before to continue discovering, innovating, educating, and leading the world as a beacon of progress and prosperity. Opportunity abounds for you, as a researcher, to participate. The tools available to you, the vast repositories of knowledge at your fingertips, and the need for creative minds to tackle society's most stimulating and compelling problems have never been greater. Seize the moment. Unleash your curiosity and desire to discover. The only limitation you face is that which you place upon yourself. As Michelangelo is said to have brilliantly stated, "The greatest danger for most of us is not that our aim is too high and we miss it, but that our aim is too low and we reach it."

Assess Your Comprehension

1. List a few measures demonstrating American leadership in research and innovation globally.
2. How many more Nobel laureates has the US produced than its nearest competitor?
3. What countries are today investing the most in research and development and how have these investments changed over the past twenty years?
4. How has the share of scholarly publications by the US changed over the past twenty years and what changes have occurred in other countries by comparison?

5. How does the US compare to other nations with regard to patents issued?

6. How does the US compare to other countries in the production of baccalaureate degrees?

7. What progress is being achieved by the US in diversifying degrees in science, technology, engineering, and mathematics (STEM) fields?

8. How does progress in diversifying STEM degrees compare with trends in population demographics?

9. How do women fare relative to men in science and engineering degrees awarded?

10. What key challenges face America's scholarly enterprise over the next several years to decades?

11. What reasons exist to be optimistic about the future of America's scholarly enterprise?

Exercises to Deepen Your Understanding

Exercise 1: The pathway toward a successful future research enterprise depends upon having a sustainable pipeline of students engaged in research. In particular, our nation's research and innovation enterprise needs greater numbers of individuals seeking degrees and expertise in science, technology, engineering, and mathematics (STEM) fields, particularly women and those from underrepresented minority groups. For this exercise, design the framework of a program that would stimulate interest, and provide for participation by K–12 students in research and creative activity, so as to ensure an adequate flow of talent into career techs, colleges, and universities. In framing your program, consider the following:

- What specific goals do you seek to achieve?
- Who is your target audience?
- What program structure will you use?
- What resources will you need?
- How is this program different from existing programs?
- How will this program improve participation by individuals from underrepresented groups? How can you most effectively ensure involvement of these groups?

Exercise 2: A recent report (National Science Board 2019b) highlighted the critical importance of a skilled technical workforce (STW) in America's science and engineering research enterprise. For this exercise, read the report and develop a strategy for ensuring an adequate supply of talent within, and an appropriate balance between, an STW that supports research and creative activity compared to education pathways for those within the enterprise who have more advanced degrees and are performing the research. How would you incentivize those wishing to enter the STW? What education and training options are available to them? Consider issues such as affordability, accessibility, lifelong earnings, and reskilling opportunities for those already in certain trades (e.g., welders, electricians, heating/ventilation/air conditioning experts, machinists).

Exercise 3: This chapter pointed to a number of trends in international science, engineering, and technology research in which other nations are gaining ground relative to the US. What actions can the US take, both in terms of funding and policy, to ensure it remains a global leader in research while also serving as a collaborative partner? Speak specifically to issues that might be inhibiting multinational collaboration, such as differences in intellectual property ownership policies among nations, concerns about the theft or misappropriation of research results (chapter 10) by some foreign governments, immigration policies, and so on. You may wish to consider examining the European Union's (EU) Horizon Europe (European Commission n.d.) program and the challenges it poses for US engagement in research.

Exercise 4: Holding a degree (or degrees) in higher education has been documented to result in greater lifelong earnings and earning potential. Additionally, higher education has long been viewed as a public good, bringing benefits to society broadly in addition to those accruing to degree holders. Yet, the focus today is much more on a college degree as a pathway to a job or career, as evidenced by decreased public investment and the growing cost of higher education. For this exercise, describe how you would go about reframing the value proposition of higher education, including research, as a public good in addition to a private (individual) good. Which stakeholders are most critical for you to reach (e.g., students, parents, faculty, university administrators, Congress, the White House, private industry), and how would you most effectively make your case given the broad array of views held by them regarding higher education?

Exercise 5: The success of America's research enterprise—across all disciplines and sectors in which research and creative activity take place—is due in no small part to individuals from other nations who come to the US., receive a college education including advanced degrees, and remain here as productive citizens. Yet today, other nations are investing heavily in research and education, thereby providing other high quality and less expensive options for their citizens even though America remains the destination of choice. How can the US ensure it continues to be viewed as an attractive destination for foreign nationals? Discuss this issue with some of your peers from other countries who are either studying or conducting research in the US and obtain their opinions and points of view. Compare their input with current policies regarding foreign nationals in education and research (e.g., H-1B visa program) and suggest changes to improve the system.

Afterword

Those of us who are scholars or scholars in training and have the privilege of undertaking research and creative activity in the US are among the most fortunate individuals on the planet because the US is a global leader in science and technology research, creative activity, and related education. Especially important to this leadership role are our American values, which are manifest in many ways in the context of scholarship. Specifically, the freedom to explore ideas, create new knowledge, perform and exhibit our works, express views and opinions openly—including those critical of others—start companies, share results, allow scholars from other nations to move freely about and utilize our resources, and transition scholarly outcomes into benefits for society.

More extraordinary, however, is the congruence between American values and those values foundational to the conduct of scholarship itself—namely, honesty, integrity, transparency, accountability, freedom of inquiry, sharing, collaboration, mutual respect, impartiality, objectivity, civil debate irrespective of the topic, openness to new ideas and approaches, reciprocity, and principled international and merit-based competition. Unfortunately, such is not the case in some countries, and thus the US has been and remains a beacon to the world with regard to values.

Yet even today, those values are being challenged. On many of our campuses, certain topics are deemed off limits for discussion. Individuals of certain political persuasions or points of view are harassed or prevented from speaking, and persons of certain races, gender identities, or other characteristics are demeaned or marginalized. This is not what America is about, and it certainly is not what the scholarly enterprise is about. Agreement with others is not the point. Mutual respect and support are.

Although research and creative activity have many reasons for existing, as described in this book, I believe one of the most important is to preserve, practice, and model for one another, and for the world, the set of values mentioned above. In that regard, three important characteristics describe the powerful role of research and creative activity in society.

First, research and creative activity *inspire*. The word means to encourage and comes from a Latin word meaning to "blow life into." Think about scholarly activities as a flame fed not with oxygen, but rather kindled by ideas and perspectives—bold thinking and creative ideas—until a raging inferno develops. And this inferno, by its very characteristics, attracts interest. Research and creative activity do just that. They motivate us to think beyond ourselves and give us a passion that draws the best out of us. We simply are not willing to settle for not knowing, and research provides us with the tools to understand! Think about examples that move and inspire you. Perhaps it was the first image of a black hole shadow, which appeared in newspapers around the world, or the development of COVID-19 vaccines with unprecedented speed, or a drama, opera, or work of art. Those and countless other examples touch each of us in different and special ways, providing hope and making life worth living.

Second, research and creative activity *unite*. To unite means to join together or come together to become one thing. This is the epitome of scholarly endeavors, which bring people together with a common goal—to explore innate curiosity, create new knowledge, solve problems, and express the amazing complexities and beauty of humanity. One's race, gender identity, sex, ethnicity, political views, religion and other characteristics should not come into play. Yet, as explained in this book, scholars still have work to do in order to ensure the veracity of that statement.

Finally, research and creative activity *guide*. In some situations, this occurs in obvious ways, say via the provision of solutions to compelling challenges such as the COVID-19 pandemic. The unprecedented speed with which vaccines were developed and distributed was made possible by decades of curiosity-driven research and coordination among local, state, federal, and corporate leaders. In other situations, the guidance from scholarly work is subtler, such as when a theater production portrays a particularly challenging time in our nation's history and reminds us of the fragility of life and the importance of loving and supporting one another.

America's scholarly enterprise is one of society's few remaining constructs in which values foundational to Western civilization are cherished and protected. Therefore, it is incumbent upon us, as scholars, to ensure these values remain a guiding North Star not only for the good of research and creative activity, but also for the very welfare of humanity.

Notes

Chapter 1

1. Academic tenure essentially is the guarantee of an academic appointment that can be terminated only under exceptional circumstances such as violation of the law, egregious violation of institutional policy, financial exigency, or discontinuation of programs or of the institution itself. Tenure was created to ensure faculty are able to pursue scholarly activities without external pressure. The foundation upon which tenure is built is academic freedom.

2. The sources of internal funding available to the SRO for allocation vary substantially, and in some cases are linked to the recovery of facilities and administrative (F&A) costs from external grants and contracts (section 6.2).

3. Most colleges and universities manage other dimensions of compliance, including those related to athletics, Title IX, auditing, and human resources.

Chapter 2

1. This book attempts to use authoritative figures and graphs based upon the most recent data available. However, in some cases, data collection mechanisms, such as surveys, lead to data sets and associated figures that lag the present by up to a few years. In other cases, figures from authoritative sources are refreshed only periodically. Fortunately, trends of data over time in most of the figures shown in this book do not change appreciably. Relevant exceptions are noted.

2. Although OMB has formal directive authority over federal agencies, OSTP does not, except in very limited circumstances. Consequently, the R&D priorities memo is created collaboratively by both and jointly issued.

3. In contrast to the US structure, many other countries have cabinet-level ministries, such as a ministry of research and technology or research and education. As a result, their budgeting and coordination processes are simplified and streamlined.

Chapter 3

1. As noted in section 2.1, however, academic institutions are expanding their portfolios in applied R&D as a way to expand the opportunity space for funding, contribute in more direct ways to the creation of products and services that benefit society, and build collaborative partnerships with the private sector (chapter 12).

2. The ultimate administrative structure of NSF was notably different than what Dr. Bush envisioned owing to President Truman's differing view.

Chapter 4

1. In science, the term "paradigm" sometimes is used to describe approaches to research involving theory, observation, experimentation, computational simulation, and data-driven discovery.

Chapter 5

1. Here, the word "laboratory" is applied very generally to all disciplines and simply refers to a notebook that captures process-oriented information about your work, as well as results as the work proceeds.

Chapter 6

1. Because the structure of grant proposals varies so dramatically among funding sources, I do not present here examples of the various components of such proposals or the many varied guidelines that exist for preparing them. Instead, exercises are provided at the end of this chapter for you to develop your own proposal by examining proposals available online using guidance provided by funding sources. In completing those exercises, it is important that you work with an experienced colleague, at your institution or another, to guide your work.

2. Exceptions do of course exist, such as with the DOE Office of Science.

3. Universities often also refer to F&A as overhead, which has an entirely different meaning in the private sector and can lead to additional confusion (Droegemeier 2018).

4. In reality, the term "modified total direct costs" is used because some budget components are excluded from the F&A calculation, including student tuition and equipment exceeding a certain value.

Chapter 7

1. Although often used interchangeably, the terms "merit review" and "peer review" are different. Peer review is a general term describing any sort of scholarly review conducted by peers. It can be applied to work being proposed, as in research grant proposals, or to research outcomes, such as journal and book manuscripts, performances, scores, technological innovations, exhibits, paintings, and sculptures. Merit review is a subset of peer review whereby scholarly activity is evaluated based upon its merits, according to stated criteria. This term typically is used in the context of research grant proposals.

2. NSF uses the term "merit review" because the review process is designed to judge the merit of submitted proposals.

3. As noted in section 4.7, reproduction of research results in some fields, based solely upon information contained in a formal publication, increasingly is difficult given the complexity of tools used (e.g., computer models) and the inability of a publication to contain all of the information associated with their application.

4. A fascinating example of overturning an established paradigm is the discovery of a mathematical error in a 100-year-old theory—conceived and developed by three giants in mathematics (Bernhard Riemann, Hermann von Helmholtz and Erwin Schrödinger)—which describes how human eyes distinguish among different colors. The new study (Poling 2022) brought together elements of psychology, biology, and mathematics and has profound implications for scientific data visualization, flat panel displays, and other applications where color interpretation is foundational (e.g., textiles and paint).

Chapter 12

1. An interesting and controversial feature of the Bayh-Dole Act is the "march-in rights" provision, which allows the federal government, acting in its interest or on behalf of another party, to bypass the ownership dimensions of the Act and grant IP licenses to others, provided certain criteria are satisfied. To date, no march-in rights have been exercised.

Chapter 14

1. According to the Organisation for Economic Co-operation and Development (http://oecd.org /sdd/purchasingpowerparities-frequentlyaskedquestionsfaqs.htm#FAQ1), "PPPs are the rates

of currency conversion that equalize the purchasing power of different currencies by eliminating the differences in price levels between countries. In their simplest form, PPPs are simply price relatives that show the ratio of the prices in national currencies of the same good or service in different countries. PPPs are also calculated for product groups and for each of the various levels of aggregation up to and including GDP."

2. According to the International Monetary Fund (https://www.imf.org/external/pubs/ft/fandd /basics/gdp.htm), "GDP measures the monetary value of final goods and services—that is, those that are bought by the final user—produced in a country in a given period of time (say a quarter or a year). It counts all of the output generated within the borders of a country. GDP is composed of goods and services produced for sale in the market and also includes some nonmarket production, such as defense or education services provided by the government."

References

Alberts, B., Cicerone, R. J., Fienberg, S. E., Kamb, A., McNutt, A., Nerem, R. M., Schekman, R., Shiffrin, R., Stodden, V., Suresh, S., et al. (2015). Self-correction in science at work. *Science, 348*(6242), 1420–1422. https://www.science.org/doi/10.1126/science.aab3847

Alberts, B., Hanson, B., & Kelner, K. L. (2008). Reviewing peer review. *Science, 231*(5885), 15. https://www.science.org/doi/pdf/10.1126/science.1162115

American Academy of Arts and Sciences (2014). *Restoring the foundation: The vital role of research in preserving the American Dream.* Cambridge, MA: American Academy of Arts and Sciences. https://www.amacad.org/multimedia/pdfs/publications/researchpapersmonographs/AmericanAcad_RestoringtheFoundation.pdf

American Academy of Arts and Sciences (2020). *The perils of complacency: America at a tipping point in science and engineering.* https://www.amacad.org/sites/default/files/publication/downloads/Perils-of-Complacency_Report-Brief_4.pdf

American Association for the Advancement of Science (2018). *Historical trends in federal R&D.* https://www.aaas.org/page/historical-trends-federal-rd

American Association for the Advancement of Science (2020, October 22). *A snapshot of U.S. R&D competitiveness: 2020 update.* https://www.aaas.org/news/snapshot-us-rd-competitiveness-2020-update

American Society for Quality (n.d.). Learn about quality. Retrieved June 27, 2022, from http://asq.org/learn-about-quality/quality-assurance-quality-control/overview/overview.html

Anania, F. A. (2015). Universities and sponsored research: Indirect cost recovery and the law of diminishing return. *Hepatology, 61*(6), 1776–1778. https://doi.org/10.1002/hep.27776

Arthur, B. (2017, April 17). *The difference between quality assurance and quality control.* Open Dialog, Dialog Information Technology. https://www.dialog.com.au/open-dialog/the-difference-between-quality-assurance-and-quality-control/

Arti (2014). *Development of education as a discipline—An analytical study.* Doctoral thesis, University of Lucknow. INFLIBNET Centre. http://hdl.handle.net/10603/70652

Association of American Medical Colleges (n.d.). *Regulatory burden provisions in the 21st century cures.* Retrieved June 27, 2022, from https://www.aamc.org/download/479546/data/regulatoryburdenprovision.pdf

Association of American Universities (2017a). *Breaking down the costs of federal research at universities.* https://www.aau.edu/sites/default/files/files/Costs-University-Research-Background-Brief_3-2017.pdf

Association of American Universities (2017b). *Frequently asked questions about facilities and administrative (F&A) costs of federally sponsored university research.* https://www.aau.edu/key-issues/frequently-asked-questions-about-facilities-and-administrative-fa-costs-federally

Association of American Universities (n.d.). *Reducing regulatory burden.* Retrieved June 27, 2022, from https://www.aau.edu/issues/reducing-regulatory-burden

Association of Public & Land-grant Universities (2016). *A guide to implementing a safety culture*. http://www.aplu.org/library/safety-culture/file

Association of University Technology Managers (n.d.-a). *AUTM licensing activity survey*. Retrieved June 27, 2022, from https://autm.net/surveys-and-tools/surveys/licensing-survey/2019 -licensing-survey/disclosures

Association of University Technology Managers (n.d.-b). *Driving the innovation economy: Academic technology transfer numbers*. Retrieved June 27, 2022, from https://autm.net/AUTM/media /Surveys-Tools/Documents/FY20-Infographic.pdf

Balietti, S., Goldstone, R. L., & Helbing, D. (2016). Peer review and competition in the art exhibition game. *PNAS, 113*(30), 8414–8419. http://www.pnas.org/cgi/doi/10.1073/pnas.1603723113

Batterbee, R. (2017). Research papers, gender bias and peer review. *Biology Letters, 13*. https:// doi.org/10.1098/rsbl.2017.0424

Beall, J. (2013). Unethical practices in scholarly, open-access publishing. *Journal of Information Ethics, 22*(1), 11–22.

Bennett, L. M., & Gadlin, H. (2012). Collaboration and team science—from theory to practice. *Journal of Investigative Medicine, 60*(5), 768–775. https://jim.bmj.com/content/60/5/768

Bennett L. M., & Gadlin, H. (2019). Conflict prevention and management in science teams. In K. Hall, A. Vogel, & R. Croyle (Eds.), *Strategies for team science success*. Springer. https://doi .org/10.1007/978-3-030-20992-6_22

Bias (n.d.-a). *Cambridge English Dictionary*. Retrieved June 27, 2022, from https://dictionary .cambridge.org/us/dictionary/english/bias

Bias (n.d.-b). *Oxford English Dictionary*. Retrieved June 27, 2022, from https://www.oed.com /view/Entry/18564?rskey=UQAvts&result=1#eid

Bienenstock, A. (2000). Some thoughts on cost sharing. *Research Management Review, 11*(1), 5–8.

Bjork, B-C. (2011). A Study of innovative features in scholarly open access journals. *Journal of Medical Internet Research, 13*(4). https://www.jmir.org/2011/4/e115/

Blakeslee, W. D. (2004). *Fundamentals of intellectual property for institutional research*. The Johns Hopkins University. https://www.google.com/url?sa=t&rct=j&q=&esrc=s&source=web &cd=&ved=2ahUKEwisv-rO4bjyAhXIWc0KHXZJCA8QFnoECBQQAQ&url=https%3 A%2F%2Fwww.higheredcompliance.org%2Fwp-content%2Fuploads%2F2018%2F10%2Fxviii -04-11-4.doc&usg=AOvVaw2tAJWsSlntS0PG1LnZD6mU

Bohannon, J. (2013). Who's afraid of peer review? *Science, 342*(6154), 60–65. https://www.science .org/doi/10.1126/science.2013.342.6154.342_60

Bornmann, L. (2013). Research misconduct—definitions, manifestations and extent. *Publications, 1*, 87–98. https://doi.org/10.3390/publications1030087

Brabin, D. W. (2004). *Pioneering research: A risk worth taking*. Hoboken, NJ: Wiley-Interscience.

Bradley, S. H., Devito, N. J., Lloyd, K. E., Richards, G. C., Romby, T., Wayant, C., & Gill, P. J. (2020). Reducing bias and improving transparency in medical research: A critical overview of the problems, progress and suggested next steps. *Journal of the Royal Society of Medicine, 113*(11), 433–443. https://doi.org/10.1177%2F0141076820956799

Bulmer, E. (Ed.) (2003). *Sociological research methods* (2nd ed.). New York: Transaction Publishers.

Burney, S. M. A., & Saleem, H., (2008, March 6). Inductive & deductive research approach [PowerPoint slides]. Lecture delivered at the University of Karachi, Pakistan. https://www.research gate.net/profile/Hussain-Saleem/publication/331330927_Inductive_and_Deductive_Research_ Approach/links/5d0749d492851c900442dcb7/Inductive-and-Deductive-Research-Approach.pdf

Burroughs Wellcome Fund & Howard Hughes Medical Institute (2006). *Making the right moves: A practical guide to scientific management for postdocs and new faculty* (2nd ed.). https://www .hhmi.org/science-education/programs/resources/making-right-moves

Bush, V. (1945). *Science, the endless frontier*. Washington, DC: US Government Printing Office. https://www.nsf.gov/about/history/nsf50/vbush1945.jsp

Callen, T. (2020, February 24). *Gross domestic product: An economy's all.* International Monetary Fund. https://www.imf.org/external/pubs/ft/fandd/basics/gdp.htm

Canadian Institutes of Health Research (n.d.). *Unconscious bias training module.* Retrieved June 27, 2022, from http://www.chairs-chaires.gc.ca/program-programme/equity-equite/bias/module -eng.aspx?pedisable=false

Cantu, R. (n.d.). *In fraud we trust: Top 5 cases of misconduct in university research.* University of Houston. Retrieved June 27, 2022, from https://research.uh.edu/the-big-idea/university -research-explained/five-cases-of-research-fraud/

Carey, S. S. (2011). *A beginner's guide to the scientific method* (4th ed.). Boston: Wadsworth, Cengage Learning.

CEBM (n.d.). *Catalog of bias.* University of Oxford. Retrieved June 27, 2022, from https:// catalogofbias.org/biases/

Christensen, L. B., Johnson R. B., & Turner, L. A. (2014). *Research methods, design and analysis* (12th ed.). Upper Saddle River, NJ: Pearson.

Cisak, A., Formanowicz, M., & Saguy, T. (2018). Bias against research on gender bias. *Scientometrics, 115,* 189–200. https://doi.org/10.1007/s11192-018-2667-0

CITI Program (n.d.). *Responsible conduct of research.* Retrieved June 27, 2022, from https://about .citiprogram.org/series/responsible-conduct-of-research-rcr/

Cohen, E., & Lloyd, S. (2014). Disciplinary evolution and the rise of the transdiscipline. *Informing Science: The International Journal of an Emerging Transdiscipline, 17,* 189–215. http://www .inform.nu/Articles/Vol17/ISJv17p189-215Cohen0702.pdf

Colby, S. L., & Ortman, J. M. (2015). *Projections of the size and composition of the U.S. population: 2014 to 2060.* https://census.gov/content/dam/Census/library/publications/2015/demo/p25-1143.pdf

Collins, F. (2018, August 23). *Statement on protecting the integrity of U.S. biomedical research.* National Institutes of Health. https://www.nih.gov/about-nih/who-we-are/nih-director/statements /statement-protecting-integrity-usbiomedical-research

Comrie, A. C. (2021). *Like nobody's business: An insider's guide to how U.S. university finances really work.* Open Book Publishers. https://doi.org/10.11647/OBP.0240

Congressional Research Service (2020a). *Department of Defense research, development, test, and evaluation (RDT&E) appropriations structure.* Report R44711. https://fas.org/sgp/crs/natsec /R44711.pdf

Congressional Research Service (2020b). *Federal research and development (R&D) funding: FY2020.* Report R45715. https://fas.org/sgp/crs/misc/R45715.pdf

Congressional Research Service (2020c). *The U.S. export control system and the export control reform initiative.* Report R41916. https://sgp.fas.org/crs/natsec/R41916.pdf

Congressional Research Service (2021a). *Defense Primer: RDT&E.* Report IF10553. https:// crsreports.congress.gov/product/pdf/IF/IF10553

Congressional Research Service (2021b). *Earmark disclosure rules in the House: Member and committee requirements.* Report RS22866. https://sgp.fas.org/crs/misc/RS22866.pdf

Cooper, C. (2014, January 3). Drugs companies "routinely withhold results of medical trials" from doctors, researchers, and patients. *Independent.* http://www.independent.co.uk/life-style/health -and-families/health-news/drugs-firms-routinely-withhold-results-of-medical-trials-from -doctors-researchers-and-patients-9035740.html

Council on Governmental Relations (2019). *Excellence in research: The funding model, F&A reimbursement, and why the system works.* https://www.cogr.edu/sites/default/files/Excellence InResearch4_12_19_0.pdf

Council on Governmental Relations (2021, April 10). *Federal regulatory changes, since 1991.* https://www.cogr.edu/sites/default/files/RegChangesSince1991_Updated%20January%20 2021%20Draft%20clean.pdf

Council on Governmental Relations (2022). *Excellence in research: Technology transfer in U.S. research universities: Dispelling common myths.* https://www.cogr.edu/sites/default/files/Myths _Final%2008-01-22.pdf

Coursera (n.d.). *Reproducible research.* Retrieved June 27, 2022, from https://www.coursera.org /course/repdata

Creswell, J. W., & Plano Clark, V. L. (2017). *Designing and conducting mixed methods research* (3rd ed.). Los Angeles: Sage Publications.

Crowther, D., & Lancaster, G. (2008). *Research methods.* New York: Routledge.

DeCoursey, T. E. (2006). The pros and cons of open peer review. *Nature.* https://doi.org/10.1038 /nature04991

Denning, P. J. (1997). A new social contract for research. *Communications of the ACM, 40*(2), 132–134. https://dl.acm.org/doi/10.1145/253671.253755

Desilver, D. (2018). *Congress has long struggled to pass spending bills on time.* Pew Research Center. https://www.pewresearch.org/fact-tank/2018/01/16/congress-has-long-struggled-to-pass -spending-bills-on-time/

Diamond, L., & Schell, O. (Eds.) (2019). *China's influence & American interests: Promoting constructive vigilance.* https://www.hoover.org/research/chinas-influence-american-interests -promoting-constructive-vigilance

Dizikes, P. (2011, February 22). When the butterfly effect took flight. *MIT Technology Review.* https://www.technologyreview.com/s/422809/when-the-butterfly-effect-took-flight/

Doyle, M. (2018, January 9). U.S. Interior Department to put academic, nonprofit grants through political review. *ScienceInsider.* http://www.sciencemag.org/news/2018/01/us-interior-department -put-academic-nonprofit-grants-through-political-review

Drawson, A. S., Toombs, E., & Mushquash, C. J. (2017). Indigenous research methods: A systematic review. *International Indigenous Policy Journal, 8*(2). https://ir.lib.uwo.ca/iipj/vol8/iss2/5

Droegemeier, K. (2020, August 19). Harnessing the power of science to fight the Coronavirus. *Washington Examiner.* https://www.washingtonexaminer.com/opinion/op-eds/harnessing-the -power-of-science-to-fight-the-coronavirus

Droegemeier, K. K. (2017, October 24). *Written testimony provided for a hearing before the United States House of Representatives Sub-Committee on Labor, Health and Human Services, Education and Related Agencies titled "The Role of Facilities and Administrative Costs in Supporting NIH-Funded Research."* https://docs.house.gov/meetings/AP/AP07/20171024/106525 /HHRG-115-AP07-Wstate-DroegemeierK-20171024.pdf

Droegemeier, K. K. (2018, May 30). Direct costs, indirect costs, overhead, G&A, and F&A: Clearing up the confusion. http://kkd.ou.edu/Overhead_G&A_and_F&A.pdf

Droegemeier, K. K., Snyder, L. A., Knoedler, A., Taylor, W., Litwiller, B., Whitacre, C., Gobstein, H., Keller, C., Hinds, T. L., & Dwyer, N. (2017). The roles of chief research officers at American research universities: A current profile and challenges for the future. *Journal of Research Administration, 48*(1), 26–64. https://files.eric.ed.gov/fulltext/EJ1152287.pdf

DuBois, J. M., Anderson, E. E., Chibnall, J., Carroll, K., Gibb, T., & Ogbuka, C. (2013). Understanding research misconduct: A comparative analysis of 120 cases of professional wrongdoing. *Accountability in Research, 20*(5–6), 320–338. https://doi.org/10.1080/08989621.2013.822248

Earhart, A. E., Risam, R., & Bruno, M. (2021). Citational politics: Quantifying the influence of gender on citation. *Digital Scholarship in the Humanities, 36*(3), 581–594. https://doi.org/10.1093 /llc/fqaa011

Editor (1996). The Bulletin interviews Professor Edward N. Lorenz. *WMO Bulletin, 45*(2), 127–137. https://eapsweb.mit.edu/sites/default/files/Bul_interview.pdf

Editor (2014). Journals unite for reproducibility. *Nature, 515*(7). https://www.nature.com/articles /515007a.pdf

Eisinger, D. (2013, August 8). The biggest accidental art discoveries of all time. *Complex.* https:// www.complex.com/style/2013/08/found-art/

Elmore, K. L., Flamig, Z. L., Lakshmanan, V., Kaney, B. T., Farmer, V., Reeves, H. D., & Rothfusz, L. P. (2013). MPING: Crowd-sourcing weather reports for research. *Bulletin of the American Meteorological Society, 95*(9), 1335–1342. https://doi.org/10.1175/BAMS-D-13-00014.1

Elmore, S. A., & Weston, E. H. (2020). Predatory journals: What are they and how to avoid them. *Toxicologic Pathology, 48*(4), 607–610. https://doi.org/10.1177/0192623320920209

Elsevier (n.d.). *What is peer review?* Retrieved June 27, 2022, from https://www.elsevier.com /reviewers/what-is-peer-review

EPSCoR/IDeA Foundation (n.d.). *Program history.* Retrieved June 27, 2022, from https://www .epscorideafoundation.org/about/overview

Esarey, J. (2017). Does peer review identify the best papers? A simulation study of editors, reviewers, and the scientific publication process. *PS: Political Science & Politics, 50*(4), 963–969. https://doi.org/10.1017/S1049096517001081

European Commission (n.d.). *Horizon Europe: Research and innovation funding programme until 2027.* https://ec.europa.eu/info/research-and-innovation/funding/funding-opportunities /funding-programmes-and-open-calls/horizon-europe_en

Farthing, M. J. G. (2013). Research misconduct: A grand global challenge for the 21st century. *Gastroenterology and Heptatology, 29,* 422–427. https://doi.org/10.1111/jgh.12500

Federal Bureau of Investigation (2019). *China: The risk to academia.* https://www.fbi.gov/file -repository/china-risk-to-academia-2019.pdf/view/

Federal Demonstration Partnership. (2014). *2012 Faculty workload survey research report.* https://sites.nationalacademies.org/cs/groups/pgasite/documents/webpage/pga_087667.pdf

Feilden, T. (2017, February 22). Most scientists "can't replicate studies by their peers." *BBC News.* https://www.bbc.com/news/science-environment-39054778

Feller, I. (2000a). The remainder of the cost sharing policy agenda. *Research Management Review, 11*(1), 31–39.

Feller, I. (2000b). Social contracts and the impact of matching fund requirements on American research universities. *Educational Evaluation and Policy Analysis, 22*(1), 91–98.

Femi, O., Jayawickrama, U., Arakpogun, E. O., Suklan, J., & Liu, S. (2022). Fake news on social media: The impact on society. *Information Systems Frontiers.* https://doi.org/10.1007/s10796-022 -10242-z

Fitzpatrick, N. (2018). Media manipulation 2.0: The impact of social media on news, competition, and accuracy. *Athens Journal of Mass Media and Communications, 4*(1), 45–62. https://doi .org/10.30958/ajmmc.4.1.3

Flake, J. (2015, January 1). *Wastebook: The farce awakens December 2015.* https://www.amazon .com/Wastebook-Farce-Awakens-December-2015/dp/B06Y4Y63JT

Flake, J. (2017, July 19). *Senator Jeff Flake presents Wastebook Porkemon Go January 2017.* https://www.amazon.com/Senator-Presents-Wastebook-Porkemon-January/dp/1973708094 /ref=tmm_pap_swatch_0?_encoding=UTF8&qid=&sr=

Fort, D., Herr, T., Shaw, P., Gutzman, K., & Starren, J. (2017). Mapping the evolving definitions of translational research. *Journal of Clinical and Translational Science, 1*(1), 60–66. https://doi .org/10.1017/cts.2016.10

Gauch, H. G., Jr. (2003). *Scientific method in practice.* Cambridge: Cambridge University Press.

Getting started with research: Is it a primary or secondary source? (n.d.). Brooklyn College. Retrieved June 27, 2022, from https://libguides.brooklyn.cuny.edu/startingresearch/primaryor secondary

Ginther, D. K., Schaffer, W. T., Schnell, J., Masimore, B., Liu, F., Haak, L. L., & Kington, R. (2011). Race, ethnicity, and NIH research awards. *Science, 333*(6045), 1015–1019. https://doi.org /10.1126/science.1196783

Godin, B. (2006). The linear model of innovation: The historical construction of an analytical framework. *Science, Technology, & Human Values, 31*(6), 639–667. http://journals.sagepub.com /doi/abs/10.1177/0162243906291865

Goodman, J., Chandna, A., & Roe, K. (2015). Trends in animal use at US research facilities. *Journal of Medical Ethics, 41,* 567–569. https://doi.org/10.1136/medethics-2014-102404

Grants.gov (n.d.). *Grant-making agencies.* Retrieved June 27, 2022, from https://www.grants.gov/web/grants/learn-grants/grant-making-agencies.html

Gray, F. D. (1998). *The Tuskegee syphilis study.* Montgomery, AL: New South Books.

Groat, L., & Wang, D. (2013). *Architectural research methods* (2nd ed). Hoboken, NJ: Wiley.

Gunsalis, C. K., McNutt, M. K., Martinson, B. C., Faulkner, L. R., & Nerem, R. M. (2019). Overdue: A U.S. advisory board for research integrity. *Nature, 566,* 173–175. https://media.nature.com/original/magazine-assets/d41586-019-00519-w/d41586-019-00519-w.pdf

Hammond, C., Gifford, W., Thomas, R., Rabaa, S., Thomas, O., & Domecq, M. C. (2018). Arts-based research methods with indigenous peoples: An international scoping review. *AlterNative, 14*(3), 260–276. https://doi.org/10.1177%2F1177180118796870

Hannas, W., Mulvernon, J., & Puglisi, A. B. (2013). *Chinese industrial espionage: Technology acquisition and military modernization.* Abingdon, UK: Routledge.

Hardy, R. B. (2000). Cost sharing—past, present and future. *Research Management Review, 11*(1), 9–19.

He, A. (2021, April 20). What do China's high patent numbers really mean? Center for International Governance Innovation. https://www.cigionline.org/articles/what-do-chinas-high-patent-numbers-really-mean/

Heaser, J. (2009). Pulled Pork: The three part attack on non-statutory earmarks. *Journal of Legislation, 35*(1), 32–47. https://heinonline.org/HOL/Page?handle=hein.journals/jleg35&id=34&collection=journals&index=

Heifetz, R. A. (1998). *Leadership without easy answers.* Cambridge, MA: Harvard University Press.

Heifetz, R. A., Grashow, A., & Linsky, M. (2009). *The practice of adaptive leadership.* Boston: Harvard Business Press.

Heifetz, R. A., & Linksy, M. (2017). *Leadership on the line.* Boston: Harvard Business Review Press.

Henderson, C., Connolly, M., Dolan, E. L., Finkelstein, N., Franklin, S., Malcom, S., Rasmussen, C., Redd, K., & St. John, K. (2017). Towards the STEM DBER alliance: Why we need a discipline-based STEM education research community. *International Journal of STEM Education, 4*(14). https://doi.org/10.1186/s40594-017-0076-1

Hey, T., & Payne, M. C. (2015). Open science decoded. *Nature Physics, 11,* 367–369. https://doi.org/10.1038/nphys3313

Hey, T., Tansley, S., & Tolle, K. (Eds.) (2009). *The fourth paradigm: data-intensive scientific discovery.* Redmond, WA: Microsoft Research.

Higher Education Compliance Alliance (n.d.). Retrieved June 27, 2022, from https://www.higheredcompliance.org/

Hill, C. T. (2012, February 23). Competitiveness and the university [PowerPoint slides]. Presentation to Council on Governmental Relations. https://www.cogr.edu/COGR/files/ccLibraryFiles/Filename/000000000237/151893.pdf

Hirsch, J. E. (2005). An index to quantify an individual's scientific research output. *PNAS, 102*(46), 16569–16572. https://doi.org/10.1073/pnas.0507655102

Hourihan, M. (2018, September 19). Federal R&D budget environment outlook. [PowerPoint slides]. https://www.aaas.org/sites/default/files/2018-10/20180919%20-%20AMO.pptx?adobe_mc=MCMID%3D405222107604605802042252676992536266644%7CMCORGID%3D242B6472541199F70A4C98A6%2540AdobeOrg%7CTS%3D1655220435

Hourihan, M. (2021, June 14). The federal R&D budget process 101. [PowerPoint slides]. https://www.aaas.org/sites/default/files/2021-08/20210614%20-%20GWU.pptx?adobe_mc=MCMID%3D26151662485914633473805786764882636500%7CMCORGID%3D242B6472541199F70A4C98A6%2540AdobeOrg%7CTS%3D1646329089

Hourihan, M., & Parkes, D. (2016, March 22). *Guide to the President's R&D budget: Research & development FY 2017.* https://www.aaas.org/news/guide-presidents-budget-research-and-development-fy-2017

Hourihan, M., & Parkes, D. (2019). *Federal R&D budget trends—A short summary.* American Association for the Advancement of Science. https://www.aaas.org/sites/default/files/2019-01/AAAS%20RD%20Primer%202019_2.pdf

Hourihan, M., & Zimmermann, A. (2022, May 10). *US R&D innovation in a global context: 2022 update.* https://www.aaas.org/sites/default/files/2022-05/AAAS%20Global%20R%26D%20Update%20May%202022.pdf

How to deal with criticism (n.d.). In Wikihow. Retrieved June 27, 2022, from https://www.wikihow.com/Deal-With-Criticism

Hsu, J. (2010, June 24). *Dark side of medical research: Widespread bias and omissions.* LiveScience. https://www.livescience.com/8365-dark-side-medical-research-widespread-bias-omissions.html

Hunter, D., & Russ, M. (1996). Peer assessment in performance studies. *British Journal of Music Education, 13*(1), 67–78. https://doi.org/10.1017/S0265051700002953

Hurston, Z. N. (1942). *Dust tracks on a road: An autobiography.* Philadelphia, PA: J. B. Lippincott.

Hvistendahl, M. (2019, April 19). Major U.S. cancer center ousts "Asian" researchers after NIH flags their foreign ties. *ScienceInsider.* https://www.sciencemag.org/news/2019/04/exclusive-major-us-cancer-center-ousts-asian-researchers-after-nih-flags-their-foreign

Institute of Medicine and National Research Council (2013). *Perspectives on research with H5N1 avian influenza: Scientific inquiry, communication, controversy: Summary of a workshop.* Washington, DC: National Academies Press. https://doi.org/10.17226/18255

Interesting Literature (n.d.). *A short history of the word serendipity.* Retrieved June 27, 2022, from https://interestingliterature.com/2015/01/28/a-short-history-of-the-word-serendipity/

Ioannidis, J. P. A., Munafo, M. R., Fusar-Poli, P., Nosek, B. A., & David, S. P. (2014). Publication and other reporting biases in cognitive sciences: Detection, prevalence and prevention. *Trends in Cognitive Sciences, 18*(5), 235–241. https://doi.org/10.1016/j.tics.2014.02.010

Jacobson, R. (2015, October 21). Many antidepressant studies found tainted by pharma company influence. *Scientific American Health.* https://www.scientificamerican.com/article/many-antidepressant-studies-found-tainted-by-pharma-company-influence/

Jane Elliott (n.d.). In Wikipedia. Retrieved June 27, 2022, from https://en.wikipedia.org/wiki/Jane_Elliott

Jasny, B. R., Wigginton, N., McNutt, M., Bubela, T., Buck, S., Cook-Deegan, R., Gardner, T., Hanson, B., Hustad, C., Kiermer, V., et al. (2017). Fostering reproducibility in industry-academia research. *Science, 357*(6353), 759–761. https://www.science.org/doi/10.1126/science.aan4906

JASON (2019). *Fundamental research security.* Report JSR-19-21. https://irp.fas.org/agency/dod/jason/fundamental.pdf

Jefferson, T., Alderson, P., Wager, E., & Davidoff, F. (2002). Effects of editorial peer review: A systematic review. *Journal of the American Medical Association, 287*(21), 2784–2786. https://doi.org/10.1001/jama.287.21.2784

Jeffres, L. W., Neuendorf, K., & Atkin, D. J. (2012). Acquiring knowledge from the media in the Internet age. *Communication Quarterly, 60*(1), 59–79. https://doi.org/10.1080/01463373.2012.641835

Jennings, C. (2006). Quality and value: The true purpose of peer review. *Nature.* https://doi.org/10.1038/nature05032

Jhangiani, R. S., & Biswas-Diener, R. (Eds.) (2017). *Open: The philosophy and practices that are revolutionizing education and science.* London: Ubiquity Press. https://doi.org/10.5334/bbc

John F. Kennedy Library (n.d.). Cuban missile crisis. Retrieved September 10, 2022, from https://www.jfklibrary.org/learn/about-jfk/jfk-in-history/cuban-missile-crisis

Kaatz, A., Gutierrez, B., & Carnes, M. (2014). Threats to objectivity in peer review: The case of gender. *Trends in Pharmacological Sciences, 35*(8), 371–373. https://doi.org/10.1016/j.tips.2014.06.005

Kaiser, J. (2018, May 31). Applicant's race or gender doesn't appear to influence NIH peer reviewers. *ScienceInsider*. https://doi.org/10.1126/science.aau3472

Kalichman, M. (2020). Survey study of research integrity officers' perceptions of research practices associated with instances of research misconduct. *Research Integrity and Peer Review*, 5(17). https://doi.org/10.1186/s41073-020-00103-1

Kamerer, J., & Wasserman, S. (2000). Cost sharing and effort reporting: Breaking the juggernaut. *Research Management Review*, 11(1), 41–44.

Kaplan-Liss, E., Lantz-Gefroh, V., Bass, E., Killebrew, D., Ponzio, N. M., Savi, C., & O'Connell, C. (2018). Teaching medical students to communicate with empathy and clarity using improvisation. *Academic Medicine*, 93(3), 440–443. https://doi.org/10.1097/ACM.0000000000002031

Kaufman, C. (n.d.). *The history of higher education in the United States*. Retrieved June 25, 2022, from https://www.coursehero.com/file/34770681/The-History-of-Higher-Education-in-the -United-Statesdocx/

Kays, J., & Phillips-Han, A. (n.d.). *Gatorade: The idea that launched an industry*. Retrieved June 25, 2022, from https://research.ufl.edu/publications/explore/v08n1/gatorade.html

Kelly, J., Sadeghieh, T., & Adeli, K. (2014). Peer review in scientific publications: Benefits, critiques, & a survival guide. *Journal of the International Federation of Clinical Chemistry and Laboratory Practice*, 25(3), 227–243. https://www.ncbi.nlm.nih.gov/pmc/articles/PMC4975196 /pdf/ejifcc-25-227.pdf

Kennedy, D., & Overholser, G. (Eds.) (2010). *Science and the media*. Cambridge, MA: American Academy of Arts and Sciences.

Kezar, A. J., & Lester, J. (2009). *Organizing higher education for collaboration*. San Francisco: Jossey-Bass.

Khaldi, K. (2017). Quantitative, qualitative, or mixed research: Which paradigm to use? *Journal of Educational and Social Research*, 7(2), 15–24. https://www.mcser.org/journal/index.php/jesr /article/view/9915

King, S. R. F. (2017). Peer review: Consultative review is worth the wait. *eLife*, 6. https://doi.org /10.7554/eLife.32012

Kligyte, V., Marcy, R. T., Waples, E. P., Sevier, S. T., Godfrey, E. S., Mumford, M. D., & Hougen, D. F. (2007). Application of a sensemaking approach to ethics training in the physical sciences and engineering. *Science and Engineering Ethics*, 14(2), 251–278. https://doi.org/10.1007 /s11948-007-9048-z

Knezo, G. J. (1994). *Indirect costs for R&D at higher education institutions: Annotated chronology of major federal policies*. Updated January 24, 1995.

Knezo, G. J. (1999). *Indirect costs at academic institutions: Background and controversy—Issue Brief*. Congressional Research Service, updated February 3.

Kuehn, B. M. (2017). Peer Review: Rooting out bias. *eLife*, 6. https://doi.org/10.7554/eLife.32014

Lankford, J. (2017). *Federal fumbles: 100 ways the government dropped the ball*. https://www .lankford.senate.gov/imo/media/doc/Federal_Fumbles_2017.pdf

Lauer, M., & Amero, S. (2019). *Breaches of peer review integrity*. National Institutes of Health. https://nexus.od.nih.gov/all/2019/06/25/breaches-of-peer-reviewintegrity/

Ledford, H. (2014). Indirect costs: Keeping the lights on. *Nature*, 515, 326–329. https://www.nature .com/news/polopoly_fs/1.16376!/menu/main/topColumns/topLeftColumn/pdf/515326a.pdf

Lee, C. J. (2015). Commensuration bias in peer review. *Philosophy of Science*, 82, 1272–1283. https://doi.org/10.1086/683652

Lee, C. J., & Moher, D. (2017). Promote scientific integrity via journal peer review data. *Science*, 357(6348), 256–257. https://www.science.org/doi/10.1126/science.aan4141

Lee, C. J., Sugimoto, C. R., Zhang, G., & Cronin, B. (2013). Bias in peer review. *Journal of the Association for Information Science and Technology*, 64(1), 2–17. https://doi.org/10.1002/asi.22784

Lerch, A., Arthur, C., Pati, A., & Gururani, S. (2020). An interdisciplinary review of music performance analysis. *Transactions of the International Society for Music Information Retrieval*, 3(1), 221–245. https://doi.org/10.5334/tismir.53

Leshner, A. (2008). Reduce administrative burden. *Science, 322*(5908), 1609. https://www.science .org/doi/10.1126/science.1168345

Levenberg, L., Neilson, T., & Rheams, D. (Eds.) (2018). *Research methods for the digital humanities.* Cham, Switzerland: Palgrave Macmillan.

Lewis, D. (2020). Australia's plan to end foreign interference in science: Did it work? *Nature, 584,* 178–179. https://media.nature.com/original/magazine-assets/d41586-020-02188-6/d41586 -020-02188-6.pdf

Lewis, D. W. (2012). The inevitability of open access. *College & Research Libraries, 73*(5), 493–506. https://doi.org/10.5860/crl-299

Lewis, M. K. (2021). Criminalizing China. *Journal of Criminal Law and Criminology, 111*(1), 145–225. https://scholarlycommons.law.northwestern.edu/jclc/vol111/iss1/3

Leyser, O., Kingsley, D., & Grange, J. (2017, March 15). The science "reproducibility crisis"—and what can be done about it. Phys.org. https://phys.org/news/2017-03-science-crisis.html

Liar! Liar! (2009, June 4). *The Economist.* http://www.economist.com/node/13776974

Lim, G. B. (2017). Warfarin: From rat poison to clinical use. *Nature Reviews Cardiology.* Epub ahead of print. https://doi.org/10.1038/nrcardio.2017.172

Litosseliti, L. (2018). *Research methods in linguistics* (2nd ed.). Bedford Square, UK: Bloomsbury Academic.

Long, J. W., Lake, F. K., & Goode, R. W. (2021). The importance of Indigenous cultural burning in forested regions of the Pacific West, USA. *Forest Ecology and Management, 500,* 119597. https://doi.org/10.1016/j.foreco.2021.119597

Lu Wang, L., Lo, K., Chandrasekhar, Y., Reas, R., Yang, J., Eide, D., Funk, K., Kinney, R., Liu, Z., Merrill, W., et al. (2020). CORD-19: The Covid-19 open research dataset. Preprint, ArXiv, arXiv:2004.10706v2.

Lyall, C., Bruce, A., Tait, J., & Meagher, L. (2011). *Interdisciplinary research journeys: Practical strategies for capturing creativity.* London: Bloomsbury Academic. https://doi.org/10.5040 /9781849661782

Lyall, C., & Meagher, L. R. (2007). *A short guide to building and managing interdisciplinary research teams.* Edinburgh Research Explorer ISSTI Briefing Note No. 3. https://www.pure.ed .ac.uk/ws/portalfiles/portal/14926368/A_Short_Guide_to_Building_and_Managing_Interdis ciplinary_Research_Teams.pdf

Lyall, C., & Meagher, L. R. (2012). A masterclass in interdisciplinarity: Research into practice in training the next generation of interdisciplinary researchers. *Futures, 44*(6), 608–617. https:// doi.org/10.1016/j.futures.2012.03.011

Mahoney, M. (1977). Publication prejudices: An experimental study of confirmatory bias in the peer review system. *Cognitive Therapy and Research, 1*(2), 161–175. https://doi.org/10.1007/BF01173636

Mandal, J., Acharya, S., & Parija, S. C. (2011). Ethics in human research. *Tropical Parasitology, 1*(1), 2–3. https://doi.org/10.4103/2229-5070.72105

Markel, H. (2013, September 27). The real story behind penicillin. *PBS News Hour.* https://www .pbs.org/newshour/health/the-real-story-behind-the-worlds-first-antibiotic

Marsh, H. W., Jayasinghe, U. W., & Bond, N. W. (2008). Improving the peer-review process for grant applications: Reliability, validity, bias and generalizability. *American Psychologist, 63*(3), 160–168. https://doi.org/10.1037/0003-066X.63.3.160

Martinson, B. C., Anderson, M. S., & de Vries, R. (2005). Scientists behaving badly. *Nature, 435,* 737–738. https://doi.org/10.1038/435737a

McAuliff, M. (2013, May 1). Lamar Smith: Science peer review process would "improve" with political oversight. *Huffpost.* https://www.huffingtonpost.com/2013/04/30/lamar-smith-science -peer-review_n_3189107.html

McClellan, J. E., III. (2005). Accident, luck, and serendipity in historical research. *Proceedings of the American Philosophical Society, 149*(1), 1–21.

McCullagh, C. B. (1984). *Justifying historical descriptions.* Cambridge: Cambridge University Press.

McElreavy, C., Tobin, V., Martin, T., Bea Damon, M., Crate N., Godines, A., & Bennett, K. (n.d.). The history of the academy and the disciplines. In R. Derosa (Ed.), *Interdisciplinary Studies: A Connected Learning Approach* (chapter 25). Retrieved June 27, 2022, from https://press.rebus.community/idsconnect/

McNutt, M. (2014). Journals unite for reproducibility. *Nature, 346*(6210), 679. https://www.science.org/doi/pdf/10.1126/science.aaa1724

McNutt, M. (2019). "Plan S" falls short for society publishers—and for the researchers they serve. *PNAS, 116*(7), 2400–2403. https://www.pnas.org/cgi/doi/10.1073/pnas.1900359116

Mehrotra, K., & Welch, D. (2017). *Why much of the car industry is under scrutiny for cheating.* Bloomberg. https://www.bloomberg.com/news/articles/2017-08-02/why-it-seems-like-open-season-on-car-companies-quicktake-q-a

Mehta, D. (2019, October 4). Highlight negative results to improve science. *Nature.* https://doi.org/10.1038/d41586-019-02960-3

Mervis, J. (2015, October 8). NSF peer review remains target for Congress. *ScienceInsider.* http://www.sciencemag.org/news/2015/10/nsf-peer-review-remains-target-congress

Miller, W. (1955, May 2). Death of a genius. *Life Magazine, 38*(18), 61–64.

Mintz, S. (2012, March 2). *The 10 greatest cases of fraud in university research.* https://www.workplaceethicsadvice.com/2012/03/the-10-greatest-cases-of-fraud-in-university-resear.html

Mligo, E. S. (2016). *Introduction to research methods and report writing: A practical guide for students and researchers in social sciences and the humanities.* Eugene, OR: Resource Publications.

Montaigne, M. (1958). Of experience. In D. M. Frame (Trans.), *The complete essays of Montaigne* (pp. 815–857). Stanford, CA: Stanford University Press.

Moore, J. C. (2019). *A brief history of universities.* Cham, Switzerland: Palgrave Macmillan. https://link.springer.com/book/10.1007/978-3-030-01319-6

Moran, J. (2010). *Interdisciplinarity* (2nd ed.). Abingdon, UK: Routledge. https://www.routledge.com/Interdisciplinarity/Moran/p/book/9780415560078

Munafo, M. R., Nosek, B. A., Bishop, D. V. M., Button, K. S., Chambers, C. D., Percie du Sert, N., Simonsohn, U., Wagenmakers, E.-J., Ware, J. J., & Ioannidis, J. P. A. (2017). A manifesto for reproducible science. *Nature Human Behavior, 1.* https://doi.org/10.1038/s41562-016-0021

National Academies of Sciences, Engineering, and Medicine (2016). *Optimizing the nation's investment in academic research: A new regulatory framework for the 21st century.* Washington, DC: National Academies Press. https://doi.org/10.17226/21824

National Academies of Sciences, Engineering, and Medicine (2017a). *Communicating science effectively: A research agenda.* Washington, DC: National Academies Press. https://doi.org/10.17226/23674

National Academies of Sciences, Engineering, and Medicine (2017b). *Fostering integrity in research.* Washington, DC: National Academies Press. https://doi.org/10.17226/21896

National Academies of Sciences, Engineering, and Medicine (2018). *Open science by design: Realizing a vision for 21st century research.* Washington, DC: National Academies Press. https://doi.org/10.17226/25116

National Academies of Sciences, Engineering, and Medicine (2019). *Reproducibility and replicability in science.* Washington, DC: National Academies Press. https://doi.org/10.17226/25303

National Academy of Sciences, National Academy of Engineering, and Institute of Medicine (2007). *Rising above the gathering storm: Energizing and employing America for a brighter economic future.* Washington, DC: National Academies Press. https://www.nap.edu/catalog/11463/rising-above-the-gathering-storm-energizing-and-employing-america-for

National Academy of Sciences, National Academy of Engineering, and Institute of Medicine (2009). *On being a scientist: A guide to responsible conduct in research.* Washington, DC: National Academies Press. https://doi.org/10.17226/12192

National Academy of Sciences, National Academy of Engineering, and Institute of Medicine (2010). *Rising above the gathering storm, revisited: Rapidly approaching category 5*. Washington, DC: National Academies Press. https://www.nap.edu/catalog/12999/rising-above-the-gathering-storm-revisited-rapidly-approaching-category-5

National Archives and Records Administration (2022, October 6). *Title 2 of Code of Federal Regulations*. https://www.ecfr.gov/current/title-2/subtitle-A/chapter-II/part-200?toc=1

National Archives and Records Administration (n.d.). *NSDD 189: National policy on transfer of scientific, technical and engineering information*. Retrieved June 28, 2022, from https://catalog.archives.gov/id/6879779

National Bureau of Asian Research (2017). *The theft of American intellectual property: Reassessments of the challenge and United States policy*. https://www.nbr.org/wp-content/uploads/pdfs/publications/IP_Commission_Report_Update.pdf

National Center for Education Statistics (2017). *Status and trends in the education of racial and ethnic groups*. https://nces.ed.gov/programs/raceindicators/index.asp

National Center for Education Statistics (2019, February). *Status and trends in the education of racial and ethnic groups*. https://nces.ed.gov/programs/raceindicators/indicator_reg.asp

National Center for Science and Engineering Statistics (2022). Universities report largest growth in federally funded R&D expenditures since FY 2011. NSF 23-303. Alexandria VA: National Science Foundation. https://ncses.nsf.gov/pubs/nsf23303#:~:text=Research%20and%20development%20spending%20by,billion%20of%20the%20total%20increase

National Endowment for the Arts (2021). *About the National Endowment for the Arts*. https://www.arts.gov/about

National Endowment for the Arts (n.d.). *Grant review process*. Retrieved September 12, 2022, from https://www.arts.gov/grants/grant-review-process

National Endowment for the Humanities (2021). *About the National Endowment for the Humanities*. https://www.neh.gov/about

National Institutes of Health (2021). *History*. https://www.nih.gov/about-nih/who-we-are/history

National Institutes of Health (n.d.-a). *Ethical conduct*. Retrieved June 28, 2022, from https://oir.nih.gov/sourcebook/ethical-conduct

National Institutes of Health (n.d.-b). *The IACUC*. Office of Laboratory Animal Welfare. Retrieved June 27, 2022, from https://olaw.nih.gov/resources/tutorial/iacuc.htm

National Institutes of Health (n.d.-c). *Peer review*. Retrieved September 12, 2022, from https://grants.nih.gov/grants/peer-review.htm

National Institutes of Health (n.d.-d). *Racial disparities in NIH funding*. Retrieved September 12, 2022, from https://diversity.nih.gov/building-evidence/racial-disparities-nih-funding

National Institutes of Health (n.d.-e). *Responsible conduct of research training*. Retrieved June 28, 2022, from https://oir.nih.gov/sourcebook/ethical-conduct/responsible-conduct-research-training

National Institutes of Health (n.d.-f). *Rigor and reproducibility*. Retrieved June 27, 2022, from https://www.nih.gov/research-training/rigor-reproducibility

National Oceanic and Atmospheric Administration (n.d.). *Cooperative observer network (COOP)*. Retrieved June 27, 2022, from https://www.ncei.noaa.gov/products/land-based-station/cooperative-observer-network

National Research Council (1983). Chapter 6, Cost sharing and indirect costs, and Appendix B, History of indirect costs and cost sharing. In *Strengthening the government-university partnership in science*, pp. 117–145 and 220–223. Washington, DC: National Academies Press. https://doi.org/10.17226/19442

National Research Council (2004). *SBIR program diversity and assessment challenges: Report of a symposium*. Washington, DC: National Academies Press. https://doi.org/10.17226/11082

National Research Council (2007). *Science and security in the post 9/11 world: A report based on regional discussions between science and security communities*. Washington, DC: National Academies Press. https://doi.org/10.17226/12013

National Research Council (2009). *Beyond fortress America: National security controls on science and technology in a globalized world.* Washington, DC: National Academies Press. https://doi.org/10.17226/12567

National Research Council (2011). *Guide for the care and use of laboratory animals* (8th ed.). Washington, DC: National Academies Press. https://grants.nih.gov/grants/olaw/guide-for-the-care-and-use-of-laboratory-animals.pdf

National Research Council (2012a). *Discipline-based education research: Understanding and improving learning in undergraduate science and engineering.* Washington, DC: National Academies Press. https://doi.org/10.17226/13362

National Research Council (2012b). *Research universities and the future of America: Ten breakthrough actions vital to our nation's prosperity and security.* Washington, DC: National Academies Press. https://www.nap.edu/catalog/13396/research-universities-and-the-future-of-america-ten-breakthrough-actions

National Research Council (2014). *Convergence: Facilitating transdisciplinary integration of life sciences, physical sciences, engineering, and beyond.* Washington, DC: National Academies Press. https://doi.org/10.17226/18722

National Research Council (2015). *Enhancing the effectiveness of team science.* Washington, DC: National Academies Press. https://doi.org/10.17226/19007

National Research Foundation (2012). *Research and human resources development funding opportunities of the NRF.* http://slideplayer.com/slide/7287570/24/images/2/Research+-+Innovation+System+Value+Chain+National+Research+Facilities.jpg

National Science and Technology Council (2019). Summary of the 2019 White House summit of the joint committee on the research environment (JCORE). https://trumpwhitehouse.archives.gov/wp-content/uploads/2019/11/Summary-of-JCORE-Summit-November-2019.pdf

National Science and Technology Council (2021). *Recommended practices for strengthening the security and integrity of America's science and technology research enterprise.* https://trumpwhitehouse.archives.gov/wp-content/uploads/2021/01/NSTC-Research-Security-Best-Practices-Jan2021.pdf

National Science and Technology Council (2022a). *Guidance for implementing National Security Presidential Memorandum 33 (NSPM-33) on National Security Strategy for United States Government-Supported Research and Development.* https://www.whitehouse.gov/wp-content/uploads/2022/01/010422-NSPM-33-Implementation-Guidance.pdf

National Science and Technology Council (2022b). *Protecting the integrity of government science.* https://www.whitehouse.gov/wp-content/uploads/2022/01/01-22-Protecting_the_Integrity_of_Government_Science.pdf

National Science Board (2007). *Enhancing support of transformative research at the National Science Foundation.* Report NSB-07-32. https://www.nsf.gov/nsb/documents/2007/tr_report.pdf

National Science Board (2009). *Investing in the future: NSF cost sharing policies for a robust federal research enterprise.* Report NSB 09-20. https://www.nsf.gov/pubs/2009/nsb0920/nsb0920.pdf

National Science Board (2012). *Diminishing funding and rising expectations: Trends and challenges for public research universities.* Report NSB-12-45. https://www.nsf.gov/nsb/sei/companion2/files/nsb1245.pdf

National Science Board (2014). *Reducing investigators' administrative workload for federally funded research.* Report NSB-14-18. https://www.nsf.gov/pubs/2014/nsb1418/nsb1418.pdf

National Science Board (2015). *Revisiting the STEM workforce.* Report NSB-2015-10. https://www.nsf.gov/pubs/2015/nsb201510/nsb201510.pdf

National Science Board (2016a). Patent activity index of selected technologies for the United States, the EU, and Japan: 2012–2014. *Science and engineering indicators.* https://www.nsf.gov/statistics/2016/nsb20161/uploads/1/9/fig06-28.pdf

National Science Board (2016b). *Science and engineering indicators 2016.* https://www.nsf.gov/statistics/2016/nsb20161/uploads/1/nsb20161.pdf

National Science Board (2016c). USPTO patents granted, by selected U.S. industry, 2012. *Science and engineering indicators*. https://www.nsf.gov/statistics/2016/nsb20161/uploads/1/9/fig06-25.pdf

National Science Board (2016d). Venture capital investment, by selected region/country/economy: 2005–2014. *Science and engineering indicators*. https://www.nsf.gov/statistics/2016/nsb20161/uploads/1/9/fig06-33.pdf

National Science Board (2016e). Venture capital investment in the United States and the rest of the world: 2005–2014. *Science and engineering indicators*. https://www.nsf.gov/statistics/2016/nsb20161/uploads/1/9/fig06-32.pdf

National Science Board (2018a). Invention: United States and comparative global trends. In *Science and engineering indicators 2018*, chapter 8: Invention, knowledge transfer and innovation. https://www.nsf.gov/statistics/2018/nsb20181/report/sections/invention-knowledge-transfer-and-innovation/invention-united-states-and-comparative-global-trends

National Science Board (2018b. *Science and engineering indicators 2018*. Figure 2-11. https://www.nsf.gov/statistics/2018/nsb20181/figures/fig02-11

National Science Board (2018c). *Science and engineering indicators 2018*. Report NSB-2020-1. https://www.nsf.gov/statistics/2018/nsb20181/assets/nsb20181.pdf

National Science Board (2019a). *Higher education in science and engineering*. Report NSB-2019-7. https://files.eric.ed.gov/fulltext/ED599398.pdf

National Science Board (2019b). *The skilled technical workforce: Crafting America's science & engineering enterprise*. Report NSB-2019-23. https://www.nsf.gov/nsb/publications/2019/nsb201923.pdf

National Science Board (2020a). Cost components of academic R&D. *Science and engineering indicators*. https://ncses.nsf.gov/pubs/nsb20202/academic-r-d-in-the-united-states#cost-components-of-academic-r-d

National Science Board (2020b). *Merit review process: Fiscal year 2020 digest*. Report NSB-2021-45. https://www.nsf.gov/nsb/publications/2021/merit_review/FY-2020/nsb202145.pdf

National Science Board (2020c). Publications output: U.S. trends and international comparisons. *Science and engineering indicators*. Figure 5a-3. https://ncses.nsf.gov/pubs/nsb20206/figure/5a-3

National Science Board (2020d). Research and development: U.S. trends and international comparisons. *Science and engineering indicators*. Figure 4-7. https://ncses.nsf.gov/pubs/nsb20203/figure/4-7

National Science Board (2020e). Research and development: U.S. trends and international comparisons. *Science and engineering indicators*. Figure 4-8. https://ncses.nsf.gov/pubs/nsb20203/figure/4-8

National Science Board (2020f). *Science and engineering indicators 2020*. https://ncses.nsf.gov/pubs/nsb20201/u-s-r-d-performance-and-funding

National Science Board (2020g). Science and technology: Public attitudes, knowledge, and interest. *Science and engineering indicators*. https://ncses.nsf.gov/pubs/nsb20207/public-attitudes-about-s-t-in-general

National Science Board (2020h). The state of U.S. science and engineering 2020. *Science and engineering indicators*. Figure 3. https://ncses.nsf.gov/pubs/nsb20201/figure/3

National Science Board (2020i). The state of U.S. science and engineering 2020. *Science and engineering indicators*. Figure 18. https://ncses.nsf.gov/pubs/nsb20201/u-s-r-d-performance-and-funding

National Science Board (2020j). *Vision 2030*. Report NSB-2020-15. https://www.nsf.gov/nsb/publications/2020/nsb202015.pdf

National Science Board (2021a). *Merit review process—Fiscal year 2020 digest*. Report NSB-2021-45. https://www.nsf.gov/nsb/publications/2021/merit_review/FY-2020/nsb202145.pdf

National Science Board (2021b). *NSB statement on training to improve peer reviewing and address unconscious biases in the merit review process*. Publication NSB-2021-8. https://www.nsf.gov/nsb/publications/2021/nsb20218.pdf

National Science Board (2022a). Higher education in science and engineering. *Science and engineering indicators.* https://ncses.nsf.gov/pubs/nsb20223/figure/HED-29

National Science Board (2022b). *Science and engineering indicators 2020.* Report NSB-2020-1. https://ncses.nsf.gov/pubs/nsb20201

National Science Foundation (2013a, May 28). *Long-term Federal investments improve severe weather prediction.* https://beta.nsf.gov/news/long-term-federal-investments-improve-severe

National Science Foundation (2013b). *Revised NSF merit review criteria.* https://www.nsf.gov/bfa/dias/policy/merit_review/overview.pdf

National Science Foundation (2014). *Survey of federal funds for research and development: Fiscal years 2012–2014.* https://www.nsf.gov/statistics/srvyfedfunds/#tabs-2

National Science Foundation (2016). *Survey of federal funds for research and development: Fiscal years 2014–2016.* https://www.nsf.gov/statistics/srvyfedfunds/#tabs-2

National Science Foundation (2017a). *Higher education R&D.* https://ncsesdata.nsf.gov/herd/2016/

National Science Foundation (2017b). *National patterns of R&D resources.* https://www.nsf.gov/statistics/2017/nsf17311/

National Science Foundation (2021a). *A timeline of NSF history.* https://www.nsf.gov/about/history/overview-50.jsp

National Science Foundation (2021b). *U.S. R&D investments.* Report NCSES 21-203. https://www.nsf.gov/statistics/natlpatterns/us-r-and-d-investments.pdf

National Science Foundation (2022). *The art and science of reviewing proposals.* https://tipsforreviewers.nsf.gov/

National Science Foundation (n.d.-a). *ADVANCE: Organizational change for gender equity in STEM academic professions (ADVANCE).* Retrieved June 27, 2022, from https://www.nsf.gov/funding/pgm_summ.jsp?pims_id=5383

National Science Foundation (n.d.-b). *Merit review.* Retrieved June 28, 2022, from https://www.nsf.gov/bfa/dias/policy/merit_review/

National Science Foundation (n.d.-c). Response to Senator Flake's "Wastebook: The Farce Awakens." Retrieved June 27, 2022, from https://www.nsf.gov/about/congress/reports/responsefederalflake.pdf

National Science Foundation (n.d.-d). Response to Senator Lankford's "Federal Fumbles, Vol. 3." Retrieved June 27, 2022, from https://www.nsf.gov/about/congress/reports/responsefederalfumbles.pdf

National Science Foundation (n.d.-e). *Responsible and ethical conduct of research.* Retrieved June 28, 2022, from https://www.nsf.gov/bfa/dias/policy/rcr.jsp

Newton, I., & Hooke, R. (1675). Isaac Newton, letter to Robert Hooke. Historical Society of Pennsylvania. Retrieved June 27, 2022, from https://discover.hsp.org/Record/dc-9792

Northwestern Office of the Provost (n.d.). *Resources on unconscious bias.* Retrieved June 27, 2022, from https://www.northwestern.edu/provost/policies-procedures/faculty-searches/resources/unconscious-bias.html

Nosek, B. A., Alter, G., Banks, G. C., Borsboom, D., Bowman, S. D., Breckler, S. J., Buck, S., Chambers, C. D., Chin, G., Christensen, G., et al. (2015). Promoting an open research culture. *Science, 348*(6242), 1422–1425. https://www.science.org/doi/10.1126/science.aab2374

Nosek, B. A., Ebersole, C. R., DeHaven, A. C., & Mellor, D. T. (2018). The preregistration revolution. *PNAS, 115*(11), 2600–2606. https://www.pnas.org/doi/pdf/10.1073/pnas.1708274114

Nuzzo, R. (2014). Scientific method: Statistical errors. *Nature, 506,* 150–152. https://www.nature.com/news/scientific-method-statistical-errors-1.14700

Oestreicher, C. (2007). A history of chaos theory. *Dialogues in Clinical Neuroscience, 9*(3), 279–289. https://www.tandfonline.com/doi/full/10.31887/DCNS.2007.9.3/coestreicher

Office of Human Research Protections (n.d.). *45 CFR 46.* Retrieved June 27, 2022 from https://www.hhs.gov/ohrp/regulations-and-policy/regulations/45-cfr-46/index.html

Office of Management and Budget (2018a). *Analytical perspectives budget of the U.S. government fiscal year 2018*. https://www.govinfo.gov/content/pkg/BUDGET-2018-PER/pdf/BUDGET -2018-PER.pdf

Office of Management and Budget (2018b). *Budget of the United States government FY 2018*. https://www.whitehouse.gov/wp-content/uploads/2017/11/budget.pdf

Office of Research Integrity (n.d.-a). *Definition of research misconduct*. Retrieved June 27, 2022, from https://ori.hhs.gov/definition-misconduct

Office of Research Integrity (n.d.-b). *Federal policies*. Retrieved June 27, 2022, from https://ori .hhs.gov/content/chapter-2-research-misconduct-federal-policies#:~:text=To%20be%20consid ered%20research%20misconduct,by%20a%20preponderance%20of%20evidence.%E2%80%9D

Office of Research Services (n.d.). *History of research ethics*. University of Missouri–Kansas City. Retrieved June 27, 2022, from https://ors.umkc.edu/services/compliance/irb/history-of -research-ethics.html

Office of Science and Technology Policy (2013). *Increasing access to the results of federally funded scientific research*. https://obamawhitehouse.archives.gov/sites/default/files/microsites /ostp/ostp_public_access_memo_2013.pdf

Office of Science and Technology Policy (2015). *Fact sheet: Empowering students and others through citizen science and crowdsourcing*. https://obamawhitehouse.archives.gov/sites/default /files/microsites/ostp/citizen_science_backgrounder_03-23-15.pdf

Office of Science and Technology Policy (2022). *Ensuring free, immediate and equitable access to federally funded research*. https://www.whitehouse.gov/wp-content/uploads/2022/08/08-2022 -OSTP-Public-Access-Memo.pdf

O'Flaherty, W. (2018). *The misquotable C. S. Lewis: What he didn't say, what he actually said, and why it matters*. Eugene, OR: Wipf & Stock.

Online Ethics Center for Engineering and Science (n.d.). Retrieved June 27, 2022, from https:// onlineethics.org/

Open Access (2022, June 22). In Wikipedia. https://en.wikipedia.org/wiki/Open_access

Open Science Collaboration (2015). Estimating the reproducibility of psychological science. *Science, 349*(6251). https://www.science.org/doi/10.1126/science.aac4716

Organisation for Economic Co-operation and Development (2017). *Main science and technology indicators*. http://www.oecd.org/sti/msti.htm

Organisation for Economic Co-operation and Development (n.d.). Purchasing power parities— frequently asked questions (FAQs). Retrieved June 27, 2022, from https://www.oecd.org/sdd /prices-ppp/purchasingpowerparities-frequentlyaskedquestionsfaqs.htm

Pannucci, C. J., & Wilkins, E. G. (2010). Identifying and avoiding bias in research. *Plastic and Reconstructive Surgery, 126*(2), 619–625. https://doi.org/10.1097/PRS.0b013e3181de24bc

Paoletti, C. R. (2000). Cost sharing—Just when I thought I knew all the answers. *Research Management Review, 11*(1), 21–29.

Patten, M. L., & Newhart, M. (2017). *Understanding research methods: An overview of the essentials* (10th ed.). New York: Routledge. https://doi.org/10.4324/9781315213033

Peck, M. S. (1978). *The road less traveled: A new psychology of love, traditional values, and spiritual growth*. New York: Simon & Schuster.

Peels, R. (2019). Replicability and replication in the humanities. *Research Integrity and Peer Review, 4*(2). https://doi.org/10.1186/s41073-018-0060-4

Peer review and fraud. (2006). *Nature, 444*(7122), 971–972. https://doi.org/10.1038/444971b

Peterson, H. (Ed.) (1954). *A treasury of the world's great speeches*. New York: Grolier.

Pettinger, T. (n.d.). 7 effective ways to deal with criticism. Retrieved June 27, 2022, from http:// www.lifehack.org/articles/featured/7-effective-ways-to-deal-with-criticism.html

Pew Research Center (2015). *Public and scientists' views on science and society.* http://assets .pewresearch.org/wp-content/uploads/sites/14/2015/01/PI_ScienceandSociety_Report_012915.pdf

Pickard, A. J. (2013). *Research methods in information* (2nd ed.). London: Facet Publishing.

Pinholster, G. (2016). Journals and funders confront implicit bias in peer review. *Science, 352*(6289), 1067–1068. https://www.science.org/doi/10.1126/science.352.6289.1067

Plan S (n.d.). Retrieved June 27, 2022, from https://www.coalition-s.org/

Poling, C. (2022, August 10). *Math error: A new study overturns 100-year-old understanding of color perception.* Los Alamos National Laboratory. https://discover.lanl.gov/news/0810-color -perception

President's Council of Advisors on Science and Technology (2021). *Industries of the future institutes: A new model for American science and technology leadership.* https://science.osti.gov /-/media/_/pdf/about/pcast/202012/PCAST---IOTFI-FINAL-Report.pdf

Primary sources: A research guide (n.d.). University of Massachusetts/Boston. Retrieved June 27, 2022, from https://umb.libguides.com/PrimarySources/secondary

Punch, K. F., & Oancea, A. (2014). *Introduction to research methods in education* (2nd ed.). Los Angeles: Sage Publications.

Quacquarelli Symonds (n.d.). *QS world university rankings 2022.* Retrieved June 27, 2022, from https://www.topuniversities.com/university-rankings/world-university-rankings/2022

Quitoriano, V., & Wald, D. J. (2020). USGS "Did You Feel It?"—Science and lessons from 20 years of citizen science-based macroseismology. *Frontiers in Earth Science, 8,* Article 120. https://doi.org/10.3389/feart.2020.00120

Rabesandratana, T. (2019). The world debates open-access mandates. *Science, 363*(6422), 11– 12. https://www.science.org/doi/10.1126/science.363.6422.11

Redman, B. K. (2018). *Research misconduct policy in biomedicine: Beyond the bad-apple approach.* Cambridge, MA: MIT Press.

Repko, A. F., Szostak, R., & Buchberger, M. P. (2020). The rise of the modern disciplines and interdisciplinarity. In *Introduction to interdisciplinary studies,* 3rd ed. Los Angeles: Sage Publications. Retrieved June 27, 2022, from https://us.sagepub.com/sites/default/files/upm-assets /109628_book_item_109628.pdf

Research (n.d.). *Merriam-Webster Dictionary.* Retrieved June 27, 2022, from https://www.mer riam-webster.com/dictionary/research

Research techniques (2015). Retrieved February 21, 2023 from http://danahollowayfilmandtv .blogspot.com/2015/12/deductive-and-inductive-research.html

Resnik, D. B. (2015). *What is ethics in research & why is it important?* National Institute of Environmental Health Sciences. https://www.niehs.nih.gov/research/resources/bioethics/whatis /index.cfm

Resnik, D. B. (2020, December 23). *What is ethics in research & why is it important?* https:// www.niehs.nih.gov/research/resources/bioethics/whatis/index.cfm

Resnik, D. B. (n.d.) *Research ethics timeline.* National Institute of Environmental Health Sciences. Retrieved June 27, 2022, from https://www.niehs.nih.gov/research/resources/bioethics/timeline /index.cfm

Roberts, L. (2001). Timeline: History of the human genome project. *Science, 291*(5), 1195–1200.

Rockwell, S. (2009). The FDP faculty burden survey. *Research Management Review, 16*(2), 29–44.

Rodgers, P. (2017). Peer review: Decisions, decisions. *eLife, 6.* https://doi.org/10.7554/eLife.32011

Rojon, C., & Saunders, M. N. K. (2015). Dealing with reviewer's comments in the publication process. *Coaching: An International Journal of Theory, Research and Practice, 8*(2), 169–180. https://doi.org/10.1080/17521882.2015.1047463

Roper, R. L. (2019). Does gender bias still affect women in science? *Microbiology and Molecular Biology Reviews, 83*(3). https://doi.org/10.1128/MMBR.00018-19

Rosenzeig, R. M. (1998). The politics of indirect costs. *Journal of Papers—Council on Government Relations.* https://www.nmt.edu/policies/docs/cost-accounting-office/The%20Politics-IDC .pdf

Roth, J. H. (1995). *Arthur Anderson study of indirect costs across sectors. Report to the Government-University-Industry Research Roundtable.* https://www.aau.edu/sites/default/files /AAU%20Files/Key%20Issues/Research%20Administration%20%26%20Regulation/Arthur -Andersen-Study-of-Indirect-Costs-Across-Sectors.pdf

Rovell, D. (2015, October 1). Royalties for Gatorade trust surpass $1 billion: "Can't let it spoil us." ESPN. http://www.espn.com/college-football/story/_/id/13789009/royalties-gatorade-inventors -surpass-1-billion

Roy E. Disney Quotes. (n.d.). BrainyQuote. Retrieved June 4, 2023, from https://www.brainy quote.com/quotes/roy_e_disney_183365

Royster, P. (2016, March 15). *A brief history of open access* [PowerPoint slides]. University of Nebraska-Lincoln. https://digitalcommons.unl.edu/library_talks/123/

Rubio, D. M., Schoenbaum, E. E., Lee, L. S., Schteingart, D. E., Marantz, P. R., Anderson, K. E., Platt, L. D., Baez, A., & Esposito, K. (2010). Defining translational research: Implications for training. *Academic Medicine, 85*(3), 470–475. https://doi.org/10.1097/ACM.0b013e3181ccd618

Ryder, C., Mackean, T., Coombs, J., Williams, H., Hunter, K., Holland, A. J. A., & Ivers, R. Q. (2020). Indigenous research methodology—weaving a research interface. *International Journal of Social Research Methodology, 23*(3), 255–267. https://doi.org/10.1080/13645579.2019.1669923

Sandewall, E. (2006). Systems: Opening up the process. *Nature.* https://doi.org/10.1038/nature04994

Sarniak, R. (2015, August). 9 types of research bias and how to avoid them. Quirk's Media, Article 20150825-2. https://www.quirks.com/articles/9-types-of-research-bias-and-how-to-avoid-them

Schneider, S. L. (2020). *2018 faculty workload survey research report: Primary findings.* https:// thefdp.org/default/assets/File/Documents/FDP%20FWS%202018%20Primary%20Report.pdf

Schwab, S., Janiaud, P., Dayan, M., Amrhein, V., Panczak, R., Palagi, P. M., Hemkens, L. G., Ramon, M., Rothen, N., Senn, S., et al. (2022). Ten simple rules for good research practice. *PLOS Computational Biology, 18*(6). https://doi.org/10.1371/journal.pcbi.1010139

Schwecherl, L. (2020, February 26). How to handle criticism like a pro. Greatist. https://greatist .com/happiness/how-handle-criticism-pro

The scientific method as an ongoing process. (2015, August 7). In Wikipedia. https://commons .wikimedia.org/wiki/File:The_Scientific_Method_as_an_Ongoing_Process.svg

Schneider, S. L. (2019). *Results of the 2018 FDP faculty workload survey: Input for optimizing time on active research* [PowerPoint slides]. Federal Demonstration Partnership. http://thefdp.org/default /assets/File/Presentations/Schneider%20FDP%20FWS3%20Results%20Plenary%20Jan19.pdf

Schneider, S. L., Ness, K. K., Rockwell, S., & Brutkiewicz, R. (2014). *2012 faculty workload survey research report.* Federal Demonstration Partnership. https://sites.nationalacademies.org /cs/groups/pgasite/documents/webpage/pga_087667.pdf

Scholarly Publishing and Academic Resources Coalition (n.d.). Open access. Retrieved June 27, 2022, from https://sparcopen.org/open-access/

Science Europe (2021). *The OA diamond journals study.* https://scienceeurope.org/media/yejfasey /20210309_coalitions_diamond_study_final.pdf

Science Europe (2022). Open access. https://www.scienceeurope.org/our-priorities/open-access.

Scoles, S. (2017, May 23). A brief history of SETI@Home. *The Atlantic.* https://www.theatlantic .com/science/archive/2017/05/aliens-on-your-packard-bell/527445/. See also https://www.seti.org/

Sedwick, S. (2009). Facilities and administrative issues: Paying for administration while under the cap, maximizing recovery, and communicating value. *Research Management Review, 16*(2), 22–28.

Seligman, R. P. (2000). An introduction to cost sharing: Why no good deed goes unpunished. *Research Management Review, 11*(1), 1–4.

Serendipity (2018). *Oxford University English Dictionary.* Retrieved June 27, 2022, from https://en .oxforddictionaries.com/definition/serendipity

Shamoo, A., & Resnik, D. (2015). *Responsible conduct of research* (3rd ed.). Oxford: Oxford University Press.

Shuster, E. (1997). Fifty years later: The significance of the Nuremburg Code. *New England Journal of Medicine, 337*, 1436–1440. https://www.nejm.org/doi/full/10.1056/nejm199711133372006

Sidik, S. M. (2022). Weaving Indigenous knowledge into the scientific method. *Nature, 601*(7892), 285–287. https://www.nature.com/articles/d41586-022-00029-2

Simundic, A.-M. (2013). Bias in research. *Biochemia Medica, 23*(1), 12–15. https://doi.org/10.11613/BM.2013.003

Singer, S., & Smith, K. A. (2013). Discipline-based education research: Understanding and improving learning in undergraduate science and engineering. *Journal of Engineering Education, 102*(4), 468–471. http://doi.org/10.1002/jee.20030

Smith, H., & Dean, R. T. (Eds.) (2009). *Practice-led research, research-led practice in the creative arts.* Edinburgh: Edinburgh University Press.

Smith, J., & Noble, H. (2014). Bias in research. *Evidence Based Nursing, 17*(4), 100–101. https://doi.org/10.1136/eb-2014-101946

Smith, L. T. (1999). *Decolonizing methodologies: Research and indigenous peoples.* London: Zed Books.

Smith, R. (2006). Peer review: A flawed process at the heart of science and journals. *Journal of the Royal Society of Medicine, 99*(4), 178–182. https://doi.org/10.1258/jrsm.99.4.178

Smith, T. L., Trapani, J., Decrappeo, A., & Kennedy, D. (2011). Reforming regulation of research universities. *Issues in Science and Technology, 27*(4), 57–64.

Snow, K. C., Hays, D. G., Caliwagan, G., Ford, D. J., Jr., Mariotti, D., Mwendwa, J. W., & Scott, W. E. (2016). Guiding principles for indigenous research practices. *Action Research, 14*(4), 357–375. https://doi.org/10.1177/1476750315622542

Soderberg, C. K., Errington, T. M., Schiavone, S. R, Bottesini, J., Thorn, F. S., Vazire, S., Esterling, K. M., & Nosek, B. A. (2021). Initial evidence of research quality of registered reports compared with the standard publishing model. *Nature Human Behavior, 5*, 990–997. https://doi.org/10.1038/s41562-021-01142-4

Sorokanich, B. (2016, May 25). The facts behind every major automaker emissions cheating scandal since VW. *Road & Track.* http://www.roadandtrack.com/new-cars/car-technology/a29293/vehicle-emissions-testing-scandal-cheating/

Spill, H., & Mason, D. (2014). Management models in the NZ software industry. *Journal of Applied Computing and Information Technology, 18*(1). https://ndhadeliver.natlib.govt.nz/delivery/DeliveryManagerServlet?dps_pid=FL21848094

Stark, J., & Tiffert, G. (2021). *Eyes wide open: Ethical risks in research collaboration with China.* The Hoover Institution. https://www.hoover.org/sites/default/files/research/docs/stoff-tiffert_eyes wideopen_web_revised.pdf

Steneck, N. H. (2006). Fostering integrity in research: Definitions, current knowledge, and future directions. *Science and Engineering Ethics, 12*(1), 53–74. https://doi.org/10.1007/pl00022268

Sterne, L. (1759). *The life and opinions of Tristram Shandy, gentleman.* Edited and with an introduction and notes by I. C. Ross. Oxford: Oxford University Press, 1983.

Stokols, D., Hall, K. L., Taylor, B. K., & Moser, R. P. (2008). The science of team science. *American Journal of Preventative Medicine, 35*(2), S77–S89. https://doi.org/10.1016/j.amepre.2008.05.002

Suk, W. (2006). Can peer review police fraud? *Nature Neuroscience, 9*(2), 149. https://doi.org/10.1038/nn0206-149

Tamborini, C. R., Kim, C., & Sakamoto, A. (2015). Education and lifetime earnings in the United States. *Demography, 52*(4), 1383–1407. https://doi.org/10.1007/s13524-015-0407-0

Tennant, J. P. (2018). The state of the art in peer review. *FEMS Microbiology Letters, 365*(19). https://doi.org/10.1093/femsle/fny204

Thibault, M. (2000). Cost sharing: A time to be traditional or a time for change? *Research Management Review, 11*(1), 45–49.

Times Higher Education (n.d.). *World university rankings 2021*. Retrieved June 27, 2022, from https://www.timeshighereducation.com/world-university-rankings/2021/world-ranking#!/page /0/length/25/sort_by/rank/sort_order/asc/cols/stats

Tricco, A. C., Thomas, S. M., Antony, J., Rios, P., Robson, R., Pattani, R., Ghassemi, M., Sullivan, S., Sevlaratnam, I., Tannenbaum, C., et al. (2017). Strategies to prevent or reduce gender bias in peer review of research grants. A rapid scoping review. *PLOS One*. https://doi.org/10.1371/journal .pone.0169718

Trochim, W. M. K. (n.d.). *Research methods knowledge base*. Retrieved June 27, 2022, from https://conjointly.com/kb/

Unreliable research: Trouble at the lab (2013, October 19). *The Economist*. https://www.economist .com/briefing/2013/10/18/trouble-at-the-lab

US Congress (2007). *Public Law 110-69—America COMPETES Act*. https://www.congress.gov /110/plaws/publ69/PLAW-110publ69.pdf

US Congress (2015). *H.R. 1806—America COMPETES Reauthorization Act of 2015*. https://www .congress.gov/bill/114th-congress/house-bill/1806

US Department of Health, Education and Welfare (1979). *The Belmont Report*. https://www.hhs .gov/ohrp/sites/default/files/the-belmont-report-508c_FINAL.pdf

US Department of Justice (2020a). Former Emory University professor and Chinese "Thousand Talents" participant convicted and sentenced for filing a false tax return. https://www.justice .gov/opa/pr/former-emory-university-professor-and-chinese-thousand-talents-participant -convicted-and

US Department of Justice (2020b). Harvard University professor and two Chinese nationals charged in three separate China related cases. https://www.justice.gov/opa/pr/harvard-university -professor-and-two-chinese-nationals-charged-three-separate-china-related

US Department of Justice (2020c). University of Arkansas professor indicted for wire fraud and passport fraud. https://www.justice.gov/opa/pr/university-arkansas-professor-indicted-wire-fraud -and-passport-fraud

US Department of State (n.d.). Overview of the U.S. export control system. Retrieved June 27, 2022, from https://2009-2017.state.gov/strategictrade/overview/index.htm

US Department of the Interior (2020, November 9). Embracing Indigenous knowledge to address the wildfire crisis. https://www.doi.gov/wildlandfire/embracing-indigenous-knowledge-address -wildfire-crisis

US Food and Drug Administration (n.d.). Institutional review boards frequently asked questions. Retrieved June 27, 2022, from https://www.fda.gov/regulatory-information/search-fda-guidance -documents/institutional-review-boards-frequently-asked-questions

US General Accounting Office (1978). *Technology transfer: Administration of the Bayh-Dole Act by research universities*. Publication RCED-98-126. https://www.gao.gov/assets/rced-98-126.pdf

US General Accounting Office (1995). *University research: Effect of indirect cost revisions and options for future changes*. Publication RCED-95-74. https://www.gao.gov/products/RCED-95-74

US Geological Survey (n.d.-a). Did you feel it? Retrieved June 27, 2022, from https://earthquake .usgs.gov/data/dyfi/

US Geological Survey (n.d.-b). Manage quality. Accessed September 20, 2022, from https://www .usgs.gov/data-management/manage-quality

US Government Accountability Office (2013). *Biomedical research: NIH should assess the impact of growth in indirect costs on its mission*. Publication GAO-13-760. https://www.gao.gov /products/GAO-13-760

US Government Accountability Office (2014). *Grants management: Programs at HHS and HUD collect administrative cost information but differences in cost caps and definitions create challenges*. Publication GAO-15-118. https://www.gao.gov/assets/gao-15-118.pdf

US Government Accountability Office (2017). *National Science Foundation: Preliminary observations on indirect costs for research*. Publication GAO-17-576T. https://www.gao.gov/products /GAO-17-576T

US Government Accountability Office (2019). *Federal research: Additional actions needed to improve public access to research results.* Publication GAO-20-81. https://www.gao.gov/products /gao-20-81

US Government Accountability Office (2020). *Open data: Agencies need guidance to establish comprehensive data inventories; Information on their progress is limited.* Publication GAO-21-29. https://www.gao.gov/products/gao-21-29

US Government Accountability Office (2022). *Research reliability: Federal actions needed to promote stronger research practices.* Publication GAO-22-104441. https://www.gao.gov/products /gao-22-104411

US House of Representatives (n.d.). *U.S. Code Chapter 18—Patent rights in inventions made with federal assistance.* Retrieved October 8, 2022, from https://uscode.house.gov/view.xhtml ?path=/prelim@title35/part2/chapter18&edition=prelim

U.S. News and World Report (n.d.). *2022 Best global universities rankings.* Retrieved June 27, 2022, from https://www.usnews.com/education/best-global-universities/rankings

US Patent and Trademark Office (n.d.). General information concerning patents. Retrieved July 27, 2022. https://www.uspto.gov/patents/basics/general-information-patents

US Senate (2019). *Threats to the U.S. research enterprise: China's talent recruitment plans.* https://www.hsdl.org/?abstract&did=831878

Validating key experimental results via independent replication (n.d.). *Science Exchange.* Retrieved June 27, 2022, from http://validation.scienceexchange.com/#/

Van Dusen, V. (2013). Intellectual property and higher education: Challenges and conflicts. *Administrative Issues Journal: Education, Practice, & Research, 3*(2), 1–13. https://files.eric.ed .gov/fulltext/EJ1057074.pdf

van Peer, W., Hakemulder, F., & Zyngier, S. (2012). *Scientific methods for the humanities.* Amsterdam: John Benjamins.

Vespa, J., Medina, L., & Armstrong, D. M. (2020). *Demographic turning points for the United States: Population projections for 2020 to 2060.* https://www.census.gov/content/dam/Census /library/publications/2020/demo/p25-1144.pdf

Walliman, N. (2010). *Research methods: The basics* (2nd ed.). London: Routledge. https://doi.org /10.4324/9780203836071

Walsh, D. (2013, May 6). Not safe for funding: The N.S.F. and the economics of science. *New Yorker.* https://www.newyorker.com/tech/elements/not-safe-for-funding-the-n-s-f-and-the -economics-of-science

Walt Disney Archives (n.d.). *Walt's quotes.* Retrieved June 27, 2022. https://d23.com/section/walt -disney-archives/walts-quotes/

Ward, A. (2015, May 2). 24 unintended scientific discoveries. Mental Floss. http://mentalfloss .com/article/53646/24-important-scientific-discoveries-happened-accident

Ware, M. (2008). Peer review: Benefits, perceptions and alternatives. *Publishing Research Consortium Summary Papers, 4,* 4–20.

Welter, B., & Egmon, J. (2005). *The prepared mind of a leader: Eight skills leaders use to innovate, make decisions, and solve problems.* San Francisco: Jossey-Bass.

White, K. S., & Carney, J. P. (2011). *Working with Congress: A scientist's guide to policy.* Washington, DC: American Association for the Advancement of Science. https://www.aaas.org/sites /default/files/AAAS_Working_with_Congress.pdf

White, T. L., & McBurney, D. H. (2013). *Research methods* (9th ed.). Belmont, CA: Wadsworth Cengage Learning.

White House (2021). *Presidential Memorandum on United States Government-supported research and development national security policy. National Security Presidential Memorandum 33.* https://trumpwhitehouse.archives.gov/presidential-actions/presidential-memorandum -united-states-government-supported-research-development-national-security-policy/

Williams, C. (2007). Research methods. *Journal of Business and Economic Research, 5*(3), 65–70. https://doi.org/10.19030/jber.v5i3.2532

Willinsky, J. (2006). *The access principle: The case for open access to research and scholarship.* Cambridge, MA: MIT Press.

Wilson, S. (2001). What is an Indigenous research methodology? *Canadian Journal of Native Education, 25*(2), 175–179.

Wilson, S. (2008). *Research is ceremony: Indigenous research methods.* Halifax, NS: Fernwood Publishing.

Wisconsin Historical Society (n.d.). Golden Fleece Awards, 1975–1987. Retrieved June 27, 2022, from https://content.wisconsinhistory.org/digital/collection/tp/id/70852/

Wolf, J. (2015, August 7). How effective leaders handle criticism. *Fast Company.* https://www.fastcompany.com/3049410/how-effective-leaders-handle-criticism

Woollaston, V. (2014, May 28). Hilarious graphics reveal how statistics can create false connections. *Daily Mail.* https://www.dailymail.co.uk/sciencetech/article-2640550/Does-sour-cream-cause-bike-accidents-No-looks-like-does-Graphs-reveal-statistics-produce-false-connections.html

World Intellectual Property Organization (2020). *What is intellectual property?* https://www.wipo.int/edocs/pubdocs/en/wipo_pub_450_2020.pdf

Wulff, D. (2010). Unquestioned answers: A review of research is ceremony: Indigenous research methods. *The Qualitative Report, 15*(5), 1290–1295. https://doi.org/10.46743/2160-3715/2010.1345

Author Biography

Dr. Kelvin K. Droegemeier is Professor of Atmospheric Science and Special Advisor to the Chancellor for Science and Policy at the University of Illinois at Urbana-Champaign. Formerly, he was Regents' Professor of Meteorology, Roger and Sherry Teigen Presidential Professor, and Weathernews Chair at the University of Oklahoma, where he served for nearly a decade as vice president for research. He cofounded and directed one of the National Science Foundation's (NSF) first eleven Science and Technology Centers and cofounded and served as deputy director of an NSF Engineering Research Center. In 2003, Dr. Droegemeier was nominated by President George W. Bush and confirmed in 2004 by the US Senate for a six-year term on the National Science Board, the governing body of NSF that also provides science policy guidance to the president and Congress. He was renominated by President Barack Obama and again confirmed by the Senate, serving a second six-year term, the last four years as vice-chairman. He has testified before Congress on numerous occasions on topics ranging from the importance of science and engineering research to STEM education and federal investments in research and development.

In 2017, Dr. Droegemeier was appointed by Governor Mary Fallin as Oklahoma's fourth Cabinet Secretary of Science and Technology. In 2018, he was nominated by President Donald J. Trump to serve as Director of The White House Office of Science and Technology Policy (OSTP) and Science Advisor to the President. He was confirmed by the US Senate and served from 2019 until 2021. As OSTP director, he coordinated planning, prioritization, and policymaking for more than two dozen federal agencies that conduct or support research and development with combined budgets of more than $130 billion. While at OSTP, he also served for two and a half months as acting director of NSF.

Dr. Droegemeier is a fellow of the American Meteorological Society and of the American Association for the Advancement of Science. He cofounded a private company and has served on and chaired numerous national boards and committees. Dr. Droegemeier has generated over \$40 million in external research funding, authoring or coauthoring more than eighty refereed journal articles and over two hundred conference publications. His research interests lie in thunderstorm dynamics and predictability, variational data assimilation, mesoscale dynamics, computational fluid dynamics, massively parallel computing, and aviation weather.

Index

Note: Page numbers in *italics* indicate figures and tables.

AA. *See* American Airlines
AAALAC. *See* Association for Assessment and Accreditation of Laboratory Animal Care International
AAAS Policy Fellowship program, 62
AAHRPP. *See* Association for the Accreditation of Human Research Protection Programs
AAMC. *See* Association of American Medical Colleges
AAU. *See* Association of American Universities
Abstracts, 96–97
Academic-corporate partnerships, 239, 251–255
  establishing, 255–259
  beyond research in, 259–262
Academic disciplines. *See also* Interdisciplinary work; Multidisciplinary work; STEM disciplines
  entrepreneurship programs and, 66
  research funding differences across, 62–64
  work at boundaries of, 204
Academic freedom, 285n1
Academic institutions, 11
  private company use of facilities and equipment, 260–261
  purposes of, 253
  research leadership at, 15–23
Academic research enterprise, 1–2
Academic tenure, 11, 285n1
Academie Royale des Sciences, 127
Accidental discoveries, 90
Accountability, 181
  ethics and, 161
ACE. *See* American Council on Education
Administrative workloads, 188, *188*, *189*, 190
ADVANCE program, 272
Affiliation bias, 152

Alan Alda Center for Communicating Science, 206
America COMPETES Act (2007), 183
American Academy of Arts and Sciences, 46, 276
  Humanities Policy Fellows program, 62
American Airlines (AA), 257
American Council of Learned Societies, 31, 113
American Council on Education (ACE), 21, 184
Analysis, 102–103
Analysis bias, 150
Anchoring bias, 150
Animal research subjects, 173–175
Antibiotics, 90
APCs. *See* Article processing charges
APLU. *See* Association of Public and Land-grant Universities
A posteriori review, 140
Apple, 10, 226
Applied research, 8–9, *9*, *10*, 52, 285n1
  federal funding for, 28
  funding of, *29*
Apprenticeships, 261
Appropriations bills, 40, *41*
A priori review, 140
Archive publications, 96, 208
  submission process, 133–134, *134*
Aristotle, 7, 126, 238
Army Research Laboratory, 11
Article processing charges (APCs), 198–199
Artificial intelligence, 44
  in data analysis, 102
  researching previous work with, 96
Assessing purpose and value, 13–15
Association for Assessment and Accreditation of Laboratory Animal Care International (AAALAC), 185

Association for the Accreditation of Human Research Protection Programs (AAHRPP), 185
Association of American Medical Colleges (AAMC), 184
Association of American Universities (AAU), 184, 216–217, 255–256
Association of Public and Land-grant Universities (APLU), 23, 184, 217
Commission on Economic and Community Engagement, 255
Office of Economic Development and Community Engagement, 222
Association of University Technology Managers (AUTM), 217, 227
Atacama Large Millimeter Array, 250
AUTM. *See* Association of University Technology Managers

BAAs. *See* Broad agency announcements
Backups, 99
"Bad apple" theory, 165
Basic research, *9, 10*. *See also* Fundamental research
Bayh-Dole Act, 215, 223, 224, 226, 286n1
Belief systems, balancing research progress with, 56–58
Bell Laboratories, 12
Belmont Report, 173
Belonging, 18, 80, 245
Bias, 145
  affiliation, 152
  analysis, 150
  anchoring, 150
  citation, 151
  commensuration, 153
  confirmation, 150, 152, 154
  conservatism, 153
  content, 152
  cultural, 149, 154
  data collection/sampling/measurement, 149
  defining and understanding, 146–147
  design, 148–149
  equity, 152
  gender, 118, 152
  historical, 149
  implicit and explicit, 148
  language, 152
  mitigating, 153–154
  nationality, 152
  prestige, 151
  procedural, 150
  proposal review and, 118
  publication, 151
  racial, 152
  selection/participant, 149
  teams and, 250

types and impacts in peer/merit review of, 151–153
types and impacts in research process of, 147–151
Bibliographies, 97
Big ideas
  peer review and, 137
  transformative research funding and, 153
Bill and Melinda Gates Foundation, 42
Biomedical engineering, 204, 239–240
Black open access model, 199
Book publication, 20
Books, 196
Boren, David L., 257
Boundary-spanning problems, 243
  engaging, 247–251
BRAIN Initiative, 37
Bridge funding, 20
Broad agency announcements (BAAs), 43
Bronze open access model, 199
Budgets
  challenges for the future, 276–277
  development of as supported by research administrative services, 19
  federal guidelines for proposals, 112–113
  federal R&D by character, *52*
  federal R&D process, 35–41
  future of R&D funding, 45–48
  peer review and, 135–136
  priorities for federal research, 33–34
  in proposals, 108, 111–116
Bush, Vannevar, 53
Business Roundtable, 205

Cancer Moonshot, 37
CAPS. *See* Science and Technology Center for Analysis and Prediction of Storms
Career paths
  ethics and, 166
  multidisciplinary work and, 244
  successful team characteristics and, 247
Carnegie Foundation for the Advancement of Teaching, 21
CARR. *See* Coordinating Administrative Research Requirements
Causality, 103
CBR. *See* Congressional Budget Resolution
Census Bureau, 272
Chamber of Commerce, 205
Chaos, 90–91
Churchill, Winston, 64
Citation bias, 151
Citation indexes, 208
CITI. *See* Collaborative Institutional Training Initiative
Citizen science, 83–84
Classified information, 139, 178–179

Classified research, 202
Climate change, 13
  policy and research on, 60
Coca-Cola, 220
COGR. *See* Council on Governmental
  Relations
COI. *See* Conflicts of interest
Cold Spring Harbor Laboratory, 12
Collaboration
  ethics and, 161
  international, 250
  lexicon, challenges, and opportunities of,
    238–241
  multisector, 251–255
  resources for creating, 248
  team characteristics and success in,
    244–247
  team development, 247–251
Collaborative Institutional Training Initiative
  (CITI), 185–186
College degrees
  multidisciplinary work and, 242–244
  production of, 270, *271*, 272
Colonialism, 80
Commensuration bias, 153
Commission on Economic and Community
  Engagement, 255
Committee of visitors, 132
Common Rule, 173, 174
Communicating outcomes
  divisive topics and, 206–207
  with expert audiences, 202–204
  with general audiences, 204–207
  importance of, 195–196
  special circumstances and helpful hints,
    207–208
  traditional and open access frameworks for,
    196–200
Community engagement, 21
Compliance checks, 133
Compliance requirements, creation of, 183
Computer models
  chaos theory and, 91
  interdisciplinary work and, 246–247
  partnerships for, 256
  reproducibility and complexity of, 86
  translational research and, 10
  validation and, 100
Computer visualization, 103
Confidentiality
  in panel review, 118, 131
  in peer review, 135, 138
Confirmation bias, 150, 152, 154
Conflicts of commitment, 177, 178, 181, 186
Conflicts of interest (COI), 129, 160, 177–178,
  186, 188, 191
  academic-corporate partnerships and, 254

Congressional Budget Resolution (CBR),
  38–39
Congressional Research Service (CRS), 59
Conservatism bias, 153
Consultative peer review, 132, 139
Consulting, 259–260
Content bias, 152
Context
  of IP, 213–217
  researching previous work for, 97
Continuing Budget Resolution (CR), 40
Contracts, 44–45
  research compliance and, 176
Controlled Unclassified Information
  (CUI), 179
Convergence, 240
Convergent research, 237
Coordinating Administrative Research
  Requirements (CARR), 22
Copernicus, 127
Copyright, 217, 218
CoR. *See* Council on Research
CORD-19. *See* COVID-19 Open Research
  Dataset
Corporate R&D, 42
Cost sharing, 113–116
Council on Governmental Relations (COGR),
  23, 217
  compliance policies and, 184
Council on Research (CoR), 23
COVID-19 Open Research Dataset
  (CORD-19), 201
COVID-19 pandemic, 47, 84, 155, 197, 284
  access to publications and data and, 201
  fundamental research and vaccines for, 66
  impact on attitudes toward research, 54
  preprint servers and, 199
  public policy during, 60
Coworking spaces, 226
CR. *See* Continuing Budget Resolution
Crandall, Robert, 257
Creative activity, 8
  as innovation foundation, 64–67
  many homes of, 10–12
  societal roles of, 284
Creative Commons, 198
Critical thinking skills, 84
Criticism. *See also* Peer review
  effective use of, 140–142
  source, 78–79
Crowd-sourced science. *See* Citizen science
CRS. *See* Congressional Research Service
Cuban missile crisis, 59
CUI. *See* Controlled Unclassified
  Information
Cultural beliefs, 57
Cultural bias, 149, 154

Cultural burning, 80
Curiosity, 6, 7

Daily life, research methods and, 83–84
Danforth Plant Science Center, 12
Data
analysis of, 102–103, 260
defining, 100
growth in, 102
open access to, 199–200
publicly accessible, 200–202
QC and QA for, 100–101
quality of, 101
Data collection bias, 149
Data mining, 103
DBER. See Discipline-based education
research
Deductive reasoning, 73, 74
Defect detection. See Quality control
Defect prevention. See Quality assurance
Deficit model of communication, 205
Department of Defense (DOD)
mission agencies in, 110
national laboratories, 11–12
research classifications, 9, 10
Department of Education, Institute for
Education Sciences, 64
Department of Energy (DOE)
mission agencies in, 110
National Laboratories, 11
Office of Science, 47
research centers, institutes, and regional
hubs, 249
Department of Health and Human Services
(DHHS), 163
Office for Human Research Protections, 174
Design bias, 148–149
Design patents, 218
Development, 9
DHHS. See Department of Health and
Human Services
Diamond open access model, 199
Digital archives, 203
Digital libraries, 96
Direct costs, 113, 115
Directed spending. See Earmarks
Disciplinary research and education,
241–244
Discipline-based education research (DBER),
82, 82–83
Discretionary spending, 33–34, 35
Discrimination, 146
Disney, Roy E., 162
Disney, Walt, 6
Diversity, 206
of scholarly enterprise, 277
team composition and, 245, 248

Divisive topics, communication about,
206–207
DOD. See Department of Defense
DOE. See Department of Energy
Double-blind model of review, 138, 154
Drug safety, 172
Dual use information, 140, 178–179

Earmarks, 41
Economic development, 21
Education
research integration with, 81–83
US statistics in, 272–275, 273–275
Education research, 64, 82
EHSO. See Environmental Health and Safety
Office
Einstein, Albert, 6, 13
Elevator speeches, 207–208
Emerging Research Institutions (ERIs), 3, 58,
113, 197, 220, 258, 277
IP resources and, 220
Empirical approach, 73–74
Enron, 257
Entitlement programs, 45
Environmental Health and Safety Office
(EHSO), 175
EPSCoR. See Established Program to
Stimulate Competitive Research
Equity, 80, 206
within federal agencies, 58
Equity bias, 152
ERIs. See Emerging Research Institutions
ESPN, 216
Established Program to Stimulate
Competitive Research (EPSCoR), 44,
58, 250
Ethical conduct of research, 160
Ethics, 162. See also Research compliance
accountability and, 161
balancing research progress with, 56–58
career paths and, 166
collaboration and, 161
public understanding of research and
personal, 56
research process and, 159, 163
scholarship programs and, 166–168
Event Horizon Telescope, 250
Experimental development, 9
Experimental research, 75
Experimentation, 77–78
Experiment design, 72
animal research rules and, 175
bias from poor, 148–149
reproducibility and, 86–87
research misconduct and, 164
Explanatory power, 79
Explanatory scope, 79

Explicit bias, 148
Export controls, 119, 178–179
Extension services, 214

Fabrication, 164
Facebook, 226
Facilities and administrative costs (F&A), *114*, 114–116
Fact-checking, 163
FAIR. *See* Findable, accessible, interoperable, and reusable
Falsification, 164
F&A. *See* Facilities and administrative costs
FDP. *See* Federal Demonstration Partnership
Federal agency funding, 28
Federal Aviation Administration, 257
Federal budgets, 33, *34, 35,* 37–40, *40,* 45–46, *47*
 R&D budgets in, 34–35, *36, 52*
Federal Data Strategy, 202
Federal Demonstration Partnership (FDP), 188, 217
Federal Fumbles, 156
Federal government, university research funding history, 214–215
Federal Register, 127
 NPRM posting in, 140, 184
Fellowships, 31
 cost sharing and, 113
Findable, accessible, interoperable, and reusable (FAIR), 197, 200
Fleming, Alexander, 90
Food, Drug, and Cosmetic Act (1938), 172
Food and Drug Administration, 184
For-profit research organizations, 11
Fraud, 164
 peer review role in detecting, 135, 136
Freedom of inquiry, 181
Fulbright Fellowships, 31, 113, 117
Fundamental research, 8, 52
 dual use information and, 178–179
 federal investments in, 28–29, *276,* 276–277
 funding of, 11, *29,* 43
 security and, 179
 taxation and, 53
 transition to practicable products and services, 65, *66*
Funding
 composition of, *29*
 future of, 45–48
 inequities in, 58
 mechanisms for obtaining, 42–45
 multidisciplinary work and, 243
 research compliance and, 176
 sources of and historic trends in, 27–33, *30–32, 40*

Galileo Galilei, 127, 238
Gatorade, 66, 216
GDP. *See* Gross domestic product
GenBank, 202
Gender bias, 152
 proposal review and, 118
Gifts, 45
Globally engaged teams, 12–13
Global Plants database, 202
Golden Fleece Award, 155–156
Golden Goose Award, 156
Golden Rule, 162
Gold open access model, 198
Google, 12
Government Accountability Office, 59
Government Patent Policy Act. *See* Bayh-Dole Act
Government relations officials, 39
Government-University-Industry Research Roundtable (GUIRR), 217, 255
Grand challenges, 37
GRANTED program, 220
Grant proposals, 44, *108,* 108–111
 consultative review and, 139
 cost sharing and, 113–116
 F&A and, 114–116
 multidisciplinary work and, 243
 project budget and, 111–116, *112*
 research compliance and, 176
 structure of, 286n1
 submission and evaluation processes, 116–119
 success rates for, 118–119
Grants, 44, 45
Great Recession, 278
Green open access, 199
Gross domestic product (GDP), 287n1
 R&D expenditures as share of, 268, *269*
GUIRR. *See* Government-University-Industry Research Roundtable

Halo effect, 150, 154
Hazardous materials, 175, 176
HBCUs. *See* Historically Black Colleges and Universities
Health Insurance Portability and Accountability Act (HIPAA), 179, 188
Helsinki Declaration (1964), 173
H-index, 97, 208
HIPAA. *See* Health Insurance Portability and Accountability Act
Hippocratic Oath, 162, 172
Hispanic Serving Institutions (HSIs), 58
Historical bias, 149
Historically Black Colleges and Universities (HBCUs), 26, 58
Historical method, 78–79

Honesty, 163, 181
Howard Hughes Medical Institute, 12
HSIs. *See* Hispanic Serving Institutions
Hub-CAPS, 257
Human Genome Project, 53
Human research subjects, 172–174
Hurston, Zora Neal, 6
Hybrid open access model, 199
Hybrid review, 140
Hypotheses
  evaluating, 78
  generation of, 77
  plausibility of, 79
  source material identification and, 98
  testing, 7
Hypothesis testing
  empiricism and, 74
  models and, 247
  quantitative methods and, 73
  research proposals documenting, 110

IACUC. *See* Institutional Animal Care and
  Use Committee
IBC. *See* Institutional Biosafety Committee
I-Corps, 227
Identity, 147
IGs. *See* Inspectors general
Immigration, 162–163
Impacts, 13–15
Impartiality, 146–147, 181
Imperfect environment theory, 165
Implicit bias, 148
Inclusion, 18, 80, 206, 245
Independent research institutes, 12
Indigenous communities, 79
  worldview of, 80
Indigenous methods, 79–81
Indirect costs, 114
Individual researchers
  global engagement and, 12–13
  research compliance and, 176
  responsible conduct and, 162
Inductive reasoning, 73, *74*
Industrial Revolution, 14
Information
  backups of, 99
  classified, 139, 178–179
  dual use, 140, 178–179
  personally identifiable, 179
  protection of sensitive, 178–179
  reporting and posting, 176–177
Innovation
  cyclic model of, 65, *66*
  research and creative activity as foundation
    for, 64–67
  traditional academic linear model of, 65, *65*
Inspectors general (IGs), 185, 186

Inspiration, 284
Institute for Education Sciences, 64
Institutional affiliation, 151
Institutional Animal Care and Use
  Committee (IACUC), 175, 188
Institutional Biosafety Committee (IBC), 176
Institutional cost sharing, 20
Institutional leadership, 15–16
  public confidence in, 54, *54*
Institutional Review Board (IRB), 174, 188
Institutional strategic planning, 17–18
Institutional subvention fees, 20
Instrument calibration
  bias from, 149
  for QA, 101
  validation and, 100
Integrity, 163
Intellectual property (IP)
  academic-corporate partnerships and, 254
  academic enterprise policies, procedures,
    and challenges, 220–223
  commercialization of, 224–227
  context, definition, and importance of,
    213–217
  disposition of, 223–227
  licensing of, 221–222, 224–225
  ownership of and royalties from, 222–223
  types of protection for, 217–220
  value to society of academic, 227, *228*, 229
Interactive methods, 74
Interdisciplinary collaboration, 239
Interdisciplinary work
  confirmation bias and, 152
  peer review and, 137
Internal funding, 19–21, 285n1
Internal R&D (IR&D), 11, 42
International collaborations, 250
International Monetary Fund, 287n1
Internet, 84
  researching previous work with, 96
Internships, 261
Interviews
  empiricism and, 74
  explaining research projects in, 120
  with focus groups, 74
  human subject rules and, 174
  with sources, 98
Intradisciplinary collaboration, 239
Inventories of American Painting and
  Sculpture, 202
IP. *See* Intellectual property
iPhone, 10
IR&D. *See* Internal R&D
IRB. *See* Institutional Review Board

Joint Committee on the Research
  Environment (JCORE), 22, 181, 182

Journal des Scavans, 127
Journal manuscripts, 128, 286n1
  open access and, 198
  review of, 129, 130
  submission process, 133–134, *134*
  traditional publication and, 196
Journals, 196–200
  open access, 199
  predatory, 167

Kennedy, John F., 59
Kettering, Charles, 14
Kiwanis Clubs, 205

Laboratories, 286n1
LAM model, 168
Land-grant universities, 214, 242
Language bias, 152
Large Hadron Collider, 238, 250
Lawrence Livermore National Laboratory, 11
Laws, 78, 171
  ethics and morality and, 162
Leadership
  academic-corporate partnerships and, 256
  development of, 247
  institutional, 15–16, 54, *54*
  research, 15–23
  team success and, 245
Lewis, C. S., 14
Licensing IP, 221–222, 224–225
Linked Environments for Atmospheric
  Discovery, 257–258
Listening, 207
Lobbyists, 39
Lorenz, Ed, 91
Los Alamos National Laboratory, 11

MacArthur Foundation, 31
Machine learning, 44
  in data analysis, 102
Maker spaces, 226
Mandatory spending, 33–34
Manhattan Project, 53
March-in rights provision, 286n1
McCullagh, C. Behan, 79
Measurement bias, 149
Media. *See also* Social media
  communicating research outcomes and, 204
  COVID-19 pandemic and, 60
  public understanding of research and, 55
Medicaid, 45
Medicare, 45
Mellon Foundation, 42
Merit-based competition, 182
Merit review, 286n1
  bias types and impacts in, 153
  definition and purpose of, 127–129

difference from peer review, 128
  NSF process for, 130–132, *131*, 133
  principles and processes of, 129–134
  of research proposals, 117–118
  strengths and weaknesses of, 135–138
  variations on, 138–140
Messenger RNA, 66
Meta-analyses, 97
Minority Serving Institutions (MSIs), 3, 58,
  113, 197, 220, 258, 277
  IP resources and, 220
Mission agencies, 11, 110–111
Mixed methods, 72, *73*, 74–75
Models. *See also* Computer models
  deficit, of communication, 205
  differences in meanings, 246–247
  double-blind, of review, 138, 154
  of innovation, 65, *65*, *66*
  LAM, 168
  of open access, 199
  single-blind, of review, 131
Monographs, 196
Montaigne, Michel de, 140–141
Morality, 162–163
Morrill Land-grant Act (1862), 214
MSIs. *See* Minority Serving Institutions
Multiagency federal programs, 250
Multidisciplinary collaboration, 4, 239
Multidisciplinary work
  communicating outcomes and, 204
  disciplinary research and education and,
    241–244
  peer review and, 137
Multisector collaborations, 251–255
Mutual benefits, 256
Mutual need, 256
Mutual trust, 256

NASA. *See* National Aeronautics and Space
  Administration
National Academies of Science, Engineering,
  and Medicine (NASEM), 35, 59
  open science vision of, 197
  on reproducibility and replicability, 85, *85*
National Academy of Inventors, 222
National Aeronautics and Space
  Administration (NASA), 43
National Archives and Records
  Administration, 179
National Centers for Environmental
  Information, 202
National Commission for the Protection of
  Human Subjects of Biomedical and
  Behavioral Research, 173
National Council of University Research
  Administrators (NCURA), 19
National Council on the Arts (NCA), 133

National Endowment for the Arts (NEA),
  19, 35
establishment of, 53
mission of funding, 111
peer review process, 133
proposal review process, 118
state and regional organizations and
  alliances supported by, 250
National Endowment for the Humanities
  (NEH), 19, 31
establishment of, 53
mission of funding, 111
National Humanities Center, 250
National Institute of Standards and
  Technology (NIST), 47
on RECR, 160–161
National Institutes of Health (NIH), 19, 47
establishment of, 53
on ethics, 163
Office of Biotechnology Activities, 176
Office of Laboratory Animal Welfare, 175
peer review process, 132–133
proposal review process, 117–118
RECR education resources, 166
research centers, institutes, and regional
  hubs, 249
Nationality bias, 152
National Library of Medicine, 202
National Oceanic and Atmospheric
  Administration (NOAA), 11
National Centers for Environmental
  Information, 202
National Organization of Research
  Development Professionals (NORDP), 18
National Renewable Energy Laboratory, 11
National Research Act (1974), 173
National Research Council, 240
National Science and Technology Council
  (NSTC), 22, 35, 161
research security and, 181
National Science Board (NSB), 23, 59, 153
merit review process and, 133
Science and Engineering Indicators,
  227, 268
National Science Foundation (NSF), 19, 43,
  46, 47, 58
administrative workloads and, 190
affiliation bias and, 152
compliance rules and, 183
cost sharing and, 113
Directorate for STEM Education, 64
Engineering Research Center for
  Collaborative Adaptive Sensing of the
  Atmosphere, 257
establishment of, 53
Federal Fumbles responses by, 156
IP resources and, 220

Large Information Technology Research
  projects, 257–258
merit review process, 130–132, *131*,
  133, 286n2
mission of funding, 111
proposal review process, 117–118
PYI award, 256
RECR education resources, 166
research centers, institutes, and regional
  hubs, 249
Research Coordination Networks
  program, 248
National Security Council (NSC), 181
National Security Decision Directive 189
  (NSDD-189), 179
National Security Presidential Memorandum
  33 (NSPM-33), 181
National Severe Storms Laboratory, 11
Naval Research Laboratory, 11–12
NCA. *See* National Council on the Arts
NCURA. *See* National Council of University
  Research Administrators
NEA. *See* National Endowment for the Arts
NEH. *See* National Endowment for the
  Humanities
Newton, Isaac, 238
NIH. *See* National Institutes of Health
Nike, 219
NIST. *See* National Institute of Standards and
  Technology
NOAA. *See* National Oceanic and
  Atmospheric Administration
Nonexperimental research, 75
Noninteractive methods, 75
Nonprofit organizations, 12
NORDP. *See* National Organization of
  Research Development Professionals
Notice of Proposed Rulemaking (NPRM),
  140, 184
NSB. *See* National Science Board
NSC. *See* National Security Council
NSDD-189. *See* National Security Decision
  Directive 189
NSF. *See* National Science Foundation
NSPM-33. *See* National Security Presidential
  Memorandum 33
NSTC. *See* National Science and Technology
  Council
Numerics, 73
Nuremberg Code, 173

Oak Ridge National Laboratory, 11
Objectivity, 163, 181
Observations
bias in, 149
in citizen science, 83
in historical method, 78–79

as primary sources, 98
in qualitative and quantitative methods, 73–75
in scientific method, *76*, 76–78
Office for Human Research Protections, 174
Office of Economic Development and Community Engagement, 222
Office of Information and Regulatory Affairs (OIRA), 183–184
Office of Management and Budget (OMB), 35, 37, 59
compliance policies and, 183–184
proposal budget guidelines by, 112–113
research compliance and, 176
Office of Research Integrity (ORI), 163, 184
Office of Science and Technology Policy (OSTP), 22, 37, 59, 61, 163, 200
compliance rules and, 183
publication policies, 177
research security and, 180
Office of sponsored programs (OSP), 19
OIRA. *See* Office of Information and Regulatory Affairs
OMB. *See* Office of Management and Budget
Open access
to data, 199–200
journals, 199
licenses, 198
policies, 84
publishing, 177, 198
Open access frameworks, 196–200
reproducibility and, 87
researching previous work and, 96
source availability and, 99
Openness, 181
peer review and, 136–137
Open peer review, 137, 138–140, 154
Open science, 197
Oral presentation, 208
ORI. *See* Office of Research Integrity
OSP. *See* Office of sponsored programs
OSTP. *See* Office of Science and Technology Policy
Outcomes, 13–15
Outreach, 120

Page charges, 199
Paradigms, 285n1, 286n4
The Parent Trap (film), 89
Participant bias, 149
Partnerships
academic-corporate, 255–256, 258
beyond academic-corporate, 259–262
as a component of grant proposals, 108
development of research, 18
international, 245, 250
multi-institutional, 67

among multiple sectors, 47, 55, 213, 237–239, 251–252, 254–255
multisector, 37
Pasteur, Louis, 90
Patent activity index, 229, *231*
Patents, 203, 217–221
design, 218
government ownership of, 224
number granted, by industrial sector, *230*
plant, 218–219
provisional, 219
rate of issuing, 227, *228*, 229
utility, 218–219
PCAST. *See* President's Council of Advisors on Science and Technology
PD. *See* Project director
Peck, M. Scott, 141
Peer review, 86, 286n1
bias types and impacts in, 153
consultative, 132, 139
definition and purpose of, 127–129
difference from merit review, 128
double-blind, 138, 154
early forms of, 127
effective use of, 140–142
NEA process, 133
NIH process, 132–133
open, 137, 138–140, 154
principles and processes of, 129–134
strengths and weaknesses of, 135–138
variations on, 138–140
Penicillin, 90
Personalized health information (PHI), 179
Personally held beliefs, 57
Personally identifiable information, 179
PHI. *See* Personalized health information
Philanthropic-based organizations, 12
Philosophical Transactions of the Royal Society (journal), 127
PI. *See* Principal investigator
Plagiarism, 164
peer review role in detecting, 135, 136
Plan-S, 197
Plant patents, 218–219
Platinum open access model, 199
Plato, 126, 238
Points of view, 154
Politicization, 60
Politics
belief systems and, 57
public understanding of research and, 56
Population samples, bias in, 149
PPP. *See* Purchasing power parity
Predatory journals, 167
Prejudice
bias and, 148
teams and, 250

Preprint or early release servers, 198, 199
Presidential Young Investigator award
   (PYI), 256
President's Budget, 34–35, 37–38, 40
President's Council of Advisors on Science
   and Technology (PCAST), 59
Press
   communicating with, 207
   COVID-19 pandemic and, 60, 199
Press releases, 204, 247
Prestige bias, 151
Previous work
   gaining familiarity with, 95–97
   sources on, 96
Primarily Undergraduate Institutions (PUIs),
   3, 11
Primary sources, 98
   protecting, 99
Principal investigator (PI), 108–111, 114
   administrative workloads on, 188, *188*,
   189, 190
   project management by, 119
Private companies
   academic institution facilities and
   equipment use by, 260–261
   consulting for, 259–260
   data analysis for, 260
   as funding sources, 43
   partnerships with, 251–255
   purposes of, 252–253
   research at, 11
   restricted funding access and, 261–262
Private foundations, 12, 20
   grant proposal budgets, 111
   research proposal calls by, 43
Procedural bias, 150
Professional reputation
   communicating research outcomes and, 196
   research misconduct consequences to, 165
Progress reports, 186
Project director (PD), 119
Project summaries, 110
Proposal reviewers, 109
Provisional patents, 219
Proxmire, William, 155–1156
Publication
   open access, 177, 198
   predatory journals, 167
   publicly accessible, 200–202
   reproducibility and pressures of, 86
   traditional and open access frameworks,
   196–200
   US share in global, 270, *270*
Publication bias, 151
Public comment
   in consultative review, 139
   open peer review and, 140

on policy proposals, 127
Public lectures, 120
Public policy, 171
   research results use and misuse in, 58–62
PUIs. *See* Primarily Undergraduate
   Institutions
Purchasing power parity (PPP), 268, 286n1
PYI. *See* Presidential Young Investigator
   award

QA. *See* Quality assurance
QC. *See* Quality control
Qualitative methods, 72–75, *73*, *74*. *See also*
   Historical method
Quality assurance (QA), 100–101
Quality control (QC), 100–101
   peer review as, 135, 136
Quantitative methods, 72–75, *73*, *74*. *See also*
   Scientific method
Quasi-experimental research, 75
Questions
   empiricism and, 74
   formulating, 76–77
   previous work and, 95–97
   serendipity and, 88–90

R2O. *See* Research to operations transition
Racial bias, 152
R&D. *See* Research and development
RAS. *See* Research administrative
   services
RCN program. *See* Research Coordination
   Networks program
RCR. *See* Responsible conduct of research
RD. *See* Research development
Reciprocity, 181
Record keeping, 163
RECR. *See* Responsible and ethical conduct
   of research
Refereed publications, 96
Regional innovation hubs, 226, 249
Registering protocols or procedures, 86
Reliability, 84–88
Religious beliefs, 57
Replicability, 84–88, *85*
Reporting
   progress, 186
   research compliance and, 176–177
Reproducibility, 84–88, *85*
Research, 6
   categories of, 72–75, *73*
   convergent, 237
   defining, 7–8
   determining priorities and budgets, 33–42
   DOD classifications, 9, *10*
   education integration with, 81–83
   federal investment in, *276*, 276–277

importance of responsible conduct of,
160–161
as innovation foundation, 64–67
many homes of, 10–12
public awareness of, 155
public understanding of, 55–56
scrutinizing, 125–127
sharing costs of, 111–116
social compact with general public and,
51–55
societal roles of, 284
structure in, 7
subclassifications in, 8–9
use and misuse of results in policy, 58–62
US government classifications, 9, *9*
Research administrative services (RAS),
5–6, 18–19
Research agreements, 225–226
Research and development (R&D), *9*
budget hearings and, 38
congressional hearings and, 37
corporate funding of, 42
domestic expenditures in, 268, *269*
federal budgets for, 34–35, *36, 52*
fending for academic, 27–29
investment in, 31, *32*, 33
"valley of death" transition in, 65
Research and development equipment, *9*
Research and development facilities, *9*
Research assistance grants, 44
Research centers, 249
Research compliance, 21–23, 171
conflicts of interest and commitment,
177–178
grant proposals, contracts, and other
funding instruments, 176
history and purpose of, 172–173
human and animal subjects and, 173–175
materials and, 176
protection of sensitive information,
processes, devices, and activities, 178–179
reforms in, 186–190
reporting and posting information and data,
176–177
research environment and, 175
researcher role in understanding and
meeting rules and regulations for,
185–186
Research Coordination Networks program
(RCN program), 248
Research development (RD), 18
Research enterprise
challenges facing, *276*, 276–278
comparing US and other nations, 267–272,
269, 271
general public trust in, 155, 161
openness in, 179–180

self-policing in, 86–87, 165
social compact with, 14
start of modern, 53
Research environment. *See also* Joint
Committee on the Research Environment
ethics training and, 167, 168
imperfect environment theory of
misconduct and, 165
project management and, 119
regulation and, 190
research compliance and, 175
Research integrity, 21–23
research security and, 180
Research leadership, 15–23
Research methods
citizen science and daily life and, 83–84
courses in, 103
education and, 81–83
general framework for, 72–75, *73*
historical, 78–79
Indigenous, 79–81
reproducibility, reliability, and replicability
and, 84–88
scientific method, 75–78
Research misconduct, 159, 163–165
analysis bias and, 150
Research process
bias types and impacts in, 147–151
critical assessment and, 141
ethics and, 159, 163
Indigenous communities and, 80
observations collected in, 77
outcomes and, 203, 220–221
RD and, 18
resource needs and management in, 98–99
Research projects
academic-corporate partnerships and,
253–255
administrative workloads in, 188
budgets, 111–116
explaining to nonexperts, 120
joint, 201
managing, 119–120
mission agencies and, 110
outcomes, 119–120
serendipity and, 89
Research proposals
budgets, 111–116, *112*
serendipity and, 87
solicitations for, 43
structure and value of, 107–111, *108*
submission and evaluation processes,
116–119
Research rules and regulations, 187, *187*
creation and enforcement of, 182–185
Research security, 179–182
Research to operations transition (R2O), 10

Research universities, 11
  proposal development assistance at, 109
  public funding for, 62, *63*
Resources
  collecting and protecting, 98–99
  for creating collaborations, 248
  IP, 98–99
  RECR education, 166
Respect, 181
Responsible and ethical conduct of research
    (RECR), 160, 168
  education resources for, 166
  required training in, 165
Responsible conduct of research (RCR),
    160–161
Restricted funding opportunities, private
    companies and, 261–262
Retention packages, 20
Revenue splits, 221–222
Review articles, 97
Rising above the Gathering Storm
    (NASEM), 46
The Road Less Traveled (Peck), 141
Rockefeller Foundation, 31
Roentgen, Wilhelm, 91
Roosevelt, Franklin D., 53
Rotary Clubs, 205
Royal Society, 127
Royalties, 222–223

Safety culture, 175
Sampling bias, 149
Sandia National Laboratory, 11
SBIR. *See* Small Business Innovation
    Research
Scholarship, 8
Science: The Endless Frontier (Bush), 53
Science and Engineering Indicators (SEI),
    227, 268, 275
Science and Technology Center for Analysis
    and Prediction of Storms (CAPS), 256–258
Science of Science and Innovation Policy, 46
Scientific method, 75–78, *76*
Scrutiny
  forms of, 127
  of research, 125–127
  value of, 125–126
Search for Extraterrestrial Intelligence
    (SETI), 83
Secondary sources, 98
Seed funding, 20
SEI. *See* Science and Engineering Indicators
Selection bias, 149
Senior research officer (SRO), 16
  internal funding and, 285n1
  roles and responsibilities of, 17–23
Serendipity, 88–92

SETI. *See* Search for Extraterrestrial
    Intelligence
SETI@home, 83
Shared vision and goals, 245–246, 251
Single-blind model of review, 131
Sleepless in Seattle (film), 89
Small Business Innovation Research (SBIR),
    44, 227, 254
Small Business Technology Transfer (STTR),
    44, 227
Smart devices, 10
Smart mobile devices, 83
Social compact, 14, 64, 214
  communicating with nonexperts and, 205
  research and, 51–55
Social media, 203
  debating on, 207
  explaining research projects on, 120
  historical bias and, 149
  identity and, 147
  morals and, 162
  sampling bias and, 149
Social Security, 45
Society of Research Administrators
    International (SRA International), 19
Socrates, 238
Source criticism, 78–79
Sources
  backups of, 99
  identifying, 98–99
  primary, 98
  protecting, 99
  reliability of, 78–79
  secondary, 98
  validation of, 99–101
Space rental, 20
SRA International. *See* Society of Research
    Administrators International
SRO. *See* Senior research officer
Stakeholders
  in CBR process, 38–39
  community engagement with, 21
  strategic planning and, 17
Start-up packages, 20
State and local government funding, 28
Statistical analysis, 103
  hypothesis formulation and, 77
  research proposals documenting, 110
Statistical correlation, 103
Statistics, 73
Stem cells, 56, 57
STEM disciplines, 8
  college degrees in, 272, *273–275*
  DBER and, 83
  funding trends and, 28, 31
  workforce and, 272
Sterne, Laurence, 7

Strategic planning, 17–18
Structured frameworks, 71
STTR. *See* Small Business Technology Transfer
Subjectivity
  design bias and, 148
  in peer review, 137
  qualitative methods and, 73
Synthesis, 102–103
Syphilis, 172

Taxation, 53
TCUs. *See* Tribal Colleges and Universities
Team-building activities, 251
Teams
  characteristics of successful, 244–247
  developing, 247–251
  diversity and, 245, 248
  globally engaged, 12–13
  trust and, 246
Technology transfer, 21
TED talks, 120, 206
Texas A&M University, 214
Theories, 78
  "bad apple," 165
  chaos, 91
  imperfect environment, 165
  testing, 7
Theory-building methods, 73, *74*
Theory-testing methods, 73, *74*
Three-minute thesis, 208
Tokenism, 80
Total budget, 115
Trademark, 217, 219
Trade secret, 217, 219–220
Transdisciplinary collaboration, 239–240
Translational research, 10
Transparency, 181
  peer review and, 136–137
Travel funding, 20
Tribal Colleges and Universities (TCUs), 26, 58
Trust
  academic-corporate partnerships and, 256
  peer review process and, 130, 135–136
  in research enterprise, 155, 161
  in research leaders, 54

  social compact and, 53
  successful teams and, 246
Tuskegee Syphilis Study, 172
21st Century Cures Act, 190

UIDP. *See* University-Industry Demonstration Partnership
Unconscious bias, 146–148
  proposal review and, 118
Unidisciplinary collaboration, 239
United States Patent and Trademark Office (USPTO), 203, 218, 219
University-Industry Demonstration Partnership (UIDP), 217, 255
University of Florida, 216
University of Oklahoma, 219
US Copyright Office, 218
USPTO. *See* United States Patent and Trademark Office
Utility patents, 218–219

Validation, of sources and data, 99–101
"Valley of death," 65, *65*
Venture capital (VC), 229, *232*
Visualization, 103

Walpole, Horace, 87–88
Warfarin, 66
Wastebook, 156
Weather Decision Technologies, 257
Wildfires, 80
Williams Energy Marketing and Trading, 257
W. M. Keck Foundation, 42, 43
Workflow, 99
Working partnerships, 182
World Intellectual Property Organization, 215, 227
World Medical Association, 173
World War II
  arts funding during, 64
  federal research funding and, 214
  multisector research enterprise after, 45, 53
  research compliance and, 173
  social compact and, 53

X-rays, 91